Women in English Society 1500–1800

Edited by
MARY PRIOR

METHUEN
London and New York

First published in 1985 by
Methuen & Co. Ltd
11 New Fetter Lane, London EC4P 4EE

Published in the USA by
Methuen & Co.
in association with Methuen, Inc.
733 Third Avenue, New York, NY 10017

Printed in Great Britain at
The University Press,
Cambridge

British Library Cataloguing in Publication Data

Women in English society 1500–1800.
  1. Women—Great Britain—Social conditions
  I. Prior, Mary
  305.4'20941   HQ1593

ISBN 0–416–35700–8
ISBN 0–416–35710–5 Pbk

Library of Congress Cataloging in Publication Data

Main entry under title:

Women in English society, 1500–1800

  Bibliography: p.
  Includes index.
  Contents: Marital fertility and lactation, 1570–1720 / Dorothy McLaren
— The remarrying widow / Barbara J. Todd — Women and the urban
economy / Mary Prior — [etc.]
  1. Women—England—History—16th century—Addresses, essays,
lectures. 2. Women—England—History—17th century—Addresses,
essays, lectures. 3. Women—England—History—18th century—
Addresses, essays, lectures. I. Prior, Mary.
HQ1599.E5W64   1985   305.4'0942   84–20547
ISBN 0–416–35700–8
ISBN 0–416–35710–5 (pbk.)

Contents

List of plates   vii
List of contributors   ix
Acknowledgements   xi
List of abbreviations   xiii
Preface   xv

Foreword   1
Joan Thirsk

1 Marital fertility and lactation 1570–1720
  Dorothy McLaren   22

  Appendix 1: Select bibliography on scientific research
  into the relation of lactation and amenorrhoea   47
  Appendix 2: Historiography of work by historical demographers on the relation between breastfeeding and fertility   48

2 The remarrying widow: a stereotype reconsidered
  Barbara J. Todd   54

  Appendix: The problem of untraced widows   86

3 Women and the urban economy: Oxford 1500–1800
  Mary Prior   93

4 Reviled and crucified marriages: the position of
   Tudor bishops' wives
   Mary Prior   118

5 Recusant women 1560–1640
   Marie B. Rowlands   149

6 Stuart women's diaries and occasional memoirs
   Sara Heller Mendelson   181

   Appendix: Annotated list of diarists and diaries   202

7 Women's published writings 1600–1700
   Patricia Crawford   211

   Appendix 1: Provisional checklist of women's published
   writings 1600–1700
   Patricia Crawford   232
   Appendix 2: Statistical analysis of women's printed
   writings 1600–1700
   Richard Bell and Patricia Crawford   265

   Index   283

Plates

(between pages 112 and 113)

1 *The Accomplish't Ladys Delight* by Hannah Wolley, 1675, showing women making medicines, preserving, beautifying themselves and cooking

2 'The house of rest' from P. Gringore, *Castell of Labore*, English edn, Wynken de Worde, 1510?, plate recut

3 Haymaking, from *The Roxburghe Ballads*

4 The wet-nurse and her charge: frontispiece to *Children's Diseases, Both Outward and Inward* by J.S. [J. Starsmare], 1664

5 Portrait of Lady Mary Verney by Van Dyck

6 Trade card of a silkman who had married and taken over his wife's business

7 Brass rubbing of Dame Joan Bradshawe and her husbands, 1598: Noke, Oxfordshire

8 Portrait of Mrs Salusbury by J. Zoffany, c. 1766

9 Portrait of Mrs Bridgman (later Mrs Mathew), sister of the founder of St John's College and the most successful female trader in Oxford

10 Machine-cut by Mrs Harrington, 1760

11 Mary Ward learns of the religious life at the house of her cousins

12 Tomb of Bishop Bentham in the parish church at Eccleshall, Staffs, showing the bishop and family at prayer

13 Tomb of Archbishop Sandys in Southwell Minster, Notts, showing Mrs Sandys and family at prayer

14 Tomb of Bishop Hough, Worcester Cathedral

15 Mary Ward praying for the conversion of England, Christmas 1626

16 A page from the diary of Sarah Savage, written on the day of her wedding

17 Memorial portrait of Sir Thomas Aston, his wife and son, by John Souch of Chester

18 Self-portrait of Lady Anne Killigrew, the frontispiece to her *Poems*, 1686

19 Title page of *The Restitution of Prophecy: that Buried Talent to be revived*, by the Lady Eleanor Douglas, 1651

20 'The London Quaker'

Contributors

PATRICIA CRAWFORD is a lecturer in History, University of Western Australia. Her publications include *Denzil Holles 1598–1680* (Whitfield Prize, 1980), 'Attitudes to Menstruation in Seventeenth-century England' (*Past and Present*, May 1981). In 1983 she edited *Exploring Women's Past: Essays in Social History* (Sisters Publishing Ltd, Carlton, South Victoria 3053, Australia). Her chapter, 'From the Women's Point of View: Pre-Industrial England, 1500–1750', provides a useful overview of the period as background in a book mainly concerned with women in Australian history.

DOROTHY McLAREN teaches local history part-time for the Bristol University Extra-Mural Department. She has explored aspects of lactation and fertility in a series of papers in *Medical History*.

SARA HELLER MENDELSON was until recently a postgraduate student at Wolfson College, Oxford, and now lives in Hamilton, Ontario. She has written 'The Weightiest Business: Marriage in an Upper Gentry Family in Seventeenth-Century England' (*Past and Present*, November 1979). She has a book on Aphra Behn, Mary Rich, Countess of Warwick and Margaret, Duchess of Newcastle, forthcoming.

MARY PRIOR teaches local history and women in history part-time for the Oxford University Department of External Studies, and is the author of *Fisher Row: Oxford Fishermen, Bargemen and Canal Boatmen 1500–1900*.

MARIE B. ROWLANDS is Principal Lecturer in History, Newman

College, Birmingham. Her publications include *Masters and Men in the West Midland Metalware Trades before the Industrial Revolution*, and articles in *Recusant History*. She edited the *Catholic Registers of Staffordshire* for the Staffordshire Parish Register Society.

JOAN THIRSK has just retired from a readership in Economic History at Oxford. She is an honorary fellow of St Hilda's College, and general editor of *The Agricultural History of England and Wales*. Her numerous publications include her 1975 Ford Lectures, *Economic Policy and Projects: the Development of a Consumer Society in Early Modern England*.

BARBARA J. TODD teaches history in the Simon Fraser University Women's Studies Program.

Acknowledgements

PATRICIA CRAWFORD

I wish to acknowledge the financial assistance of the University of Western Australia and the Australian Research Grants Scheme. Many people have helped me in a number of libraries, especially Malcolm Thomas at the Friends' Library and Mike Crump at the British Library. Richard Bell carried out the computer analysis. Among the many friends who have read and commented upon this chapter, I am especially grateful to Mary Prior, Sara Mendelson and Carolyn Polizzotto.

DOROTHY MCLAREN

I am indebted to the SSRC and the Wellcome Trust for grants towards the original family reconstitution of Minehead; to Jane Evans, Division of Genetics, University of Manitoba, Winnipeg, for help and advice, especially with statistical analysis; to Mary Siraut, assistant editor of the *Victoria County History* of Somerset, for many references, especially to the Trevelyan and Willoughby families; to Valerie Fildes at the Wellcome Institute for the History of Medicine; to the staff of the Somerset Record Office, especially Steve Hobbs; and to the staff of the Gloucestershire and Hertfordshire Record Offices. Any errors of interpretation from the statistics and references are entirely my own. The editor of *Medical History* gave permission to reprint figures for Caversham, Mapledurham and Chesham, for which I am grateful.

SARA HELLER MENDELSON

I would like to thank Patricia Crawford, Alan Mendelson, Mary Prior and Keith Thomas for helpful comments on previous drafts of this article, and Michael MacDonald for his generosity in sharing sources.

MARY PRIOR

Chapter 3: My thanks are due to Patricia Crawford, Barbara Todd, Sara Mendelson, Miranda Chaytor, Joan Thirsk and Mavis Oddie for their comments and encouragement.
Chapter 4: My thanks are due to the Oxford University Women's Studies Committee which, through one of their Small Grants, enabled me to make initial soundings. Felicity Heal, Tony Kenny, Sara Mendelson and Joan Thirsk made helpful comments; and Janet Cooper photographed monuments to bishops' wives.

BARBARA J. TODD

I would like to thank St Hilda's College, Oxford for a grant from the Elizabeth Levett Memorial Fund.

The editor and publishers would like to thank the following for permission to reproduce illustrations in the plates section:

The Curators of the Bodleian Library, Oxford, for plates 1, 2, 4, 6 (John Johnson Coll., Trade Cards VIII, Haberdashers), 9 (Manning 4°40), 19 and 20 (J.J. Coll., Trades I, Cries of London, ser. I, 27); The Mary Evans Picture Library for plate 3; The Oxford University Archaeological Society for plate 7; The President, St John's College, Oxford, for plate 9; The Institute of the Blessed Virgin Mary, Augsburg, West Germany, for plates 11 and 15; Chester City Record Office for plate 16; The City Art Gallery, Manchester, for plate 17; and the Alexander Turnbull Library, Wellington, New Zealand, for plate 18. Plate 5 appears by kind permission of Sir Ralph Verney, Bt; photograph: Courtauld Institute of Art. Plate 8 appears by courtesy of the Earl of Shelburne.

Abbreviations

Entries marked with an asterisk are Wing abbreviations for book locations

APC	*Acts of the Privy Council*
BI	Borthwick Institute, York
BL	British Library
BMC	*British Museum Catalogue*
Bodl.	Bodleian Library
BRO	Berkshire Record Office
brs	broadside
C	Proceedings in the Court of Chancery, PRO
CCRO	Chester City Record Office
CPR	*Calendar of Patent Rolls*
CRS	Catholic Record Society
CS	Camden Society
CSPD	*Calendar of State Papers Domestic*
DNB	*Dictionary of National Biography*
EETS	Early English Text Society
EcHr	*Economic History Review*
EHR	*English History Review*
EU	United Free, Church College, Edinburgh*
Foxe, *A & M*	John Foxe, *Acts and Monuments*, ed. G. Townsend and R.S. Cattley, 8 vols (1837–9)
HS	Harleian Society
JOJ	*Jackson's Oxford Journal*
L	British Library, London*
LF	Friends' Library, London*

LP	*Letters and Papers Foreign and Domestic of the Reign of Henry VIII, 1509–47*
LPS	*Local Population Studies*
NS	new series
O	Bodleian Library, Oxford*
OCA	Oxford City Archives
OED	*Oxford English Dictionary*
OHS	Oxford Historical Society
P & P	*Past and Present*
PRO	Public Record Office
PROB	Probate Records of the Prerogative Court of Canterbury, PRO
PS	Parker Society
RO	Record Office
SHC	Staffordshire Record Society (formerly William Salt Archaeological Society), Staffordshire Historical Collections
STC	A.F. Pollard and F.W. Redgrave, *A Short-title Catalogue of Books printed in England, Scotland and Ireland ... 1475–1640*
TC	Edward Arber, *The Term Catalogues, 1668–1709*
TLS	*The Times Literary Supplement*
TTC	*Catalogue of the Pamphlets, Books, etc. relating to the Civil War, Commonwealth and Restoration*, collected by George Thomason
VCH Oxon, IV	*The Victoria History of the Counties of England, Oxfordshire IV, The City of Oxford*
Wilts RO	Wiltshire Record Office
Wing	Donald Wing, *Short-title Catalogue of Books printed in England, Scotland, etc., 1641–1700*

Preface

Research on women in the period 1500–1800 is still at an early stage. Records for women are always more sparse than those for men, and for the period before 1800 more so than after. Research has tended to concentrate on subjects for which material is readily available, or on women who appear prominently in the records. Thus men's attitudes to women have been studied from literary sources, such as plays, poems, sermons and advice books. Studies of actual women have tended to concentrate on queens and aristocrats on the one hand and women who fell foul of the law on the other. The great mass of women in between have received little attention.

Until we have studied such women too, any generalizations about women in this period must be regarded simply as hypotheses to be tested. Nevertheless studies of individual women also present difficulties, for it is difficult to evaluate behaviour and attitudes. What is typical and what idiosyncratic? If, however, we examine small groups of women intensively we can overcome this problem at least within such limits. In the past two decades social and local historians and historical demographers have made a breakthrough in the study of small groups, and shown the rich rewards they can offer, not least for the study of women.

It was indeed the work of two historians using the methods of the historical demographer and local historian which first suggested this book. Further contributors were sought who were interested in surveying particular groups intensively, though the methods naturally varied with the subject. An attempt was made to cover a wide range of women's activity and condition. As the idea of the book arose in discussion with Joan Thirsk, it seemed fitting to ask her to contribute a foreword. Although she has made her name as an agricultural historian, not only has she encouraged and helped women in many fields of history and in many countries, but her shrewd remarks on women's strengths as historians, and her indignation over their failure to receive adequate academic recognition, suggested the result would be interesting.

As a group the contributors, and I not least, would like to thank the following institutions and persons: the Nuffield Foundation, who funded the research, St Hilda's College, Oxford, who administered the grant, and Rita Harris their Treasurer, for her practical and helpful advice; the Oxford University Women's Studies Committee and Shirley Ardener for advice when the project was under consideration; Eleanor Chance for typing contributors' papers with cheerful efficiency, and Betty Milburn who patiently made mountains of photocopies. The intellectual, financial and other indebtednesses of individual contributors are recorded in the acknowledgements section.

Mary Prior

Foreword

JOAN THIRSK

In the last century and a half no more than spasmodic attention has been given to the history of women. But those spasms of interest have reflected far-reaching changes in the organization of the English economy and of society, and have been accompanied by an improvement in women's position within it. The present reappraisal of women's history and role in society again accompanies large-scale changes in the economy. Will future historians see some concomitant improvement in women's position? The hope persists that they will, even though the present outlook is bleak, and the legislation promising women equal opportunities appears to be largely ineffective. The changes required, however, involve such a fundamental overturning of deep-seated attitudes that change will surely proceed at a snail-like pace, too slowly, perhaps, for one generation of women to notice much difference. But whatever the final outcome, a better knowledge of women's history cannot but help to advance understanding and sharpen consciousness, both of the obstacles that lie ahead and the injustices of the present situation.

The essays in this book explore aspects of women's history in the sixteenth to eighteenth centuries. Can they be said to illuminate in a fresh way the life of women in the past? As always, it is easier to frame direct and simple questions than to answer them with the same brevity. To set the scene, we need to summarize the judgements of earlier historians who have already surveyed women's lives in the same period. Their viewpoint, in turn, cannot be fully understood without some account of the circumstances which first inspired their curiosity, and so induced them to choose one rather than another avenue of approach. This introduction, therefore, strives to fill in the historical background to these essays. In doing so, it should explain why historians were preoccupied with certain themes in the past and not with others, and clarify the reasons why the same matters are not a major issue in this present volume. At the outset, it should be said that women historians in the 1980s see the period in a fresh perspective, and hope to illuminate the lives of their predecessors by approaching the subject from new directions.

The difficulties in writing on the history of women have been rehearsed many times, and nothing in the future will ever remove them. The records of women of the past are sparse, and every kind of ingenuity is needed to reconstruct even fragments of their lives. Domestic routines of life were, and still are, labour-intensive, and responsibility for them fell to women. In consequence, their time was fully engaged, leaving them little energy to write about themselves. If they did write, they were lucky if their manuscripts were preserved, let alone published. Writers' hopes of documenting women's lives will always outrun the possibilities of achievement.

Given these difficulties in re-creating women's experiences some three to five hundred years ago, it is not surprising that women have taken a long time to reach the present position where they will attempt, as in this volume of essays, to explore the lives of small groups of ordinary women—widows in Abingdon, tradeswomen in Oxford, or wet nurses in Buckinghamshire. Their predecessors started by writing of grander women, who left much more in the way of documentary evidence. Nevertheless, those nineteenth-century historians laid foundations on which we build, and they deserve credit for the substantial contribution they made to a historical literature on women that is far from voluminous. Their works were widely read in their time (though they are totally neglected now), and they were veritable pioneers in their indefatigable search for original documents as evidence.[1]

The first in this line of nineteenth-century women historians were Agnes and Elizabeth Strickland, who chose to write mainly on the queens and princesses of England.[2] The presence of Queen Victoria on the throne at the time encouraged them in their work and they attracted large numbers of readers. Their twelve volumes on the queens from the Norman Conquest onwards, first published in 1840–8, were reissued in a cheap edition of six volumes in Bohn's Library in 1864–5, and sold eleven thousand copies.

Born of well-to-do middle-class parents, the Stricklands were

educated at home by a father who encouraged historical and anti-
quarian studies. Exhilaration and a zestful excitement in the re-creation
of past events were more in evidence in their work than a broadly
conceived, calm, and objective judgment; and Agnes's uncritical
admiration and championship of Mary Queen of Scots in her later life
deprived her of much of the sympathy and respect which she enjoyed
earlier in her literary career. A heavy shadow, in consequence, rests
over her reputation as a historian. Nevertheless, the Stricklands were
in the forefront of scholars searching out original documents and
insisting on letting the documents speak for themselves. The
calendaring of state papers and private archives did not begin until the
1860s, whereas their first books date from the 1840s. Thus they had
to fight to gain access to original archives; their request to Lord John
Russell for permission to enter the State Paper Office was at first
refused. In the end, however, they gained entry to the State Paper
Office, the British Museum, the Bodleian Library, and the muniments of private landowners and collectors. Agnes's searches also
took her to Paris where an interview with Guizot opened the door to
the French archives.[3]

Sympathy will always be given to Agnes Strickland, who firmly
enunciated the view that the reader must have the evidence laid before
him and not be defrauded by 'declamations about the dignity of
history' and summaries of information which make 'everything sub-
servient to a political system'. It was unfortunate that she did not
escape a similar error herself. But her untiring search for original
documents was impressive and exemplary at that date. Lingard, her
contemporary, wrote history without making the same efforts.
Moreover, the Stricklands deemed it essential to see for themselves
the places where historical events had been enacted, and, in this
second respect, they established a routine that is now taken for
granted by local historians.[4]

A distinguished contemporary of the Strickland sisters was Mrs
Mary Anne Everett Green, née Wood, who was educated at home in
a staunchly Wesleyan household and embarked on a similar series of
histories of royal ladies, attaching the same importance as the Stricklands to the consultation of original archives. When she married and
settled in Gower Street in London, the main British archive reposi-
tories were readily accessible to her, and her exhaustive use of them is
reflected in her books. Her *Lives of the Princesses of England* (1849–
55), starting in 1066 and continuing to the end of Charles II's reign,
included an outstanding biography of Elizabeth, Queen of Bohemia,

described by Sir Adolphus Ward in the *Dictionary of National Biography* as 'the most exhaustive which the subject has yet received.' On her own admission, she investigated the available documents 'in almost every civilized country in Europe.'[5]

Before the *Lives of the Princesses* appeared, Mrs Green had edited for publication in 1846 *Letters of Royal Ladies of Great Britain from the 11th Century to the Close of Queen Mary's Reign*. This and other editorial work brought her scholarly recognition when she was appointed in 1853 one of the editors of the calendars of state papers. But it put an end to her original writing. In forty years she edited forty-one volumes of calendars of documents of the early modern period. They brought to naught her intention to write the histories of the queens of the House of Hanover, even though she had collected voluminous material.[6]

It is plainly a mistake for women to show themselves good editors, for they may never emerge from that role. This was the fate of other nineteenth-century women historians who became the *amanuenses* of their fathers or husbands, and who are hardly ever discernible behind the more bulky masculine presence of their literary partners. Lucy Toulmin Smith is one such example. Mrs J. R. Green (Alice Stopford) might have been another, but for her long widowhood. Only in brief sentences does an interest in women's history escape from the pages that they edited; for Lucy Toulmin Smith the opportunity was seized when she edited for her father, after his death, *English Gilds. The Original Ordinances of more than one Hundred Early English Gilds*. 'It is worth noticing', she wrote in the introduction (1870), 'who were the persons who composed the gilds. Scarcely five out of the five hundred were not formed equally of men and women, which, in these times of the discovery of the neglect of ages heaped upon woman, is a noteworthy fact.'[7]

Another author who entered the field of women's history from a less scholarly direction was Georgiana Hill. She forms a bridge between those who had concentrated on royalty and those who were next to explore the history of middle- and working-class women. No biographical details of Georgiana Hill appear in the *DNB*, and her dates of birth and death are unknown to the library cataloguers, but something can be gleaned from her books. Her extraordinary success as an author started with her cookery books which sold cheaply – at six pence apiece – and in very large numbers. The first was a cookery book for the kitchen and cottage (1860) and was plainly not aiming to satisfy the expensive tastes of the gourmet. But subsequent manuals, giving over one hundred recipes for cooking rabbit, or fish, or preparing salads, sent her searching through many foreign cookery books, raised the culinary standards of her publications, and build up a picture of the author as a considerable linguist, who was also probably an experienced traveller in Spain and France. Her continued literary success from the 1860s onwards must have left her by the 1890s looking for fresh fields to conquer, for no more cookery books appeared, and instead she turned to an investigation of *The History of English Dress* (2 vols, 1893). In the concluding paragraphs of that work, in which she summarized recent changes in women's lives that had imposed increasing simplicity on their dress, yet another project came into view. Women, she explained, now travelled on trams and buses, climbed mountains, played tennis, kept shops and sat on committees. Plainly, she was already thinking ahead to her next task. *Women in English Life from Mediaeval to Modern Times* was published in two volumes in 1896, and displayed yet again the clarity, force, and considered judgement that characterized all the writing of Georgiana Hill. In discussing the fortunes of women in the early modern period (1500–1800), she established the general direction in which historians have since conducted the discussion of their lives. She saw the Renaissance as a liberating force, opening to women a larger intellectual world, drawing them out from the narrow confines in which religious teaching had held them during the Middle Ages, and introducing them into the wider life of the political nation. But her view of the period was, perhaps, somewhat more optimistic than the evidence allowed, being coloured by her own optimism in the 1890s when she saw women taking an active part 'in all the great movements, political, religious, and philanthropic'. She did not seem to envisage the possibility of any further setbacks.[8]

At the same time in the 1890s a fresh stimulus to women studying women's history emerged from an unexpected direction. Academic historians in the universities embarked on a whole new branch of investigation into economic and social life, one that would for the first time bring the life of ordinary people out into the light. Since women are so much involved in the practicalities of everyday living, this new subject in its pioneering days attracted a number of able women, who combined their more general studies of the economy with an interest in the history of women. Thus the role of women in the economic life of the nation began to dominate the next group of publications on women's history.

The new breed of economic and social historians in the 1890s belonged to one of two circles. Either they had a connection with William Cunningham, and had been taught by him at Cambridge, or they were connected with the London School of Economics.[9] More likely, they were associated with both Cambridge and London, for close contact was maintained between the two centres; scholars from both places approached the subject from a similar viewpoint, and shared a common set of assumptions. William Cunningham was as much at home in the medieval as in modern periods, and his students moved freely through all centuries. But at the London School of Economics, predictably in view of its associations with Sidney and Beatrice Webb and the Fabians, most scholarly effort was devoted to the later eighteenth and nineteenth centuries, and was invested in uncovering the course and consequences of the industrial and agricultural revolutions. This meant that those women historians who carried out their researches at LSE focused their attention likewise on the period 1760 to 1900, and when they turned their attention to the history of women, this remained the favoured period for study.

One of the pioneers in these early days was Lilian Knowles, who had studied under William Cunningham at Girton College, Cambridge, and was already a research student at LSE before the turn of the century. She finally became a professor there, and died in 1926. Her book on the *Industrial and Commercial Revolutions in Great Britain during the Nineteenth Century*, which appeared in 1921, was dedicated to the memory of Cunningham, 'a great teacher and master of English economic history'.[10] Under the persisting influence of older historical conventions, Lilian Knowles chose a semi-political approach to her research, seeking to explore the impact of the industrial revolution on world trade and the relations of states.[11] But a clearly expressed opinion on women's lives emerged in the course of her remarks on the domestic system of industrial production and the move into factories. She had evidently arrived at a firm view, which, we must suppose, was woven into her lectures at LSE. Thus she gave a fresh slant to the discussion of women's history; one that visibly influenced the work of the two historians who then wrote full-length studies of women that have since become classics, Alice Clark in 1919 and Ivy Pinchbeck in 1930. Both these authors carried out their research at LSE under her inspiration and encouragement, and the second of these, Ivy Pinchbeck, chose much the same period as Lilian Knowles. She hardly differed in any important respect from her in her conclusions.[12]

The central concern in Lilian Knowles's discussion of women's lives in the past was their role in industry outside the home. This was natural enough for a scholar immersed in the nineteenth century. Women had first been recruited into industry under the domestic system, which had employed them in the home. Recruitment had been a long, slow process, starting in the Middle Ages. But when finally the factory was adopted as the workplace, it took women out of the home, fundamentally changed their lives, and altered their role in society.

Lilian Knowles's knowledge of the domestic system rested on the reports in nineteenth-century parliamentary papers, when home-based industry was in a debased state. Viewing the industrial revolution against this background, she passed an optimistic verdict on the coming of the factories and its consequences. Comparing dank, dirty workshops in private houses, representing life under the domestic system, with light, clean, well-ventilated factories under the factory system, she set store by the consequent improvement in working conditions, and the removal of dust and the smell of industry from the home. She also thought that domestic happiness had been increased when family members were dispersed into factories instead of jostling each other in one crowded room. On the debit side, she granted that women at home were deprived of their chance to earn money, and recognized that that meant a loss of self-esteem for them and of cash for their families. But unmarried women reaped advantages; they enjoyed the independence afforded by a steady job and a regular wage. As for middle-class women, she admitted that they had lost more than they gained. They had been partners of their husbands in business, when home was the centre of activity, but when the home was separated from the workplace, women found their lives narrowed and lost touch with the business world. When once their children grew up, they had to seek their satisfactions in social work, craftwork, and the social round. In short, the industrial revolution had mixed results. But for working-class women the benefits outweighed the losses.[13]

Since Lilian Knowles concentrated her studies on the years between 1780 and 1914 she did not claim to offer a full account of women's lives in the preceding 250 years. In that sense, her work lay beyond the period with which this book is concerned. Yet indirectly she passed a judgement on it, for in her final analysis she broadly welcomed the changes caused by the industrial revolution. This implied some adverse comment on the earlier conditions, which the industrial revolution had fundamentally transformed. It is not difficult to see why Lilian Knowles's work prompted another scholar to investigate the earlier period more thoroughly.

This investigator was Alice Clark, whose book on the *Working Life of Women in the Seventeenth Century* was published in 1919. She delved deeper than any earlier writer on women into the national and local archives of economic and social history; and, although her research sprang from within Professor Knowles's framework of argument, it was informed with a curiosity and imaginative understanding that plainly derived from another world of experience. Alice Clark had had many years of work in her Quaker family's shoe factory at Street in Somerset, where she had worked as supervisor of the machine room. She was also politically alert, and engaged, like her mother, in the suffrage movement. A bout of illness had obliged her to suspend work in the factory, and in 1912 she undertook research into the history of seventeenth-century women, with the aid of a scholarship at LSE, endowed by Mrs Bernard Shaw.[14]

Thus Alice Clark began a systematic study of the period before the age of factories and congested urban tenements, when the industrial revolution was casting no more than a small shadow. She surveyed a world where manufacturing activity for a national market was intruding more than ever before upon country lives, but as yet did not threaten to destroy their deep roots in the land. In other words, she had a view of a transitional period in economic life, poised between the medieval and the modern, when the material comforts of life were being improved, but the underlying demands that were to be made upon the kingdom's labour resources were not yet undermining the traditional family economy. From a seventeenth- rather than a twentieth-century viewpoint, Alice Clark perceived, with greater clarity than did Lilian Knowles, features of women's lives in the past which had given them more dignity and status than was granted them after the industrial revolution. Through her association with Eileen Power, moreover, she had a perspective on a still longer process of change; she could compare the lives of medieval women with those of the seventeenth century.[15]

At the London School of Economics, where man is perceived as an economic animal whose first instinct is the pursuit of material gain, Alice Clark took her cue from the economists. Her prime task, she explained, was to investigate women's productivity. How, she asked, had economic development in the seventeenth century affected the productive capacity of women? Sensibly, she gave a broader than usual definition of this term, considering women's work in the home

as well as outside it, asking herself how the changes of the period
affected women's success, not simply as producers of goods for the
market, but as mothers and builders of a stable family life. Here, as
Miranda Chaytor and Jane Lewis have recently explained in their
new edition of Alice Clark's book, she revealed the influence of
contemporary debate. Lively discussion was then in progress on
ways by which women could possibly combine motherhood and
management of their households with work outside the home.[16]

The mode of thought of the economist directed Alice Clark in the
initial stages of her work, but another set of personal convictions
broke through her written text. In many places she revealed the
qualities in life and in people that she most esteemed, not all of them
concerned with stern economic efficiency. They seem to have their
source in her Quaker upbringing in a small town that cannot have
been wholly estranged from its seventeenth-century past. She clearly
admired thrift, hard work, self-help, and good business sense, but
she also took pride in the perpetuation of country skills and traditions. Thus a broad, rather than narrow, view of women's economic
achievements emerged from her even-handed account of women,
seen at close quarters in the kitchen, in the parlour, and in the fields,
as well as at the spinning wheel and weaving loom. She also differen-
tiated sensitively between women of the upper, middle and working
classes, and gave a whole chapter to the productive achievements of
middle-class women in the professions.[17]

Alice Clark's final verdict on the changes wrought in women's
lives between the seventeenth and nineteenth centuries did not
coincide with that of Lilian Knowles. Viewing their experience from
many different angles, and offering many different reasons, she
concluded that women's practical skills, as well as their qualities of
mind and temperament, had been far more effectively used before the
industrial revolution than after. Before the changes of the mid-
eighteenth century, she argued, an orderly sequence of training had
set women on life's course, in the same way as men. Unmarried
women had been virtually apprenticed trainees of married women,
learning from them the many domestic arts that were needed to feed,
clothe and educate a household. Subsequently, industrial work had
taken the unmarried women away from the home, and demoted and
devalued household skills. These were, in any case, being diminished,
and some of them outmoded, by new technologies. Thus, women's
resources of energy and ingenuity were no longer stretched as before.
They lost their role as teachers and organizers in their households,

and became instead the lonely performers of a much smaller, and less demanding, round of domestic duties. They could no longer be regarded as the economic equals of their husbands, and, instead, had to accept a condition of dependence. The whole family now relied for its main support on the wage which the husband alone could earn. 'The triumph of capitalistic organization', she concluded, wrought the downgrading of women's status.[18]

Men, too, suffered losses under the new regime. They had once been able to contribute more to their family life, educating and training their children and their apprentices in the circle of the home. But as they shifted their activities into a more public world, they accepted a reduction of their role in family life. Society attached greater significance to these public, as opposed to private, activities, and the change thus elevated the status of men *vis-à-vis* women. Greater formality in a world of increasing complexity also led to a further tightening of institutional structures, causing women to be more positively excluded from public life.

Alice Clark's toughest criticism of these developments was reserved for her last chapter on the professions. A controlled, but deep indignation flows through her description of the way one profession after another, slowly but relentlessly, shut the door upon women. For different reasons they were excluded from the law, from the church, and from medicine; even midwifery, which had been 'women's inviolable mystery', was, by the later seventeenth century, mastered by male medical doctors. Women lost their commanding position because they were excluded from the education necessary to keep them in touch with advancing scientific knowledge.[19]

And the causes of this turn of events, so damaging to women? It was not, she emphasized, deliberately engineered by anyone. It simply happened, inexorably, under the constraints imposed by a host of changes, in political and religious, as well as economic life. The expanding economy also expanded the role of the state; this heightened the importance of formal education and of professional institutions for those employed in its service. The commercial needs of a developing national economy were now best served by singling out individuals for employment, rather than family groups. Both the exclusion of women from the professions and the rise of factory employment, in short, were inextricably linked with the decline of the household economy. As the public world increased its demand for people to work in it, women found themselves confined in a shrinking circle. Lacking the new educational opportunities open to men, their intellectual capacity atrophied and their moral influence was weakened. All these tendencies inevitably fostered a growing belief in the inferiority of women. Alice Clark's final verdict was a devastating critique of capitalism and the effects of the industrial revolution as it had affected women. It was just as positive as the entirely contrary judgement of Lilian Knowles. How could they be reconciled? [20]

Both accounts expose the weaknesses in all large generalizations; they cannot accommodate too much diversity. Lilian Knowles's conclusions must appear entirely reasonable to anyone who has thoroughly read mid- to late- nineteenth-century parliamentary reports. Her verdict on the advantages of factory industry would have been endorsed by many working-class women of the time who still eked out a living in cottage workshops against the competition of large-scale factory production. Alice Clark's judgement was equally understandable in the light of her better knowledge of the seventeenth and earlier centuries, when a more harmonious blend of industrial work and farming was achieved that yielded to many families a satisfactory living and considerable independence. Lilian Knowles accepted twentieth-century lifestyles and gave more weight to the trends in the nineteenth century which wrought that outcome. The two centuries before were, to her, all of a piece, and she did not fully appreciate the changes that occurred within that long period of time, between the arrival of the domestic system and its decay in the face of an overwhelming factory system. Alice Clark, for her part, gave a somewhat idealistic picture of family life under a regime of near self-sufficiency in the seventeenth century. It amounted to a fair representation of the households of yeomen, even husbandmen and urban craftsmen in calm, crisis-free times. But it did not contemplate all the drawbacks of a family-based economy, experienced by those who were permanently impoverished and rootless. It paid no attention to the many severe legal disabilities which denied women control over their property, their children, and, indeed, over the way they conducted their own lives. If they had to earn the entire living for the family, it allowed them nothing more than a livelihood of makeshifts. She had nothing to say about the heavy burden of constant child-bearing, and the high rate of infant mortality. And even though she was aware of the writings of seventeenth-century theorists who upheld the notion of men as the rightful heads of families, and she recognized the ambiguities in this literature, yet she sidestepped this muddy pool by assuming that, in practice, in the home, the equality of husband and wife prevailed. [21]

Alice Clark's picture, in short, painted some features in the landscape with too broad a brush, and entirely omitted others. Yet, in its broad outlines, it was a magisterial survey, and its arguments substantial and cogent. The more self-sufficient households of the seventeenth century undoubtedly made greater demands on women's natural gifts and skills than the modern world in which their tasks became narrowly domestic. Women who had nursed and doctored, taught their children, produced and preserved vegetables and fruit, spun flax and wool, brewed beer, run dairies, and generally shared equally in getting the family's livelihood, whether from land, a craft, or trade, had been managers of a considerable enterprise. In the ordering of the family economy, they were, indeed, equal partners with their husbands. Moreover, the great diversity of skills which they commanded enabled them to contribute valued practical help in their local communities. In their way they were as important as village constables or poor-law overseers who held publicly recognized offices.

Historians since Alice Clark's day, who have more closely examined the constituent parts of the nation, would not deny the essential validity of her account of the challenges that life offered to women in the seventeenth century. Rather, they would elaborate upon her descriptions. They see women in a great miscellany of different economic and social contexts in the two hundred and fifty years between 1500 and 1750. Alice Clark concentrated on the intrusion of industrial work and capitalist organization. But 'industrial work' and 'capitalist organization' are deceptively simple terms, masking a complex reality. England was a collection of highly varied regions, whose distinctive farming economies accommodated industrial work and capital enterprise in many different guises, and at different levels of intensity. Different rural environments were matched by others equally varied in large towns, mean market towns, and fishing ports, and in new manufacturing centres that were transforming themselves from villages into towns. Families which lived by a craft, by shop-keeping, by innkeeping, by fishing or by market gardening all worked to different rhythms. The routines of these different lives inevitably made varied demands on the womenfolk.[22]

To picture women divided into two types only, the one trapped in a dull routine of fetching water, cooking pottage, and spinning wool, and the other entertaining the court in manor houses, gardens and parks, bears little relation to reality. Regional and occupational differences were legion. And while many of the alternative lifestyles, indicated at random above, existed long before 1500, the period up to

1800 presented a fresh range of challenges that further diversified women's lives.

From some time in the early sixteenth century, England began to bustle with innovations that harnessed energies in many new enterprises, and created fresh possibilities for human development. Women, whose lives have always obliged them to be the most adaptable creatures under the sun, did not neglect the fresh chances that came their way. In a highly fragmented kingdom of self-governing villages and towns, over which the state imposed as yet no uniform rules of government, let alone uniform standards of social behaviour and responsibility, many anomalies crept in. Thus when boys' education in the schools was more generously provided in the sixteenth century than hitherto, some girls also, adventitiously, received an education. That some took advantage of their chance to learn to read and write is made clear in this volume. Sara Mendelson selects for attention the writers of diaries; Patricia Crawford shows in her list and survey of surviving books by women the surprising number of those who went into print. For other women a practical training was provided, sometimes by apprenticeships for girls, but much of it in the workhouses, newly set up under the Elizabethan poor laws. These taught skills such as knitting, lacemaking, and button-making, which might lead to nothing more than ill-paid drudgery, but at least gave women more ways of earning cash in their own support.[23]

In agriculture, women's responses to the challenges of the market were no less positive. The remarkable growth of the dairying business in the seventeenth century could not have occurred without the efforts of women – the acknowledged mistresses of the dairy house. The market in vegetables and fruit could not have expanded as it did without the efforts of women in planting, weeding, and harvesting the crops of market gardens and orchards, and in carrying the produce on their shoulders to market. They were also the discriminating buyers of the same produce, who experimented in ways of cooking novel foodstuffs in the kitchen and helped to boost the demand for quantity and the improvement of its quality. Asparagus, pumpkins and artichokes, for example, were unfamiliar gastronomic experiences in the sixteenth century. They had to be coaxed and encouraged to survive both in the garden and at the cooking hearth. Similarly, the cultivation of fruits, and their preservation so that they might last through the winter, taxed the ingenuity and energy of increasing numbers of women, as these one-time luxuries of the gentry came within the reach and the purse of more people among the lower ranks of society. Yet another range of skills was publicized and tested when wider interest was shown in the preparation of aromatic waters, herbal infusions, and distillations for medicinal and culinary purposes. These tasks were more elaborately and professionally performed when once instructions appeared in printed books.[24]

Thus in the interstices of a more complex economy a host of fastidious tastes and pleasures were cultivated that could be enjoyed by more people than before. They imposed fresh domestic and commercial demands on women's energies, and offered them, if they chose, many new sources of cash. In two small items of expenditure and income in the diary of Joyce Jeffreys of Hereford in 1638 and 1639, we glimpse the broadening range of consumer goods, giving work and an income to someone somewhere. In the 'twigger cage' that she bought for her 'throstle' – in step with the fashion that took hold in England in the later sixteenth century for keeping caged birds – and in the 20 shillings that she earned from selling 2 ounces of saffron from her ground, we see the work, and the reward for work, for one woman, and perhaps two.[25]

In short, women were deeply involved in the expanding consumer society, stimulating the taste for more consumer wares and satisfying it. Yet the work that women did was still mostly unhampered by authority, especially when the enterprise was novel. The guilds mostly ignored women, taking action against them erratically, when they felt their interests threatened, but in an arbitrary and unsystematic way. Town councils only occasionally took cognizance of them, as Mary Prior shows in her essay on women at work in Oxford.[26] The provinces of the kingdom all enjoyed much freedom in developing their economies and in governing themselves, even though a loose network of trading links and official supervision was cast over all, holding the nation together in some kind of unity. When it ignored women, officialdom deprived them of many opportunities, but its negligence also sometimes gave them others.

Gradually the net of government tightened, however, and between 1500 and 1750 continuing economic and political changes broke down decentralized rule and the relative autarchy of local communities. Public affairs of all kinds intruded more aggressively into the private world of the family, robbed it of half its sphere of influence, broke its unity, and deprived the women of half their functions. It carried the male members away to rule more flamboyantly in the public world. The whole process proved extremely damaging to women, as Alice Clark fervently demonstrated.

Alice Clark's distinction between the role of women in private and public worlds goes to the heart of their problem, for if society had somehow continued to attach the same value to productive work in the home as it attached to work in the factory and office, women would not have found themselves reduced to a position of economic and social inferiority. Seeing the seventeenth century in this way, as a watershed in the development of women, was Alice Clark's boldest insight. And now, in the later twentieth century, it has a special interest when another technological revolution looms that could well return large numbers of people to occupations that can be carried on from home, possibly permitting a duality of occupations, reminiscent of circumstances in the early modern period. Such a return to a domestic economy, wearing a new guise, but bearing similarities to a past experience, gives Alice Clark's account of the seventeenth century a greater immediacy in the 1980s than it had sixty years ago. It is not the reason why the book was reprinted in 1982, but it can certainly be re-read with a new perception.

The searchlight which, for a large part of the present century, has been directed on the history of economic development, has affected the writing of women's history, and left many other facets of their lives in darkness. When the struggle for women's suffrage was won, moreover, published books on women's history dwindled; Ivy Pinchbeck's in 1930 was unusual. The present phase of renewed interest was first discernible in the late 1950s, and has swollen gradually in the last two decades.[27] It has turned its attention away from an overwhelming preoccupation with economic concerns, and confronts instead other aspects of women's lives which were either constrained or liberated by the changes taking place in the world around them.

We are now in a better position to answer our original question: what is new in this volume about women's lives between the sixteenth and eighteenth centuries? As the contents show, it does not divide women into two basic groups, working women on the one hand, and well-to-do gentlewomen on the other. A scheme which discusses professional openings for the second group and industrial work for the first touches only one segment of women's activities. The bulk of women in the early modern period lived private lives or entered the job market in an improvising, casual, and impermanent way, infiltrating the interstices of an employment structure that only occasionally noticed them or invited them to participate. They certainly took advantage of every chink in the edifice, but they had to be arch-improvisers and entirely flexible. Indeed, it is centuries of this kind of training that has made them the more adaptable of the two sexes, and has doubtless prepared them best for the next revolutionary phase in our economic development. From one point of view, then, the essays in this volume could be summed up as studies in women's adaptation to changing circumstances.

This volume adopts a fresh approach by examining women in smaller groups, not dominated by economic categories. Within these we can recognize the faces of individuals – an essential of sympathetic historical writing – and yet retain a basis for important generalizations. Dr McLaren examines the childbearing experiences of women, and reveals the differences between those of ordinary womenfolk who breastfed their babies, and of the gentlewomen who sent their children away to wet-nurses, suffered their many deaths, and, in consequence, underwent frequent pregnancies. At the edge of this picture (which must broaden the demographer's investigations of women's fertility rates) we glimpse a group of women who acted as wet-nurses and earned some cash from this dire convention of the gentry class.[28]

Marie Rowlands writes of the deeply committed Catholic women who were turned by the Reformation into lawbreakers but whom the state generally was powerless to discipline, simply because of its illogical treatment of them in law. It illustrates the strained contortions of officialdom, which were made necessary by the ambiguous position allotted to women – an ambiguity which they exploited with ingenuity as well as moral courage.[29]

Barbara Todd examines the lives of widows in Abingdon who re-married less often in the seventeenth, than in the sixteenth, century. Among the reasons for this was a growing desire in society as a whole to preserve property in the family. This led husbands to insert provisions in their wills that penalized women if they re-married; and women who shared the same concern for their children's inheritances avoided second marriages that would disadvantage their offspring. Choosing to remain independent was made easier by the emergence of more varied types of work for women, and, for the indigent, the institution of a public system of poor relief came to their aid. In practice, they and their children proved to be the main beneficiaries of the weekly dole.[30]

Mary Prior sheds light on the brave women who became the first wives of churchmen when clerics were once allowed to marry. They faced more than private trials of their fortitude, they had to carve out for themselves and their successors a place in the hierarchy of ranks and orders where none before existed. Dr Prior, in another essay, also uncovers the precarious position of women in trade in the city of

Oxford. They were fortunate, inasmuch as Oxford was undergoing economic and social upheaval, and so had a fairly open framework of government. Women successfully probed the weak points in its institutional structure of crafts and marketing, and seized their chance whenever new developments unwittingly yielded an entry into novel trades. But these entrances did not long remain open, and it was then usually impossible for women to move on in search of another less formally structured town. Her account supports a generally observed fact of life that women frequently play a significant part in the founding of new enterprises, before they become institutionalized and harden their structures. Then rules are devised, or other factors intervene, that effectively exclude them.[31]

The women who used their education to write diaries and publish books are studied in the essays of Sara Mendelson and Patricia Crawford. Urged to be silent in public, such women found through their pens a means of expression for their feelings. Their writings deserve more attention than they have yet received, but we are already shown in these essays how their political horizons expanded and their political discernment sharpened.[32]

Adaptable women managed and made the best of the opportunities that came their way in the changing world of early modern England. Some doors opened; others firmly closed. Life was enriched in many directions, and women played a large part in improving its material comforts. But in innumerable ways they were newly constrained and confined. Considering how many possibilities for human development opened up in the period, women secured only a very small share; they had to wait another century and a half before they were allowed to partake of the scientific, educational and political advances that stimulated the lives of men.

Now as we face an electronic revolution that will match, if it does not outstrip, the industrial revolution in the scale of economic and social changes it will impose, deep uncertainties arise again concerning the benefits that women will derive from the new technology. They are now receiving the same education as men, but they do not make an equal contribution with men in any single branch of public life. Will they be the first to be called upon to adapt to the hardships, without equally sharing the benefits, of the electronic revolution?

In a world which is composed of almost equal numbers of men and women, the special qualities of both sexes are needed equally in public and private life, if humanity is to make the most use of its resources and create the best environment for all. Such equality has never yet existed in historic time, and the obstacles in the way of achieving it should not be underestimated. But despite setbacks over the centuries, progress has been made. Women who now write new chapters of their past history do so in the firm belief that they can assist further progress through a better understanding of the territory that has already been traversed.

NOTES

[1] For an account of an eighteenth-century woman historian, similarly neglected now, but who showed some of the same qualities as the nineteenth-century historians cited below, in particular, a care for searching out original documents and a vigorous, lively, practical style of writing, see Bridget and Christopher Hill, 'Catherine Macaulay and the Seventeenth Century', *Welsh History Review*, III, 4 (1967), pp. 381–402. Catherine Macaulay wrote general political history, but missed no anecdote that did 'honour to the female sex' (p. 389).

[2] Mention should also be made of another scholarly historian of women, writing at the same time as Agnes Strickland, but less popular than her, Mrs Hannah Lawrance. She wrote *Historical Memoirs of the Queens of England from the Commencement of the Twelfth Century*, 2 vols (London, 1838–40), and *The History of Woman in England and her Influence on Society and Literature from the earliest Period*, vol. I (London, 1843). No second volume appeared. Like Agnes Strickland, she set great store by the collection of contemporary evidence from every available and authentic source; see *The History of Woman*, Preface, p. vi.

[3] See Agnes Strickland in *DNB*; and biographical introduction by John Foster Kirk of Strickland, *Lives of the Queens of England from the Norman Conquest* (Philadelphia, 1907).

[4] A. Strickland, *Lives of the Queens of England from the Norman Conquest*, Bohn's Library, 6 vols (London, 1864), I, p. ix; J. Foster Kirk, op. cit., vol. I, pp. xix–xx.

[5] See the account of M. A. E. Wood in *DNB* by Sir Adolphus William Ward, Professor of History and English Literature at Manchester, later Master of Peterhouse, and one of the editors of the Cambridge Modern History. A. W. Ward also wrote the prefatory note when Mrs Green's life of Elizabeth, Queen of Bohemia, was revised by her niece, Mrs S. C. Lomas, and reissued separately in 1909. He described it as 'the gem, I make bold to say, of her *Lives of the Princesses of England*'. M. A. E. Green, *Elizabeth, Electress Palatine and Queen of Bohemia* (London, 1909), p. vii.

[6] Mrs Green's *Lives of the Princesses*, vol. I (London, 1849), contained a notice opposite the preface announcing her *Lives of the Queens of England of the House of Brunswick*, 2 vols, as though it were imminent, but by volume VI (1855), it was described as 'preparing for publication'.

⁷ Toulmin Smith, ed., with introduction and glossary by Lucy Toulmin Smith, *English Gilds. The Original Ordinances of More than One Hundred Early English Gilds*, EETS, XV (1870), Introduction, p. xxx. I wish to thank Mary Prior for drawing my attention to this passage. Mrs J. R. Green (Alice Stopford) did not find her literary skills until after her husband's death, when she fulfilled a promise to him to study further certain problems of medieval history, and published in 1894 *Town Life in the Fifteenth Century*. See her Preface, pp. xii–xiii, describing her diffident steps towards authorship. She became much bolder during her long widowhood, when she wrote on Irish history, espoused the cause of Home Rule in Ireland, and in 1916 removed from London to Dublin. Her most candid remarks on women's position in society occur in *Woman's Place in the World of Letters* (London, 1913), an essay originally published in the journal *Nineteenth Century* in June 1897. She said almost nothing about women historians, but she saw the nineteenth century as 'a new age' for women writers in general. These she felt to be oppressed by conventions that were alien to them. Hence they chose 'precaution and disguise'. She was arguing for women's sensibilities and perceptions that were different from men's, but she took an optimistic view of the future, in which women's intervention would become 'more and more decisive in human affairs' (ibid., pp. 6, 10, 11, 13–14, 16, 23, 29).

⁸ Georgiana Hill, *A History of English Dress from the Saxon Period to the Present Day* (London, 1893), II, pp. 335–7; idem, *Women in English Life from Mediaeval to Modern Times* (London, 1896), I, pp. viii, xi–xii, 114. A stinging review appeared in 1896 of this last work by an anonymous critic who could not stomach Georgiana Hill's strictures against the Anglican church and its attitude to women, nor did he approve of modern women's aspirations. He grudgingly admitted, however, 'so far as her history is concerned, that it is generally accurate': *Athenaeum*, 108, no. 3591 (August 1896), pp. 252–3. Despite the very large sales of Georgiana Hill's cookery books, the Bodleian Library has very few, and most of those held by the British Library were unfortunately destroyed during the last war.

⁹ I leave out of these brief remarks any reference to earlier political economists who read much history, but did not use that knowledge to write it, preferring to construct theories of economic development.

¹⁰ L. C. A. Knowles, *The Industrial and Commercial Revolutions in Great Britain during the Nineteenth Century* (London, 1921), Dedication.

¹¹ Ibid., Preface. Lilian Knowles's later work dealt with the economies of countries in the British Empire. See L. C. A. Knowles, *The Economic Development of the British Overseas Empire*, London, 1924.

¹² L. C. A. Knowles, *Industrial and Commercial Revolutions*, pp. 96ff.; Ivy Pinchbeck, *Women Workers and the Industrial Revolution, 1750–1850* (London, 1930), p. 307ff.

¹³ L. C. A. Knowles, *Industrial and Commercial Revolutions*, Preface, pp. viii, 91, 86, 96–7, 99–100.

[14] Alice Clark, *Working Life of Women in the Seventeenth Century*, new edn (London, 1982), Preface, p. viii; new introduction by Miranda Chaytor and Jane Lewis, pp. ix–xi. Alice Clark received research assistance from Dorothy George, who used some of the material so collected for her *London Life in the XVIIIth Century* (London, 1925). See the prefaces to the books of both authors.

[15] Clark, op. cit., p. vii. For Eileen Power's writings on women, see 'The Position of Women', in C. G. Crump and E. F. Jacob, *The Legacy of the Middle Ages* (Oxford, 1926), pp. 401–33; E. Power, *Medieval Women*, ed. M. M. Postan (Cambridge, 1975).

[16] Clark, op. cit., pp. 3, 4, 8–9, xv, xviii.

[17] Ibid., *passim*, also p. xxviii.

[18] Ibid., *passim*, but especially Introduction and Conclusion.

[19] Ibid., Chapter VI, pp. 236–89; on midwifery, p. 265*ff.*, 284. For a recent study of the rivalry in midwifery, see Jean Donnison, *Midwives and Medical Men. A History of Inter-Professional Rivalries and Women's Rights* (New York, 1977).

[20] Clark, op. cit., pp. 299–301, 286–7.

[21] Ibid., pp. 40–1, 300–1. For more recent comment on the theorists and their influence, see L. Stone, 'The Rise of the Nuclear Family in early Modern England. The Patriarchal Stage', in Charles E. Rosenberg (ed.), *The Family in History* (Pennsylvania, 1975), p. 49*ff.* For insights into women's control, or lack of it, over their lives, see Ivy Pinchbeck and Margaret Hewitt, *Children in English Society. Volume I. From Tudor Times to the Eighteenth Century* (London, 1969), p. 50*ff.* and *passim*.

[22] For illustrations of diverse regional economies and social structures, see Joan Thirsk (ed.), *The Agrarian History of England and Wales*, IV, *1500–1640* (Cambridge, 1967); and V, *1640–1750* (Cambridge, 1984). For an account of the work rhythm governing the lives of fishermen and bargemen on the river, see Mary Prior, *Fisher Row. Fishermen, Bargemen, and Canal Boatmen in Oxford, 1500–1900* (Oxford, 1982).

[23] See Chapters 6 and 7. For girls' education in local schools, see Margaret Spufford, 'The Schooling of the Peasantry in Cambridgeshire, 1575–1700', in Joan Thirsk (ed.), *Land, Church, and People*, Supplement of *The Agricultural History Review*, 18 (1970), pp. 140, 141. For an apprenticeship of girls in the bonelace industry, see Joan Thirsk and J. P. Cooper (eds), *Seventeenth-Century Economic Documents* (Oxford, 1972), pp. 234–5. For handicraft teaching in workhouses, and the manufacture of new consumer goods generally, see Joan Thirsk, *Economic Policy and Projects. The Development of a Consumer Society in Early Modern England* (Oxford, 1978), pp. 65–6 and *passim*.

[24] On dairying and horticulture, see Joan Thirsk, *Agrarian History*, V, Chapters 18 and 19. A growing interest in distillations is mirrored in two sixteenth-century editions of Fitzherbert's *Book of Husbandry*. In the first (1523), these subjects were barely mentioned, but in a newly corrected and

amended edition by I.R. in 1598 wholly new chapters were added on gardening and the distilling of herbs, vegetables and fruits, flowers and wild plants. *The Book of Husbandry by Master Fitzherbert*, ed. W. W. Skeat, English Dialect Soc., Series D, Miscellaneous (1882), pp. 144*ff.*

[25] BL, Egerton MS 3054.

[26] See Chapter 3, below.

[27] For the 1950s, see Jean E. Gagen, *The New Woman. Her Emergence in English Drama, 1600–1730* (New York, 1954); Ruth Kelso, *Doctrine for the Lady of the Renaissance* (Urbana, 1956); K. Thomas, 'The Double Standard', *Journal of the History of Ideas*, XX (1959), pp. 195–216. For the most recent general survey of women's position in the early modern period, see Patricia Crawford, 'From the Woman's View: Pre-Industrial England, 1500–1750', in Patricia Crawford (ed.), *Exploring Women's Past* (Carlton, Australia, 1983). For two recent bibliographical essays, see Rosemary Masek, 'Women in an Age of Transition, 1485–1714', in Barbara Kanner (ed.), *The Women of England from Anglo-Saxon Times to the Present* (London, 1980), p. 138*ff.*; Olwen Hufton, 'Survey Articles. Women in History I. Early Modern Europe', *P & P*, CI (November 1983), pp. 125–41.

[28] Chapter 1, below.

[29] Chapter 4, below.

[30] Chapter 2, below.

[31] Chapters 5 and 3, below. For a seventeenth-century example of the hardening structures of organizations that start with liberal attitudes and admit women on equal terms, see the radical religious sects: K. Thomas, 'Women and the Civil War Sects', *P & P*, XIII (1958), pp. 50, 53. The same course of events overtook the historical profession, in which so many scholarly women were represented, alongside men, in the nineteenth century. The writing of history was then entering upon a new phase, stimulated by the opening of the archives. When it became more formally professionalized in the universities, however, the ranks of the women were thinned. Apart from a reference to Alice Stopford Green, wife of J. R. Green, the women are all passed over in silence by John Kenyon in his recent survey: *The History Men. The Historical Profession in England since the Renaissance* (London, 1983).

[32] Chapters 6 and 7.

1 Marital fertility and lactation 1570–1720

DOROTHY McLAREN

There is no doubt that the fertility of rich women between 1570 and 1720 was often appallingly high. It was not uncommon for a rich woman to bear twenty children, and at least one gave birth to thirty infants.[1] This knowledge has led some to believe that in the eighteenth century 'a rise in fertility could not have occurred simply because fertility behaviour was already unrestricted and had always been so'.[2] However, at local level, it has long been recognized that the majority of women in pre-industrial society did not have large families.[3]

For many years the families of the élite have been reconstituted by heralds and genealogists. Now that the method may be extended to all families in a given parish, it is possible to say that the majority of women had a fertility rate that lagged far behind their fecundity – that is, their reproductive capacity. Although abstention, *coitus interruptus*, abortion and infanticide are frequently canvassed as causes of low fertility, obviously none of these can be well documented. Nuns and many single women, as well as the wives of seamen and other absentees, did abstain, *coitus interruptus* did take place,[4] and abortion and infanticide did occur, though in the last case often outside marriage.[5] It is clear that infertility was not artificially induced by abstaining from sexual intercourse while suckling an infant. The view that one ought to abstain was held in some circles, but was by no means general:

> A nurse that lives with her husband is allowed coition and congress with him, lest she be disturbed by the desire of it, and by experience we see that Mothers that live with their Husbands, and use congress, Nurse the Child without hurt.[6]

This study will deal with the natural control of female marital fertility. The aim is, first, to show that the amenorrhoea of lactation (the period of infertility during breastfeeding) is a biological fact revealed by worldwide research and is more intense than the amenorrhoea of malnutrition; although amenorrhoea of lactation was recognized in the seventeenth century, the old knowledge and the new scientific evidence have not yet been adequately used by historians to explain family and population change. The second aim is to show that prolonged and non-exclusive breastfeeding was customary and woven into the English economy and society during the pre-industrial period, and was a basic part of the reproductive pattern for the majority of women. The third aim is to show from demographic evidence from various parishes in Oxfordshire, Buckinghamshire and Hertfordshire, and from recent family re-constitution in Somerset, that the majority of normal, healthy women, well proven to be fecund, had long birth intervals; shorter intervals did occur, however, when an infant died. The fourth and final aim is to show that rich women of the period had an entirely different reproductive pattern, which was mainly due to their having abandoned maternal breastfeeding.

The results indicate that the majority of women could control their fertility in a natural way, but how far the women themselves consciously exercised this control we may never know.

THE SCIENTIFIC EVIDENCE

It was stated at Geneva in 1982 that 'The changing history of breastfeeding is the history of the human population explosion.'[7] For at least a quarter of a century it has been recognized by scientists that fertility is delayed in women who suckle their infants. Biologists have now clarified the process whereby the hormone prolactin, a product of the pituitary gland, promotes the production of milk and inhibits the ovarian function. Empirical studies involving lactating and non-lactating mothers have led Professor Short to state that 'throughout the world as a whole more births are prevented by lactation than all other forms of contraception put together.'[8] Space does not permit discussion of these investigations; the literature is voluminous, and the references given here are highly selective.[9] It is hardly surprising that, while historical demographers had noted the effect of lactation on fertility quite early they were slow to attach much weight to it,[10] for prolactin was not discovered in humans until recently, and there was some justification for believing that the contraceptive effect of breastfeeding was 'a myth of the working class'.[11]

The scepticism is understandable. In our society it is not uncommon for women to conceive while breastfeeding, but the western habit of scheduled feeding, rather than feeding on demand, the abandoning of night feeding and the early introduction of solids, reduces the extent of the contraceptive effect of the suckling stimulus.[12] It is the suckling stimulus that is now thought to be of paramount importance in the process of lactation and ovulation. In the early modern period we are, however, dealing with a society that fed on demand, when the alternatives to breast milk were neither economic nor desirable, and where babies often slept in bed with their mothers or wet-nurses. It was then much easier to suckle during the night. Lady Anne Clifford may have had her daughter Margaret in bed with her all night when she was 3 years old for the first time since she was born, but Margaret had slept in a bed with Mary Hicken, her nurse, before then and did so until she was 5 years old.[13] We are dealing also with a society where the majority of women probably believed that by sustaining lactation they could delay the next pregnancy. The idea that this was 'a myth of the working class' may have arisen with industrialization, when women had to reduce suckling to work in factories and sweatshops.

Since biblical times the contraceptive properties of lactation have been observed. In Hosea 1: 8 it is written of Gomer, the wife of Hosea, who had born him a daughter: 'Now when she had weaned Loruhamah, she conceived, and bare a son.' Hints are also found in medical texts throughout the period under discussion. In the seventeenth century William Petty, Tomlins Professor of Anatomy, wrote that prolonged lactation hindered propagation. His work on fertility was noted by Kuczynski in 1935, along with the opinions of other British demographers on fertility between 1660 and 1760. Evidence that women knew that prolonged lactation was nature's way of protecting them from an early pregnancy is not easy to find outside the medical profession. However, by the end of the seventeenth century, Newcome made a comment that shows it was current, even if not taken seriously by the upper classes:

> So vain is that popular pretense that nursing is an impediment to fruitfulness, and to be declin'd by great persons for the better securing of succession, by a numerous posterity: for if those bear

faster who dry up their breasts, they that nurse their children commonly bear longer, and bring up more to maturity.

In fact, Newcome wrote at length to persuade mothers of the importance of breastfeeding their infants.[15] At the end of the eighteenth century Mary Wollstonecraft wrote:

> Nature has so wisely ordered things that did women suckle their children, they would preserve their own health, and there would be such an interval between the birth of each child, that we should seldom see a houseful of babes.[16]

It seems unlikely that most women in pre-industrial England were unaware that prolonged lactation reduced their fertility. The possible effect of poor maternal nutrition on fertility must also be considered. Professor Short summarizes his findings in the statement that 'Even under conditions of frank malnutrition or actual starvation, lactation is scarcely affected.'[17] Obviously the quality and quantity of milk is influenced by maternal nutrition, but, while malnutrition affects the duration of lactational amenorrhoea, the difference in fertility between poorly and well-nourished women is slight in developing countries.[18] It is now generally agreed that the amenorrhoea of lactation is more intense than the amenorrhoea of famine.[19] The very high fertility of the well-nourished Hutterite women of North America who breastfeed has almost certainly given rise to the suggestion that English women before industrialization, whose fertility was much lower than that of Hutterite women, were undernourished.[20] However, although twentieth-century Hutterite women breastfeed their infants,[21] they do not practise the prolonged, non-exclusive breastfeeding of English women in our period. Probably the suckling habits of English women were more akin to those of Kung women of the Kalahari who suckle on demand for three to four years.[22] The Kung women use no artificial contraception, menarche comes late, and the amenorrhoea of lactation keeps birth intervals at about four years. The majority of English women at this time had a somewhat similar pattern of reproduction, as had many Japanese women of the same period.[23]

Before leaving scientific fact and turning to historical interpretation, we may look very briefly at two important and very relevant properties of prolactin. First, strenuous exertion leads to a greater release of prolactin.[24] No one can doubt the amount of physical labour required of poorer English women in rearing their infants and performing numerous other duties expected of wives of the period. Their intense activity increased the secretion of the hormone prolactin and protected them from early pregnancy while they were breast-feeding. Second, when prolactin was discovered in animals it was called 'the mother-love hormone'.[25] Animals who were prevented from suckling consistently rejected their young. Breastfeeding is now said to be important in creating a bond between mother and infant. However, the apparent maternal indifference to their babies of women who did not breastfeed may well be a matter of chemistry rather than being purely psychological in origin. The suppression of the flow of milk to their breasts enabled them to produce infants annually but may have restricted their maternal instincts. We shall note later Mary Verney's concern about her infant's journey to the wet-nurse. Mary, for all her problems during the Civil War and her own ill health, appears to have been a caring, gentle mother. How, then, we may ask, could she put her infant aside, knowing the risks? Of his second wet-nurse, she writes:

> She lookes like a slatterne but she sayeth that if she takes the child she will have a mighty care of itt, and truly she hath toe as fine children of her owne as evor I sawe. The nurse is to have 4s a week and two loads of wood; truly tis as little as we can offer her ... for nurses are much dearer than they ever were ... poor child I pray god bless him and make him a hapy Man, for he hath had butt a troublesom begining, yett I prayse god he thrives well, and is a lovely baby.[26]

He did not thrive, and her grief when he died just four months after his birth was terrible.[27] This apparent indifference of women to sepa-ration from their newborns has no doubt led to the statement that 'good mothering is an invention of modernization'.[28] If by good mothering one means the successful care and nurturing of children, this is not a prerogative of modern women, and there is good evidence of strong maternal instincts in women in history, especially those who nursed their own infants.

THE USE OF HUMAN MILK

Except among wealthy women, maternal breastfeeding was customary. It was usual to feed on demand and often until the child was 3 years old, certainly until all the milk teeth had arrived. This varied; generally, the teeth appeared by the time the child was 2 years old. Weaning was traumatic and dangerous, and physicians never 'discussed early weaning as a possibility'. Breastfeeding was safe and was maintained until the child was strong enough to resist the diseases transmitted by food and drink.'[29] The Welsh physician, John Jones, wrote in 1579 that there were good reasons for delaying weaning until three years after birth. He also discussed the relatively robust condition of the infants of poorer mothers. Colostrum, the first milk, was once highly valued and inspired the Latin endearment – 'Meum mel, meum cor, mea colostra' ('My honey, my heart, my colostrum')[30] – but there is no consensus of opinion regarding its use or abuse during the period. Many physicians advised against its use; some were undecided. Mauriceau knew that 'Poor people cannot observe so many precautions and such mothers are obliged to give their child suck from the very first day.'[31] James McMath wavered. Although he observed that some thought it good for 'carrying off the excrements therein', he was clearly trapped between what he had read and what he had observed. He wrote: 'Some will give suck from the very first day … to wit, robust healthful Woman and in easie Labours.'[32] It is a fact that poorer women were seldom faced with the excessively high neonatal mortality of the infants of richer women. It cannot yet be proved that this was because from the very first day, like their domestic animals, they gave their first milk to their newborns, but, probably helped over this first hurdle, the newborns of poorer women more often went on to suckle for two to three years. Artificial feeding was rare in this period and believed to be dangerous. There was, therefore, a steady demand for women who were willing to breastfeed.

The position of upper-class women was very different. They used wet-nurses, and they had a reproductive pattern of ever-recurrent births. Poets and playwrights eulogized their fertility. Artists painted them caressing their big bellies. Monuments proudly depicted their numerous boys and girls. Even their priests and physicians do not seem to have discouraged their productivity. The latter did note their sufferings, and the easier labours of poorer women. There was pressure to produce heirs because so many rich infants perished. Some of these women may have realized that maternal breastfeeding would reduce their fertility and save more of their infants, but the pressure on them to deny the breast to their numerous issue was as great as the pressure to beget them; 'as the Renaissance advanced, the image of the nursing Virgin waned in popularity'.[33] Believing that sexual intercourse would corrupt the milk, but that the conjugal debt had priority above the welfare of the infant, the church had condoned wet-nursing. Rich women who wanted to feed their infants had a

battle, especially with husbands and friends. Anne Newdigate's first
child was born in 1598. Her men friends, Leveson, Knollys and Fulke
Greville, and her father disapproved of her breastfeeding. Her mother
wrote:

> I have sent you a nourse's rewarde. ... I longe to heer how all
> thinges abowte your new Charge goeth, for I parswaed myself
> that my sonne Newdygat wyll not go backe wth hys worde. I pray
> God send you well to doe with it.[34]

It seems that Anne's husband had promised to allow Anne to
breastfeed.

The Countess of Lincoln wrote that she did not lack the will to breastfeed but was overruled by others and misled by bad advice until it
was too late. Her treatise advising women to suckle was published in
1622 and dedicated to her daughter-in-law, who was breastfeeding.
She was a rare example. The Countess met with moral and physical
objections but stood her ground. In reply to the objection that it was
'noysome to ones clothes, that it makes one looke old', she wrote, 'ask
any one they carry their age and hold their beautie', and then she gave
as examples Sarah, Hannah and the Virgin Mary.[35] Also, the instruction
in the 1612 English translation of Guillemeau was clear with its 'preface
to Ladies, wherein they are exhorted to nurse their children themselves'.[36]

In spite of advice from physicians and theologians to breastfeed,
most rich women of the period did not go against the pressures to give
their infants to surrogate mothers, and throughout the period and
beyond it those rich women who breastfed their infants remained rare
examples. It is difficult for us to understand how women like Mary
Verney could give their tiny, weak and sometimes sickly infants to
wet-nurses, often miles from home. If opinions like those of Sir John
Acton in the eighteenth century were common, however, it is not so
very difficult to understand why rich women succumbed to the temptation to remove their newborns from the house. Sir John expressed
revulsion at the sight of a wet-nurse giving suck and said that 'A
sucking child makes a most dreadful spectacle'.[37] It was as well for him
that he was often at sea and not exposed to the Bedfordshire parishes
where women's 'whole employment consists in nursing their children'.[38]

Although knowledge of the extent of breastfeeding in pre-industrial
England is only slowly accumulating, it can be said that it was
prolonged and not necessarily restricted by the mother to her own
baby. It was extended to the infants of relatives and neighbours, and
to orphaned or abandoned parish infants. Mercenary wet-nursing of
rich women's infants was common, and in certain areas within reach

of London the wholesale suckling of infants from the city was highly organized. Breastfeeding also included the suckling of weak women in labour and after parturition, and the suckling of ailing adults was also practised. In a book originally written in the sixteenth century by Thomas Moffat and published posthumously in 1655, the use of a wet-nurse is clearly testified. Dr John Caius died in London on 29 July 1573. He was said to have been the most important physician before Harvey. Thomas Moffat wrote:

> What made Dr Cajus in his last sickness so peevish and so full of frets at Cambridge, when he suckt one woman (whom I spare to name) froward of conditions and of bad diet; and contrariwise so quiet and well, when he suckt another of contrary dispositon; verily the diversity of their milks and conditions, which being contrary one to the other, wrought also in him that sucked them contrary effects.[39]

It is not possible to assess how widespread the custom of adult suckling was. Throughout the period there are numerous suggested remedies that include the use of milk direct from the breast if possible. This was especially important for pulmonary tuberculosis, and it was often recommended that breast milk should be expressed directly into sore or diseased eyes.[40] As the breast became increasingly a symbol of eroticism, it may have declined as a remedy for sickness.

While it is possible to give some details of the background of rich women who employed wet-nurses, it is rare to discover much information about the wet-nurses themselves. It is only by chance that details about a number of wet-nurses in Chesham, Buckinghamshire, have come to light. The occupations of some of the husbands of Chesham wet-nurses and the place of origin of some of the infants are given in Table 1.1. Infants were fostered out at parishes all around London, and are said to have been fostered out from Norwich and Bristol.[41] Sadly, almost all of the evidence comes from burial registers; and, of bastards put out to nurse, the evidence (even more sadly) comes from Coroners' Rolls and Quarter Sessions. It is clear from at least one study that infanticide caused by neglect and starvation at the hands of wet-nurses was very much restricted to the infants of unmarried mothers.[42] Infection, intemperance and impoverishment also affected sucklings, especially when they were congregated in a semi-urban situation.

> In this year following, 1597, began the great plague of Cranbrook, the which continued from April the y^r afs^d to July, 13, 1598 ... ended in House of one Henry Grynnock, who was a pott com-

panion, and his wife noted much for incontinence, which both died excommunicated. That this infection gott almost into all the Inns and Suckling Houses of the Town, places then of much misorder.... Together with this infection, there was a great dearth at the same time, which was cause also of much wailing and sorrow.[43]

I do not know of any other appearance of the term 'Suckling House' in this sense; the *OED* refers to a 'suckling-house' as a place where calves were reared. There may have been a 'suckling house' in Reading, Berkshire, in the period, but the evidence is not clear. The term 'suckling house' may not mean anything more organized than the home of a wet-nurse. More research needs to be done on this subject.

There is no doubt that in many parishes within reach of London women were habitually employed in wet-nursing. It amounted to a form of by-employment, and if wet-nursing may be defined as 'useful work' then the term 'domestic industry' is appropriate. The author of *The Parish Registers of England* noted the burials of nurse children in twenty-seven separate parishes 'without making any special search'.[44] They were mostly in the Home Counties. He mentioned only Aldenham in Hertfordshire, but it is clear from a preliminary search of the registers that Aldenham was by no means atypical of Hertfordshire. The business of wet-nursing London infants was very well established in that county during the period, as one may judge from the parish registers. In Elstree 'in the peak decade 1700–1709 of 177 burials no less than eighty-three were of nurse children.'[45] My own study alighted on Chesham, in the neighbouring county of Buckinghamshire, where, between 1578 and 1601, 6 per cent of the total burials were of nurse children. But it is impossible to say at the moment from the variety of evidence whether wet-nursing as a domestic industry was increasing or declining, whether it was shifting from parish to parish, and whether the mortality of the nurse children increased or declined throughout the period. We can, however, observe the geographical concentration of wet-nursing. Is it simply coincidence that five Hertfordshire parishes noted for processing grain for London[46] took in large numbers of London nurse children? Did the wagons return not only with mer-chandise but with a human payload? It is possible that country glovers, hatters, tailors, shoemakers and a host of other craftsmen took their wares to London and came back with nurse children for country wives. There is no doubt that the thoroughfares to and from the metropolis were very busy. Some of the parishes with a substantial number of nurse children from London are no longer on main roads, but the old roads to the city can still be traced. The journey on

Table 1.1 Nurse children buried at Chesham 1585–1594

26.3.1585	Jaane daughter of one Robert White of London nursed first by the wife of Adrian Goodchild and lastly by Ric. Smythes wife.
26.4.1585	A nurse child of ones of London nursed by Ric. Twytchells wife.
12.5.1585	John Gallopp a nurse child of London nursed by the wife of Adrian Goodchild.
5.9.1585	Anthony son of John Edwardes of Tetsworth in the county of Oxford and nursed by John Lewys wife, tailor.
17.3.1586	Adam a nurse child of the widow Taylor junior.
10.9.1586	Susan daughter of Henry and Ellen Walton of London and nursed by the wife of Richard Harding of Botley.
4.12.1586	Wynefreede daughter of one Carnock of London and nursed by the wife of Henry Doddes.
2.12.1587	Mary daughter of Gerard price of London and nursed by the wife of Thomas Dell tiler.
28.1.1589	Sara daughter of Richard favell of London victualler and nursed by the wife of John Lochremas.
13.3.1589	Mary Roper of London nursed by the wife of Zachary Gosham.
17.3.1589	Rychard son of Rychard Mathew of London and nursed by the wife of henry Reeding.
24.1.1590	A nurse child of the wife of Zacherie Gosham.
7.10.1590	A nurse child of the wife of John Randoll.
18.10.1590	A nurse child of the wife of Robt. Dyllam.
30.11.1590	A nurse child from London nursed by the wife of John Edwardes shovel-maker.
12.9.1591	Michael a nurse child of the wife of henry Awby.
14.12.1591	Thomas Hill a nurse child of the wife of Ric. Gaate.
20.3.1592	Thomas Cordell a nurse child of Wm Edwardes wife.
13.5.1593	Gother verna of London nursed by Elyzab. wheatly.
10.2.1594	Edward Tarr son of an haberdasher of London and nursed by the wife of henry Gosham.
30.6.1594	Agnes walker of London nursed by Jo. Edwardes wife shovel-maker.

Note
Modern spelling except for proper names.

Source
J. W. Garrett-Pegge, *A transcript of the first volume, 1538–1636 of the parish register of Chesham in the county of Buckingham* (London, 1904).

25 June 1647 of one tiny infant into the country by way of St Albans to be suckled has been recorded.

> The nurse sayeth that her husband hath a very easy-going horse, and she thinks itt will be best for him to carry the child before upon pillows, because she cannott ride between toe panniers and hold the child.... If her husband doth carry the child, she cannott ride behind him, soe you must provide a horse for her; my sister Mary goes downe with them, soe you must bring up a pillion to carry her downe behind.... Pray doe you see that they take a great care of the child, and that they goe very softly, for the weather is very hott ...[47]

Mary Verney's son Ralph survived that journey, but died at the house of his second wet-nurse three months later.

Comments on successful wet-nursing are so rare that we may perhaps infer that it was so commonplace as not to call for remark; in other words, the tragic and infamous have had a disproportionate share of the publicity. References to nurse children who survived are often brief and indirect. Thorough investigation of the parish documents of Caversham in South Oxfordshire, for example, gave no indication whatsoever of prolonged or non-exclusive breastfeeding. Yet a paternity suit regarding the son of Elizabeth Knollys, lady of the manor, revealed that he had been suckled for fifteen months by Mary Ogden. In court, when he was 31 years old, Mary said she was present at his birth; she nursed him, and, when questioned, 'How know you that this petic'oner is the child you nursed?', she replied: 'I have known him all along as well as my owne child.'[48] The family reconstitution of Mary Ogden reveals that her fourth child, Robert, was born in May 1630 and was about six months old when Nicholas Knollys was born. Birth intervals for Mary had been almost a regular thirty months. Mary may have nursed other infants of whom we know nothing. What we do know is that, although fecund, Mary did not produce another child for six years after Robert was born. In 1671 Dorothy Andrews died soon after delivering an infant. Her husband John was an innholder in the parish of Stogumber, Somerset. Dorothy's baby was wet-nursed by Joan Jenkins, wife of John, a tailor in the same parish. Yet it is only the theft of baby clothes by a servant of John Andrews that reveals that Joan Jenkins was suckling the Andrews baby, and that Joan was in the habit of dressing the Andrews children and laundering their clothes.[49] Two survivors do not, of course, indicate successful wet-nursing, but we would probably know nothing of the rearing of these two children had their wet-nurses not been compelled to testify in court.

It may be questioned whether women were capable of producing milk for all and sundry. In fact a modern wet-nurse is known to have produced 5700 ml of milk in one day, and was able to maintain seven babies at a time with the quantity produced.[50] However, the picture of frequent and prolonged breastfeeding by wet-nurses is not an easy one to visualize. The recent popularity of maternal breastfeeding in the western world is a return to traditional practices, but the maternal suckling of one or two infants within thirty years cannot be compared with the prolonged and non-exclusive breastfeeding by English women in the period under review.

THE DEMOGRAPHIC EVIDENCE: (1) THE NORMAL EXPERIENCE

Conventional demographic evidence does not offer any direct information on breastfeeding practices and their consequences, but it may provide clues. One example came from Caversham and Mapledurham, two Thamesside parishes in South Oxfordshire. The data revealed that the intervals between births were almost always reduced when the first of two siblings failed to survive (see Table 1.2). No information on the customs of breastfeeding was available, but the possibility that the length of these intervals was affected by breastfeeding was raised.[51] After she had seen the paper on this material, Joan Thirsk drew my attention to the habit of the Whitelocke family in Buckinghamshire in sending their babies to be wet-nursed in the county. It then became evident from Buckinghamshire parish registers that not only upper-class infants were sent to a wet-nurse; the infants of many middle-class Londoners also were often seen in the burial registers. Partial reconstitution of the population of Chesham parish was carried out, and this also indicated that, when a nurse child was taken in, the intervals between the births of the wet-nurse's children doubled (see Table 1.3).[52] It can be seen that the interval when no nurse child was taken but the child survived two years was approximately two and a half years for the first interval, rising to approximately two years and nine months for later intervals. If a nurse child was taken, the intervals were doubled, indicating that prolonged suckling of another newborn infant caused a lengthening of the interval. When the first of two children died, the interval fell at all birth orders but was shortest at the earlier birth orders. These intervals were, however, increased again and were close to the figures for when a child survived and a nurse child was taken.

Table 1.2   Caversham and Mapledurham birth intervals (in months)

	Birth order				$(n-1)-n$*	Between baptisms
	1–2	2–3	3–4	4–5		
Caversham: yeomen and gentry	23.76	28.9	27.35	31.27	39.04	*If the first of the two children attained two years of age*
Caversham: husbandmen and cottagers	23.75	34.05	26.32	32.9	35.68	
Caversham: tradesmen and watermen	26.58	24.6	31.35	27.4	34.27	
Mapledurham: all families	23.35	27.36	28.15	31.7	38.24	
Mean of the four groups	24.36	28.73	28.29	30.82	36.81	
Number of observations	(86)	(93)	(93)	(95)	(93)=(460)	
Caversham and Mapledurham	23.39	17.69	21.5	27.81	28.48	*If the first of the two children did not attain two years of age*
Number of observations	(17)	(12)	(13)	(12)	(13)=(67)	

Notes
1 Completed families with six or more confinements: Caversham 1635–1706; Mapledurham 1628–1715.
2 Number of families in the sample 107: Mapledurham 39; Caversham, yeoman and gentry 25; husbandmen and cottagers 31; trade 12.
* The total observations do not total 535 intervals (107 families with six confinements) because in eight cases the month of the baptism was questionable because of wear and tear on the register, although in every other respect the family was suitable.

Source
Dorothy McLaren, 'Fertility, Infant Mortality and Breast Feeding in the Seventeenth Century', *Medical History*, XXII (1979).

Table 1.3 Birth intervals (in weeks) of Chesham mothers who nursed children from London and Oxford 1578–1601

| Mean interval | *Birth order* | | | |
	1–2	*2–3* 3–4 4–5	*5–6* 6–7 7–8 8–9	*Total intervals*
First child survived; no nurse child taken	127.0 (13)*	141.5 (33)	135.6 (11)	137.1 (57)
First child survived; nurse child taken	231.3 (3)	317.7 (6)	252.6 (4)	277.7 (13)
First child died in less than two years; no nurse child taken	71.4 (4)	101.1 (6)	128.3 (6)	103.9 (16)
First child died in less than two years; nurse child taken	97.0 (1)	152.5 (3)	292.0 (1)	169.3 (5)

Notes
1 There were twenty-one families in the sample: 112 confinements, one set of twins, hence 113 natural children.
2 The infant mortality of the natural children was 226 per thousand live births.
3 There were ninety-one total intergenesic intervals used.
* Numbers in parentheses represent the number of observations.

Source
Dorothy McLaren, 'Nature's Contraceptive: Wet Nursing and Prolonged Lactation: The Case of Chesham, Buckinghamshire, 1578–1801', *Medical History*, XXIII (1979).

We have already noticed the proliferation of nurse children in Hertfordshire, although no statistical analysis of these data has yet been attempted, apart from a brief note by Frank Dulley.[53] The main study of population was, however, carried out on the parish of Minehead in Somerset. The parish contained a port that was very busy in the seventeenth century and was surrounded by rich arable and pasture lands. Shipping to Wales, Ireland and the Americas was well organized. In particular, wool came from Ireland for the cloth industry of Somerset and Devon, going by pack-horse to the cloth centres of Dunster, Dulverton, Taunton, Tiverton and Exeter. Although there were fluctuations, the population of the parish probably doubled during the period 1570–1720. During its growth period the number of families increased dramatically. More shipping meant more shipwrights, chandlers, warehousemen, customs men, hosteliers, farriers and pack-horse men. Masons, surgeons, apothecaries and a host of other occupational groups increased, some forming occupational dynasties. They were supported by men and women in agriculture, fishing, butchering, brewing and baking. Because the children of Minehead could often find employment and a home, they did not need to leave the parish. This resulted in a fairly stable population, an essential for the reconstitution of complete families.

The method of family reconstitution pioneered by Louis Henry in France and followed by Anthony Wrigley for the Colyton parish registers was scrupulously followed for Minehead. Every marriage, baptism and burial was entered on a form and eventually transferred to a family reconstitution form, especially designed and used by the Cambridge Group for the Study of Population and Social Structure. The parish registers of Minehead are of adequate coverage, of good quality, and none was lost or destroyed during the Civil War and Interregnum. Only the marriage register was partly obliterated between 1665 and 1678. The period under review is relatively short for family reconstitution but was chosen in order to compare birth intervals with those of Oxfordshire and Buckinghamshire parishes. The loss of marriage registration between 1665 and 1678 reduced the numbers of women who could be used to determine age at marriage and, therefore, age-specific fertility.

For this survey, only complete families with six or more live births have been studied. A 'complete family' in this case requires the record of burial of husband and/or wife or the baptism of a seventh child. If a multiple birth was involved, there would, of course, be more infants, but the number of intervals would remain the same. Use of complete families with five live births was considered. While this would have increased the number of families, it would have reduced the number of intervals under review. Since the length of the birth interval is undeniably the most important aspect of this study, and in determining fertility in pre-industrial society in general, the number of families was sacrificed in favour of a greater number of intervals. A further influence was that other workers in this field had used complete families with six live births. The one indisputable problem for family reconstitution with regard to birth intervals is the possible non-registration of stillbirths. As far as Minehead is concerned, the register never makes this distinction. Baptism is, of course, not the same as date of birth, but experience of parish registers has convinced me that baptism followed very closely after birth in the period 1570–1720. Any error regarding stillbirths or delay in baptism must be considered as a risk taken with any quantitative analysis of historical documents. Perhaps it is no more of a risk than that taken with statistics from newly developing countries of today, where women often cannot remember the dates of birth or death of some of their children, or how many children were born. For this reason the demographer Louis Henry 'turned to history out of frustration with the difficulty of finding accurate modern data for a population in which there was little or no deliberate control of conception'.[54] We cannot count those who got away, but bearing this and the pitfalls of counting in mind, it still seemed worthwhile to study the fertility of the women who stayed and reared families in Minehead.

The 179 women who fulfilled the criteria of having six or more live births by one marriage were taken from all the socio-economic groups and encompassed many of the occupations mentioned earlier. No noble families appeared in the sample and only one that could be described as wealthy. Infant mortality was not considered for its own sake in this study, but noted solely for its interaction with female fertility. The two main areas covered are marital fertility and inter-genesic intervals.

Table 1.4   Fertility by live births per thousand woman years: Minehead 1600–1720

(a) Overall fertility

| Age at marriage | Date of marriage | | | |
	1600–39	1640–79	1680–1719	Total
Under 25 years	246.4	311.3	289.4	286.9
Over 25 years	311.1	353.9	335.3	355.4
All mothers	271.7	327.1	301.7	302.9

(b) Age-specific fertility

| Age at marriage | Age of mother in years | | | | | |
	15–19	20–4	25–9	30–4	35–9	40–9
Under 25 years	333.3	453.1	410.8	378.4	302.9	97.2
Over 25 years	0	0	476.7	450.0	393.2	131.2
All mothers	333.3	453.1	431.7	406.6	339.0	109.4

Marital fertility

The age of each woman at marriage was noted, where this could be ascertained from family reconstitution. When age of marriage was known, families were divided into those where the woman was under 25 years at marriage and those where she was older. Overall fertility (births per thousand women years lived) was calculated for these two groups, depending on the date of marriage: 1600–39, 1640–79 and 1680–1719. These data are given in Table 1.4(a). In addition, age-specific fertility of these women was calculated for six age spans: 15–19, 20–4, 25–9, 30–4, 35–9 and 40–9 years. These data are given in Table 1.4(b). It was not possible to cover the social and economic background of all the 179 families in the sample. A crude analysis was attempted to grade the mothers into richer or poorer from a number of parish documents as well as hearth-tax returns, lists of inhabitants and the 1641 poll tax. It does appear that the richer women married at a slightly lower mean age than the poorer women. It also appears that premarital conception was not uncommon, nor was it limited to any particular level of society.

Two main points arise from the data. First, fertility was highest in 1640–79 in both age groups. Clearly all the women in the sample were successful in bearing infants and probably successful in breast-feeding them, as for many of the women the births were spread over twenty years. Since many of the women lived long after the final birth, it seems likely that they were strong and healthy. The fact that there are only forty families in the period 1600–39 and almost double that number in the other two periods perhaps indicates that the overall population and the number of families were smaller at the beginning of the seventeenth century; the method of extracting and using the data was identical for all three periods. It is significant that in the period 1600–39 the highest number of births to any one woman was nine. Five women achieved this, eight women had eight children, fifteen had seven and twelve had six. Of the sixty-six women in the next period, 1640–79, half of the women had six or seven children, nineteen women had eight or nine children and fourteen women had more than nine children. The last group included Frances Crockford, the wife of a wealthy Minehead merchant and mother of eighteen children. Of the seventy-three women in the third period, 1680–1720, more than half the women had six or seven children, but only nine women had more than nine children. Family size was clearly larger in 1640–79. This is consistent with the high fertility of this period (Table 1.4(a)), despite the higher mean age at marriage of these mothers. It may indicate a decline in prolonged lactation and wet-nursing, as women began to find more lucrative and less demanding opportunities for employment. This awaits investigation in Somerset.

The second point is that in all three periods, the younger a woman was at marriage, the lower her overall fertility and her age-specific fertility as measured by length of birth intervals, not by number of children born (Table 1.4(b)). The fertility of the women who married under 25 years of age was highest between 20 and 24 years. However, women who were older at marriage were most fertile between 25 and 29. Fertility was therefore apparently highest in the first five years of marriage, as mean age at marriage for those under 25 was 20.9 years, and for women 25 and older at marriage it was 26.4 years. Fertility was relatively low between 15 and 19 years. This corresponds with the fact that menarche was late in the seventeenth century but may also reflect problems for young women bearing their first child at this time and thus omits unrecognized foetal loss.

Intergenesic intervals

Intergenesic intervals (the periods between births) were calculated separately for the births between the first and second, second and third, third and fourth, fourth and fifth, and fifth and sixth child. The intervals between the sixth and seventh and subsequent sibships were calculated separately and pooled. This was also done for the penultimate and ultimate children in each sibship. The intergenesic intervals when the first child of a pair survived two years and when he or she died before this age were separately assessed for each of the forty-year periods. In each case the first baptism in the families took place between 1600–39, 1640–79 and 1680–1720. Intergenesic intervals were also assessed for the whole period 1600–1720.

Table 1.5 summarizes these data and shows that there was a marked reduction in the intergenesic interval when the first child of a pair failed to survive two years. For example, between 1680 and 1720 there were seventy-three families with six or more live births. In the fifty-five families where the first child survived more than two years, the interval to the second birth was 110.2 weeks. In the eighteen families where the first child died, the mean interval was reduced to 97 weeks.

At the personal level we may look more closely at one of these eighteen families. John Connebere married Elizabeth Putham on

Table 1.5   Mean birth intervals (in weeks), Minehead 1600–1720

	Order of birth within family						
	1–2	2–3	3–4	4–5	5–6	6–18	Penulti-mate –ultimate
Total 1600–1720 (179 families)							
First child sur-	110.9	124.0	125.0	146.1	139.3	143.0	161.7
vives two years	(146)*	(165)	(160)	(153)	(148)	(257)	(161)
First child dies	108.0	98.4	104.0	99.3	109.5	95.2	99.5
before two years	(33)	(14)	(18)	(24)	(30)	(36)	(18)
1600–39 (40 families)							
First child sur-	107.0	124.5	127.0	156.3	153.2	150.9	163.5
vives two years	(36)	(37)	(38)	(35)	(32)	(43)	(39)
First child dies	162.0	88.3	76.0	186.3	131.0	90.3	82.0
before two years	(4)	(3)	(1)	(3)	(7)	(3)	(1)
1640–79 (66 families)							
First child sur-	114.1	115.3	122.9	136.0	128.7	139.3	156.2
vives two years	(55)	(63)	(59)	(53)	(52)	(118)	(58)
First child dies	106.5	127.3	91.1	91.2	95.1	96.1	93.5
before two years	(11)	(3)	(7)	(13)	(14)	(18)	(8)
1680–1720 (73 families)							
First child sur-	110.2	132.2	125.7	148.8	140.9	143.9	165.6
vives two years	(55)	(65)	(63)	(65)	(64)	(96)	(64)
First child dies	97.0	91.4	115.8	117.4	115.1	95.1	106.7
before two years	(18)	(8)	(10)	(8)	(9)	(15)	(9)

Note

179 complete families with six or more confinements

* Parentheses denote number of observations

26 January 1697. John was 25 and Elizabeth just 24. Their daughter Elizabeth was baptized two weeks after they were married but was buried within four months. A son was born less than a year after the death of the infant Elizabeth, and was baptized John. Four more children were born with almost exactly a three-year gap between each one; the seventh and last child arrived after a four-year gap; and all survived. The only time that the intergenesic intervals strayed far from a regular three years was after the death of Elizabeth, the first-born, when it was drastically reduced, and at the end of Elizabeth

Connebere's fecund period, when it lengthened. The last observation is in keeping with most findings regarding the penultimate and ultimate intergenesic intervals.

The numbers are small in Table 1.5 for the period 1640–79 and under-registration is possible due to the Civil War, typhus and plague. The interval between the second and third births in this period shows an increase rather than a reduction when the first child of a pair died. Although there are no obvious gaps in the parish register at this time, the numbers are small and some infant burials may have gone unrecorded.

It can generally be seen that the intergenesic interval increases with birth order, and, as with the Connebere family, penultimate to ultimate births always show the greatest interval. The increased intergenesic interval when the first child of a pair survives two years is probably physiologically determined and less affected by increasing birth order than by maternal age. However, when the first child of a pair dies before two years the intervals are closely tied to infant mortality. Thus it is likely that the age of the infant at death would be more pertinent to birth intervals than birth order or maternal age. Indeed in this study intergenesic intervals rose with increasing length of survival. The interval from the death of the first child of a pair to the birth of the second gradually fell with increasing length of survival. If the first child of a pair died between twelve and twenty-four months the interval to the next child was in fact no less than if the first child had survived two years. Many factors determine whether parents

Table 1.6   Mean intervals between the death of the first child and the birth of the second child of a pair (in weeks), Minehead 1600–1720

	Age at which child dies				
	Under 1 month	1–6 months	7–12 months	13–24 months	Over 24 months
Interval number					
1st or 2nd	85.0	81.5	75.5	67.8	117.9
3rd or 4th	87.3	86.0	77.7	54.4	135.3
5th or subsequent	77.8	78.6	73.0	83.7	141.6
Total (all intervals)	83.3	81.0	75.2	70.0	132.4

Note
179 families with six or more confinements

attempt to replace a lost child, or if they do so at all. Whilst today pregnancies may be planned, such decisions were limited in the period 1570–1720. It is likely that physiological factors were more important than psychological factors. Although postpartum infertility is a biological fact, its duration is determined by the length and intensity of the suckling stimulus and to a lesser degree by the nutritional health of the mother. It would seem that there was a definite physiological barrier to the Minehead mothers conceiving another child whilst they had young infants. If the child died young the mother conceived much more quickly than if it survived. The most important consideration of the birth/death/birth interval is that very few Minehead mothers can be seen to have conceived prior to the death of the first child of a pair. This was not so with rich Somerset women who frequently became pregnant before the deaths of their unweaned infants, whose suckling provided a contraceptive stimulus to a surrogate breast.

Intergenesic intervals are obviously related to age at marriage and age-specific fertility. Women who married late showed a higher age-specific fertility at all ages but had a lower mean family size. It is unlikely that the selection of only families with six or more infants severely biased the sample towards highly fertile older women as all were under thirty at marriage and therefore had a physiological minimum of about twelve years in which to complete their families. Women who were young at marriage had larger families but these were spread over longer periods, as was demonstrated by the longer birth intervals in such cases. At all intervals except the first, women who married young had longer birth intervals than women who married at a later age. It is possible that, except for very young women, it was easier to sustain lactation and that, being young, fit and with few children, they may have taken a nurse child, provided that they had succeeded in rearing one child successfully.

The two factors of long birth intervals and low age-specific fertility are obviously interrelated. The relationship is probably one where the long intervals contribute to the reduced fertility rather than the other way round. In other words, because these young women tended, by prolonged lactation, to delay another pregnancy, their observed fertility was lowered. There appears to be no biological reason why women who married earlier (except perhaps teenage brides) should have had intrinsically lower fertility. It seems clear, therefore, that prolonged lactation leads to low fertility, not that low fertility leads to long birth intervals. From the vital statistics of the

179 Minehead mothers who produced six or more infants between 1570 and 1720, there is abundant evidence that they had good reproductive ability, and that they were successful at motherhood and child-rearing. The statistics also reflect a controlled fertility. The extent to which this was consciously controlled is not known.

THE DEMOGRAPHIC EVIDENCE: (2) THE ABERRANT CASES – RICH WOMEN AND WET-NURSES

It is certain that wet-nursing was the normal procedure for rearing the children of rich women in the period 1570–1720. How does this tie up with demographic facts? We have noted the lack of evidence of a wet-nursing domestic industry in Somerset. Having studied the vital statistics of the 179 fecund women of Minehead who were almost certainly breastfeeding their infants, it seemed important to look at the background of equally fecund women of the same county who were using wet-nurses. As in the parish of Minehead, only women having six or more live births of one union, terminated by the death of a partner, were used. Fourteen rich women met those criteria; many had to be excluded because their families could not be reconstituted. The Arundell, Trevelyan, Steyning and Hobbes families are in the sample; but they did baptize some infants before 1570, and some Arundell infants were baptized in Cornwall. There is no evidence yet that any of the rich mothers breastfed their children at all. They may have done so for a short time, but from their family papers it is clear that many used a wet-nurse soon after birth. Unlike the majority of the Minehead mothers they often became pregnant before the death of their last-born infant, a strong indication that maternal suckling was not taking place. The fourteen rich women of Somerset, who almost certainly gave their infants to wet-nurses or had one to stay in the house, had an overall fertility of 700.2 per thousand women years lived. This is twice as high as the fertility of the Minehead mothers overall, and much higher than the most fertile group of Minehead mothers aged 25–29 years, as shown in Table 1.4(b).

Two mothers died during or soon after their last delivery and deserve special attention. Sir John Arundell married Catherine Cosworth in May 1562. Their first child, Juliana, was baptized nine months later in February 1563. John, the only son, was baptized and buried on 12 July 1564. Six daughters followed, and Catherine died giving birth to her seventh daughter on 15 June 1572. Seven girls and one boy had been baptized in just over nine years. Urith Chichester married John Trevelyan in 1571. Ten infants arrived almost annually. Urith died soon after the birth of her last child.

The other twelve highly fertile women fared well on the whole. The grand multigravida, who is generally supposed to face serious danger, often lived for very many years after her last delivery. One typical example will suffice to show the lifestyle of most of these rich women. Alice Frye, the daughter of William Frye of Membury, married Philip Steyning of Selworthy, one of the parishes that border on Minehead. Alice was 25 when her first son Charles was born, and eight more sons and five daughters followed. An infant arrived every year until Alice was 35 years old; thereafter, the intervals lengthened until her fourteenth child Alexander was born when she was 44 years old. Her husband Philip died twenty years later, but Alice was 72 when she died, twenty-eight years after the birth of Alexander. Alice did not leave a diary and we do not know much about the quality of her life or how she felt about being almost always pregnant. We can assume, however, that annual deliveries did not shorten her life. 'Repeated pregnancies *per se* do not seem to damage the mother's health provided that she is adequately fed.'[55] There is no doubt that Alice and the other rich Somerset women were well fed. Testimony from local family documents reveals a very high degree of nourishment from fish, meat and a variety of vegetables. Clearly maternal mortality and/or longevity is important in any discussion on fertility. There is no evidence from this study to show extremely high maternal mortality. The authors of *Poverty and Piety in an English Village* arrived at a similar conclusion regarding the women of Terling.[56]

Apart from overall fertility figures, it seems important to show that the rich women did not suckle their own infants. Although a full-scale wet-nursing industry in Somerset has not been revealed, in the family papers of the rich women there is sufficient qualitative evidence to show that they did use wet-nurses. Moreover, it is possible occasionally to show the relative socio-economic background of the mothers and their relative fertility. George Trevelyan, the second son of John Trevelyan and Urith *née* Chichester, was baptized on 11 May 1579. George was given to Elizabeth, the wife of Nicholas Gilbert, to be nursed. Payments fell into arrears and were offset by the rent of a meadow to the Gilbert family. The third son born to Urith, Ames, was baptized on 6 May 1580, less than a year after his brother George. The Trevelyan commonplace book gives details of the payments to Nicholas Gilbert for Ames's nursing. Ten shillings were paid for the twelve weeks from 6 May to 29 July 1580. It is quite clear from the accounts that Ames Trevelyan was suckled by Elizabeth Gilbert from birth.[57] The maternal ages of Urith Trevelyan and Elizabeth Gilbert have not been established with accuracy, but, while Urith produced ten children in just over ten years, her wet-nurse produced eight children in twenty-two years.

On 18 November 1707 another George Trevelyan was baptized at Nettlecombe. He was suckled by the wife of the churchwarden of nearby Sampford Brett. Her name was Elizabeth Vicary, and years later George left her an annuity of five pounds in his will.[58] Although Elizabeth lived and died in the parish of Sampford Brett there is no record of any more children being born to her after she took George Trevelyan to wet-nurse. If more children were born, they were not baptized in the surrounding Somerset parishes.

Employing good wet-nurses was a costly business, especially by the middle of the seventeenth century. The account paid for nursing Katherine Poulett in 1650 for eighteen months was thirty pounds, and there were often extras such as rent, clothing and presents of all kinds. John Willoughby paid highly when his wife Margaret *née* Steyning gave birth to Susan Willoughby in 1604; he wrote: 'for the Mydwyfe, and Nurse, I am to pay for them whyle they are heere at the same Rate by the weeke as I now pay for myselfe'.[59] Outlays did not end with the lying-in; christening dinners, keep and extras for maids, midwives and nurses had to be found. When Julian Willoughby was given to her wet-nurse in 1630, more than 120 articles for her and her wet-nurse accompanied her. They included shirts, sheets, head-cloths, lace stomachers, neckcloths, silk and wrought sleeves, navel cloths, lace handkerchiefs, dowlas aprons, gloves, girdles, pillows, a counterpane and a whistle.[60] In addition to the high cost of the annual birth and nurture of infants, the funeral expenses of so many of them had also to be met. The maternal matters of poorer women were not nearly as wasteful of physical or financial resources. Any woman who could afford and desired a wet-nurse risked an annual delivery for many years and often the early death of the infant as well. A picture is emerging of rich mothers tied to perpetual pregnancy and poor mothers to perpetual suckling.

Although the wet-nursing domestic industry noted in Hertford-shire has not yet been found in Somerset, it is known that on 27 June 1604 Robert Yarde, a nurse child of Taunton, was buried in the parish of North Curry, not very far from Taunton where he was baptized at the parish church of St Mary on 29 March 1604. This note may be the beginning of a trail of discovery. It is just possible, however, that the Somerset parishes so far investigated were very healthy indeed and, if nurse children from the towns came to them, perhaps they did not die as often as London children in the Home Counties.

CONCLUSION

The use and abuse of human milk was so linked with infant mortality and therefore fertility that it was an important ingredient – perhaps the most important ingredient – in the history of population change in the transition to an industrialized England. Babies within the wombs of mothers who had become dead drunk for twopence, and who soon after birth were handed to foster mothers to starve, are often pictured in accounts of mid-eighteenth-century city life. Infant mortality had reached alarming proportions by 1760 and is attributed to incorrect infant nutrition and the abandonment of breastfeeding.[61] However, the majority of mothers in our period did not live in cities. The evidence from the parishes discussed indicates a fertility controlled by prolonged and non-exclusive lactation. This in itself kept infant mortality relatively low for the majority of mothers. Had this silent majority had the time or the ability to write of their maternal experiences, very few could justifiably have wailed, like rich mothers, 'always going to bed, always pregnant, always giving birth'.[62] Obstetric tragedies through bad presentation and malformation affected rich and poor women alike; difficult births were agonizing for all concerned. But the tragedy should not be overplayed. Only two of the fourteen rich women in this study died as a result of childbirth after producing ten and eight infants respectively at almost annual intervals. Of the 179 Minehead mothers, all of whom produced six or more infants, possibly ten died as a direct result of childbirth, but the longevity of many mothers has been noted. The choice for wives during their teeming years in pre-industrial England was an infant in the womb or at the breast. Since most wives chose to have an infant at the breast, their fertility lagged well behind their fecundity. Small changes in the lives of ordinary women could, however, lead to alterations in breastfeeding patterns which affected fertility, and so bring about major population change.[63]

APPENDIX 1: SELECT BIBLIOGRAPHY ON SCIENTIFIC RESEARCH
INTO THE RELATION OF LACTATION AND AMENORRHOEA

Titles are given in chronological order because of the importance of dates for the development of the subject.

SALBER, EVA J., FEINLEIB, MANNING and MACMAHON, BRIAN. 'The Duration of Postpartum Amenorrhoea', *American Journal of Epidemiology*, LXXXII (1966), pp. 347–58.

CRONIN, T. J. 'Influence of Lactation upon Ovulation', *The Lancet*, no. 7565, 24 August 1968, pp. 422–4.

OSTERIA, TRINIDAD S. 'Lactation and Postpartum Amenorrhoea in a Rural Community', *Acta Medica Philippina*, IX, pt 2, no. 4 (1973), pp. 144–51.

KIPPLEY, SHEILA. *Breast Feeding and Natural Child Spacing*, New York, 1974.

BONTE, M. *et al.* 'Influence of the Socio-Economic Level on the Conception Rate during Lactation', *International Journal of Fertility*, XIX (1974), pp. 97–102.

KNODEL, J. and PRACHUABMOH, V. 'Demographic Aspects of Fertility in Thailand', *Population Studies*, XXVIII (1974), pp. 423–48.

Population Reports, Department of Medical and Public Affairs, George Washington University Medical Centre, Washington, DC, 1975.

SHORT, R. V. 'Lactation – the Central Control of Reproduction', *Breast Feeding and the Mother*, Ciba Foundation Symposium, NS, XLV (1976), pp. 73–86.

BLEEK, WOLF. 'Spacing of Children, Sexual Abstinence and Breast Feeding in Rural Ghana', *Social Science and Medicine*, X (1976), pp. 225–30.

TYSON, JOHN. 'Mechanisms of Puerperal Lactation', *The Medical Clinics of North America*, LXI (1977), pp. 153–63.

DELGADO, HERNAN *et al.* 'Nutrition, Lactation and Postpartum Amenorrhoea', *American Journal of Clinical Nutrition*, XXXI (1978), pp. 322–7.

SHORT, R. V. 'Lactation as a Reproductive Strategy', *11th Hannah Lecture*, University of Glasgow, 1981.

OJOFEITIMI, E. O. 'Effect of Duration and Frequency of Breast Feeding on Postpartum Amenorrhoea', *Pediatrics*, LXIX (1982), p. 2.

APPENDIX 2: HISTORIOGRAPHY OF WORK BY HISTORICAL DEMO-
GRAPHERS ON THE RELATION BETWEEN BREASTFEEDING AND
FERTILITY

The link between lactation and fertility was noted by E. Gautier and L. Henry a quarter of a century ago in a study of a French village in the early modern period, *La population de Crulai, Paroisse Normande*, Institut National d'Etudes Démographiques: Travaux et Documents, XXXIII (1958). J. T. Krause mentioned that prolonged nursing of infants could, among other methods, be used to limit fertility, in papers in 1959 and 1960 ('Some Implications of Recent Work in Historical Demography', *Comparative Studies in Historical Demography*, I (1959), pp. 183n., 184; 'Some Neglected Factors in the English Industrial Revolution', reprinted in Michael Drake (ed.), *Population in Industrialization* (London, 1969), pp. 103–17). It was left, however, to medical research to realize the importance of Henry and Gautier's work. Using their evidence for Crulai, 1674–1742, Christopher Tietze came to the conclusion that breastfeeding was a more reliable contraceptive than any other method in a rural population ('The Effect of Breast Feeding on the Rate of Conception', *Proceedings of the International Population Conference, New York, 1961*, II (London, 1963), pp. 129–36).

Brief references to the relation of lactation and amenorrhoea had already appeared in scientific journals, but after 1961 work tumbled out of the scientific presses from all corners of the world (see Appendix 1). Although Tietze had leaned on historical evidence, historians themselves were slow to follow it up. The challenge of trying to understand population changes with this knowledge in hand has not been taken up with enthusiasm, although brief mention of the effect of lactation on fertility continued to be made. D. V. Glass wrote that 'the probability of conception may be reduced by prolonged breast feeding' (D. V. Glass and D. E. C. Eversley (eds), *Population in History* (London, 1965), Introduction, p. 16); while E. A. Wrigley conceded that 'For example a fall in marital fertility might simply reflect a change in suckling habits' ('Family Limitation in Pre-Industrial England', *EcHR*, 2nd ser., XIX (1966), p. 100). Only in 1967 was the subject carried forward by historical research, with the publication of John Knodel and E. van de Walle, 'Breastfeeding, Fertility and Infant Mortality: An Analysis of Some Early German Data' (*Population Studies*, XXI (1967), pp. 109–31, and carried further in John Knodel, 'Breast Feeding and Population Growth', *Science*, CXCVIII (1977), pp. 1111–15).

My own early work on this subject appeared in 'Stuart Caversham: a Thames-side Community in Oxfordshire During the Seventeenth Century' (unpublished Ph.D. thesis, University of Reading (1975), pp. 257–63) and made use of the medical evidence. An abstract of these findings was published in the *Bulletin of the Society for the Social History of Medicine*, XX (June 1977), pp. 12–16, and a more detailed article followed: 'Fertility, Infant Mortality and Breast Feeding in the Seventeenth Century', *Medical History*, XXII (1978), pp. 378–96.

NOTES

[1] Charlotte Fell Smith, *Mary Rich, Countess of Warwick, 1625–1678, her Family and Friends* (London, 1901), p. 303.
[2] Brian Benson, a review of *The Modern Rise of Population* by Thomas McKeown, *LPS*, XVII (1976), pp. 44–7.
[3] D. V. Glass, 'Two Papers on Gregory King', in D. V. Glass and D. E. C. Eversley (eds), *Population in History* (London, 1974), p. 199; C. W. Chalklin, *Seventeenth-Century Kent: A Social and Economic History* (London, 1965), pp. 35–8; J. D. Chambers, *Population, Economy and Society in Pre-Industrial England* (London, 1972), p. 70; L. Stone, *Family, Sex and Marriage in England 1500–1800* (London, 1977), p. 64.
[4] G. R. Quaife, *Wanton Wenches and Wayward Wives, Peasants and Illicit Sex in Early Seventeenth-Century England* (London, 1979), p. 171. The whole of the book is based on evidence from Somerset. 'Contraception within marriage was evident but rarely mentioned. Abstinence and withdrawal were the methods most commonly used. This was put most bluntly by a frustrated wife who complained "that her husband did not deal with her in bed as befitted a married man ... for that he carnally coupled with her of late years but once a quarter and then what seed should be sown in the right ground he spent about the outward part of her body".'

[5] K. Wrightson, 'Infanticide in Early Seventeenth-Century England', *LPS*, XV (1975), pp. 10–21.

[6] J. Starsmare, *Childrens Diseases both Outward and Inward from the Time of their Birth to Fourteen Years of Age* (Oundle, Northampton, 1664), Introduction.

[7] R. V. Short, 'The Biological Basis for the Contraceptive Effects of Breast Feeding', background document for World Health Organization workshop on breastfeeding and fertility regulation (Geneva, February 1982, in press).

[8] R. V. Short, 'The Evolution of Human Reproduction', *Proceedings of the Royal Society*, ser. B, CXCV, no. 3 (1976), pp. 3–24.

[9] See Appendix 1.

[10] See Appendix 2.

[11] In 1965 theologians doubted 'that there was proof of any natural mechanism preventing ovulation in lactation' (John Noonan, *Contraception* (Harvard, 1965), p. 468). In a personal communication of 1980, Dr R. Blaney of the Queen's University, Belfast, wrote that he found it was still thought of by many as 'a myth of the working class'.

[12] D. B. Jelliffe and E. F. P. Jelliffe, *Human Milk in the Modern World* (London, 1978), pp. 118–19.

[13] V. Sackville-West (ed.), *The Diary of Lady Anne Clifford, 1616–1619* (London, 1923), pp. 30, 67.

[14] R. Kuczynski, 'British Demographers' Opinions on Fertility, 1660–1760', *Annals of Eugenics*, VI (1935), pp. 137–71.

[15] I am indebted to Dr Valerie Fildes for her reference to the diary of Henry Newcome, edited by Thomas Heywood for the Chetham Society in 1849.

[16] Mary Wollstonecraft, *Vindication of the Rights of Women* (1792), ed. Miriam Kramnick (Harmondsworth, 1978), p. 315. See also her letters.

[17] R. V. Short, 'Evolution of Human Reproduction', p. 14.

[18] J. Bongaarts, 'Does Malnutrition Affect Fecundity?', *Science*, CCVIII (1980), pp. 564–9. I am indebted to Professor Short, who wrote to me after the publication of Bongaarts's paper that 'once again this underlines the point that it is the suckling frequency, far more than nutrition, that is responsible for the long inter-birth intervals in some communities.' This is not the same interpretation as E. A. Wrigley and R. S. Schofield give to Bongaarts's paper. These writers have stressed nutrition rather than suckling in *The Population History of England 1541–1871* (Cambridge, Mass., 1981), p. 306.

[19] W. H. Mosley (ed.), *Nutrition and Reproduction* (New York, 1978), esp. pp. 179–229, but full accounts of the subject are given by many workers in the field. See especially Sandra Huffman, 'Postpartum Amenorrhoea: How is it Affected by Maternal Nutritional Status?', *Science*, CC (1978), pp. 1155–7.

[20] Rose E. Frisch, 'Nutrition, Fatness and Fertility: The Effect of Food Intake on Reproductive Ability', in Mosley, op. cit., pp. 91–122.

[21] J. W. Eaton and A. J. Mayer, 'The Social Biology of Very High Fertility among the Hutterites: The Demography of a Unique Population', *Human Biology*, XXV (1953), pp. 206–64.

[22] G. B. Kolata, 'Kung Hunter Gatherers: Feminism, Diet and Birth Control, *Science*, CLXXXV (1974), pp. 932–4.

[23] Susan B. Hanley and Kozo Yamamure, *Economic and Demographic Change in Pre-Industrial Japan, 1600–1868* (Princeton, NJ, 1977), p. 244.

[24] Barbara Harrell, 'Lactation and Menstruation in Cultural Perspective', *American Anthropologist*, LXXXIII (1981), p. 805.

[25] Henry G. Friesen, reported in the *Winnipeg Tribune*, 30 September 1977.

[26] Frances and Margaret Verney, *Memoirs of the Verney Family during the Seventeenth Century* (London, 1907), p. 380.

[27] Ibid., p. 382.

[28] Edward Shorter, *The Making of the Modern Family* (London, 1976), p. 168.

[29] Valerie Fildes, 'Weaning the Elizabethan Child', *Nursing Times*, LXXVI (1980), p. 1358.

[30] Jelliffe and Jelliffe, op. cit., p. 162.

[31] François Mauriceau, *The Accomplisht Midwife, Treating of the Diseases of Women with Child and in Childbed with Fit Remedies for the Several Indispositions of New-born Babes* (1668), trans. Hugh Chamberlen (1673), pp. 295–389.

[32] James McMath, *The Expert Midwife: A Treatise of the Diseases of Women with Child and in Childbed ... with the Fit Remedies for the Various Maladies of New-born Babes* (Edinburgh, 1694), p. 324. See also Audrey Eccles, *Obstetrics and Gynaecology in Tudor and Stuart England* (Ohio, 1982), p. 99.

[33] Marina Warner, *Alone of All Her Sex* (London, 1976), p. 203.

[34] Lady Newdigate-Newdigate, *Gossip from a Muniment Room* (London, 1897), p. 17.

[35] Elizabeth Clinton, Countess of Lincoln, *The Countess of Lincolns Nurserie* (Oxford, 1622).

[36] [J. Guillemeau], *Childbirth; or the Happie Delivery of Women* (1612), Preface.

[37] Nora Lofts, *Emma Hamilton* (London, 1978), p. 76.

[38] Ivy Pinchbeck, *Women Workers and the Industrial Revolution, 1750–1850* (1930), 3rd edn (London, 1981), p. 238.

[39] Thomas Mo(u)ffat, *Health's Improvement* (London, 1655).

[40] I am indebted to Valerie Fildes for this information.

[41] J. C. Cox, *The Parish Registers of England* (London, 1910), pp. 68–9.

[42] Wrightson, op. cit., pp. 10–21.

[43] J. S. Burn, *The History of Parish Registers in England* (1829), 2nd edn (repr. Wakefield, 1976), p. 137.

[44] Cox, op. cit., pp. 68–9.

[45] Franklyn Dulley, 'Nurse Children: A Forgotten Cottage Industry', *Hertfordshire Countryside*, XXXVII, no. 274 (1982), pp. 14–15; Roger A. P. Finlay, 'Population and Fertility in London, 1580–1650', *Journal of Family History*, IV (1979), pp. 26–38.

[46] J. F. Fisher, 'The London Food Market', in E. M. Carus Wilson (ed.), *Essays in Economic History*, 3 vols, I (London, 1954), p. 148. 'London had no facilities for malting, and in the absence of adequate running water, few for milling. Consequently a number of country towns found their major employment in the processing of the city's corn. ... Hertford was a flourishing milling centre. Hatfield, Hitchin, St Albans, Hexton, Cheshunt, Aldenham, Elstree ... "were onely upholden and maynteyned by the trade of making Maults and the cariage thereof up to London by horse and carts". By the time of Charles I, the more distant Royston was buying "a very great parte of the Corne in Cambridgeshire" and sending 180 great malt waggons to the city every week.'

[47] Verney and Verney, op. cit., p. 361.

[48] H. N. Nicholas, *A Treatise on the Law of Aldulterine Bastardy, with a Report of the Banbury Case, and of all other Cases bearing upon the Subject* (London, 1839), pp. 331–2.

[49] Somerset Record Office, Q/SR 115/52–4.

[50] Ronald Illingworth, *The Normal Child* (London, 1975), p. 10.

[51] Dorothy McLaren, 'Stuart Caversham: a Thames-side Community in Oxfordshire During the Seventeenth Century', unpublished Ph.D. thesis, University of Reading (1975), and 'Fertility, Infant Mortality and Breast Feeding in the Seventeenth Century', *Medical History*, XXII (1978), pp. 378–96.

[52] Dorothy McLaren, 'Nature's Contraceptive: Wet Nursing and Prolonged Lactation, the Case of Chesham, Buckinghamshire, 1578–1601', *Medical History*, XXIII (1979), pp. 426–41.

[53] Dulley, op. cit.

[54] E. A. Wrigley, 'Population History in the 1980s', *Journal of Interdisciplinary History*, XII (1981), pp. 207–26.

[55] R. V. Short, personal communication, 1981.

[56] K. Wrightson and D. Levine, *Poverty and Piety in an English Village: Terling 1525–1700* (Toronto, 1979), p. 58. The extent of maternal mortality has been discussed in B. M. Willmott Dobbie, 'An Attempt to Estimate the True Rate of Maternal Mortality, Sixteenth to Eighteenth Centuries', *Medical History*, XXVI (1982), pp. 79–90. It may not have been as grave as this writer suggests. Gregory King assumed that it was common knowledge that women in England on average lived longer than men: R. Thompson, 'Seventeenth-Century English and Colonial Sex Ratios', *Population Studies*, XXVIII (1974), pp. 162–3.

[57] Somerset Record Office, DD/WO 61/5.

[58] Ibid., 62/13.

[59] Ibid., 56/8.

[60] Ibid., 61/5.

[61] Roger Short, personal communication, 11 August 1980; G. F. Still, *The History of Paediatrics* (Oxford, 1931), p. 455.

[62] Jean-Louis Flandrin, *Families in Former Times*, trans. Richard Southern (Cambridge, 1979), p. 217.
[63] George D. Sussman's important book, *Selling Mother's Milk: The Wet-Nursing Business in France, 1715–1914* (Illinois, 1982), came to my attention too late to be considered in this paper.

The remarrying widow: a stereotype reconsidered

2

BARBARA J. TODD

For playwrights of the early modern period, a remarrying widow was a subject for comedy. In one of the earliest surviving English comic plays, *Ralph Roister-Doister* (written in the 1550s), the widow Christian Custance was the object of Ralph's ridiculous attentions. She had many successors. In the early Stuart period she emerged as Lady Plus in *The Puritaine* or Lady Allworth in Philip Massinger's *A New Way to Pay Old Debts*, and re-emerged in the many comic widows of the Restoration stage, of whom Widow Blackacre in William Wycherley's *The Plain Dealer* and Lady Wishfort in William Congreve's *The Way of the World* are only two of the best known.[1] They made the old woman who would remarry a stock character of the comedy of manners.

It was a genre that discouraged the playwright from showing any sympathy for the pain and loneliness of widowhood. Contempt was substituted for sympathy. The condemnation of all remarrying widows, after Lady Plus has been saved from an unsuitable match, shows plainly the feeling that was otherwise often only implied:

> Such is the blind besotting in the state of an unheaded woman that's a widow! For it is the property of all you that are widows ... to hate those that honestly and carefully love you ... and strongly to dote on those that only love you to undo you ... such is the peevish moon that rules your bloods.[2]

Among these stage widows, a few like Christian Custance and Lady Allworth are sensible women, but most are drawn as foolish, pathetic creatures. Yet so effective are they as comic characters that they have

engendered an enduring stereotype of the early modern widow as a
woman who anxiously sought a husband at any cost.

The present-day observer cannot help but feel sympathy for the
dilemma of these fictional women, who are expected by their creators
to seek to remarry, but who are treated with contempt because they
try to do so. So to discover that a few of these theatrical widows break
the stereotype by rejecting matrimony comes as a pleasant surprise.
They are particularly interesting because they also articulate some of
the reasons why a seventeenth-century widow might choose not to
remarry. Wycherley's Widow Blackacre, for instance, wishes to
protect her rights to her property and her legal independence. Lady
Haughty in the Duke of Newcastle's *The Triumphant Widow* (1677)
rejects her suitors because she relishes the personal freedom her
widowed state allows.

As Widow Blackacre and Lady Haughty were well aware, marital
status had important legal implications for the early modern woman.
A married woman was legally and personally subject to her husband.
A widow was free from such control. Even if she was poor, she was
her own woman and could run her life as she saw fit. If she was lucky
enough to have inherited or succeeded to property, she was able to
control her independent means in her own interest and on behalf of
her children and others for whom she chose to act.

But the independent widow was also an anomaly. English patriarchal society required that, like the state, the household should be
headed by a man. The woman heading her own household contra-
dicted the patriarchal theory; the ungoverned woman was a threat to
the social order. Hence the great pressure on young single women to
marry, and the mockery of the 'old maid' who failed to do so. The
situation of the widow, however, was much more ambiguous. She
too should have been urged to remarry quickly: not only was she a
threat to the theoretical order, but without the support of a man's
earnings she and her family were likely to become a financial burden
on the community. Yet it was the widow who did remarry who was
criticized; for, as men realized, the remarriage of any widow confronted every man with the threatening prospect of his own death
and the entry of another into his place. The comic widows of the
stage personify these contradictory feelings.

The stage thus not only created a stereotype of the remarrying
widow but also gives us grounds to question whether early modern
widows did indeed marry as readily as the comedies suggest. It is not
easy, however, to measure just how common remarriage was in the

past. A recent estimate suggests that some scepticism is justified, and that the remarriage of widows was becoming increasingly less common in the seventeenth century when the stage widows flourished. Using the sparse evidence on remarriage available in parish registers, E. A. Wrigley and Roger Schofield have calculated that in the mid-sixteenth century 30 per cent of brides and grooms had already been married at least once before. By the mid-nineteenth century, when dependable central statistics become available, this proportion had dropped to 11.27 per cent.[3] These figures are for men and women combined; remarriage rates for widows seem to have fallen even lower.[4] Evidence on the rate of change is very scanty, and Wrigley and Schofield have postulated that it occurred as a linear decline.[5] This alteration of remarriage patterns was a 'very substantial change' with profound implications for the lives of the widowed themselves and for their families and their communities.

What could have caused such a change? At first glance one would assume that greater longevity was the simple cause. People widowed young were very likely to remarry in the sixteenth century. This was also true in the nineteenth century, but if, as a result of reduced mortality, fewer people were widowed young, fewer would have remarried. However, as Wrigley and Schofield observe, what is in question is not gross mortality, but mortality among adults old enough to marry. And this in fact changed very little between the sixteenth and nineteenth centuries – far too little to explain the major change in remarriage rates.[6]

If the simple explanation based on changing mortality rates does not suffice, then some more subtle and complex factors must have been at work. But, hard though it is to measure change in remarriage rates, it is even harder to assess the reasons that led widows in the past to marry or to decide against matrimony. Remarriage is something that involves many intangibles which normal historical sources rarely document. Love and a sense of duty to the dead husband, on the one hand, and loneliness and the need for affection and security, on the other, were surely important factors that it is now impossible to evaluate fully. Economic and social factors also played a part. To assess their effect one must also understand the social status and economic circumstances of those widows who remarried and those who did not. These features can best be studied in a specific local context, using a fairly small and clearly identifiable group of women. There is therefore much to learn from studying remarriage in terms of the lives of widows of one community. This essay focuses on the

women of Abingdon, Berkshire, between 1540 and 1720, and it con-
centrates on the factors that may have influenced the widows' own
decisions about remarriage. Some of these factors may also have
affected the widowers and bachelors who were the widows' potential
partners. But though a widow obviously could not marry without a
willing partner she too had to be willing to wed. The factors discussed
here would have influenced widows, whether or not a potential
suitor was at hand.[7]

REMARRIAGE RATES IN ABINGDON

Abingdon is well suited for such a study for several reasons. Its
population, which remained at around 1500 from the mid-sixteenth
to the mid-seventeenth century and then increased to more than 2000
by 1720,[8] was large enough to provide a good sample. Yet it was
almost all comprehended within one large parish, St Helen's. The
other parish, St Nicholas's, had only about a hundred residents.
Most people thus can be traced within a single set of parochial
records, leaving only a few to be pursued further in the other parish.
The historian of Abingdon is also blessed with a rich and wide range
of other documents relevant to the study of widowhood and remarriage. The probate records are excellent; there are superb series of
poor-relief accounts; the minute and account books of the town's
charitable corporation, Christ's Hospital, are extremely well preserved; and the minute and account books of the borough itself
survive. Christ's Hospital and the borough were the two main land-
lords of a town where most property was held by lease, so their
records contain a vast amount of information about accommodation
for the town's residents. Records of tradespeople appear in borough
minute books and in many lists of those summoned to the market
court.[9] All in all, it is possible to learn a great deal about the characteristics of Abingdon widows who are known to have remarried or
known not to have done so, and also much about even those women
who cannot be traced completely to the end of their widowhood.

Remarriage rates of widows can be studied in two ways: by estimating
either what proportion of brides were already widows or what
proportion of widows eventually married again. For the first method
one must have parish registers that consistently record the marital
status of all brides. English registers that do this are very rare indeed;
the Cambridge demographers have so far found only two that do so

for extended periods.[10] Abingdon's registers are typical in that information on marital status is only very rarely included, so this measure of remarriage cannot be used. The difficulties with the second way of measuring are also great, because one must follow a large number of women from the death of the husband to the end of widowhood, when they either remarried or died as widows. In theory this information should be recoverable from parish registers, but in fact widowed people were particularly likely to disappear from the records of their home parishes – because they moved away, because their deaths were not registered, or because they cannot be positively identified.[11] Widows are particularly difficult to trace in English records because of the propensity to identify them only as 'Widow So-and-so', without using a Christian name. But, however difficult, this is the only measure of remarriage that can be used for Abingdon and most other English communities.

The first task is to identify a large group of widows to be traced. This exercise is more difficult than at first appears, since it was most unusual in Abingdon, as elsewhere, for the parish clerk to record the marital status of the men who were buried. Married men and the widows who survived them must be identified in some other way. A family reconstitution could provide this information, but would be very time-consuming as a way of identifying a group of widows. Luckily there exists a manuscript index of the Abingdon parish registers in which entries under each surname have been arranged as far as possible by family units, and which includes all information in the original registers.[12] With such an index it is scarcely more difficult to identify people than if a full reconstitution had been undertaken.

Two techniques were finally chosen to secure a group of widows for study. One sample was obtained by using probate records and includes the widows of the 650 married Abingdon men whose estates were proved in the court of the Archdeacon of Berkshire from 1540 to 1720 and in the Prerogative Court of Canterbury from 1540 to 1700. From this number widows of Nonconformists who died before 1700 have been excluded, since the deaths of some of these women were recorded in parish registers or probate records while the marriages of others may have been lost because they did not wed in the parish church.[13] Omitting the Nonconformists leaves a total of 622 widows to be studied. The obvious advantage of using a group of widows identified from probate records is that a great deal is known about their social and economic situation – the value of their husbands' inventories, how much they acquired as executors, administrators or legatees, their husbands' occupations, and often something about the number and ages of children. All these are factors that might affect the likelihood of remarriage. Although a group selected from probate records can also be expected to include a disproportionate number of the wealthier members of the community, a surprisingly large number of estates of poor Abingdon men were proved. A quarter of husbands' inventories in the sixteenth century were worth less than £6. 11s. 7d. In the later seventeenth century, after years of inflation, a quarter of the husbands still had inventories worth less than £21. 2s. 5d. Evidence about the wives of these men gives some indication of remarriage patterns among poor widows, even though it cannot take full account of the very poorest, whose husbands' estates were rarely proved.

Because of this, a second sample less subject to the selectivity of probate was obtained for comparison by abstracting cohorts of couples from the parish registers. These cohorts included all couples married in St Helen's parish in three decades: 1541–50, 1571–80 and 1691–1700. Each couple was followed to the decease of the first partner, and then each surviving widow was traced to the end of her widowhood. The cohorts chosen were from decades that were the least likely to be affected by manifest lapses in registration, while still corresponding roughly to the three periods used to study the probate widows. Although 415 couples made up the original cohorts, only about a third (144) could be traced through to the end of the marriage, and an even smaller group (63) to the fate of the widow. The cohort study is thus useful mainly for comparison with the much larger probate sample.

Since the reason for using the cohort group was to minimize bias, only information in the parish registers has been used to investigate the fate of these widows. On the other hand, all possible sources were used to identify and trace widows in the probate group – other probates, leases, marriage bonds, other registers, court records, and so forth. Nevertheless a large proportion of Abingdon widows (40 per cent in the probate group, 20 per cent in the cohort sample) cannot be traced, even if a wide range of documentation is used. This is due in large part to a long period of poor registration in the mid-seventeenth century. Many women were also counted as un-traced, not because they disappeared from the records, but because of ambiguity of identification. From all that can be learned about the untraced women from their husband's wills and elsewhere, it is clear that the group of probate widows who disappeared was very similar in structure to the group that remained in view (see Appendix and

Table 2.8); and, while it is possible that some widows disappeared because they went away to remarry, there is no evidence in records of marriage licences and registers of nearby communities to suggest that this was necessarily the case for many. Even had their behaviour differed radically from that of the women who remained in view, it would still not have negated the overall pattern of change shown below. (See Appendix.)

The whole group of probate widows whose fate is known is shown in Table 2.1. A little more than a third (about 36 per cent) of these women remarried, while two-thirds died as widows. However, if

Table 2.1 Remarriage of widows of Abingdon men whose estates were proved

| | Date of husband's probate | | | |
	1540–99	1600–59	1660–1720*	Total
All husbands' probates	149	270	203	622
No. of traced widows†	100	144	132	376
No. of widows remarried	50	54	31	135
Widows remarried as percentage of widows traced	50.0	37.5	23.5	35.9

* Omits Nonconformists' probates before 1700
† That is, those known to have remarried or to have died as widows

these women are divided into three groups according to the date of the husband's probate (1540–99, 1600–59 and 1660–1720), it is clear that these proportions altered considerably as time passed. In the sixteenth century fully half of the women traced married again; in the first half of the seventeenth century this proportion dropped to a little more than a third (37.5 per cent). After the Restoration, less than a quarter (23.5 per cent) married again. A similar pattern occurred with the cohort widows shown in Table 2.2. Of the widows traced who originally married in the 1540s, not quite half married again; of those married in the 1570s more than a third (38.5 per cent) and of those who first married in the 1690s only about a sixth (15.8 per cent) took another husband. This is the pattern one would expect in the light of the changes in remarriage rates that Wrigley and Schofield have posited for the country as a whole, using the nineteenth-century statistics of the Registrar General to show changes over three

Table 2.2 Remarriage of widows from cohorts of couples married at St Helen's, Abingdon

| | Date of original marriage* | | |
	1541–50	1571–80	1691–1700
All marriages in decade	163	136	178
Couples traced to death of husband or wife	56	42	46
Marriages ended by death of husband	36	18	24
Widows traced to remarriage or burial as widow	31	13	19
Widows remarried	15	5	3
Widows remarried as percentage of widows traced	48.4	38.5	15.8

* Year beginning 25 March

centuries. Since this study of Abingdon widows uses different methods and data, the statistics collected in the Registrar General's reports are of little use for comparison here. However, in 1840 the statistician William Farr used the mortality and remarriage statistics for that year to calculate that one-quarter of women widowed then would eventually remarry.[14] If Farr's estimates are correct, Abingdon widows at the end of the seventeenth century remarried at the same rate as their nineteenth-century counterparts.

LONGEVITY AND REMARRIAGE IN ABINGDON

It seems fair to assume that remarriage rates and the factors that fostered change varied considerably from place to place. Any explanation of change must take that into account. This is true, for instance, of the effects of changing longevity. Despite the fact that differences in mortality rates do not explain the decline in remarriage on the national scale, it does appear that among these Abingdonians, over this shorter period, increasing longevity may have had some effect. Studies that measure the age of widows who remarried indicate that younger widows were the most likely to wed again.[15] Thus when fewer women were widowed young in the later seventeenth century, when marriages lasted longer than formerly (as is shown in Tables 2.3 and 2.4), remarriage rates of Abingdon widows should have declined.

Table 2.3 Length of marriages and intervals to remarriage: probate group

	Date of husband's probate		
	1540–99	1600–59	1660–1720
*From marriage to husband's death*****			
Mean interval (months)	146.6	238.8	234.4
Median interval (months)	125	224	180
Number	45	61	49
*From husband's death***** *to remarriage of widow*			
Mean interval (months)	28.4	21.2	30
Median interval (months)	11	16	23
Number	34	20	21

* Using registered date of burial if available, or date of probate if it occurred within one calendar month of the writing of the will

Table 2.4 Length of marriages and intervals to remarriage: cohort couples

	Date of original marriage*****		
	1541–50	1571–80	1691–1700
Marriage ended by death of husband			
Mean length (months)	150.8	210.1	277.2
Median length (months)	111	158	175
Number	36	18	24
From burial of husband to remarriage of widow			
Mean interval (months)	18.5	8	13
Median interval (months)	11	9	10
Number	15	5	3

* Year beginning 25 March

Table 2.3 shows the length of marriages of couples in the probate group that could be traced back to their weddings. The marriages of women widowed in the sixteenth century lasted about 10–12 years on average (a mean of about 147 months, a median of 125 months), while the average length of marriage of women widowed in the early seventeenth century increased to 18–20 years (about 239 months mean, 224 months median), despite the effects of plague and epidemic disease in 1625 and the 1640s. Between 1660 and 1720 the mean length of marriage in the group continued to be about 20 years (about 234 months). The same pattern of increasingly long marriages is shown in the cohort sample (Table 2.4). Here the mean length of marriage ended by the death of the husband increased from around 151 months to around 277 months, and the median length from 111 months to 175 months. This Abingdon evidence is surprising, because nationally the later seventeenth century was a period of very high mortality, when life expectancy declined even among men who had reached the age of 30.[16] Our Abingdon couples may have been going against a national pattern, although the fact that the median length of marriage in the probate group in the later seventeenth century was only 180 months suggests that, in Abingdon too, years of generally high mortality had some impact.[17]

Does the increasing length of the marriages of these widows serve to explain the change in remarriage rates? This question can be answered by comparing the record of the widows in the probate group whose first marriages had been brief with the record of women whose marriages had lasted longer. The same kind of comparison could be made by using the age of the widows, but the actual ages of few of these women could be calculated, since only a small group could be traced back to their births. As it is, it has been possible to discover both the length of the marriage and the fate of only some 18 per cent of our 622 probate widows. None the less it does appear to be true that Abingdon widows whose first marriage lasted ten years or less were very likely to marry again.[18] Such women would have been mainly about 35 years old or younger. As can be seen from Table 2.5, in the sixteenth century 73 per cent of these widows married again, and the rate was fairly similar (around 71 per cent) in the later seventeenth century. The smaller proportion (50 per cent) remarrying in the early seventeenth century probably reflects the small sample rather than a change in behaviour. The fact that so many young Abingdon widows did remarry suggests that, indeed, when marriages lasted longer in the later seventeenth century, the group of widows most likely to wed became smaller and overall remarriage rates declined.

Table 2.5 Remarriage of widows in probate group, by length of preceding marriage

| | 1540–99 Widows | | 1600–59 Widows | | 1660–1720* Widows | |
	Traced† No.	Remarried No. %	Traced† No.	Remarried No. %	Traced† No.	Remarried No. %
All cases	100	50 50.0	144	54 37.5	132	31 23.5
Preceding marriage lasted:						
10 years or less‡	11	8 72.7	8	4 50.0	7	5 71.4
10–20 years	9	7 77.8	15	7 46.7	10	3 30.0
More than 20 years	11	3 27.3	24	4 16.7	14	0 0.0

* Omits widows of Nonconformists whose estates were proved before 1700
† That is, widows traced to remarriage or to death as a widow. Only some couples could be traced back to their weddings, and only some of those widows could be traced to their fate. The total number of probates in each category is shown in Table 2.8. Marriages known to have ended within each period are included, even if the exact length of the marriage is not known.
‡ Wife not previously married

What is surprising, however, is what happened to remarriage rates among the older widows – that is, those whose marriages had lasted longer. This is where the biggest change occurred. In the sixteenth century a quarter of the women whose marriages had lasted more than twenty years remarried, but in the later period no woman in this oldest age group is known to have married again. In the sixteenth century seven of the nine widows whose marriages are known to have lasted 10–20 years married again; in the later seventeenth century, only three among ten. The mean length of all the preceding marriages of widows who remarried fell from 130 months to 92 months.

The record of these older widows provides evidence that the increasing longevity of husbands is only part of the explanation for changes in remarriage patterns. The proportion of older widows who remarried dropped so precipitously that even if the number of older widows had not increased, remarriage rates overall would still have declined. For example let us suppose that the same proportion of women were widowed within ten years in the seventeenth century as in the sixteenth. Let us also suppose that such young widows continued to remarry at the same rate as in the sixteenth century (as seems to have been the case). Nevertheless, because the change in remarriage rates amongst older widows was so great, the proportion of all widows who married again would still have dropped from 59 per cent in the sixteenth century to 36 per cent after the Restoration. It appears, then, that two things were happening: fewer women in the seventeenth century were widowed after brief marriages, but at the same time older widows, who in the sixteenth century had been quite likely to marry again, were much less likely to do so later on. Forces other than a simple increase in husbands' longevity must thus have contributed to such a change.

SOCIO-ECONOMIC CHARACTERISTICS OF REMARRYING WIDOWS

Something about how and why changes in remarriage rates occurred may be learned from studying the familial, social and economic situations of the widows in the probate group who remarried. Surprisingly, when the widows are grouped according to certain socio-economic characteristics (in Table 2.6), it is clear that remarriage rates declined among all groups. It is true that the tendency to remarry was higher overall for some groups than others, and this suggests some of the reasons for the change. But the general

Table 2.6 Remarriage of widows in probate group, by various socio-economic characteristics

	1540–99 Widows			1600–59 Widows			1660–1720* Widows		
	Traced† No.	Remarried No.	%	Traced† No.	Remarried No.	%	Traced† No.	Remarried No.	%
All cases	100	50	50.0	144	54	37.5	132	31	23.5
Children									
All minors	23	16	69.6	31	18	58.1	18	7	38.9
None	14	6	42.9	19	8	42.1	17	5	29.4
Husband's probate inventory									
In lowest quarter	20	11	55.0	26	9	34.6	21	6	28.6
In highest quarter	19	10	52.6	27	13	48.1	23	7	30.4
Low-income occupations‡	11	6	54.5	14	4	28.6	13	3	23.1
Widow was									
Executor or administrator	85	49	57.6	124	51	41.1	98	29	29.6
Not executor or administrator	15	1	6.7	20	3	15.0	34	2	5.9

Husband's occupation									
Artisan	33	17	51.5	48	16	33.3	52	13	25.0
Catering, transport, milling	4	3	75.0	21	13	61.9	23	9	39.1
Merchant, maltster	15	10	66.7	15	6	40.0	20	3	15.0
Gentleman or professional	15	4	26.7	23	4	17.4	23	2	8.7
Other or not known	33	16	48.5	37	15	40.5	14	4	28.6

* Omits widows of Nonconformists whose estates were proved before 1700

† That is, widows known to have remarried or to have died without remarrying; total number of probates in each category is shown in Table 2.8

‡ Labourers, clothworkers, tailors, cordwainers, shoemakers

consistency of the decline indicates that we may also have to look beyond these particular social and economic factors for a complete explanation.

One group that was more likely to remarry were widows with young children. The second line of Table 2.6 shows the record of widows whose husbands' wills mention children who were all minors; the third line gives the rates for the widows who had the least familial responsibilities, those whose husbands' wills mention no children at all.[19] It is clear that in the sixteenth century young children were no obstacle to remarriage and perhaps encouraged it: nearly 70 per cent (16 out of 23) of widows with young families married again. But, though this group continued to remarry more readily than the average, their tendency to do so declined quite sharply in the seventeenth century, and in the later period less than 40 per cent remarried. We shall consider reasons for this in due course. Women with no children were not so likely to remarry in the sixteenth century, but the likelihood that they would do so also changed less. Widows who remarried after brief marriages in the latest period tended to be childless.

Wealth seems to have had less effect on changing remarriage patterns than one would expect, considering the popular if cynical belief that widows were married mainly for their money. Table 2.6 compares the record of women whose husbands' probate inventories were in the poorest 25 per cent with the record of women whose husbands were part of the richest 25 per cent. Both groups followed the general trend of change, and both groups were surprisingly close to average in each period (though wealthier widows were rather more likely than poorer widows to remarry in the early seventeenth century). A similar general pattern appears when the median values of the husbands' inventories are compared in Table 2.7, although the evidence here suggests that in the sixteenth century widows who remarried tended to be rather poorer than those who did not, while in the seventeenth century they were almost as wealthy or wealthier. The remarriage rates of widows of men who followed low-income occupations, such as labourers, clothworkers or shoemakers (Table 2.6), also followed the overall pattern, but were rather lower than average in the early seventeenth century.

The seventh and eighth lines of Table 2.6 show one characteristic that was closely correlated with remarriage rates. The vast majority of widows of Abingdon testators were named executor or co-executor in their husbands' wills (89 per cent in the sixteenth century, 74 per

Table 2.7 Median value of probate inventories of men whose widows were traced

	1540–99	1600–59	1660–1720*
Widows married	£15 8s. 0d. (43)†	£46 13s. 2d. (38)	£46 1s. 0d. (20)
Widows died as widows	£19 17s. 10d. (30)	£29 4s. 10d. (64)	£51 0s. 8d. (60)

* Omits inventories of Nonconformists before 1700
† Parentheses indicate number of cases

cent after 1660), and so succeeded to all or most of their husbands' goods. Widows were also almost always appointed administrator if their husbands died intestate. Women who were not named, or who surrendered their powers of administration, were extremely unlikely to marry again. This is not in fact surprising, since, in the early periods especially, when a widow was not made executor it was usually because she was incapacitated by age or infirmity, and her husband made other provision for her care. The failure of such women to remarry thus does not reflect the plight of the widow cut out of her husband's will and left with nothing. That happened to just three of the 622 widows. Women who renounced administration also sometimes did so because of infirmity or age, but more often because their husbands' debts were too great to make administration worthwhile. The latter widows were slightly more likely to remarry than those who were not named to act as executor.

A glance at the last five lines of Table 2.6, in which widows are divided according to their husbands' occupations, shows that each of these groups followed the same trend, although remarriage rates among widows of merchants and maltsters (grouped together because of the importance of liquid capital in these callings) fell more abruptly. However, the behaviour of two groups should be particularly noted: the widows of men in catering and transport (innkeepers, boatmen, millers, and so on) were decidedly more likely to marry in all periods (the number in the group was extremely small in the first period); while, on the other hand, widows of gentlemen and men who followed professional callings (mainly clerics, but also a few scriveners and physicians) were in all periods much less likely to marry again.

The record of widows of men in catering and transport may in part be a function of documentary visibility. Widows who succeeded to an inn or a mill could not easily move their wealth to another community to marry there. That alone, however, would not make them more likely to marry again. Such a tendency more likely reflects the peculiar difficulties of running a catering or transport business. As wives, these women had probably been involved in running the family enterprise, and were expected by their husbands to carry on in the trade (four-fifths of their husbands asked this specifically in their wills or implied it by naming the widow as executor). But, although a number of Abingdon widows successfully ran alehouses, wharfs and mills for long periods, operating a mill or running a large inn with a sizeable indoor and outdoor staff to supervise seems to have been difficult for a woman working alone. They were thus less inclined than the widows of merchants and maltsters, for instance, to continue in business by themselves, but more likely to marry men who were in, or entered, the trade. Merchandising and malting involved investment that seems to have been relatively easy for a woman to manage; 87 per cent of testators in these occupations specifically expected or implied that their widows should continue, and many of the widows did so.

The group of tradesmen's widows who were the least likely to remarry were the widows of artisans. This may at first seem surprising, since one might assume that they would be the least able to continue in trade on their own. Many artisans' trades demanded physical skills that few women were likely to acquire (a widow of a baker or a glover might well have learned all aspects of the trade, but the widow of a carpenter or a tanner would probably have been involved only on the financial side of her husband's business, if at all; the wives of journeymen who worked away from home were probably occupied in entirely different work from that of their husbands).[20] Such women could only carry on the business by relying on employees, and it would seemingly have been more efficient to marry a workman already skilled in the trade. However, artisans' wills suggest they were aware of the difficulties a widow might have, and they were rather less likely than men in other occupational groups to pass their affairs over to their widows as executors (barely half did so in the later seventeenth century). Without an ongoing business, an artisan's widow had less need to remarry someone in the same trade and could bring little in the way of trading assets. Instead of remarrying, artisans' widows often turned to alehouse-keeping. Keeping a front-room alehouse was a common by-employment in this market town,[21] and, since many artisans' wives were probably already part-time victuallers catering for market crowds and fair-goers long before their husbands died, they would have continued the work in which they were already established. Others undoubtedly worked for wages at a variety of jobs, as they had done when their husbands were alive.[22]

The record of the artisans' widows suggests that remarrying within the trade was perhaps not so common as the conventional image of the marriage of the widow and her apprentice suggests. It has not been possible to identify the occupations of many pairs of Abingdon husbands,[23] but, of forty-eight widows for whom the occupations of both husbands are known, nineteen married men in the same trade as their deceased husband, and eight others married men in a related field (a baker's widow marrying a victualler, a millwright's widow marrying a sawyer, and so forth). This is a higher proportion than pure chance would have produced, but indicates that decisions about remarriage made by widows of Abingdon tradesmen were not guided only by a desire to perpetuate an existing business.[24]

The situation of widows of gentlemen and men in the professions (the penultimate line of Table 2.6) deserves consideration because it raises some interesting questions about changing attitudes towards remarriage. Only four among fifteen of these women remarried in the sixteenth century, and only two out of twenty-three after the Restoration. This may have been partly because of greater longevity among the élite (although the few gentlemen's marriages that can be traced to their inception were no longer than average), or because of some special sensitivity to the traditions and honour of a gentleman's family. Lack of space forbids discussion of the rules of land tenure that may have discouraged remarriage, but the possibility that gentlemen's widows held more of their wealth in land may have affected their propensity to wed. The reasons why such widows were less likely to marry are not so important here as the possible (though unprovable) effect they may have had in setting an example that other widows later emulated.

The case of the widows of clergymen is interesting because it seems to show attitudes toward remarriage among the gentry. Though their calling gave them gentle status, members of the lower clergy were often quite poor. The situation of their widows was often particularly pathetic, since they simultaneously lost both husband and home. It would hardly be surprising if such women found refuge in another marriage, even if, because of their poverty, they could scarcely expect to remarry in the gentle classes. Two of the four widows in the 'gentleman or professional' group who remarried in the sixteenth century were widows of vicars of Abingdon. One, Magdalen Wolf, whose husband's inventory totalled only £11. 6s. 2d., married a blacksmith; the other, Dorothy Scottesford, married a glover even before she proved her first husband's estate.[25] Though seventeenth-century vicars were not necessarily wealthier, none of their widows are known to have married. This may have been due in part to the fact that in the later seventeenth century poor widows of clergymen had a means of support without remarriage because the gentle classes had joined together to provide for them and their children. In 1678 the Sons of the Clergy was founded as a result of this concern,[26] and numerous institutions were set up to aid or house clerical widows, such as Seth Ward's College of Matrons, founded in 1682 for widows of clergy in the diocese of Salisbury, where Abingdon was then located.[27] It was no longer necessary for a clerical widow to marry beneath herself for lack of an alternative. That the founding of such charities was motivated by a sense that remarriage out of sheer necessity was distasteful is suggested by evidence relating to a similar development in Scandinavia. After the Reformation there the incoming clergyman had traditionally entered into his post by marrying his predecessor's wife or daughter, so supplying support for the family. In the eighteenth century this way of providing for clergymen's widows was discredited and, with the growth of charities to provide for them, the practice disappeared.[28]

ECONOMIC FACTORS THAT DISCOURAGED REMARRIAGE

We may now consider factors that could have deterred Abingdon widows from remarrying and how attitudes towards remarriage changed. Attitudes are difficult to document, of course, but in Abingdon men's wills some very interesting evidence survives of the views of those most likely to have influenced widow's actions – their late husbands. Since a will often not only expresses an opinion but reinforces it with economic rewards or penalties, these wills merit extra attention. Only a minority (a little more than 10 per cent) of Abingdon men's wills refer to the question of remarriage, but the trend of change in this minority is so clear that it deserves notice.

The wills of men in the mid-sixteenth century who referred to the possibility of remarriage make it clear that they viewed it calmly as a predictable, even desirable, event. The will of one man, for instance, anticipates the time 'when it shall seem good to her to marry'; another refers to the man 'who soon marrieth my wife next';[29] and numerous wills refer to the future husband with complete serenity. Such references usually appear in the wills of men who made bequests to their young children, and who required that the widow or her new husband enter into a bond to pay any legacies. Otherwise most sixteenth-century testators simply named their wives as their executors and left it to their discretion to protect the children and their fortunes. It was unheard of to deprive a widow of her rights of guardianship if she should remarry, although in a few cases she might have to surrender the management of children's legacies.[30] It was most unusual to make a widow's right to a share of the estate contingent on continued widowhood. Provision for the widow's remarriage was made without malice and only out of concern that the children's share of the estate might be at risk if the mother should lose control of her financial affairs by marrying again.

After about 1570 an interesting change began to occur, first in the wills of men of greater wealth and social standing, and later, in the seventeenth century, of men of all social ranks. Rather than depending on the good offices of a future husband, these testators made certain that their wives should take none of their wealth into a new marriage by inserting a penalty withholding or reducing the wife's share of the estate if she remarried.[31] Sometimes she was to lose her right to her house, sometimes to her land, sometimes to household goods. In the rare instances when a testator left his widow a room or keep in the household of a son or daughter,[32] it was common to limit the widow's right of residence to her widowhood to avoid the possible inconvenience of having a new husband added to the household. It doubtless also seemed reasonable to ensure that the estate would not be wasted by a later husband or stepfather, and to prevent conflict between the children of two marriages. Occasionally one finds penalties against remarriage in the wills of childless testators, betraying more a desire to secure the sexual loyalty of the wives than to guarantee the estates of the 'right heirs'.[33] Such clauses recall Ralegh's advice: 'if [thy wife] love again let her not enjoy her second love in the same bed wherein she loved thee'.[34] These scruples surprisingly seem to have increased at a time when a widow's legal capacity to secure her separate estate by trustees was being strengthened, reinforcing the impression that the motivation was at least as much possessiveness as economic concern.

These wills suggest a new trend of thought; it had come to seem quite reasonable to penalize a widow for remarrying, on the grounds that she was apparently deserting the interests of her first husband and family. In the sixteenth century, Abingdonians had seen the widow mainly as the absolute successor to her husband's wealth, to make of it the best she could for her children and herself; in the seventeenth century, the widow's tenure was conceived more as a temporary custody, and the way she was to use the property was more circumscribed. Since her possible remarriage was one of the greatest threats to the rights of the children, the widow's right to decide for herself whether remarriage was the most suitable course was restrained. But, while a desire to retain patriarchal control over a woman even in her widowhood may have inspired this, it may also be that there was little specific desire to limit the widow's freedom. It was simply that a greater concern about passing property successfully to the next generation had this consequence. This is one more way in which the sense of individualism and the desire to perpetuate family and wealth into the next generation negatively affected women's situation.[35] There is no reason to assume, however, that many widows did not concur with these priorities; many doubtless delayed or declined marriage precisely in order to protect the estates of which they were custodians. For these women, deterrent penalties merely reinforced decisions already taken.

It is clear that economic penalties did tend to discourage remarriage. Only six of the forty-one Abingdon widows who faced such disincentives are known to have married. For three of these women the penalty was not a severe obstacle (for example, the widow was to lose her house but not her land), and the women in fact married men more prosperous or prominent than their previous husbands. The others were to pay their children's portions at once, and presumably found it possible to do so. The effect of economic deterrents is also shown very clearly in the manor of Long Wittenham near Abingdon, where in the 1580s the widow's customary right to retain her husband's copyhold as long as she lived was changed to allow her to have it only as long as she remained a widow. Before the change a number of widows had remarried and held their lands; thereafter through the seventeenth century, in nearly forty cases in which widows succeeded, only one married again, and in that case the new husband took title to the land with reversion to the son of the first marriage.[36] It might be argued that such penalties might sometimes lead those who would profit from the forfeiture to encourage or force the widow to marry.[37]

I have found no evidence that Abingdon widows thus acted against their economic interests, nor any sign that they were encouraged to do so. Doubtless it must sometimes have occurred to householders or heirs that it would be convenient to marry off a difficult widow lodger or long-lived widow landholder, but no evidence has come to light that the idea was put into practice by Abingdon families.

There were other economic factors that could have discouraged Abingdon widows from marrying, but evidence for these is more circumstantial and analysis of the effects must be more conjectural. For propertied women the disadvantages of remarriage were obvious. If they married they risked losing control of property that had come to them from a previous husband or by inheritance from their own kin. It is possible, but difficult to prove, that seventeenth-century women came to be more aware of this implication of matrimony. As Widow Blackacre observed, 'Matrimony to a woman is worse than excommunication in depriving her of the benefit of the law.'[38] The legal disabilities of marriage are well known. It is also well known that the trust was becoming a perfectly viable way of protecting a woman's separate estate if she chose to remarry. Wealthier widows undoubtedly were also aware of that. But what if, after a woman remarried, somehow her estate were lost – by confiscation, for instance, or by a lawsuit? As a married woman she would have surrendered the capacity to act personally to recover her wealth, or to use her energies and talents to rebuild it. At the very least she would have been profoundly handicapped by lack of a legal identity. The confiscations and lost fortunes of the Civil War and Interregnum were poignant memories to the women of the Restoration years; Abingdon women and their families had suffered direct loss by sequestration and by years of military occupation.[39] A sense of insecurity could deter remarriage as well as foster it, no matter what protection could be made for a separate estate. Poorer women too may have shared some of these concerns. The amount of money involved may have been only their pitifully small earnings, but they could also have seen the importance of being able to use their talents and energy for the benefit of their children, rather than surrendering their rights to a new husband. True, remarriage would gain a woman the support of a man whose powers of earning were greater than hers; but a new husband might also be a spendthrift or a drunkard, fall ill or be injured at work. The married woman's legal vulnerability could affect the poor working woman as well as the rich heiress.

At the same time Abingdon women probably observed that

widowhood gave new financial opportunities to some of the women they knew. A number of Abingdon widows were successful in trade. A few earned small fortunes by investing in malt. Others were notable merchants and innkeepers. One such was the brewer's widow, Isabel Pophley, who acquired and ran a series of inns during the thirty years of her second widowhood; when she died she owned several houses, giltware, diamond jewellery and substantial investments.[40] Other Abingdon widows, ambitious for themselves and their families, must have taken note of these examples.

There were also widows who demonstrated other advantages of widowhood. In an age when religious issues were of great importance, women would have been aware that the widow was particularly well situated to follow her own theological beliefs, and to use her wealth to benefit those who shared her convictions. In his study of the records of early Nonconformity, G. Lyon Turner remarked upon the important role played by widows.[41] In dissenting congregations widows had particular opportunities to use their homes and their wealth to sustain and defend their faith. Three Abingdon women (a spinster and two widows) were among those noted by Turner. They owned houses that were licensed for use as meeting places for conventicles.[42] One of them, Catherine Peck, was a particularly prominent member of the town's large Baptist congregation; she faced indictment and risked arrest many times in a widowhood that lasted from 1672 to 1708.[43] Such women were important figures in their community, and it was because they were widows who could control their own lives and estates that they were able to play such a leading role in the religious life of the later seventeenth century.

No Abingdon widow left a record of how such advantages and disadvantages influenced her decision about remarriage, but a diary written by a London widow deals precisely with this subject and shows how important these issues were.[44] Katherine Austen was wealthier than most Abingdon widows, but otherwise the circumstances of her life differed little from those of many Abingdon women. She was only 29 years old when she was widowed and left with three young children. Provisions for her children in her husband's will made it financially prohibitive for her to marry during the first seven years of her widowhood.[45] By 1665, the year for which her diary survives, this period had elapsed. She had a suitor and was considering remarriage. Four things restrained her. First, her love for her dead husband, her 'Dear Friend', was still strong, as was the respect she owed the 'name and Kindred' into which she had been 'grafted'. Secondly, she felt that if she married now it would appear that the seven years of her widowhood had been merely a cynical interlude. Thirdly, she was intensely aware of the general opinion that the marriage of a wealthy widow was likely to be 'a disparagement'.[46] But by far the most important factor was her awareness that marriage would rob her of her capacity to preserve and increase the fortunes of her daughter and two sons. She was much beset at law over various properties, and felt that, if they were lost, as a married woman she would not be free to rebuild her children's fortunes, and in any case would never be able to increase them. 'If my children should find lose [sic] in their estates, by Gods blesing [I] should be able to make a supply to them ... which I could never doe by ingaiging myself away from them.' It was this concern about losing her legal identity which eventually decided her against remarrying. 'For my part I doe noe Injury to none by not Loveing. But if I doe I may doe real Injuries where I am already engadged. To my Deceased friends posterity.'[47] Katherine Austen died in 1683 after a widowhood lasting twenty-five years.[48]

It might be supposed that because of the legal disabilities of marriage early modern widows preferred extramarital liaisons,[49] and that this was the source of the many contemporary notions about widows' sexual promiscuity.[50] Yet little evidence has ever been adduced to indicate that English widows were particularly likely to transgress sexual rules. In Abingdon the churchwardens never had occasion to present a widow for living in an unlawful union, and in only two cases over two centuries are widows recorded as having borne illegitimate children. This is a remarkably low proportion, but other studies of bastardy indicate that it was uncommon for widows to bear children out of wedlock.[51]

Concern about such matters as the loss of legal rights would have had little effect, however, unless widows had the economic resources to support themselves and their families. The economic history of Abingdon provides useful evidence of how the material situation of widows changed to make it more feasible for them to decide against remarriage. In the early sixteenth century, the town experienced a major economic crisis as a result of the dissolution of its abbey and the collapse of its cloth industry. Both of these changes were particularly hard on women, since catering for the abbey and its visitors had been one important source of employment for them, and spinning for the cloth trade another. In the later sixteenth century the cloth industry was replaced by malting. This was very profitable for

investors, and, as we shall see, it was a promising change for widows with capital. But it was disastrous as far as employment of poor widows and their children was concerned. Even though a few women could be employed as malt maids, most work in commercial malting was done by men,[52] and in any event malting was far less labour-intensive than the manufacture of cloth. As a result, unemployment was high in Abingdon through the second half of the sixteenth century. The same shift from cloth-making to malting occurred in Warwick, and there it was suggested that labour-intensive industries like capping be introduced to create jobs.[53] Though some similar employment schemes were tried in Abingdon, no such substitute was found in the sixteenth century, and as a result those widows who did not succeed to a business or sufficient wealth to support themselves had few chances for employment, nor could their children contribute much by their labour. Remarriage was the alternative to the direst poverty.

In the later seventeenth century, however, this picture changed. Though malt remained the town's main product, sacking and the processing of hemp and flax were introduced along with silk-weaving, and came to form an increasingly important, labour-intensive, element in the economy. Here was the source of employment for women and children that had been lacking in the sixteenth century. When we see that women with children and poor women were less likely to marry again in the later seventeenth century, the hemp industry provides one part of the explanation. At the same time, prosperity, engendered by the malt market and the development of Abingdon as a trade centre as the navigation of the Thames was improved, meant that the catering trade – a mainstay for working women – also revived in the seventeenth century.

On the other hand, the malt industry itself made self-supporting widowhood more feasible for those widows who had capital to invest. This was true even for widows who had only a few pounds to lay out, since it was possible for a woman to buy barley and make it into malt in her own home, drying it in her fireplace, which could be adapted to serve as a kiln.[54] In Hertfordshire, another malting area, it was reported that such widows who malted in a small way depended completely on the malt trade for a small but regular income.[55] Widows with large amounts of money could invest in barley to be malted by the town's commercial maltsters; and some widows owned malt-houses and kilns.[56] The inventories of several Abingdon widows show that this was extremely profitable;[57] and it was a source of an income almost as secure as they would have gained from investing in stocks and bonds in a later era.

Even if they were unable to find employment, the poorest widows of Abingdon in the seventeenth century could count on another source of support. In the sixteenth century, poor relief in Abingdon consisted only of the almshouses for the elderly infirm and *ad hoc* payments upon appeal from the funds of Christ's Hospital and the poor box of St Helen's. But beginning in the last decades of the 1500s a remarkable change occurred. The records of Christ's Hospital and then of St Helen's parish began to include ever-longer lists of recipients of regular weekly institutional relief, testifying to the growth of a well-organized and substantial system of regular aid for the poor. Widows and their children, the quintessential 'deserving poor', were the main recipients of the ever-increasing funds dispensed by these institutions.[58] Many older widows were housed in the town's almshouses. The payment of stipends to residents of the almshouse that had not been previously endowed was regularized in the seventeenth century, and the salaries increased. Regular relief provided poor widows with an effective alternative to matrimony.

FURTHER FACTORS DISCOURAGING REMARRIAGE

Once it was economically viable to remain unmarried without great sacrifice, a complex mixture of other factors discouraging remarriage could come into play. Fear of losing legal rights was one of these. There were also emotional factors. There are, of course, many emotions that encourage remarriage: women fall in love; they experience great loneliness, sexual deprivation and the need for affection. But there were also emotions that deterred the widow. Katherine Austen's diary testifies to the effect of the enduring love she felt for her former husband and the loyalty she owed to his name. The notebooks of the astrologer-physician Richard Napier record the intense attachment some seventeenth-century widows felt for their dead husbands, sometimes even after they had married again.[59] If marriage came to be an even more emotional phenomenon in the later seventeenth and eighteenth centuries, as Lawrence Stone has argued,[60] it would have further enhanced the effects of those emotional deterrents that were already important factors in many widows' lives. Similarly, if a widow's neighbours disapproved of remarriage, their opinions would have carried more weight as the economic necessity for remarrying became less. We have little evidence to indicate that there was very much neighbourly disapproval. Daniel Rogers observed that one of the difficulties of second marriages was 'the world frowning'.[61] Richard Bernard remarked of the remarriage of a poor old widow, 'we dislike it and speak against it'.[62] But it does not appear that English widows often suffered the indignity of protests in the form of rough music or charivari. Historians have so far not found any examples of this occurring in England;[63] it seems most unlikely that Abingdonians ever demonstrated against a widow's remarriage in this way.

Although specific evidence of the feelings of neighbours is sparse, many early modern widows would have been aware of the strong traditions of religious criticism of remarriage. Certainly the clergymen who counselled widows would have known these arguments. Ideas taken from the Bible and the writings of the church fathers obviously were not new in this period, but they may have come to be more influential as the economic difficulties of living as a widow diminished. The text from the Bible most often cited was from Paul's first letter to Timothy.[64] There Paul was critical of the marriages of widows, although he made an exception for young widows, who could marry lest they 'wax wanton'. The good widow, the true widow, would not marry, however, and Paul's injunction to 'Honour widows that are widows indeed' echoes through most discussions of widowhood as an implied censure of remarriage. It was this phrase that Lady Hungerford used when she refused to marry Bulstrode Whitelocke, erstwhile Recorder of Abingdon.[65] The biblical idea that remarriage was generally undesirable but that an exception could be made for young widows was a theme developed by Vives in his *Instruction of a Christian Woman*.[66] There, drawing heavily on the writings of the church fathers, he praised loyalty to the dead husband and the piety of widowhood. But his stress on the importance of chastity and a reputation for sexual purity led Vives to acknowledge that remarriage was the best course for those widows whose reputations might otherwise be most under assault.[67] Thomas Becon, the early Puritan, also followed St Paul in counselling against remarriage, and he too made the familiar exception for young widows who might otherwise only be 'prattlers and busybodies'.[68] That young widows remarried readily and continued to do so is not surprising in the light of these opinions, but clearly the weight of religious advice was against remarriage.

Two new arguments were added in the early modern period. On

the one hand, Puritan thinkers extended their ideas about marriage for mutual comfort to support the remarriage of older widows as well as their younger sisters.[69] These views may have eased the consciences of older widows who decided to remarry, and perhaps served to reprove those who criticized them for doing so. But it seems that these more generous opinions had little effect on remarriage rates in Abingdon, even though the town was a noted centre of Puritanism and radical Nonconformity. A second argument was based on the observation that widowhood gave a woman a rare personal liberty; she was free from the control of another. At its most elevated, this theme developed the Renaissance idea that being free to rule one's destiny allowed an individual – in this case the widowed woman – the opportunity to exercise her talents and demonstrate her abilities for self-discipline and careful government. Ruth Kelso discusses how Horatio Fusco developed the theme in an Italian work, *La Vedova* (1570).[70] The same argument was used by William Page at Oxford in the 1620s. In the second half of his treatise 'The Widdowe Indeed', he argued against remarriage on these grounds, stressing that widowhood gave the responsibilities but also 'the prerogative and preheminence' of a man. He concluded, if 'a woman that is a widow may be able to deale in the greatest matters of the com[m]onwealth, if she can order a battle and rule whole kingdomes, so much more may shee be able of her self to rule a family a little kingdom.'[71] In the 1630s Abingdon people may have been introduced to Page's ideas, or ideas that were very similar, by their liberal-minded vicar, Christopher Newstead, who may well have known Page at Oxford, and who had himself published a treatise in praise of women's abilities.[72]

This argument could also extend to an observation that may have had more immediate meaning for ordinary widows: that widowhood allowed a woman the freedom to order all the details of her life as best suited her needs and responsibilities. In *The Seven Sorowes that Women have when theyr Husbandes be Deade* (1568) Robert Copland satirized widows who reasoned this way; but the very existence of a satire suggests that some widows recognized that widowhood did allow a woman room for self-government.

Me thynke I lede a metely mery lyfe[73]
Whiche I should not yf that I whre [*sic*] a wyfe
To bed I go and ryse whan I wyll
All that I do is reason and skyll
I commande others but none commandeth me
And like I stand at myne owne liberte.

A similar tone is struck by Lady Haughty's defence of her decision not to marry:

> I ne're will wear a matrimonial chain
> But safe and quiet in this Throne remain
> And absolute Monarch o're my self will raign.[74]

Such a view of widowhood contrasted sharply with women's role in early modern marriage. Widows were reminded of how much matrimony cost women in 'griefs and pains' by the words of the 'Homily on Matrimony', which had been read in English churches since the time of Elizabeth. To marry, widows were told, was 'to relinquish the liberty of their own rule'.[75]

The idea that freedom was among the advantages of widowhood was an exception in the general pattern of arguments against remarriage. Not surprisingly, given the patriarchal tenor of the times, it appears only in obscure works, not widely circulated. But Copland's satire suggests it had some appeal to women. It was an idea that would increase in importance as greater weight was given to the value of individualism in a later era, and shows one way in which this new trend of thought touched on the condition of women. It is worth noting that in the twentieth century, when poor working-class widows in America were asked why they did not want to remarry, the most common reply was that a widow was free and independent;[76] the tone of their answers eerily echoes the words of Copland's widow 300 years before.

There are at least two reasons for suspecting that Abingdon widows may have been sensitive to this aspect of widowhood. The fact that a forthright defender of women's abilities had been their vicar was one. The other was the example of the women around them. It was the personal independence of widowhood that made it possible for some widows to become powerful businesswomen and for others to be important actors in the central religious issues of the day. Prominent widows in public life showed several generations of Abingdon women that there was a positive aspect to the freedom of widowhood, a freedom that more obscure widows experienced only in their private lives. Their example was one more element in the complex equation that altered remarriage rates in the later seventeenth century.

CONCLUSION

This study of one community in detail, like the estimates made by
Wrigley and Schofield on a wider scale, has shown that through the
early modern period widows came to be less likely to remarry. We
have described some reasons why this change may have occurred in
this particular locality. Doubtless the chronology and precise
causes varied from place to place, but everywhere the same change
eventually occurred. In Abingdon a number of factors contributed.
Greater longevity was probably one source of change. But it does not
provide the whole explanation, and it certainly does not explain
long-term trends on the national scale. It may be, too, that the men
who might have married widows came to prefer other partners. Their
views have been outside the scope of this study. There were also
strong reasons, both material and intangible, that deterred the widow
herself. Love and duty to the dead husband were important, and
were reinforced by the doctrine of the proprietorial hold that a man
should have on his widow's affections. Economic deterrents could be
used to buttress this patriarchal principle. Many widows doubtless
shared these beliefs, but they were also aware of the consequences of
their subordination should they marry again.

But to eschew matrimony the widow also had to have the means to
survive on her own. For poor widows good opportunities for
employment were necessary; equally important was the development of regular parish poor relief and specially endowed charities.
For wealthier women who lacked the will to continue on in business
alone, easy and secure ways to invest their wealth for dependable
returns were needed. These were the things that made it possible for
most widows, not just those of superior courage, talent and energy,
to survive on their own. Doubtless there continued to be widows not
unlike characters in Restoration plays who anxiously sought
husbands and willingly assented to their suitors. But a careful consideration of the widow's economic circumstances and the implications of matrimony for women in the past shows that there were
many good reasons why the remarrying widow eventually came to be
a much less familiar figure on the stage of everyday life.

Table 2.8 Proportions of traced and untraced probate widows, by characteristics used in Tables 2.5 and 2.6

	1540–99			1600–59			1660–1720*		
	Husbands' probates	Widows		Husbands' probates	Widows		Husbands' probates	Widows	
		Traced	Un-traced		Traced	Un-traced		Traced	Un-traced
	No.	%	%	No.	%	%	No.	%	%
All cases	149	67.1	32.9	270	53.5	46.7	203	65.0	35.0
Marriage lasted									
Less than 10 years†	18	61.1	38.8	22	36.4	63.6	13	53.8	46.2
10–20 years	15	60.0	40.0	29	51.7	48.3	16	62.5	37.5
More than 20 years	12	91.7	8.3	42	57.1	42.9	25	56.0	44.0
Children									
All minors	39	59.0	41.0	62	50.0	50.0	33	54.5	45.5
None	24	58.3	41.7	39	48.7	51.3	27	63.0	37.0
Husband's probate inventory‡									
In lowest quarter	26	76.9	23.0	48	54.2	45.8	31	67.7	32.3
In highest quarter	26	73.1	26.9	48	56.3	43.8	31	74.2	25.8
Low-income occupations	19	57.9	42.1	32	43.8	56.3	22	59.1	40.9

Widow was

Executor or administrator	128	66.4	33.6	232	53.4	46.6	153	64.1	35.9
Not executor or administrator	21	71.4	28.6	38	52.6	47.4	50	68.0	32.0

Husband's occupation

Artisan	49	67.3	32.7	100	48.0	52.0	77	67.5	32.5
Catering, transport, milling	7	57.1	42.9	31	67.7	32.3	38	60.5	39.5
Merchant, maltster	22	68.2	31.8	32	46.9	53.1	35	57.1	42.9
Gentleman or professional	18	83.3	16.7	31	74.2	25.8	30	76.7	23.3
Other or not known	53	62.3	37.7	76	48.7	53.3	23	60.9	39.1

* Omits Nonconformists' probates before 1700
† Wife not previously married
‡ Median values of inventories in the three periods:

Traced	£18 14s. 6d.	£32 11s. 9d.	£50 3s. 5d.
Untraced	£18 3s. 8d.	£37 0s. 11d.	£46 14s. 4d.

APPENDIX: THE PROBLEM OF UNTRACED WIDOWS

That the group of untraced widows was similar in many ways to the widows whose fates are known is clear from Table 2.8, which shows the proportions traced and untraced according to each characteristic examined in Tables 2.5 and 2.6. In only a few categories were a disproportionate number consistently untraced. This was true of women who had been married for less than ten years. Gentlemen's widows, by contrast, wère somewhat more likely to be traceable. Since the former group was more likely to remarry, and the latter less likely, this difference may indicate a somewhat greater propensity to remarry among the untraced group. However, since the proportions of untraced young widows and gentle widows varied in the same way in both the first and last periods, it seems unlikely that it would greatly affect the general pattern of change. Even had the record of the untraced women differed greatly, remarriage rates would still have declined. If every untraced woman had remarried, for instance, 66 per cent of Abingdon probate widows would have married in the sixteenth century, but only 50 per cent in the later seventeenth century. If, on the other hand, remarriage rates of the traced and the untraced group were identical in the sixteenth century, and if this same high proportion remarrying had carried through after the Restoration, all seventy-one of the untraced widows would have had to have remarried then – a most unlikely premiss.

It might be argued none the less that, if attitudes towards remarriage changed, widows increasingly would have left their parishes to marry elsewhere. Obtaining a marriage licence in this period usually reflected a desire to be married away from one's home parish or to avoid the public notoriety or familial opposition that would result from the calling of banns. Did an increasing proportion of those Abingdon widows whose marriages are known marry by licence? Using evidence from marriage licences for the Archdeaconry of Berkshire is somewhat problematic, since all the filed original bonds and affidavits for licences were destroyed by bombing in the Second World War, and only an index survives.[77] The index records bonds filed for thirteen years in the period 1600–59, and for fifty years between 1660 and 1720. In the thirteen years early in the century five Abingdon widows are recorded as remarrying by licence. Only six are recorded over the entire fifty years indexed for the later period. If records survived for all years of both periods, extrapolation would lead one to expect that twenty-three widows would have remarried by licence in the first part of the century, but only seven between 1660 and 1720. Not all widows named in the bonds may have planned to marry elsewhere, but this evidence surely suggests that it was not more common for Abingdon widows to marry outside Abingdon at the end of the seventeenth century than it had been earlier.[78]

NOTES

[1] See J. E. Gagen, *The New Woman: Her Emergence in English Drama, 1600–1730* (New York, 1954); E. Mignon, *Crabbed Age and Youth: The Old Men and Women in the Restoration Comedy of Manners* (Durham, NC, 1947); C. Carlton, 'The Widow's Tale: Male Myths and Female Reality', *Albion*, X (1978), pp. 118–29.

[2] *The Puritaine; or, the Widow of Watling Street*, IV. iv.

[3] E. A. Wrigley and Roger Schofield, *The Population History of England, 1541–1871* (London, 1981), pp. 258–9; see also Roger Schofield and E. A. Wrigley, 'Remarriage Intervals and the Effect of Marriage Order on Fertility', in J. Dupâquier et al. (eds), *Marriage and Remarriage in Populations of the Past* (London, 1981), p. 212; Lawrence Stone, *The Family, Sex and Marriage in England, 1500–1800* (London, 1977), p. 56.

[4] Between 1841 and 1851 (*Fourteenth Annual Report of the Registrar General of Births, Deaths, and Marriages in England* (London, 1855), p. 111) 12–14 per cent of grooms were already widowed, but only 8–9 per cent of brides. The figure reported by Wrigley and Schofield is the mean of the proportions. It may be that this difference between brides and grooms was greater than in the sixteenth century, and that remarriage rates for widows and widowers changed differently over time. According to a personal communication from Dr Schofield, that was the case in the two parishes cited in *Population History*, p. 258, n. 101.

[5] Wrigley and Schofield, *Population History*, p. 259.

[6] Schofield and Wrigley, 'Remarriage Intervals', p. 212.

[7] The decision not to remarry is considered from the widow's point of view by M. Segalen, 'Mentalité populaire et remariage en Europe occidentale'. in Dupâquier *et al.*, op. cit., pp. 69–72; and by D. Gaunt and O. Löfgren, 'Remarriage in the Nordic Countries: The Cultural and Socio-Economic Background', in ibid., pp. 49–60.

[8] See Barbara Todd, 'Widowhood in a Market Town: Abingdon, 1540–1720', unpublished Oxford University D.Phil. thesis (1983), pp. 22–8. Throughout this paper remarks about women in Abingdon society are based on findings documented in more detail in this thesis.

[9] Important collections of Abingdon records are held by St Helen's parish (registers and churchwardens' accounts), by the Abingdon town clerk (borough minute and account books, leases, etc.), by Christ's Hospital (minute and account books and leases), and by the Berkshire Record Office (St Nicholas's parish material, borough account books, records of various Abingdon courts, probate and archdeaconry material, etc.).

[10] Wrigley and Schofield, *Population History*, p. 258, n. 101.

[11] The problem is discussed by L. Henry, 'Le fonctionnement du marché matrimonial', in Dupâquier, *et al.*, op. cit., pp. 191–7; Schofield and Wrigley, 'Remarriage Intervals', pp. 212–13.

[12] Bodl. MS Top. Berks. d. 20, 21, 23. Long periods of poor registration in the mid-seventeenth century would in any case make a reconstitution very unsatisfactory.

[13] Nonconformists were identified from presentments and other legal documents relating to dissent in Abingdon held in the BRO as a separate series, A/JQ z 11; also from the Abingdon Quarter Sessions sessions book 1664–80, A/JQ s 2, and the list of subscribers to the oath against transubstantiation, A/JQ o 13. Cf. Wrigley and Schofield, *Population History*, pp. 28–9, 428, n. 52.

[14] *Fourth Annual Report of the Registrar General of Births, Deaths, and Marriages in England* (London, 1842), p. 136.

[15] Schofield and Wrigley, in 'Remarriage Intervals', p. 213, adopt this generalization; cf., for example, G. Cabourdin, 'Le remariage en France sous l'Ancien Régime (seizième–dix-huitième siècles)', in Dupâquier *et al.*, op. cit., pp. 279, 284.

[16] From a further 29.2 years in the sixteenth century to 28.4 years; Wrigley and Schofield, *Population History*, p. 250 (based on twelve reconstituted parishes).

[17] Abingdon women were living longer as well. For instance marriages in the cohort group ended by the death of the wife increased in length from 145 months for the 1540s cohort to 259 months for those married in the 1690s. Probate widows who did not remarry lived as widows 130 months in the sixteenth century, but for 175 months in the later seventeenth century, a change that would have increased any problems their presence may have caused for their families or the town. Changing remarriage rates and greater

longevity clearly increased the proportion of Abingdon properties occupied by widows, as is shown in St Helen's parish rate lists, where the average proportion of widowed female rate payers increased from 7.7 per cent in lists from 1606–56 to 9.9 per cent between 1664 and 1701.

[18] All women known to have been previously married have been eliminated. The group may include a few whose earlier marriages were not discovered, but the elimination of any such older widows would only increase the high remarriage rate of this group.

[19] Generally children described as under 21 were considered minors. A child could act as executor at 17; those named executor were considered as of age when the exact age was not known. Where it appeared that a child's portion had been paid, it was assumed that the child was not a minor. In a few cases where the will was ambiguous and could not be clarified by reference to the parish registers, children were assumed to be minors.

[20] Alice Clark, *The Working Life of Women in the Seventeenth Century* (London, 1919; repr. 1968), pp. 156–235; and cf. C. Phythian-Adams, *Desolation of a City: Coventry and the Urban Crisis of the Late Middle Ages* (Cambridge, 1979), pp. 87–91.

[21] See e.g. inventories of Thomas Mathew, a sieve-maker, BRO, D/A1/97/31 (1612), and Thomas Bradford, a linen-draper, D/A1/176 (2 November 1625).

[22] See Todd, op. cit., pp. 28–60, 184–224.

[23] The records of freemen and of apprenticeships that might have supplied them are unfortunately incomplete.

[24] Abingdon did not follow the custom known elsewhere (e.g. Northampton: see A. Everitt, 'The English Urban Inn, 1560–1760', in A. Everitt (ed.), *Perspectives in English Urban History* (London, 1973), p. 134), by which the freedom was granted to a tradesman who married a freeman's widow. There were only two instances in which this occurred in Abingdon, both in the 1640s, when the town was recovering from the effects of plague and war (Abingdon Borough Minute Book, I, p. 31).

[25] BRO, D/A1/220 (22 October 1576), D/A1/212 (31 March 1598).

[26] E. H. Pearce, *The Sons of the Clergy*, 2nd edn (London, 1928).

[27] *A Brief Account of the Charity called the College of Matrons* (Salisbury, 1879); and cf. Daniel Defoe, *A Tour through the Whole Island of Great Britain*, ed. G. D. H. Cole (London, 1927), I, p. 157.

[28] Gaunt and Löfgren, op. cit., pp. 55–6.

[29] Richard Tesdale, BRO, D/A1/126/186 (1597); Richard Bide, D/A1/40/21 (1573). An interesting parallel can be seen in the moving advice about remarrying given by two Protestant martyrs to their wives (Foxe, *A. & M.*, VI, p. 692; VII, p. 117).

[30] See e.g. John Adams, BRO, D/A1/9, f. 185 (1570).

[31] See e.g. Alexander Bisley, a gentleman, BRO, D/A1/43/53 (1621), and John Moore, a boatman, D/A1/99/59 (1700). See M. Cioni, 'The Elizabethan Chancery and Women's Rights', in D. J. Guth and J. W. McKenna (eds),

Tudor Rule and Revolution (Cambridge, 1982), p. 169, on the legal viability of such clauses.

[32] Only 12 of 398 wills did so, while 16 other husbands asked the widow to share equally with a son or daughter.

[33] See e.g. Thomas Capenhurst, BRO, D/A1/13, p. 401 (1599), and Stephen Peck, D/A1/108/31 (1708).

[34] *Advice to a Son*, ed. L. B. Wright (London, 1962), p. 22.

[35] The abolition of the customary rule of legitim is a good example of how the claims of men to have the right to dispose of their estates as they wished, especially in the interests of their children, worked to the possible detriment of wives and widows; see J. Unger, 'The Inheritance Act and the Family'; *Modern Law Review*, VI (1943), pp. 215–28; A. Macfarlane, *The Origins of English Individualism: The Family, Property and Social Transition* (Oxford, 1978), p. 81.

[36] Based on a reconstruction of histories of copyholds in the manor from the muniments of St John's College, Oxford.

[37] Cf. M. Chaytor, 'Household and Kinship: Ryton in the late 16th and early 17th centuries', *History Workshop*, X (1980), pp. 43–4.

[38] William Wycherley, *The Plain Dealer*, v, iii.

[39] Occupation successively by both sides in a civil war may be presumed to cause losses to most of the populace and perhaps profit for a few. An account of losses by Royalist occupation, obviously exaggerated for propaganda purposes, occurs in *Abingtons and Alisburies Present Miseries* (London, [1642]). Sequestrations of land from various families in the Abingdon area are documented in the records of the Committee for Compounding, PRO, SP 23/G92, pp. 395–420, 476–503 *passim*; SP 23/G146 ff. 279, 427–9, 469–79, 489–93; SP 23/G196, pp. 803–11.

[40] PROB 11/307, f. 186; Todd, op. cit., pp. 207–8.

[41] G. Lyon Turner, *Original Records of Early Nonconformity* (London, 1911–14), III, pp. 747, 757.

[42] Ibid., II, pp. 941–2.

[43] See MS sources cited in n. 13, and A. E. Preston, *St Nicholas, Abingdon and Other Papers*, OHS, XCIX (1935), pp. 129–30, 135; cf. probates of Simon Peck (BRO, D/A1/107/110) and Catherine Peck (D/A1/108/162).

[44] BL Add. MS 4454. I owe this reference to Sara Mendelson.

[45] Thomas Austen, PROB 11/285, f. 338 (15 December 1658).

[46] BL Add. MS 4454, ff. 79^v, 110^v, 50.

[47] Ibid., ff. 69^v, 95.

[48] See her will, PROB 11/375, f. 1.

[49] A. P. Wolf, 'Women, Widowhood and Fertility in Pre-modern China', in Dupâquier *et al.*, op. cit., pp. 139–46, esp. p. 142, has noted the way widows in Taiwan chose this course; their culture permitted a much wider range of socially viable unions than was available to widows in early modern England.

[50] See e.g. Stone, op. cit., pp. 281–2.

[51] Low bastardy rates among widows are reported in studies of Terling,

Banbury and Hartland in Peter Laslett *et al.* (eds), *Bastardy and its Comparative History* (Cambridge, Mass., 1980), pp. 127, 129, 163 n. 5, 169 n. 16, and 187. Cf. also P. E. Hair, 'Bridal Pregnancy in Earlier Rural England Further Examined', *Population Studies*, XXIV (1970), p. 64.

[52] G. Markham, *The English House-wife*, 5th edn (London, 1649), p. 207.

[53] *The Black Book of Warwick*, trans. and ed. Thomas Kemp (Warwick, 1898), pp. 47–8.

[54] Markham, op. cit., p. 218.

[55] *VCH Hertfordshire*, IV, p. 243.

[56] See St Helen's parish rate lists, particularly in the 1690s.

[57] E.g. Catharine Hasler, BRO, D/A1/83/14 (1692), and Margaret Hulcott, BRO, D/A1/195/32 (1609).

[58] For instance, in 1664, of 26 regular recipients of relief from St Helen's parish, 24 were women, of whom 22 were widows. In 1676, all 13 regular recipients were women, 11 of them widows. In 1683, 28 of the 32 were women (18 widows), and in 1691, of a total of 28, 22 were women (19 widows).

[59] M. MacDonald, *Mystical Bedlam: Madness, Anxiety, and Healing in Seventeenth-Century England* (Cambridge, 1981), pp. 103–4.

[60] In Stone, op. cit.

[61] Daniel Rogers, *Matrimoniall Honour* (London, 1642), pp. 27–8.

[62] Richard Bernard, *Ruths Recompence; or, a Commentarie upon the Booke of Ruth* (London, 1628), p. 65.

[63] E. P. Thompson, 'Rough Music: Le Charivari Anglais', *Annales, Économies, Sociétés, Civilisations*, XXVII (1972), p. 296. I have found no evidence of anything of this sort in north Berkshire.

[64] 1 Timothy, 5: 3, 11, 12.

[65] R. Spalding, *The Improbable Puritan: A Life of Bulstrode Whitelocke, 1605–1675* (London, 1975), pp. 122–3.

[66] Vives, *Instruction of a Christian Woman*, first published in England in 1529 with many later editions.

[67] Ibid., f. 140^v (1557 edn).

[68] *The Catechism of Thomas Becon*, ed. J. Ayre, PS (1844), p. 365; cf. 1 Timothy 5:13.

[69] Cf. K. M. Davies, 'The Sacred Condition of Equality: How Original were Puritan Doctrines of Marriage?', *Social History*, I–II (1976–7), pp. 563–79; and see e.g. J. Bailey and W. Axon (eds), *The Collected Sermons of Thomas Fuller D.D., 1631–1659* (London, 1891), I, p. 41; and W. Gouge, *Of Domesticall Duties* (1622; repr. Amsterdam, 1976), p. 186.

[70] Ruth Kelso, *Doctrine for the Lady of the Renaissance* (Urbana, Ill., 1956), pp. 127, 133.

[71] Bodl. MS Bodl. 115, ff. 191, 194.

[72] Cf. Biographies of Page and Newstead in *DNB*. They were at Oxford at the same time, though at different colleges. Newstead published his defence of women's abilities, *An Apology for Women* (London, 1620), shortly after

leaving Oxford. It was about the same time that Page must have written his treatise 'A Woman's Worth' (Bodl. MS. Bodl. 1030), which parallels Newstead's work, although Page relied entirely on religious and biblical sources, while Newstead used only classical and historical evidence.

[73] I.e. a meetly pleasant life (*OED*).

[74] W. Cavendish, Duke of Newcastle, *The Triumphant Widow* (London, 1677), V. i.

[75] *The Two Books of Homilies Appointed to be Read in Churches*, ed. J. Griffiths (Oxford, 1859), p. 505.

[76] H. Lopata, *Widowhood in an American City* (Cambridge, Mass., 1973), pp. 63, 75–6, 319.

[77] Bodl. 2262 c. 10 = R.3.540 Ind. 5.

[78] The remarriages of three more Abingdon probate widows (and two others) were discovered in indexes and abstracts of Oxford diocesan and archdeaconry marriage bonds, in those of Salisbury diocesan bonds (Wilts RO), and those of the Buckinghamshire archdeaconry. Searches of marriage registers of nearby Berkshire parishes yielded five more marriages of Abingdon widows, and one more was found in indexed Oxfordshire marriage registers (all except Salisbury bonds available in the Bodleian).

Women and the urban economy:
3   Oxford 1500–1800

MARY PRIOR

In the agitation to include female suffrage in the Reform Bill of 1867 and in the attempt to place women on the register for the next election, an argument for granting the vote to women was provided by the existence of women as freemen in some towns and cities of the medieval and early modern periods. It was argued by Thomas Chisholm Anstey that, in those places where having the freedom of the town entitled a person to vote for Members of Parliament, women's sex had not been an obstacle to their exercising this right.[1] The records of towns and courts were ransacked to provide evidence. The same evidence was used to show that in the past women had been able to play a more active and responsible part in the economic life of towns than was later allowed to them. Women of the late nineteenth and early twentieth century looked to the past to provide them with precedents, and they were less concerned with the actual extent of women's participation. That women had been active, and had been successful in trade was more important to their purpose.

The best account of women's work in the early modern period is still Alice Clark's *Working Life of Women in the Seventeenth Century*, and even that book is not entirely free from this fault.[2] This is not surprising when we consider that it was published in 1919, the year in which women were able for the first time to exercise the vote.

Alice Clark attempted to show why the position of women had changed, and saw the explanation in the rise of capitalism. Before the industrial revolution the most common method of production had been what she called Family Industry, though she never claimed that this was the only mode in operation. In this system the family shared in the work, and the profits of the family's labour belonged to the family, even if they were usually vested in the head of the family. Family Industry was notable for the unity of capital and labour, for the workers themselves owned stock and tools. The workshop and home were under the same roof. When the husband died the widow was able to carry on the business. This method of working did not vanish with the industrial revolution. It continued, but became less important. In Capitalistic Industry or Industrialism, which Alice Clark contrasted with Family Industry, production was controlled by the owners of capital, and the workpeople received individual wages. Workshop and home were divorced, and it became difficult for married women to continue working under such a system. Middle-class women aped the aristocracy in withdrawing from the world of work. The typical female worker was unmarried. There was no position of responsibility for women under Capitalistic Industry to compare with that found under the older system.[3] Alice Clark's explanation of this situation was monocausal. Had her work been followed up by systematic surveys, the complexity of the situation and the forces at play would have become clearer. Patriarchal attitudes also placed limits on women's work, while recession and boom caused fluctuations even within the pre-industrial period.

In order to attempt systematically to survey the extent of women's participation, evidence must be sought in towns and parishes where suitable records are available. Oxford has records well suited to our purpose, and it has therefore been chosen for this investigation.

Before turning to Oxford, however, it is necessary to describe the division of labour between men and women and also to see work as it was viewed in our period, for to some extent people of both sexes today share the attitude of the work-hungry middle-class feminists of the nineteenth century. In an age when waged employment is hard to come by, we regard work in itself as good. Our very identity is defined by the work we do. There has been a change in attitudes to work. Work has become pleasanter, and with the growth of the professions the range and volume of interesting work has increased. In the past, work was, far more than now, hard, monotonous, dirty, brutish and cold. To enjoy work was an uncovenanted mercy. The Bible, which was taken literally, itself taught that work was the curse which God laid on Adam when he drove him out of the Garden of Eden:

cursed is the ground for thy sake; in sorrow shalt thou eat of it all the days of thy life; thorns also and thistles shalt it bring forth to thee; and thou shalt eat of the herbs of the field; in the sweat of thy face shalt thou eat bread, till thou return into the ground, for out of it wast thou taken... (Genesis 3: 17–19)

Gentlemen, however, seemed somewhat less cursed than others. Men then would have understood very well Charles Lamb's feelings when he wrote in his poem 'Work':

Who first invented work and bound the free
And holiday rejoicing spirit down?

Work was a necessity for nearly everyone, though it was not always called work. Adam had sinned by listening to the voice of Eve rather than God. Part of the curse laid on her was that she should be ruled by her husband. Whatever a man did, therefore, was work, and what a woman did was her duty. The division of labour between the sexes was efficient and inequitable. It depended on the obedience of the woman to the man, as Eve to Adam. Men decided what they would do and left the rest to women. The realm of work was therefore divided into two parts. What men did was definite, well-defined, limited – let us call it A. What the women did was everything else – non-A. So the realm of work was divided without residue. We might call it the Jack Sprat Principle of the Division of Labour. According to this, if, for instance, a man was a glover, his work was clearly defined, and whatever else had to be done to keep the home fires burning was his wife's duty. If he became ill and could do less and less, then she must do more and more, supervising the apprentices, seeing the orders were fulfilled; or even by some employment, like taking in washing, she must supplement a failing business.

Asymmetry bred asymmetry. Because a man's work was clearly demarcated and limited, his day had a beginning and an end, and he was therefore more likely to have leisure than a woman. 'A woman's work is never done.'[1] Even when sitting down, women spun, knitted or sewed. To this day this asymmetry is found in ordinary life, if not to so marked a degree. Who has not seen the husband, at the end of a holiday, stand by the car, jingling those symbols of power, the keys, waiting impatiently for his wife who is finishing tidying up the rented holiday house?

Daughters understudied wives, helping their mothers, or were sent out to service. There was no place in early modern society any more than in medieval society for the single, independent woman, and her wages assumed she did not have to provide a roof over her head. The problem of the 'redundant woman' arose in the nineteenth century, not because the number of women who never married had reached an unprecedented level, for the number had been higher in the sixteenth and seventeenth centuries; it arose because, with the decline of family industry and the separation of home and workplace under capitalism it was no longer possible for them to be absorbed into the work of the family, at that level in society to which they belonged.[5]

This division of labour presupposed a double standard over a wide field, not merely on sexual matters. Different qualities were required in men and women. Men must be single-minded, thrusting, persistent, indomitable (unless they were servants, when they were pseudo-women). Wives must be adaptable, ready to turn their hands to anything, selfless, patient and obedient. Under the family mode of production the adaptability of the wife reached its peak when the husband died, and she assumed the 'masculine' qualities needed in running the family business. Yet in running the business she was never fully accepted in the trading community. In the craft guilds widows were tacitly excluded from office, and in Oxford, which was probably typical, there is no evidence that they attended the regular meetings of the guilds and companies. This put them at a disadvantage, as did the fact that they had been given no formal training. Thus male superiority could be demonstrated and maintained. When the widow died, she may have run the business for years but she was described in her will simply as a widow.

Demands on women were elastic. In time of crisis a woman's life might be one of bewildering and endless work, but in prosperity the success of the husband was symbolized by the idleness of the wife and daughters; for the husband's power was shown most clearly where all was done by servants paid from his purse. This became more practicable as methods of investment developed under capitalism. Conversely, for the husband to be forced to take over his wife's 'duties' was to exhibit a total lack of command, which the community found impossible to countenance. The man who accepted the situation was mocked as a 'cot-quean' or even as effeminate.[6] Men must be 'looked after'. It will be seen that the part women played in the economic life of the town in this period was not just a matter of a separate compartment of trade. They held everything together. It was important to good order that this was never recognized. Like Mr Bagnet in *Bleak House*, men felt 'Discipline must be maintained.'

It is not easy to find examples of the division of labour within the household. What is habitual and domestic is seldom recorded. Only in time of crisis are the dispositions of the household likely to be described. In the case we shall examine efforts had to be made to restore the household to working order in the face of family tragedy. The family had lost its mother, and the father was dying.

The dying man was John Davenant, a vintner and, at the time of his death, Mayor of Oxford. He came from a prosperous family of London merchant tailors. Shakespeare was his friend and one of his second cousins was Bishop of Salisbury. His son William was to become a poet and playwright. He kept The Crown, now 3 Cornmarket Street, in the very heart of Oxford, overlooking Carfax and St Martin's church, the centre of civic ceremonial. As he lay dying he was aware that, despite every appearance of material prosperity, his family was on the verge of disintegration. His wife had died two weeks previously, and when he died he would leave a family of seven young people, the eldest, Jane, having just turned 21. On the decisions he made in his will depended the future of the family.

His will therefore provides us with a clear picture of the division of labour between males and females in an urban household at the end of the reign of James I.[7] First, the house must have a head. Normally when the husband died his widow would take over, or if she was dead an adult son would inherit. Neither of these alternatives was open to him. As usual in such an emergency, some woman filled the gap. 'Sister Hatton', who had always been 'to me and my wife loving just and kind', was summoned to take charge of the household and run the tavern 'for the better releefe of my children' until his apprentice, Thomas Hallom, should have completed his apprenticeship. This would not happen for well over a year. Then the profits of the tavern over and above the costs of housekeeping were to be divided between the seven children. The sons were intended for careers which had nothing to do with the tavern: Nicholas was to inherit a property at Deptford; William, the future poet, who seems to have been bigheaded, was to be apprenticed to some reputable London merchant within three months of his father's death, 'for avoyding of Inconvenience in my house for mastership when I am gone'. Another son, Robert, was at university. He was not to have anything to do with the business, 'but have entertainment as a brother for meal tydes and the like ... or if he should call for wine and the like with his friends and acquaintance that he presently pay for it'. The youngest son, still at school, was also to be apprenticed in due course. Nothing was to disturb the sons' careers.

With the daughters things were different. They were not sent out into the world as the sons were, nor were they to live in genteel idleness as the daughters of a Victorian Mayor of Oxford would have been expected to do. They were to continue at The Crown with their aunt Hatton and 'to keepe the barre by turns and sett down every night under her hande the dayes taking in the viewe of Thomas Hallom my servant'. A room was to be set aside in the tavern to entertain the sisters when they were married, and the tavern was charged with the paying of the various legacies. If a daughter married with the consent of the overseers of Davenant's will, she was then to receive her portion, but the one remaining longest in the house was to receive hers when Thomas Hallom completed his apprenticeship, or 'if he and she can fancy one another my will is that they shall marry together'. Part of her portion would then go into the business, and the other part to the two youngest sons, Hallom being allowed the lease on advantageous terms.

Despite all John Davenant's care, he overlooked two important factors when he made his will. He failed to name an executor, and he overlooked the fact that after his death there would be no freeman to head his business. Matters were, however, soon remedied. Thomas Hallom was granted his freedom early[8] and he then married Jane, Davenant's eldest, but almost certainly not the last-to-be-married, daughter. As Jane Hallom alias Davenant she proved her father's will together with her brother Robert, 'seeing that no executor was named in the will'. Thomas Hallom continued the business. He died in 1636, and Jane took five apprentices during her widowhood, which put her among the most active of Oxford businesswomen.[9]

The case of the Davenant family shows how the women of the family, though tightly controlled in some ways, were given considerable responsibility. Indeed, the responsibility for the family business, on which the careers of the upwardly mobile sons depended, was very much in the hands of women, who provided the family with continuity and economic stability. Their lives were accommodated to family circumstance in a way not demanded of their brothers.

Such a case shows how sensitive the position of women was to economic change within the family. Their position was also particularly sensitive to change in the economic fortunes of the town, and it is therefore necessary to sketch briefly its economic development during our period before we consider the position of women in the wider community.

Throughout the Middle Ages Oxford had developed as a centre for learning, and the town's economy was to become increasingly dependent on the university throughout our period, sharing its vicissitudes. It might be said to be a town with one product, students, for its trades were largely geared to the service of the university. After a period of stagnation, the university began to expand in the early sixteenth century under the stimulus of humanism, and two new colleges, Brasenose and Corpus Christi, were founded. The dissolution of the monasteries affected the town seriously, since it contained many monastic establishments. It passed through a period of much difficulty and considerable flux, but, with the Elizabethan boom in education, town and gown prospered together. Oxford became a place of opportunity, and its numbers increased rapidly. In 1524 it had been a small town of about 3000 inhabitants, and ranked about twenty-ninth by wealth on the basis of the Poll Tax of 1523–7. By 1580 the population was perhaps about 5000, and over 9000 by 1630. During the Civil War, when it was occupied by each side in turn, the life of the town was dislocated; but this seems to have been but a temporary setback. By 1667 the population had risen to about 10,000, and, according to the Hearth Tax of 1662, it then stood ninth among English towns.[10]

The university began to decline, however, in the 1670s, the first indication of this being, as Lawrence Stone has demonstrated, a drop in student admissions.[11] As numbers fell the university became indolent, its life easy and increasingly luxurious as the choice of consumables increased in the eighteenth century. Although the town had always been a consumer society, in earlier centuries cloth was made in Oxford, and in the sixteenth and seventeenth centuries it had been noted for glove-making. By the eighteenth century this manufacture was declining, and the town was dependent on the university for its living. Or, rather, it was a case of mutual dependence, for, if the town was dependent on the members of the university for custom, the members of the university expected to live long on the townsmen's credit.[12] The conditions of trade were difficult. The population, which had more than tripled in the century and a half up to 1667, increased by only 10 per cent in the next hundred years. It started to grow again in the late eighteenth century, and was just under 12,000 in 1801.

After the difficult years of the mid-sixteenth century (for which records are sparse anyway), our period falls into two parts – one of boom, and one of relative depression. We shall be examining women first in a rapidly expanding economy, and then in a period when the economy was almost stagnant. Because it was of the nature of women's work and life to adapt themselves to the contingencies of their situation, we must expect a different response in each period.

The situation of the town is revealed in the way men became freemen. The three main methods of entry into the freedom of Oxford were by patrimony, apprenticeship and purchase. In the period of rapid expansion, when there were many immigrants, the entry of freemen's sons by patrimony was the least common method of entry. In the 1580s only 7 per cent entered in this way, and even in the 1660s only 16 per cent. By contrast, about 80 per cent of apprentices were immigrants until the 1590s, and entry by purchase, a method more likely to appeal to immigrants than to local men, was the commonest method of entry.[13]

It is not surprising that in a town in so great a state of change the structure of government was fairly open. Carl Hammer has observed that only one sixteenth-century mayor had a son who became mayor,[14] while in 1600 only one-fifth of councillors were sons of councillors.[15] It might be thought that, if other men found the city of Oxford a place of opportunity, so would its sons; but in fact many sons, like John Davenant's, either went to university or sought their fortunes elsewhere. University towns are not easy for young adolescents to grow up in, to this day. A century later Gregory King was to make a shrewd observation on wealthy parishes which seems to describe the situation of Oxford very well in its expansive years: 'The Richer ye parish ye more Females, by reason ye Daurs remain more at home, and there are more Maid servants [;] But ye sons are more disposed of abroad to Schools, Universities Trades & Imployments.'[16]

We may thus expect to find the prosperity of Oxford reflected in the marriage patterns of its daughters. Where the sons of at least the more prosperous inhabitants were emigrating, and the daughters were staying at home, it is likely that these young women would seek husbands who resembled their own menfolk – thrusting and ambitious migrants, such as their fathers had been, and as their brothers were in their turn. So they would marry immigrants, and, for this was still a very traditional world, often men in the same line of business. Through marriage, therefore, continuity was provided, and newcomers were assimilated into the community. Such was the case with Jane Davenant's marriage to Thomas Hallom, an immigrant from Amerton in Staffordshire.

It is not easy to construct matrilineal trees unless sufficient wills can be found, as parish registers are patchy at this period, but the family of the first Elizabethan Mayor of Oxford will serve as an example. His name was Richard Whittington, and he was a mercer who had come from Lancashire. His family tree over three generations shows most of the characteristics we have just discussed (see Figure 3.1). His only known child, Ursula, married twice, and both her husbands were immigrants. Her first husband was a graduate, Thomas Tatham, who became a mercer, perhaps when he married her; her second was William Levinz, a native of Croke, near Kendal, and, like her father, mayor more than once. They had several children. One daughter married Matthew Harrison, who came from Tibshelf in Derbyshire. He was a mercer who also served a term as mayor. Thus in three generations the men were immigrants, and in two generations at least they married local women. In each generation there was a mercer who became mayor. Richard Whittington is not known to have had any sons, but his grandsons were not freemen. Two great-grandsons married the daughters of gentry. One was executed in 1650 for his royalist activities.[17]

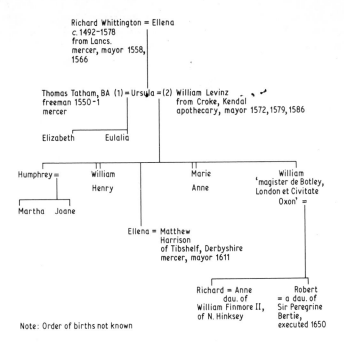

Figure 3.1 The Whittington – Levinz – Harrison connection

The life of Dick Whittington, Lord Mayor of London, involved, in legend, if not in fact, just such a marriage as was found in the family of Richard Whittington, Mayor of Oxford, and many other immigrants. As hero of the apprentice subculture we must see his marriage to a wealthy citizen's daughter as part of the ambitious young apprentice's dream.[18] The marriages of such immigrants were surely common enough in other expanding economies. In Exeter, for instance, where there was a more developed oligarchy than in Oxford, most of the leading families were founded by sixteenth-century immigrants, and, according to Wallace MacCaffrey, 'Marriage was not an unusual way of obtaining entrance into the ranks of the oligarchy itself.'[19]

As the economy of Oxford became more static and attracted fewer immigrants, its social structure became more patriarchal. More sons followed their fathers in their trades and in local government. In the eighteenth century more than half those who reached the inner council were sons of councillors.[20]

In the years of prosperity women had an important part to play in the very structure of the trading and political community. Through their marriages immigrants were absorbed into the kinship networks of the community and rose to eminence, and in a time of rapid change they provided stability and continuity. The relationships of the women provided a hidden web of family influence.

Though this traditional form of female influence was encouraged by the economic situation of Oxford, it is not even certain that this would have assisted women who were themselves in trade, for this pillow power started and ended with husbands. It had an importance not commonly recognized, but it did not necessarily provide support from women for women, and indeed dependent women might be insensitive to the position of women on their own. On the other hand, in a time of prosperity widows could be financially supported by the kinship network, which ramified most extensively on the female side and may have cushioned them from hardship.

How far did women as wives, widows, or spinsters, participate in trade themselves, and how far did the level of participation change over the years? The legal position of women in trade was governed by common law and borough custom. Under common law *feme sole*, that is the single woman or widow, suffered no legal constraints which would handicap her in trade. Things were very different for married women. Under common law the legal identity of the married woman was merged with that of her husband. The wife was described as *feme coverte*. Her husband, her *baron*, was both her 'sovereign' and 'guardian'. She was incapable of owning property or making contracts. Under such restraints it would have been impossible for a married woman to conduct a business in her own right had not common law recognized borough custom which prevailed in certain towns whereby a married woman was entitled to own property for the purpose of trade if the husband agreed to it. In this case he forfeited the legal right to his wife's business assets, though, as the wife could not be held responsible for her business contracts, he was responsible for them. Under such conditions it is not surprising that though borough custom allowed wives, together with widows and single women, to trade in many places in the medieval period, including Oxford, this right gradually fell into disuse. By the nineteenth century it only held in London.[21] There are no cases of married women trading in their own right in Oxford in our period, though they might be party to apprenticeship agreements together with their husbands.

Whilst common law might not hinder single women and widows from trading, borough custom might do so. In Oxford the council controlled entry into the trading community. Those it admitted as freemen could trade in the town, and so could their widows. Apprentices and those who bought their freedom were proposed by guilds, though the council retained the right to grant the freedom to others. Freemen could present their sons for admission.[22] In our period women were not enrolled as freemen. If a widow wished to continue her husband's trade she was expected to pay quarterage to her husband's guild, if he had been member of one, and obey its regulations. There is no evidence of widows attending ordinary meetings, and, indeed, often no widows are listed as members over long periods, though some are known to have been active in trade from other sources.

Widows of freemen could also take apprentices who were able to take up their freedom when they completed their time, just as freemen's apprentices could do. It was important that widows supported themselves and their children if possible, rather than becoming a burden on the community. Such apprenticeships must be clearly distinguished from others, like many parish apprenticeships which did not equip children to enter trade in their own right when they grew up. These apprenticeships were all too often a form of cheap labour and training was minimal. They were often used in employments beneath the notice of guilds, like housework.

As a single source, the city's apprenticeship agreements provide our best overview of the activity of wives and widows in the economic life of Oxford. These records survive from 1520.[23] They give the following information: the name of the boy and his father, together with the father's occupation and parish. They also give the name of the person or persons taking the apprentice and their craft. They are particularly valuable because they provide a continuous series which can be considered statistically. They do not, however, provide a cross-section of the community, but only of persons in trade in their own right, and those aspiring to that condition. They also excluded 'privileged persons'.[24]

At first the apprenticeship enrolments are somewhat erratic, and there seems to be much under-registration before the 1560s. After this, until the early seventeenth century, entries were plentiful but rather chaotic, and there may be some omissions on this account, but despite this, and though there are one or two short gaps, and a rather unsatisfactory book for 1698–1717, they form, as a whole, a rather impressive sequence.

In the earliest agreements the names of both husband and wife usually appear, as though they were partners in taking an apprentice, but after 1540 the name of the wife or the words *et uxore* were normally omitted. Just before the abbreviated form was commonly introduced a very full agreement of the *et uxore* form was set out, as if to act as a pattern for subsequent agreements.[25] Some people seem to have suspected some curtailment of rights and demanded the *et uxore* form. Twice, when these words had been omitted they must have been insisted on with particular force, for the clerk had inserted them later. One of those who insisted on their later insertion was the formidable Maria Bridgman (née White), later Mathew, sister of the founder of St John's College Oxford, of whom we shall hear more.[26] The parents of Orlando Gibbons, Maria and William Gibbons, were amongst those taking apprentices jointly to practise their craft. It seems quite likely Maria Gibbons was herself a musician.[27]

Out of about 175 agreements made in Henry VIII's reign, 69 were made to husband and wife, and 57 of the 70 made before 1540 were of this form. There were few in the reigns of Edward and Mary, and no cases in Elizabeth's reign after 1583. It would be unwise to make much of these figures, especially as there is probably a good deal of under-registration in the early period. When further records of this type are studied in detail for other towns, they may fit into a wider pattern.

We are on firmer ground with widows. When a freeman died his widow was legally responsible for seeing any apprentice through his apprenticeship herself, or turning him over to another master.[28] This was probably as much as many an aged widow was prepared to do, but widows were also entitled to take on new apprentices, as if they were freemen. There were many other intermediate arrangements between helpless renunciation of the role of successor to the husband's business and such vigorous acceptance. These are not usually visible in the records. The widow might continue the trade alone or with the help of such members of the family as the guild might countenance, or even without their blessing, risking prosecution. She might employ journeymen, or take up some business outside guild regulation, such as laundrywork, employing merely parish apprentices or other labour.

The number of widows enrolling apprentices with the city was therefore only a proportion of the widows in trade on their own account. Normally we have no means of estimating this proportion, but for the year 1667 it is possible to compare a listing of the inhabitants with the list of apprenticeships and arrive at some sort of rough figure.

The Poll Tax of 1667 [29] listed the inhabitants of each parish in turn by household, giving the amount of tax for which they were assessed. The number of members of a family was stated, though not necessarily all their names were given. At its simplest one finds such entries as 'John Smith, wife and seven children'. Often, though, individuals were named, relationships within the family given, and the members of the family and its servants and dependants indicated, the members of a household being bracketed together. In some parishes this was done carelessly, so it does not provide a reliable guide in counting households. Nor is this listing complete, for it excluded two categories of the poor: those receiving alms from the parish, and those children under sixteen whose parents were exempted from paying church and poor rates. Using this listing as a basis for calculation, and making due allowance, the Victoria County History puts the population of Oxford in 1667 at roughly 10,000, or 8000 persons, excluding the University.[30] Laslett found in his study of a hundred communities that the average household size was 4.7 persons. If Oxford conformed to this mean there would be about 1700 households of townspeople. In the same study he found that on average 12.9 per cent of households were headed by widows.[31] This would give us about 220 widows' households in Oxford. In fact the number of such households which can be unequivocally identified only amounted to just over 100. This low figure must be due largely to the problems of identifying widows' households. Many widows would be too poor to be taxed, and would be omitted, or as their children were omitted they would appear on the listing as if they lived alone. The erratic bracketing of members of households, and the failure to identify widows explicitly also reduced the numbers.

However, 103 households were identified as being headed by widows, and 22 of the women were clearly running their own businesses.[32] If there were around 220 widows' households in Oxford, 10 per cent were headed by women running their own businesses, and this is a minimum figure. However, of these 22 women only 3, or perhaps 4 actually appear in the apprenticeship enrolments as having apprentices at that time. There were, however, in 1667 also 3 widows who were no longer active in trade and we can view their lives retrospectively. They give us some idea of the *cursus vitae* of the widow who ran her own business in Oxford.

These three widows were Susan Townsend, Jane Hallom and Anne Turton. The first, Susan Townsend (formerly the widow Rance) had been a mercer. She was living in her son's household in 1667. He had been one of her apprentices, and was to be mayor in 1669 and 1688. The Poll Tax recorded Jane Hallom as now very aged and in retirement. She had left The Crown and lived in the parish of St Peter-le-Bailey with a servant. Her sister lived next door and her niece next along the street. All were probably widows, though not so identified and therefore not included in our statistics. Though bracketed as separate households, it is probable that they lived in a subdivided house. When Jane died later in 1667 she left very little, and what little there was she left to those relatives who were present when she made her nuncupative will. Anne Turton had remarried. She lived with her second husband, William Morrell, a daughter and several apprentices at The Crown, Jane Hallom's former tavern, while her other children and one of the apprentices, Thomas Slatter, lived together further up the street. As Anne Turton she had been active in her first widowhood, and was to be active again in her second. Her career will be discussed more fully later.[33]

Between 1520 and 1800 the apprenticeship enrolments show that 144–6 widows took apprentices. Minor problems of identification make it impossible to be exact. The occupations of those taking apprentices are not always given, but it is possible to get an idea of the commonest types of business run by women. Trades involving food and drink topped the list with 29, then came leather working (mainly glove and shoe making) with 25, 20 in the distributive trades, and 12 in clothing (mainly tailoring). With men, clothing ranked second, food and drink fourth.[34] The occupations of both men and women reflected the town's main function of servicing the university. The comparatively low number of women in the clothing trades are, we shall see later, of particular interest.

The number of apprentices taken by women varied. One took twelve, one took ten, three took five, two or three took four, and six or seven took three apprentices. About twenty-six took two and the remainder one. The total number of apprenticeships to women from 1520 to 1800 was 236.

The two who took most were exceptional, for they had connections outside Oxford which account for their pre-eminence. Here their continuance in trade served the wider interests of their relatives, and they themselves seem to have had commerce in their veins. Maria Mathew, who was a mercer, took twelve apprentices during her second widowhood, and was involved with others jointly with her first husband, John Bridgman, and with her second husband, William Mathew. William Mathew had been Mayor of Abingdon, and seems to have moved to Oxford when he married her. He was Mayor of Oxford in the year of his death. She was the sister of Sir Thomas White, merchant tailor and sometime Lord Mayor of London.[35] This family connection must have been useful in the trade of a mercer. Family connections with the cloth trade may have stretched down into the West Country, for exactly the same names as those of her successive husbands are to be found two generations earlier as signatories to an ordinance of the Guild of Tailors at Exeter. The sole apprentice to make the long journey from Devon to Oxford in the period 1559–99 served his time with her.[36] Maria Mathew was an influential woman, and men danced attendance on her. So in 1580 the Visitor wrote to the President of St John's, the college founded by her brother, 'Commend me to old Mrs. Mathewe. I would have you often resort to her and put in remembrance of the goodwill she hath shewed to the College, & trust that she will leave some monument thereof, if God take her away.'[37]

The extent of internal trade and the ramifications of family certainly played an important part in the success of Anne Turton, ironmonger, later Anne Morrell. Her husband Thomas Turton was a member of an important family of ironmasters whose family spread throughout the Midlands and beyond.[38] After the death of her husband in 1652 she was surely their woman in Oxford. As an ironmonger she enrolled three apprentices after her husband's death and issued her own trade tokens. She became a vintner, fought a long battle with the university over a wine licence, finally being granted a city licence in 1659. The following year she married William Morrell, who took over both businesses. In 1665 they took over The Crown from Jane Hallom. He was mayor in 1677, and apparently suffered a heavy financial loss on this account, so that the city renewed his wine licence without the usual fine.[39] He died in 1679, and his wife, who had been left with little apart from a property in Birmingham and the lease of The Crown, carried on the business vigorously, taking seven more apprentices as a vintner.[40]

Anne Morrell may have entered her second widowhood in somewhat straitened circumstances, but apparently with the goodwill of the council. Not all widows found it so easy to carry on. Her neighbour, Jane Slatter, had difficulties with the Tailors' Company. Jane Slatter was the widow of Anthony Slatter, a Warden of the Tailors' Company,[41] which seems to have discouraged the widows on its books from carrying on businesses of any size by passing an ordinance limiting a widow to one journeyman.[42] Quite a number of widows belonged to the company, but only three took apprentices in the seventeenth century. Jane was not one of these. In 1660 she was in trouble with the company for setting her son to work for her without paying her quarterage fees. Shortly after this her son was apprenticed to William Morrell (Anne's second husband) as an ironmonger. She had therefore no son to carry on the business in the future. In 1666 she was fined for employing a journeyman who was not 'sworn in' to the company. In 1667 the Poll Tax shows that her daughter Phillis was living at home with her.[43] She probably worked for her mother, because in 1674, the year before her death, Jane Slatter asked the Tailors' Company to admit her daughter. This was an unprecedented request. In Oxford one could trade only if a freeman or the widow of a freeman. The company agreed to admit her, provided she obtained her freedom of the city; but as the city admitted no women as freemen it is not surprising that no more is heard of this application.[44] Jane Slatter died in 1675, worth £56. 4s. 1d. One of her administrators was Phillis Kendal alias Slatter. Unable to carry on her trade as a spinster after her mother's death, she seems to have married.[45] A man called Kendal had lived with the family in 1667.

The proportion of widows taking apprentices was not static, but in the sixteenth century no very clear picture emerges, perhaps in part because until after 1560 there seems to have been some under-registration. Then in Elizabeth's reign Maria Mathew took twelve apprentices, twice as many as the rest taken together. It is only when we turn to the seventeenth and eighteenth centuries that we can see clear trends (see Table 3.1). Here an expanding economy is linked with a low incidence of widows in trade, while a stagnant economy is linked with a higher incidence. The percentages were

Table 3.1 Oxford widows taking apprentices as a percentage of the total 1601–1800

	% of widows		% of widows
1601–10	0.2*	1701–10	2.8
1611–20	0.8	1711–20	3.6*
1621–30	0.4	1721–30	8.5
1631–40	0.9	1731–40	4.4
1641–50	1.8	1741–50	4.4
1651–60	1.7	1751–60	2.6
1661–70	1.3	1761–70	3.0
1671–80	2.9	1771–80	2.7
1681–90	4.2	1781–90	1.6
1691–1700	3.4*	1791–1800	1.3

* Chronological order sometimes not observed, and therefore perhaps incomplete

miniscule, but they tend upwards until the decade 1671–80 when they reached over 2.5 per cent for the first time, and remain above this level until after 1780; they then fell below 2.5 per cent. They turned down two decades after, according to Stone, the freshman admissions to the university began to increase. Town and gown were recovering from the stagnant years which had set in in the late seventeenth century.

The highest percentage of women taking apprentices occurred in the decade 1721–30. It was then 8.5 per cent, almost double that of the next-highest decade. According to our theory, this should have been a particularly difficult period. The figures for one of Oxford's poorest parishes suggest it was also a decade of high mortality.[46] There would be more widows than usual. As well, Oxford citizens appear to have suffered severely at the time of the South Sea Bubble. On 24 April 1721 the city presented a petition to parliament concerning the 'miseries and calamities' brought on the nation by the malpractices of the South Sea directors. Some widows may have been

ruined and forced to work through hardship, others may have felt
they had had a warning and continued in business rather than trust in
investments and savings.[47] Nascent capitalism had still to provide better
safeguards for investors. These high figures, in the aftermath of the
South Sea Bubble, give striking confirmation that in hard times more
widows had to work to provide for the family than in easier times.[48]

Now if it is generally true that the state of the economy affected the
number of women in trade, then it should be true in other towns as
well as in Oxford, and it should be possible to find similar sources, so
that like can be compared with like. To make a comparison, a town
with long runs of well-kept apprenticeship agreements or freemen's
rolls is necessary. It is also important to have a town exhibiting clear
periods of economic expansion and decline. The city of York satisfies
these requirements. From Dr Palliser's figures the sixteenth century
showed a very marked change in the fortunes of York. In the early
sixteenth century it was a town in serious decline, but in 1562 the
Council of the North was established in York and the economy was
rapidly transformed. York became exceedingly prosperous, and
continued so until the Council of the North ended with the Civil
War. We should expect a marked fall in the number of women
freemen in the decades of prosperity after 1560. This is in fact what
happens. The numbers we are dealing with are small, but the effect is
clear. In the first six decades of the sixteenth century – decades of
decline – the proportion of freemen who were women was 0.9 per
cent, but in the last four decades of the century – decades of prosperity
– it was less than half this – 0.4 per cent. The total number of women
involved is only forty-two – thirty-one in the first six decades and
eleven in the last four decades.[49]

The independent spinster had no place in the Oxford commercial
community. This is clearly seen in the case of that traditional female
activity, sewing. Jane Slatter, the widow, might be a member of the
Tailors' Company, but her unmarried daughter could not. A daughter
might understudy her widowed mother and work in her trade, but
only during the mother's life. After this she must look elsewhere for a
living or, like Phillis Slatter, marry. Nevertheless the single woman
remained a threat to the guild system in Oxford, for, like the widow,
under common law, she was *feme sole*. Her problem can be seen in
the records of the Tailors' and Mercers' Companies in Oxford.

Until the end of the seventeenth century the making of all clothes,
including women's clothes, was a male preserve. The accounts of

Nathaniel Bacon of Stiffkey in the sixteenth century and Joyce Jeffreys of Ham Castle in Herefordshire in the seventeenth century both show this.[50] Originally the boning of women's clothes was incorporated into the dress itself, and making such garments required the training given to apprentices, but normally denied to girls. With the arrival of the fashionable mantua about 1676 the situation changed, for the mantua was a loose-fitting over-garment worn with stays. It was more or less blown together with as little cutting and stitching as possible. Rich materials were used which the owner could make and remake as fashion changed.[51] Mantuas did not need to be fitted, and could be made up and sold ready-made outside the regulation of the guilds, unlike the bespoke clothes of the traditional tailor. Stays still had to be made individually, and were boned as dresses had been in former times. Staymaking therefore remained a masculine occupation (Tom Paine was originally a stay-maker, it will be remembered). But mantua-making, and its later development, dressmaking, passed into the hands of women. Here we have an example of women seizing an opportunity to insert themselves in the interstices of the changing occupational structure. In Oxford, a town requiring rather more tailors for men than most places, the change came later than elsewhere, but the struggle can be followed clearly in the records of the Tailors' and Mercers' Companies. Long before the development of the mantua, ready-made clothes posed a problem for the Tailors' Guild. In 1632 the wife of a journeyman-tailor was making petticoats and selling them in Oxford market; in 1648 a 'foreign' merchant appeared at 'All Holland Fair' with ready-made suits of clothes, while in the same year the soldiers in the garrison who were tailors by trade were working in a 'disorderly' way.[52] In 1668 an action was mooted against 'the pretended milliners' for selling clothes and other commodities, and one James Hall was prosecuted for selling old and new ready-to-wear clothes. In 1669 it was decided to set money aside to prosecute milliners; by 1702 they were desperate and prepared to consult with tailors from other towns about getting an Act of Parliament to suppress the 'Manto-makers'.[53] It was about this time that they began to find traitors in their own camp. Members of the company were employing women. There were prosecutions in 1703, 1706, 1709, 1711 and 1712 against various women, mainly single women.[54] And so it continued. In 1712 the company ceased to list widows as members of the company for forty-four years, although the city records show that eight widows enrolled apprentices in tailoring during that time – more than ever before. Prosecutions against members' infringements were probably doing the company more harm than good now, since they alienated members by not recognizing the realities of the craft's position. By 1751 there were only eight members of the Commonalty, and in 1756 only four. They seem to have had a recruitment drive at this point, for in 1757 membership stood at thirteen commons and seven widows. From this time the widows formed a largish element, equalling the number of the commons in some years, but never exceeding it.[55] The Tailors' Company was now in a feeble condition. Opposition to spinsters, who were outside all companies, came now from the Mercers' Company. This company now also included tailors as well as mercers, haberdashers, milliners, ironmongers and grocers. In 1747 there had been mutterings against persons trading who were not free of the company, but at some time after this they seem to have become prepared to admit women. In January 1770 they informed three single women who were trading outside the company that they must pay the usual fines and fees and join the company. Presumably the city would have been prepared to allow them to trade, though it would not have admitted them as freemen, but this is not made clear anywhere. The spinsters did not respond, and in August it was decided to prosecute them.[56]

In September 1771 a spirited letter appeared in *Jackson's Oxford Journal* by one Ann ******, who said she was an Oxford milliner. Her father, she said, had been mayor more than once, and the family's finances had suffered from the expense of office (the story so far sounds not unlike Mrs Morrell's). To support herself she set up as a milliner, and was just becoming established when

> I received a letter from an Attorney, sent, as I am therein
> informed, by the Authority of the City, and the Order of one of
> their Companies, I think he calls them the *Mercer's*, (but much
> more properly the *Merciless* Company) threatening me with an
> immediate Distress, if I do not leave off my Business or purchase a
> Freedom of the Company, which would cost about 20 l.; a Sum
> almost equal to the whole I possess, and which money they would
> most probably use in oppressing other distressed Objects like
> myself, or spending [sic] in luxurious Entertainments, where it is
> not customary, or indeed decent for a Female to appear.

She appealed to the reader's sense of justice: should not the daughter receive as much advantage as the son of a freeman? Should not the daughter 'who is more helpless, and cannot by any means be made

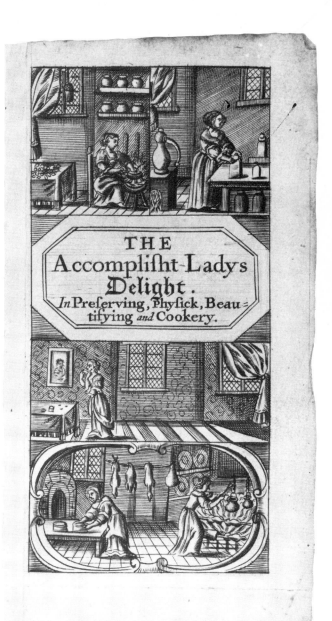

THE
Accomplisht-Ladys
Delight.
In Preserving, Physick, Beau=
tifying *and* Cookery.

1 The housewife's skills set forth

The house of rest

2 Women's work was often not recognized

3 Women's work extended beyond the household

4 The wet-nurse and her charge

5 Lady Mary Verney

Iohn Wildblood at the Rainbow &
3 pidgons in St Clements Lane
In Lombard Street London who
Married the Widdow Harrinton
Silk Dyer

6 The trade continued

HERE LYETH THE BODYE OF IOHAN BRADSHAWE DAVGHTER
AND COHEIRE OF IOHN HVRSTE OF KINGSTON ON TEMES IN
THE COVNTIE OF SVRRY GENT. WHO HAD TO HER FIRST HVS⸱
BAND WILLIAM MANWAYRINGE OF EASTHAM IN THE COVNTY
OF ESSEX GENT. WHO DIED THE 10 DAY OF OCTOBER A 1529
AND TO HER SECOND HVSBAND HENRY BRADSHAWE ESQ. LATE
LORD CHEIFE BARRON OF THEXCHEQVER WHO HAD ISSVE BE⸱
TWENE THEM 4 SONNES & 4 DAVGHTERS, WHO DYED 27 DAY
OF IVLYE 1553. THE SAID IOHAN ALL HER LIFE WAS VERY CHA⸱
RITABLE TO THE POORE AND PCHASED LANDS & RENTS FOR
EVER TO THE VSE OF THE POORE OF THE TOWNE OF NOKE IN
THE COVNTIE OF OXON. & TO HALTON & WENDOVER IN THE
COVNTIE OF BVCK. AND AT HER CHARDGS NEWLYE BVILTE
THIS CHAPPELL AND DYED 27 DAY OF FEBRVARY A 1598.
A RÑE ELIZABETHE 41

7 A sixteenth-century widow: Dame Joan Bradshawe, Noke, 1598

8 An eighteenth-century widow: Mrs Salusbury by J. Zoffany

9 Mrs Bridgman, later Mrs Mathew, Oxford's most successful woman trader

10

10 An unknown woman,
machine-cut, by Mrs Harrington,
the itinerant silhouettist

11 An English recusant household:
Mary Ward learns of the religious
life from a pious woman at the
house of her cousins, the
Babthorpes

11

12 Bishop Bentham joins his wife and family in prayer on his tomb at Eccleshall, Staffordshire

13 Archbishop Sandys, however, does not join his wife and family in prayer on his tomb in Southwell Minster

14 The trend continued: Bishop Hough is attended by an allegorical
figure. His wife's portrait is on the medallion by his left foot

15 Mary Ward prays for the conversion of England at the Capuchin Church, Feldkirch, Christmas, 1626 (detail)

16 The diary of Sarah Savage showing the entry for her wedding day

Munday, march. 28. 1687. wee were solemnly
married at whitewell Chap. with ye consent &
approbation of most of our Friends, At night Ihired
this argum.t wth God (to this purpose) Lord I have had
the presence, blessing, & approbation of my earthly
Parents, in wt I have bin doing to day, & I beg thine,
Mr Wilson gave us a short sermon on Gen. 2. 22.
o brought her to the man I hope God hath manifested
him in a special manner his bringing us together,
thirf I hope hee will make it comfortable
—— whatever God brings to us — 1. Hee will bless
to us — 2. Hee will fit for us, I am very sensible
what need I have of thy special help (oh my
dear God) to fill up my new Relation with duty,
esp. I see gr. need of wisdom & humility

ye night I was married a little surprized with
my Dear being not well, I heartily resigned
my interest in him to God, twas quickly over, God
be praised, I was about yt time like one come
into a new world, God give mee a new w for
my new condition, help mee to discharge yt duties
yt, as a wife, a Mother, & a daughter in law
I still find comfort by referring my self to God &
trusting the whole matter wth him. Tues.d.
Fath. went from home —— a witness to Flint Assizes.
Wednesday Mr. Sam Lawr, from London was here
Thursd. my Dear went to his own house to see how
all doe there, the Lord of H. go along wth him & bless
him — I beg for him yt ye Love of God & heavenly things
may eat out ye inordinate love of every
thing else, —— Thurs. my dear left us & went
home Friday, returned safe as also did dear
Fath. from Flint Assizes, a comfortable meeting,
blessed bee God, God is pleased to give mee a
cheerful spt so yt I have a good w on my new
condition, Saturd. slightly in preparation for ye Sab.

17 Women feared death in childbirth: this memorial picture shows the wife of Sir Thomas Aston in life and in death, the mourning husband and son, with many emblems of mortality

18 Self-portrait of Lady Anne Killigrew, the poet

THE
RESTITUTION
OF
PROPHECY;
THAT
Buried Talent to be revived.

By the Lady *Eleanor*.

John 16.
*He shall glorifie me; for he shall receive
of mine, and shall shew unto you.*

Printed in the Year, 1651.

19 Title page of one of the prophetic
books of Lady Eleanor Douglas

71

20 'The London Quaker'

free ... have the Privilege of following such Business as the general Laws of the Kingdom admit, without a Freedom?'[57]

The only reply to this from the Mercers' Company was a resolution two months later to distrain on those still refusing to enter the company for the penalties they had incurred for trading outside the regulation of the company.[58] The Mercers' Company won this round in Oxford, but things were different elsewhere, for in country towns there were no guilds to limit women's activities. In Banbury, for instance, the spinster Mary Hirons had an extensive millinery business in the 1740s.[59]

In the 1780s the female milliners and mantua-makers boldly took the initiative again. In 1784, for instance, M. Stringer, from the establishment of Mrs Wright, milliner to the Queen, advertised that she had returned to Oxford from London with many new fashions. In 1785 she advertised that she had now a French assistant, Mme Roget.[60] In 1886 E. Clare, from Mrs Amey's at Bath, and her sister Mary Olave set up in St Clements. Exotic gowns were the rage. In 1788 M. Parker was making Italian gowns and fancy dress of all descriptions.[61] None of these joined the Mercers' Company, and only against M. Parker do they seem to have contemplated a prosecution. Before all this dash and enterprise they seem to have been at least temporarily nonplussed. It may be that the visits of these women were brief and seasonal like those of the female silhouettists who visited Oxford in the late eighteenth century. In the 1780s M. L. Kelfe of Bond Street, Bath, took rooms at a grocer's in the High Street as did Mrs Harrington, who had also invented a machine for making likenesses.[62] Such independent women were free to make their own terms, were modestly successful, and their work is still valued by collectors of this minor art-form, but the milliners' case was very different. For a few women these trades provided an independent career, but the situation of their employees deteriorated. Where the wages of tailors were regulated through guilds, and later unions, there was none for these women, for the market was flooded, other alternatives for women were few, and their need was urgent. In the next century they were hideously exploited, and the lowness of their wages ultimately affected those of the men who had failed to come to terms with women working in this field.[63] This, though, lies outside our period.

In the nineteenth century the middle-class women envied the women of previous centuries for their opportunities to do the sort of responsible work which in their own age was the preserve of men, and they regarded them as an inspiring precedent. Yet it was not so much people's attitudes as circumstances that had changed. When women worked it was from need rather than choice, even though some enjoyed it and achieved success. This might be encouraged in wives, and tolerated because of need in the case of widows and sometimes, because of the business conditions of a far-flung network of kin, rich women might be involved, but the need for spinsters to work outside the shelter of the household received little understanding. By the end of the eighteenth century some possibilities were opening up for the independent spinster, even though the position was unstable, and the future, sadly, offered no guarantees.

NOTES

[1] Ray Strachey, *The Cause* (1928; repr. London, 1979), pp. 113–14; Thomas Chisholm Anstey, *Notes upon 'The Representation of the People Act, 1867'* (London, 1867); C. C. Stokes, *British Freewomen* (London, 1894), pp. 77–98.

[2] See, for instance, a hopeful reading of a passage which she claimed showed the wife's work was a necessary cost in the making of a loaf of bread. In Henry VII's reign it was allowed for 'everie quarter of wheate baking, for furnace and wood vi d., the Miller foure pence, for two journeymen and two pages five pence, for salt, yest, candle & sandbandes two pence. For himselfe, his house, his wife, his dog & his catte seven pence, and the branne to his advantage' (quoted from John Powell, *The Assize of Bread* (London, 1600), in Alice Clark, *The Working Life of Women in the Seventeenth Century* (1919), this edn with introduction by Miranda Chaytor and Jane Lewis (London, 1982), pp. 211–12).

[3] Clark, op. cit., pp. 1–41.

[4] An excellent description of the relation of women's work to men's is to be found in Mary Collier, *The Womans Labour, an Epistle to Mr Stephen Duck; in Answer to his Late Poem Called 'The Thresher's Labour'* (London, 1739). Mary Collier was a Petersfield washerwoman. This is a more dynamic picture of the relationship than is found in such a blacksheet ballad as *The Woman to the Plough and The Man and the Hen Roost or, A Fine Way to Cure a Cot-quean* (printed for F. Coles, T. Vere, J. Wright, I. Clarke, W. Thackeray and T. Passenger, n.p., n.d.). Unfortunately it is rural rather than urban. A nineteenth-century urban example can be found in E. P. Thompson and E. Yeo (eds), *The Unknown Mayhew* (Harmondsworth, 1973), p. 251. See also Louise A. Tilly and Joan W. Scott, *Women, Work and Family* (New York, 1978), pp. 50–1; Jean-Louis Flandrin, *Families in Former Times*, trans. R. Southern (Cambridge, 1979), pp. 107–9.

[5] E. A. Wrigley and R. S. Schofield, *The Population History of England, 1541–1871* (Cambridge, 1981), pp. 256–65, 424. The problem of 'redundant

women' is discussed in A. James Hammerton, *Emigrant Gentlewomen* (London, 1979), pp. 20–52; see also George Gissing, *The Odd Women* (London, 1893).

⁶ Alice Clark thought that under family industry men were active in home life, but no evidence is given; Clark, op. cit., p. 5.

⁷ E. T. Leeds, appendix to Arthur Acheson, *Shakespeare's Sonnet Story* (London, 1922), pp. 613–21, 658–67; Anthony Wood, *Survey of the Antiquities of Oxford*, ed. Andrew Clark, III, OHS, XXXVII (1899), p. 173.

⁸ Hallom's apprenticeship, 9 November 1616, OCA, A.5.2, f. 32; admitted a freeman, 20 August 1622; see H. E. Salter (ed.), *Oxford Council Acts, 1583–1626*, OHS, LXXXVII (1927), p. 309.

⁹ OCA, L.5.3, ff. 21ᵛ, 25, 105ᵛ, 142, 186ᵛ.

¹⁰ *VCH Oxon*, IV, pp. 74–6, 181.

¹¹ Lawrence Stone, 'The Size and Composition of the Oxford Student Body, 1580–1910', in L. Stone (ed.), *The University in Society*, I (Oxford, 1975), p. 91.

¹² W. N. Hargreaves-Mawdsley (ed.), *Woodforde at Oxford 1759–1776*, OHS, NS, XXI (1969), *passim; VCH Oxon*, IV, p. 119.

¹³ *VCH Oxon*, IV, p. 128.

¹⁴ Carl I. Hammer, Jr, 'Some Social and Institutional Aspects of Town–Gown Relations in Late Medieval and Tudor Oxford', unpublished Toronto University Ph.D. thesis (1973), p. 194.

¹⁵ *VCH Oxon*, IV, p. 138.

¹⁶ Gregory King, 'Manuscript Notebook, 1695–1700', in *The Earliest Classics: John Graunt and Gregory King*, facs. (n.p., 1973), p. 59. Barbara Todd drew my attention to this passage.

¹⁷ Bodl. MS Wills Oxon 41/2/41; Bodl. MSS Films R. 1468/181/91 and R. 1469/185/54; Diana Swayne, *The Story of North Hinksey* (n.p., 1973), pp. 36–41; Wood, op. cit., III, pp. 151–2.

¹⁸ DNB (Richard Whittington); Steven R. Smith, 'The London Apprentices as Seventeenth-Century Adolescents', *P & P*, LXI (1963).

¹⁹ Wallace T. MacCaffrey, *Exeter, 1540–1640*, 2nd edn (Harvard, 1975), p. 254.

²⁰ *VCH Oxon*, IV, pp. 118, 139; Stone, op. cit., pp. 18–23.

²¹ J. H. Baker, *An Introduction to English Legal History* (London, 1971), pp. 258–62; Lee Holcombe, *Wives and Property* (Oxford, 1983), pp. 18–36. Though women with a separate property in equity had rights denied under common law, only wealthy persons could afford the expense of establishing equity in property: ibid., pp. 37–47; *VCH Oxon*, IV, p. 19, quoting from OCA, University College husting rolls, bdle 4.

²² *VCH Oxon*, IV, pp. 126–7.

²³ OCA, A.5.3, L.5.1–6; F.4.9.

²⁴ Those falling under the jurisdiction of the university rather than the city, i.e. members of the university and its employees and certain tradesmen such as booksellers and barbers.

²⁵ OCA, A.5.3, f. 38.

[26] OCA, A.5.3, f. 45ᵛ.

[27] OCA, A.5.3, ff. 320ᵛ, 323. William Gibbons took other apprentices, but his wife is not mentioned in the agreements.

[28] City Quarter Session Minutes, OCA, 0.2.1, f. 98ᵛ.

[29] OCA, P.5.7, transcribed with minor omissions in 'The Poll Tax, March 1667', in H. E. Salter (ed.), *Surveys and Tokens*, OHS, LXXV (1920), pp. 213–307; OCA, L.5.3–4.

[30] Salter (ed.), *Surveys and Tokens*, p. 213; *VCH Oxon*, IV, p. 76.

[31] Peter Laslett, 'Mean Household Size in England since the Sixteenth Century', in Peter Laslett and Richard Wall (eds), *Household and Family in Past Time* (Cambridge, 1974), pp. 125–58.

[32] Widows running businesses were traced through wills; the records of craft guilds and companies; E. T. Leeds 'Oxford Tradesmen's Tokens' in Salter (ed.), *Surveys and Tokens*; apprenticeships; internal evidence.

[33] Salter (ed.), *Surveys and Tokens*, p. 225; OCA, L.5.3, f. 74ᵛ (Townsend); *Surveys and Tokens*, pp. 187, 275; Bodl. MS Wills Oxon 33/2/12 (Hallom); *Surveys and Tokens*, pp. 224, 423; PROB 11/431/52 (Morrell, formerly Turton).

[34] *VCH Oxon*, IV, p. 108.

[35] *DNB*.

[36] Toulmin Smith (ed.), *English Gilds*, EETS, XV (1870), p. 329. For the apprentice's journey from Devon *see* OCA, A.5.3, f. 273ᵛ; unpublished paper by Alan Crossley delivered at Keith Thomas's Seminar, Oxford, 1976.

[37] H. W. Stevenson and H. E. Salter, *The Early History of St John's College*, OHS, NS, I (1939), p. 495.

[38] M. B. Rowlands, *Masters and Men in the West Midland Metalware Trades* (Manchester, 1975), pp. 110–14; F. A. Homer and C. H. James, *Pedigree of Turton of Staffordshire, etc.* (London, 1924). I owe this last reference to Marie Rowlands.

[39] OCA, L.5.3, ff. 115ᵛ, 129, 176; Salter (ed.), *Surveys and Tokens*, pp. 423–5, 445–6; PROB 11/360/118; PROB 11/431/52.

[40] OCA, L.5.4, 316, 336, 366, 396, 419, 423, 458.

[41] Salter (ed.), *Surveys and Tokens*, p. 224.

[42] Bodl. MS Morrell 6, f. 90.

[43] OCA, L.5.3, f. 190ᵛ; Bodl. MS Morrell 6, ff. 169, 188; Salter (ed.), *Surveys and Tokens*, p. 224.

[44] Bodl. MS Morrell 6, f. 208.

[45] Bodl. MS Wills Oxon 300/2/13.

[46] Stone, op. cit., p. 91; Mary Prior, *Fisher Row: The Oxford Community of Fishermen, Bargemen and Canal Boatmen 1500–1900* (Oxford, 1982), p. 193.

[47] M. G. Hobson (ed.), *Oxford Council Acts 1701–52*, OHS, NS, X (1954), pp. 124–5; *Scandal no Argument: An Oxford Annuitant's Letter to Sir Richard Steele* (London, 1720); 'On the 3% Schemes' (Bodl. MS Firth b. 22,

f. 35); *An Epistle from Dick Franklin, Bookseller to Nich Amhurst, Poet up Three-Pair of Stairs* (London, 1721).

[48] Cf. Strachey, op. cit., p. 60, which points out the effect of bank failures on Victorian women of the middle and upper classes.

[49] D. M. Palliser, *Tudor York* (Oxford, 1979), p. 156; Rebecca Scott, 'Women in the Stuart Economy', unpublished M.Phil. thesis (London, 1973), p. 85. I am grateful to Miranda Chaytor for this reference.

[50] Elizabeth Stern, 'Peckover and Gallyard, Two Sixteenth-Century Norfolk Tailors', *Costume*, XV (1981), pp. 12–23; R. G. Griffiths, 'Joyce Jeffreys of Ham Castle', *Transactions of Worcestershire Archaeological Society*, X (1933), pp. 18–20; ibid., XII (1935), pp. 1–14.

[51] Janet Arnold, 'A Mantua *c*. 1708–9, Clive House Museum, College Hill, Shrewsbury', *Costume* IV (1970), pp. 26–31.

[52] Bodl. MS Morrell 6, ff. 110, 137, 142.

[53] Ibid., ff. 194^v, 282^v.

[54] Bodl. MS Morrell 16, ff. 32, 35^v, 38^v, 44, 48, 52^v.

[55] Bodl. MS Morrell 7. Lists of members are chronological.

[56] OCA, F.4.3, *passim*. The order is chronological.

[57] *JOJ*, 28 September 1771.

[58] OCA, F.4.3, *passim*.

[59] Bodl. MS Wills Peculiars 43/1/31.

[60] *JOJ*, 4 June 1784, 7 May 1785.

[61] *JOJ*, 2 December 1780, 22 March 1788.

[62] Mrs E. Neville Jackson, *Silhouette: Notes and Dictionary* (London, 1938), pp. 113–14, 121; see also the various and extensive entries on Mrs Kelfe and Mrs Harrington in Sue McKechnie, *British Silhouette Artists and their Work* (London, 1978), pp. 223–30, 413–14, 423–4.

[63] M. Ginsberg, 'The Tailoring and Dressmaking Trades, 1700–1850', *Costume*, VI (1972), pp. 64–71; Barbara Taylor, *Eve and the New Jerusalem* (London, 1983), pp. 101–17.

Reviled and crucified marriages: the position of
4 Tudor bishops' wives

MARY PRIOR

When the clergy began to marry in England at the Reformation, it was part and parcel of the change which resulted from the radical reappraisal of doctrine undertaken by the reformers. It resulted in the emergence of a new group of women, the wives of the clergy, which had to be accorded some sort of place within the structure of a hierarchic society. Their position was bound to reflect the attitude of society both to women and to the church, and of the church to both. In England the problems were most acute for the bishops' wives, the wives of the leaders of the newly established Anglican Church. Whereas the lives of most of the clergy are irretrievably lost to the record, there is enough information about the wives of bishops to reconstruct something of the problems they faced, and the compromises and solutions achieved in absorbing them into the structure of church and state.

Although clerical celibacy was not practised throughout Christendom, by the Middle Ages it was a prerequisite of priesthood under the papacy. All too many priests found the ideal of chastity beyond them, and even the penitence of the incontinent priest created a problem for the medieval church. Where penances were commuted to fines they all too easily became *de facto* licences to sin, and in a diocese like Constance, where the level of incontinency seems to have been high, the profits to the church of priestly incontinence were embarrassingly large.[1]

Such a situation was bound to have critics within the church, some of whom, like Erasmus, advocated clerical marriage. It was better to marry than to burn. However, in 1562–3 at the Council of Trent, the advocates of this policy were overruled, and the Catholic Church sought reform through a heightened spirituality and revitalization of monastic life.[2]

At the Reformation the marriage of the clergy formed an important item in the programme of reform. The extremist Karlstadt initiated an attack on clerical celibacy, but Luther in his treatise *On Monastic Vows*, published in 1521, integrated his own attack so closely with other doctrines of the reformers that it must have been difficult for an objective consideration of the topic to have been given at the Council of Trent. The priest's vow of celibacy, said Luther, was unscriptural: therefore it went beyond the commands of God and was wrong. It was right to break wrong vows. Further, the effect of such vows was to set the priest apart from the congregation, establishing a hierarchy where there should be none. By such vows priests sought to gain salvation by works, whereas men were justified by faith alone.[3] In the following year, in his treatise *On the Married Life* he stressed the spiritual value of godly matrimony, which he said had fallen universally into disrepute. Pagan books stressing the depravity of women were popular.[4] But those who recognized the estate of matrimony as God's good will and work would find in it delight, love and joy without end. It was honourable to be in the estate which God had ordained.

> Now you tell me, when a father goes ahead and washes the diapers or performs some other mean task for his child, and someone ridicules him as an effeminate fool ... God with all his angels is smiling – not because that father is washing diapers, but because he is doing so in Christian faith.[5]

At this moment Luther was perhaps remembering and reminding his readers of those pictures of the Holy Family to be found in France and Germany, in which Joseph undertook all kinds of household tasks: a gently comic but tender figure.[6] If the father might undertake all kinds of menial tasks for his family, yet Luther still saw him as head of the household. Like other reformers he placed a new dignity on marriage.

In England at the end of the fourteenth century John Wyclif had criticized clerical incontinency and advocated the marriage of priests,[7] and it was in areas where Lollardy still survived that Lutheranism took root most firmly in Henry VIII's reign. Lutheran books and

New Testaments translated into English by Luther's English disciple, William Tyndale, were distributed widely.[8] It was in attacking their subversive doctrines that Sir Thomas More was to claim that marrying defiled the priest 'more than dowble or treble horedom, syth that hys maryage beying as it is unlawfull, and thereby none other but horedome, doth openlye rebuke and shame two sacraments there at ones, that is both presthed and matrimony.'[9] 'O poor women,' Tyndale replied, 'how despise ye them! The viler the better welcome unto you. An whore had ye lever than an honest wife.'[10] The toleration of concubinage for the élite of the church had done nothing to raise the esteem in which marriage was held in the unreformed church. The sin of breaking the vow of celibacy was, however, to be regarded as the most serious charge against the reformers in Mary's reign.

The position of both women and the laity in general was enhanced by the Reformation doctrine of the priesthood of all believers, but because the wife was still regarded as subject to her husband this left an unresolved conflict between her position as a believer and as a wife. This was almost wholly latent in our period, but the tension is not entirely absent.[11]

There were, however, problems enough to resolve for the bishop's wife. Many of these arose from the attempt of the Anglican Church to combine reformed doctrine with a hierarchical form of church government taken over almost intact from the unreformed church and from the still feudal character of Tudor society, the headship of both being vested in the monarch. By the nature of the case, no previous discussion of the position of the bishop's wife existed, and there were no precedents. Women were subject to their husbands, as the church was to God, but what was the position of the wife to a husband who was a priest or a bishop? And what of the position of the bishop's wife in relation to the lower clergy? The position of a lord to an esquire was clear, and of the lord's wife to the esquire, but was that of the bishop's wife to a curate analogous? The bishop ranked as a peer; what of his wife and his children? The pattern of labour among ordinary people was based on the domestic workshop, where the master was aided by his wife, who, in his absence or after his death, might take his place.[12] Similarly, in her husband's absence a gentlewoman might act as his proxy. Until the sixteenth century most of the professions were in the hands of the clergy, who, being celibate, provided no patterns and precedents for the bishop's wife. What part, then, did the bishop's wife play in his work? Again, it was regarded as right and proper for men to help and succour their children and other kin socially and financially. Was not the bishop entitled to do the same? Would not the bishop, in maintaining the port of the bishop, be a figure of scorn if his wife and children were in rags? Yet no provision was made for the support of the bishop's family in a period made difficult by inflation, reduced episcopal estates, and new and heavy taxation.[13]

The first priests to marry were continental reformers, and their wives set a high standard. Some were former nuns who left their convents convinced, by the arguments for reform, of the uselessness of convent life.[14] These ex-nuns included Katharine von Bora, the wife of Martin Luther, and Elizabeth Silberstein, Martin Bucer's first wife. They were educated, energetic women, given to good works, widely hospitable; Katharine Luther bought land and farmed it to support her large and ever-changing household. She was Luther's adviser and confidante, and in his letters he often addressed her in a form (which Luther's translator has rendered as 'Sir Katie') used in the sixteenth century as a title for a priest,[15] recalling the doctrine of the priesthood of all believers. Another reformer's wife came to Protestantism by reading Luther's works. This was Katharine Schütze, the wife of Matthew Zell, the Strasbourg pastor. She cared for refugees, nursed the sick, wrote, and even preached the funeral sermon for a heretic, when others did not dare to do so.[16]

The reformers saw their marriages as setting precedents and standards. This is clearly expressed in a letter from Martin Bucer to Ottilie von Hohenheim, whose hand he sought in marriage for his friend the reformer Capito. Although, he said, some priests were capable of continence, and had no need to marry, yet even these had a special duty to marry to render the marriage of the clergy reputable. They needed suitable partners. Her deportment was exemplary: 'You will crown your witness by assuming a reviled and crucified marriage. I beseech you in the name of Christ, crucified and accursed.' Ottilie von Hohenheim did not, however, take up this challenge.[17]

A strong sense of camaraderie united the wives of the leading reformers. When Elizabeth Bucer lay dying, and heard from Katharine Zell of the death of Capito, she urged her husband to marry Capito's widow, Wibrandis, after her death. Later, Wibrandis did marry Bucer. It was Bucer's second marriage, and her fourth.[18] In Edward's reign she came to England with Martin Bucer, bringing briefly to Cambridge something of the example of the continental reformer's wife. Margaret Parker, the wife of Elizabeth's first archbishop, met her then, when her husband was master of Corpus Christi College.[19]

Thomas Cranmer married in 1532 while still a fellow of Jesus College, Cambridge. He was then on the embassy to continental universities to canvass their opinions on the royal divorce. His bride, Margaret, was the niece of the wife of a prominent reformer, Andreas Osiander of Nuremberg. In 1533, not long after his marriage, Cranmer was recalled to England to become Archbishop of Canterbury: a married priest, and the leader of a still celibate church. He married at a time when it might be thought that Henry VIII was moving towards a full-blown Protestantism, under the influence of Anne Boleyn's circle. Cranmer himself was the king's lieutenant in the final stages of the breach with Rome, but in other matters of religion the king remained essentially conservative.

In the past the celibacy of the clergy had been regarded as a disciplinary regulation and not a divine law. The Pope had occasionally issued dispensations. Once the Pope was no longer recognized as head of the church in England, responsibility for dispensations fell to Cranmer as archbishop.[20] His brother Edmund Cranmer, Archdeacon of Canterbury, married, presumably with a dispensation, and it seems most likely that Bishop Barlow also married in this way, for his wife would have been too old to produce his large brood if they had waited to marry until Edward's reign,[21] when clerical marriage was first legalized by Act of Parliament. Dispensations were no substitute for the legalization of clerical marriage, and the more radical bishops urged it on the king.[22]

The king had, however, political reasons for resisting the introduction of clerical marriage, for he feared the bishops would intermarry with the nobility and that a powerful class holding benefices and ecclesiastical property by inheritance would develop, and so alter the political balance of power and undermine the position of the king.[23]

Margaret Cranmer's marriage to the archbishop had, therefore, to be kept secret. If she had imagined her life would follow the pattern of the vigorous wives of the continental reformers, she was sadly disillusioned. She lived in the deepest seclusion. Her position became more difficult as the king's opposition to clerical marriage hardened. This declared itself to the bishops first in a letter of November 1536, followed two years later by a proclamation establishing certain penalties for breaking the vow of celibacy. In the summer of 1539 the Act of Six Articles provided the death penalty for obstinate offenders.[24] Cranmer sent his wife abroad at this time, and though the severity of the Act was reduced in the following year she does not seem to have returned until 1543, when it was clear that, though the king knew of the marriage, he would take no action.[25]

When the Act of Six Articles was first put before Convocation, Nicholas Shaxton led the opposition with Hugh Latimer, and they resigned their sees in protest when it was passed. They were imprisoned, and after his release Shaxton seems to have moved to Hadleigh, perhaps as rector. At some time he married. In the spring of 1546 he was accused of heresy along with some other favourers of Protestantism, including Anne Askew, the Protestant martyr. Although he had assured 'the faithful in Suffolk' when he was summoned to London for examination that either he would burn or else he must be seen as forsaking God's truth, he recanted. He repudiated his wife, giving her a poem advising her on how she should conduct herself in the future. It embodies to the full the medieval conception of women as seething caldrons of lust:[26]

> Receyve this little ingredience
> Agaynst the griefe of incontinence
> Suffer honger, thurste, labore
> Voyde evil thoughtes, studie in scripture
> Kepe thine eye, ill companye eschue
> Least delite and desire them do ensue,
> Whyche if they get in theyr head,
> The body liuing, the soule gostly is dead.
> If thy britle fleshe doth rage,
> Twyg it sharply till that it doth swage[27]

Mrs Shaxton gave the poem to the radical priest and printer, Robert Crowley, who published it in 1548. It seems, therefore, that she continued to move in strongly Protestant circles.

When Edward VI came to the throne early in 1547, Henrician conservatism gave way to a thoroughgoing Protestantism. A Bill to legalize clerical marriage passed Convocation and the Commons that year, but failed to pass the Lords for lack of time. It was seen as inevitable, and many, like Matthew Parker, married before it became law in 1549. The Act, 2 & 3 Ed. VI, c. 21, failed to deal with the legitimacy of the clergy's children or explicitly spell out the widow's right of dower. This may have been regarded as unnecessary. It is not clear whether anyone shared Henry's fear of powerful hereditary dynasties. Schemes were put forward in some circles which would have radically reduced the temporal powers of bishops by giving them salaries rather than estates. Such ideas found favour among those who regarded bishops as essentially godly superintendents.[28]

We know very little about the relations of bishops and their wives and families at this period. For some, like Holgate, marriage was a matter of solidarity with Protestantism;[29] for others it may have seemed an unexpected blessing for God to have given them back what they had renounced in his service. There are a few glimpses of the bishops' pleasure in fatherhood, as in the perhaps fatuous pride of Bishop Hooper in the prowess of his two-year-old daughter. 'Our little Rachel', he wrote to Henry Bullinger, her godfather, 'is making progress in both body and mind. She understands the English, German, French and Latin languages very tolerably, and especially the Latin.'[30] We have, though, no sources like Luther's letters to his wife which could provide us with a sustained record of the relation of bishops and their wives at this time.

Fitting into or, rather, inventing the role of the bishop's wife was not easy. The continental reformers had not been bishops, but they provided the only pattern available. It was probably easier for the bishops' wives who came from the continent. John Hooper, Miles Coverdale and Thomas Cranmer had married relatives of continental reformers. Anne de Tserclas, wife of John Hooper, Bishop of Worcester and Gloucester, was the sister-in-law of Valérand Poullain, the successor to Calvin at Strasbourg. He came to England in Edward's reign and became superintendent of the colony of Flemish weavers at Glastonbury. Anne herself was a women of considerable intelligence. According to Foxe, she studied Hebrew and she also corresponded with the Bullingers, her daughter Rachel's godparents.[31] Elizabeth Coverdale, wife of Miles Coverdale, the translator of the Bible and Bishop of Exeter, was the sister-in-law of John Maccabeus, chaplain to the King of Denmark. Like the Cranmers and the Hoopers they married abroad.

John Hooker has left a picture of the Coverdales at Exeter:

> He kept great Hospitality at this House, considering his Income; was very moderate in Diet, godly in Life, friendly to the godly, liberal to the Poor, and courteous to all Men.... His wife was a most sober, chaste and godly Matron, his House and Household another Church, in which was exercised Godliness and Virtue.[32]

Foxe described the household of Bishop Hooper in somewhat similar terms, except that no mention is made of Mrs Hooper.[33] She herself wrote to Bullinger from Gloucester of being 'overwhelmed by so many and urgent engagements' that she had scarcely any leisure.[34] It seems likely that these wives of two of the most radical of the

Edwardian bishops were following the example of the continental reformers' wives.

Very little is known of most of the English wives in the Edwardian period. Only in one case can we show the wife came from a family with Protestant sympathies. Not so much as the Christian names of Mrs Birde, Mrs Harley, Mrs Ferrar and the first Mrs Ponet have survived. Mrs Scory's name was Elizabeth, and Mrs Holbeach alias Randes was Joan, the daughter of Richard Mannett; but we know nothing else of their backgrounds. Sparse details are known of the backgrounds of the remaining wives. Two or three came from gentry families:[35] one was the daughter of a mayor, another of a lawyer. Agatha Wellesbourne, who had married Bishop Barlow in Henry's reign, was the daughter of Humphrey Wellesbourne, Mayor of High Wycombe.[36] The town lies in the Chilterns in an area associated with Lollardy, but geographical proximity is not enough to link her family with this local Lollard tradition. There is strong evidence for the Protestant sympathies of only one family – that of Maria Heyman, the second wife of Bishop Ponet. She was the daughter of Peter Heyman, the steward of Cranmer's liberties and son-in-law of Sir William Hawte. Sir William's four daughters had married four radical Kentish Protestants: Thomas Culpepper, Walter Mantel, Sir Thomas Wyatt and Peter Heyman himself. They formed, as Peter Clark has pointed out, a strong Protestant kinship group.[37]

The bishops who took English wives did not marry women of their own rank, for the bishops counted as peers. Normally men married long before they became bishops, but most of the Edwardian bishops married after their elevation. The aristocracy showed no tendency to marry their daughters to them. Catholic commentators were very aware of this, and were quick to remark that clergy wives were women of doubtful character, and only such would marry priests.[38] Undoubtedly some of the lower clergy married their concubines, but there is no known case of this sort among the Edwardian bishops. It would not have passed without very explicit comment.

Two of the bishops were nevertheless involved in scandalous marriage suits. The first case was against Bishop Ponet, the author of *A Defense of the Marriage of Priestes* (1549). About all that is known or rumoured of the case is that on 27 July 1551 he was divorced from the wife of a Nottingham butcher 'with shame enough', and that on this account he was to pay the butcher a yearly sum for the rest of his life.[39] At this time the law on marriage was complex and confusing, and it was possible for people to commit bigamy unintentionally, through failing to appreciate their true marital position. Bishop Ponet seems to have blundered into some such situation. He married his second wife, Maria Heyman, soon after, and Cranmer himself was at the wedding. He would not have been there if he thought Ponet's first marriage discreditable.[40] The butcher's success in obtaining damages, however, seems to have inspired a similar attempt against Archbishop Holgate and his wife, but the case was without any solid foundation. Professor Dickens has unravelled the course of the proceedings.[41]

Catholic writers enjoyed such embarrassments, but this was only one aspect of the antagonism the married clergy faced. Protestantism had not yet taken a wide hold of the populace, except where Lollardy supplied a fertile soil.[42] A fairly widespread anti-clericalism, dating from the Middle Ages, now combined with a superstitious fear of desecration. The abuse hurled at clergy wives lacked the cheerful bawdiness of popular songs and tales about lascivious friars.[43] It suggested pollution and uncleanness. Dr Tyler is surely right when he maintains that ordinary people saw the right performance of sacraments as essential to the well-being of the community, and clerical marriage as destroying ritual purity.[44] To the Prayer Book rebels of the West Country the dearth of the times was surely felt to be a punishment for the pollution of the sacraments. On the level of daily life the clergy wives were much abused. Midwives even refused them their help.[45] Such was the hostility to clerical marriage that it was necessary to pass another Act in 1553 to spell out the legitimacy of the children of the clergy and the right of clergy wives to dower.[46] The stigma of being children of the clergy was long dying. It is still seen in a poem published in the reign of Charles I and addressed by Henry King, the son of one bishop, to George Sandys, the son of another:

> Some more like you might pow'rfully confute
> Th' Opposers of Priestes' Marriage by the Fruit.[47]

The first bishops' wives must often have felt their marriages to be 'accursed and crucified'. Worse was in store.

Edward VI died, and the attempt to place Lady Jane Grey on the throne collapsed, deeply compromising the Protestant cause. Mary ascended the throne on 19 July 1553. Cranmer was arrested for treason and his estates attainted. The legislation allowing the marriage of priests was repealed,[48] but even before this some of the married bishops were in gaol. The continental reformers invited to England in the previous reign were allowed to leave unmolested, and many of the Protestant clergy fled into exile. Friend sought friend, not always knowing even where to find them; husbands and wives fled separately. John Jewel wrote to John Parkhurst, the future Bishop of Norwich, about two months after Mary's accession:

> not long ago, when I was looking for you at Cleeve, at your house, you were not at home, for, as some told me, you had yielded to the times, as others said, you had simply fled. I found your wife alone, shut up in the house, guarded by a not very large body of servants, unconcerned about herself, wretchedly anxious about you. What else can I add. O immortal God! Nothing is happening that I would dare to commit to writing ...[49]

The choice before the married clergy was stark: defiance or conformity. If they conformed they were deprived of their cures, and must live apart from their 'pretensed' wives. Former monks were forced to divorce them. Then, after performing the usual penance exacted for sexual offences, they might seek other cures.[50] Holgate, Bushe and Birde – who had been thrown into the Tower on 3 October 1553 – conformed. Bushe's wife died five days after. He later became a parish priest. Birde and Holgate repudiated their wives.

The wife and family of a bishop who conformed seem to have escaped further harassment. In 1558 Barbara Holgate was still in possession of Scrooby, which she held in survivorship after the archbishop's death.[51] The son of Bishop Bushe was provided for by his father through a grant made in trust by letters patent to Sir Henry Ashley and others for the benefit of the bishop and later for Paul Ashley, son of Edith Ashley deceased, alias Paul Bushe.[52] In Bristol Cathedral there used to be a small plaque, 'Of your Charity pray for the Soul of Edith Bushe otherwise called Ashley, who deceased the 8th Day of October A.D. 1553.' An epigram by Parkhurst, 'Of Editha', raises the possibility that she gave birth to a child about the time her husband conformed.[53]

Four bishops – Coverdale, Scory, Barlow and Ponet – went into exile, and their wives with them. The Coverdales escaped serious persecution through the intervention of the King of Denmark. Scory and Barlow conformed, later escaped, and lived on to be bishops under Elizabeth. Ponet escaped abroad too, but returned to join his kinsfolk in Wyatt's abortive rebellion of January 1554, then fled again. He died in 1556 and his widow Maria sold his library to another exile, Sir Anthony Cooke. Since her brother-in-law, William

Hammond of Acres in Kent, was also abroad, Maria Ponet was not entirely cut off from her kinsfolk. At some stage, perhaps still in exile, she married one John Hill, a cleric.[54]

There were six obdurate Protestant bishops, four of whom were married. Bishop Harley was deprived, but somehow slipped away into obscurity, perhaps as an itinerant preacher. He died soon after.[55] The others were imprisoned. Robert Ferrar was burnt at Carmarthen in March 1555, the first to be executed. Nothing is known of his wife's fate, but they had two children who survived to adulthood.[56]

Hooper and Cranmer sent their wives abroad early in Mary's reign. It was not easy for women with young children to make the trip, and no doubt the bishops' wives had similar problems to other women exiles. Rose Hickman, a merchant's wife, was pregnant, and went into hiding until her child was born, whilst her sister, Elizabeth Hill, later Bishop Bullingham's wife, had to leave her youngest child in England, as it was too delicate to face the journey.[57] Anne Hooper also had to leave her younger child, Daniel, to be brought to her later.

In England, Protestant women played an active part in Mary's short reign, just as Catholic recusant women were to do in Elizabeth's. Some died at the stake. Through their sufferings some came to claim an equality not normally recognized. John Foxe tells of an unnamed gentlewoman who exhorted women to be steadfast in faith, for 'ye were redeemed with as dear a price as men, yet be you all his flesh: so that also in the case and trial of your faith towards God, ye ought to be as strong.'[58] Women were active in various centres. In Canterbury Lady Fane and Joyce Hales, daughter-in-law of Sir James Hales, formed a Protestant cell, which also included the widows of Richard Neville and Walter Mantel (aunt to Maria Ponet).[59] At Stoke by Nayland, in Suffolk, women in large numbers refused to attend Catholic services. Alice Warner's Thames-side hostel, the King's Head, was a meeting place. Women visited prisoners, bringing clean linen[60] and even intellectual stimulation. The widows Jane Wilkinson and Anne Warcup, her kinswoman, visited Cranmer, Hooper and the unmarried bishops Latimer and Ridley in gaol in Oxford, and Mrs Wilkinson lent books to Hooper.[61] Latimer's letter of farewell to her, just before his death, has been preserved: 'If the gift of a pot of water shall not be in oblivion with God, how can God forget your manifold and bountiful gifts'.[62] After the bishops were burnt she went to Frankfurt, where she died in the household of Cuthbert Warcup, the son of her friend Anne Warcup, and his wife Agnes.

The bishops' wives who fled abroad, and the wives of the clergy in exile, many of whom became bishops under Elizabeth, had no part in such activities. Anne Hooper (with her daughter, Rachel) reached Frankfurt early in 1554, and there she rented a house near her kinsman Valérand Poullain, who had left England with the other continental reformers. Here she lived 'all but dead with grief', awaiting news of her husband. She was surrounded by friends, kin and fellow exiles, while Bullinger kept in touch by letter. Anne Hooper died on 7 December 1555 and Rachel some time in 1555 or 1556.[63] Edward Oldsworth, who came from Stonehouse in her husband's diocese, and Valérand Poullain became guardians of the Hoopers' son, Daniel.[64] Jane Wilkinson left the child a legacy, but the little boy did not live to receive it.[65]

Although the English churches established in various German and Swiss cities by the exiles were riven by theological dissension, and the manoeuvring of power groups, it was a time of intellectual excitement and stimulation. In the cramped quarters the women were exposed to a heady intellectual climate such as few English women had known up to this time. Here they met the leaders of the continental Reformation, and sat, if not at their feet, at their tables. Here, in the city-states where the social structure was less rigidly hierarchic than in English society, Luther had found an image for the church: 'Christ and all his church are one spiritual body, just as the inhabitants of a city are one community and body, each citizen being a member of the other and a member of the entire city.'[66] It may be a rosy image of the city, but nevertheless it was compelling. Years later, when Cuthbert Warcup's widow, Agnes, long returned from exile, made her will she declared her assurance of salvation through the only merits of Christ 'in whose Kingdom I do unfeignedly beleve to be a citizen'.[67] Such thoughts were easier for women to think in some places than others, but on Agnes Warcup they made an indelible impression.

Margaret Cranmer's refuge lay outside the towns where most of the exiles were granted asylum. Her kinsman Osiander was now dead, but it seems likely she returned to her family wherever they were living. She had been an isolated figure in England. She remained so in exile.

With Elizabeth's accession in November 1558 Protestantism was restored, and within a brief period all but two of the Marian bishops had been replaced. Nineteen of the new bishops were married men, and twelve of these had been exiles. They therefore formed an important group. Office, however, divided them from the other returning exiles, whose power was relatively slight. In the crisis of exile, and of the fugitive and secret life of Protestants in England in the Marian years, women had played an active part, as they were to do in other periods of crisis, such as the Civil War.[68] With the restoration of Protestantism, women lost this important role. Their position was not unlike that of the exiles from Geneva, and others who received no preferment under Elizabeth. On Mary's death the Genevan exiles, the most radical group of exiles, had delayed their return to finish the translation of the Bible on which they were engaged, but also because they doubted Elizabeth's commitment to Protestantism. Few of them were in England when the new bishops were appointed. They formed with the women of the exile the nucleus of the early Puritan movement, a self-appointed conscience to the Elizabethan church.

The wives of many of the Elizabethan bishops who had been in exile were committed Protestants. Some had also been in exile with their husbands, while the three bishops who married abroad or immediately after their return chose wives from the circle of the exile. Two of the brides came from parishes with a strong Protestant tradition. Mawde Fawcon, who married Thomas Bentham in Geneva in 1557, and was in exile in her own right, was from Hadleigh in Essex, the parish of Shaxton, from which several martyrs were drawn.[69] Cicely Wilford or Wilsford, who married Edwin Sandys, later Archbishop of York, came from a gentry family in Cranbrook, in the Kentish Weald. Like Hadleigh, Cranbrook had its martyrs and a long tradition of Lollardy. Three families of Wilfords were in exile.[70] Alice Kingsmill, the third bride, married James Pilkington, Bishop of Durham. She was the daughter of Sir John Kingsmill, Chief Justice of Common Pleas. The Protestant sympathies of her four brothers appear in various ways. Henry had been an exile, and both he and his brother Richard held seats in the Parliament of 1563 through the patronage of Bishop Horne, another former exile. Andrew was a Protestant divine, who lived his later life in Geneva, while Thomas married a daughter of Anne Warcup. J. E. Neale described them as 'truly a puritan family'.[71] The only other exile who may have married about this time was Thomas Younge, Archbishop of York. His first wife was a daughter of George Constantine, the distributor of Lutheran books in Henry VIII's reign,[72] but his second wife came from a vastly ramified gentry family in Shropshire, the Kynastons.

Though the Marian exiles who became bishops often modified their attitudes and beliefs when faced with the complexities of power,

Richard Cox and Nicholas Bullingham who married a second time in later life chose wives from the very centre of the Puritan tradition.

Nicholas Bullingham, Bishop of Lincoln and then of Worcester, married into an interesting London merchant family, that of Sir William Locke, mercer. Bullingham married Elizabeth, the youngest daughter, the widow of Richard Hill. She and her sister, Rose Hickman, who left a memoir of this period of her life, had gone into exile with their husbands in Mary's reign. Two of her sisters-in-law were interesting women. Anne Vaughan, who married her brother Henry, was an intimate friend of John Knox. Another sister-in-law was Jane, daughter and heiress of Jane Wilkinson, the friend of Cranmer and Hooper. She had married Michael Locke, merchant, traveller and associate of Martin Frobisher. Jane Locke's will showed a close-knit web of relationships between certain of the exiles.[73]

Jane Turner, the second wife of Richard Cox, Bishop of Ely was the daughter of George Awder, a Cambridge alderman, who owned property in Kent as well as Cambridge. Her first husband was one of the most distinguished of the exiles. William Turner was an uncompromising and radical Protestant, a witty and scurrilous contraversialist (who had even taken on Stephen Gardiner himself) and the first English botanist of note. Their son Peter was a noted physician and MP, and also an extreme Calvinist.[74]

When Margaret Cranmer returned at the beginning of Elizabeth's reign, she too was absorbed into extreme Protestant circles, though hers was rather different from that we have already glimpsed, since she moved among booksellers rather than merchants. She was not English and the person she turned to for help over and over again in her widowhood was her compatriot, Reyner Wolfe, one of Cranmer's publishers – that 'flower of all the London booksellers', as Parkhurst called him. He had on occasion acted as a courier for Cranmer on his business trips to Frankfurt Fair. In Mary's reign Mrs Cranmer made use of him to obtain for her covertly a lease from the crown of the abbey of Kirkstall, near Leeds, one of her husband's attainted estates.[75]

Like Wibrandis Bucer, Margaret Cranmer married several times. Changing attitudes to remarriage made the Victorian Dean Hook censorious:

> She was not a woman of much sensibility or refinement. One would have supposed that the widow of such a man as Cranmer would have retained her weeds to the hour of her death, and

would have regarded them with pride, but after the Archbishop's execution she was twice married.[76]

Her second husband, Edward Whitchurch, whom she married about the time of her return to England, was a printer and bookseller who had published many of the works of the Edwardian Reformation[77] and was thus intimately associated with Cranmer. They settled in a manor house at Camberwell belonging to their friend Edward Scott. Margaret Cranmer's daughter, Margaret, married Whitchurch's friend, the lawyer and MP Thomas Norton, co-author of *Gorboduc*, who was living in the Whitchurches' house at the time he translated Calvin's *Institutes*.[78] When Edward Whitchurch died in 1562, his widow continued to live on at Camberwell. Whitchurch's death seems to have revived earlier sorrows. She found solace in the sympathy of Edward Scott's younger brother Bartholomew. With 'much Wepyng and cryeing' he 'enticed and flattered the poor gentlewoman' into marriage.[79] It became clear all too soon that he had married her for her money and had no intention of keeping the terms of her marriage contract which preserved her an independent income, and provided for the education of her son, Thomas Cranmer the younger. She soon left her young husband and took refuge in the household of Reyner Wolfe and his wife. Her daughter had died and Norton remarried. Perhaps it tells us something of the narrow circle in which the family moved that when her son Thomas Cranmer was involved in a case of adultery it was with Judith Barwick (*née* Best), the daughter of another bishop's widow, Elizabeth Best. Judith's father, John Best, had been Bishop of Carlisle.[80]

When first Reyner and then Joan Wolfe died in 1574, Margaret Cranmer was still living in their house. When their son-in-law John Hunne was engaged in making an inventory of household goods for probate he examined a trunk belonging to Mrs Cranmer. As well as two gold chains it contained only a few oddments, a psalter and five rings he thought had belonged to the archbishop. The story emerged in evidence before the Court of Chancery, where Bartholomew Scott had brought a case against Thomas Norton and John Hunne for encouraging his wife to leave him, depriving him of jewels and household stuff, which he claimed were his by law:

and this defendant Hunne having nothing to do further she took the chest and goods out of the house and conveyed it away whether this defendant knoweth not. Only the little saltre which she left behind her ... in consideration of 3*li* she was behind with me for money lent and laid out for her necessaries ...[81]

Where she died is not known. On his grandiose tomb at Camberwell it was recorded tersely that Bartholomew Scott's first wife had been the widow of the right reverend prelate and martyr Thomas Cranmer, Archbishop of Canterbury.

The accession of a Protestant queen was not, as the exiles anticipated, the end of opposition to clerical marriage, for Elizabeth disapproved of it, and no concession was made to it in the Elizabethan church. The Edwardian legislation, repealed under Mary, was not put back on the statute book.[82] In 1559 the clergy found to their dismay that the queen would not be 'so far brought to Countenance the Conjugal state of her clergy.' Bishop Sandys summed up the situation:

> no Law was made concerning the Marriage of Priests, but that it was left, as it were, in Medio; and that the Queen would wink at it, but not establish it by Law. Which is nothing else but to bastard our children.[83]

However, an injunction was issued in 1559 which established a method of vetting the prospective wives of bishops and other clergy.[84] The Thirty-Nine Articles, ratified by the queen in 1571, stated that it was lawful for priests, as for all other Christian men, to marry at their own discretion, though the continued use of vetting procedures scarcely accorded with this bold claim.

With our monolithic legal system it is difficult to understand the workings of one in which a state of affairs could be recognized in one court and not in another.[85] This can be seen over the matter of the *de facto* bastardizing of the children of the clergy, of which Bishop Sandys complained. This seems to have been seen as more of a problem at first than later. Archbishop Parker legalized the birth of his eldest child by a private Act of Parliament. However, bastardy was normally a matter for ecclesiastical courts and not those of common law, so that problems were likely to arise only if cases were brought in such a form that they passed into the jurisdiction of common law. This was pointed out by the lawyers in a case of disputed inheritance involving Rose Simonds, the daughter of a cleric, which came up in the Court of Common Pleas.

Bendloes moved another matter, viz. Henry Simonds was a Priest, and therefore Rose was a Bastard; and if so, then she cannot be vouched as heir: but I would not trust the Bishop to certify the Bastardy, if I should plead it generally, and therefore I will plead the special matter, and so it shall be tried by the Country.[86]

Most bishops relied on making wills to protect the inheritance of their wives as well as their children, for in cases of intestacy their wives had no clear right to dower.[87] There were fifty-eight married bishops in Elizabeth's reign out of a total of seventy-six (excluding those of Sodor and Man), and forty-three of these left wills.[88] Twelve of the fifteen intestates died in Elizabeth's reign. At least eleven were in serious financial trouble at some time in their lives, and were probably still in debt at their deaths. Felicity Heal has given details of the debts to the crown of five of these: Bentham, John Bullingham, Nicholas Bullingham, Thomas Godwin and William Wykeham. Some of these had other substantial debts.[89] As well, Curteys and Middleton were crown debtors.[90] Bishop Best's widow was left destitute,[91] Downham died heavily in debt,[92] and it was said that Bishop Coldwell was so deeply in debt that his friends buried him secretly, presumably to avoid funeral expenses.[93]

The other way in which bishops could provide for their wives was by marriage settlements, trusts or contracts. The evidence is scattered, and no systematic study is possible, but they were used by some of the wealthier bishops. Thus in his will Matthew Hutton left various bequests to his wife 'for the increase of her jointure'. He had married as his third wife the widow of a member of one of York's patrician families, Martin Bowes, the son of Sir Martin Bowes, goldsmith and alderman of London, benefactor of the city of York. Such a woman would not marry without a marriage settlement. Frances Parker was not particularly well off when she married Toby Mathew, later Archbishop of York, though she was the widow of the younger son of an archbishop herself. Documents in the possession of the Lawson–Tancred family show that at some time a trust had been set up for her benefit of which her brother John and her brother-in-law Bishop Westfaling became trustees.[94]

Legally bishops' wives were close to being invisible, and it was Elizabeth's policy, conscious or unconscious, that they should be so in other spheres as well. In a period of great formality, an age which loved processions, the order of precedence was of great importance. When a temporal lord married, his wife normally took his rank, but, though bishops ranked fairly high and archbishops took precedence over all lords temporal, their wives had no rank whatever.[95] They had, therefore, no place on state occasions.

When Elizabeth thanked Archbishop Parker's wife for her hospitality with the famous words, 'Madam I may not call you; mistress I am ashamed to call you; but yet I thank you', she administered a double snub. She expressed doubt of her marital status, and made it clear she had no rank. John Seldon put the position with brutal clarity:

> You shall see a Monkey sometime that has been playing Upp and down the garden att length leapp upp to the Topp of the Wall, but his Clogg hangs a great way below on this side. The Bishopps wife is like that Monkeys Clogg, himself is gott upp very high, takes place of the Temporall Barons, but his wife comes a great way behind.[96]

The physical presence of the wives and children of the clergy was offensive to Elizabeth, and in 1561 she sought to banish them from the precincts of cathedrals and colleges. Cecil believed that at this time she was very near to forbidding clerical marriage altogether and would have done so if he had not been very 'stiff' with her. It was, however, somewhat late for such a decision. Richard Cox wrote warning her that, in undermining the position of her bishops in this matter, she undermined her own position too, for they were her loyal servants; but this thought must have occurred to her too.[97] Yet she could not resist exploiting her dislike of clerical marriage to render them compliant, and she openly enjoyed any story against married bishops and their wives.[98]

It was remarked by contemporaries that the queen took particular exception to the remarriage of bishops, but possibly it was a calculated caprice. Often there were other grounds for friction, and remarriage provided occasion for retaliation. This seems to have been the case with Bishops Cox and Fletcher, who had been less than eager to provide her courtiers with advantageous leases of their lands. The compliant Bishop of Limerick, Thornborough, was favoured despite his scandalous divorce and remarriage.[99] Despite her opposition to remarriage, fourteen (almost 25 per cent) of her bishops married more than once.[100] However, only twenty-three are known to have been in a position to marry a second time, thirty-one being known to have been outlived by their only wife, and the position of five being unknown. If these five were widowers, then 50 per cent of those who could remarried; otherwise a rather higher percentage, not exceeding 61 per cent, could have remarried. The queen's dislike of remarriage does not seem to have had much effect.

The remarriage of bishops was on occasion capable of raising old fears. If a bishop married while still a bishop, as was likely to be the case with second marriages, there was a danger he might ally himself with the nobility, as Henry VIII had feared. Elizabeth's bitter opposition to Fletcher's remarriage may have been because of Lady Baker's social position. Fletcher was said to be the first bishop to marry a titled lady.[101]

As a result of the queen's policies, the Elizabethan bishops did not form a hereditary caste allied to the temporal lords. Sons received such appointments as their fathers and fathers-in-law could provide as officials of the diocese, but in Elizabeth's reign only one bishop's son was made a bishop. Since bishops were often drawn from the higher officials of the dioceses, this looks like discrimination against bishops' sons. The position of the bishop's daughter was different. In a society where inheritance passed through the male line, the marriage of daughters did not adversely affect the careers of sons-in-law. Bishop Barlow's five daughters all married men who ultimately became bishops: Bishops Day, Wykeham, Overton and Westfaling, and Archbishop Mathew. At least three other bishops' wives were the daughters of bishops: Dorothy Jegon was the daughter of Bishop Vaughan, Susan Godwin of Bishop Wolton and Anne Blethin was the daughter or stepdaughter of Archbishop Younge. Compared with the interconnections of families in inherited occupations, this is not very impressive. The degree of intermarriage within the cathedral close was, however, quite dense.[102]

The relationship between a bishop and his successor did not encourage marriage between their children, for their relations were likely to be strained. Though a bishop might have several palaces at his command, these were only for use during his lifetime. A bishop's wife lost her home and living when her husband died. There was no 'annate' or 'ann' as in Scotland to cushion the first months of widowhood;[103] dilapidations often amounted to hundreds of pounds, and had to be paid at a time when arrears of taxes and other debts also had to be settled.[104] Often little cash was available. Katharine Chaderton attempted to reduce the erosion of her capital by payment in kind wherever possible. She sold her husband's successor £50. 14s. 6d. of household goods, corn worth £178 at 20s. an acre (and worth £50 more!), and the lease of a property worth £30. This all but made up the full sum of £266. 18s. By the time negotiations were completed the new bishop had died, and final details had to be settled with his widow.[105]

Many bishops' wives were left in penury, especially in the earlier part of Elizabeth's reign when the disruptions of the mid-century religious crisis, and the inexperience of the new bishops in ecclesiastical administration added to their problems. Felicity Heal has shown that 45 per cent of the Elizabethan bishops who died before 1580 died poor or in debt, and only 5 per cent died wealthy, including those who never married. Even after 1580 only 14 per cent died rich men, while 35 per cent died poor or in debt.[106] The plight of such wives as Mrs Bentham must have caused considerable concern in episcopal palaces. Bishop Bentham's debts could not be met by the estate, and so the queen's commissioners seized his goods:

> which goods and chattells wee sett to sale according to our said Commission, but we could not sell the same for ready money at the particular values spied in the said schedules. And thereupon we dealt with the Widow of the said Bishop for the buying thereof, and after conference with her friends for their aid therein she offered for the residue of the said goods and chattles in respect to have days for payment of the same.... And to give Bonds with good surety to her Majesty for the true payment thereof at such days as this Court (in pitiful Compassion of herself and Six destitute Children that lie on her hands and have nothing to live of) will assign and appoint.[107]

Provision for wives and children were a new demand on bishops, and they came at a time when their estates were diminished by royal rapacity, heavy taxation and the effects of inflation. Elizabeth did not want her bishops to live merely like godly superintendents. The demands on them to live in medieval pomp, to employ large retinues of servants and exercise a wide hospitality were undiminished, and, even without a family to provide for, most bishops had difficulty in meeting the demands laid upon them.[108] Attempts to economize, to raise rents, to increase their revenues or to assist their family by beneficial leases were blamed upon their wives and families by courtiers and Puritans alike. The Puritans were critical, maintaining that the wives encouraged their husbands in a lifestyle that had little to do with the simplicities of the life of the godly superintendent as envisaged in their exile. The courtiers complained because the bishops were slow to grant them the leases the queen regarded as hers to dispose of. While the demands of the Puritans were at least consistent, others applied a double standard. As Bishop Cooper remarked:

> Divers persons of other callings by the exercise of an office onely
> in fewe yeares, can purchase for wife and children many hundreds
> [of acres?], and all very well thought of: But if a bishop that by the
> state of the lawe hath the right use of a living many yeeres do
> purchase one hundred Markes [worth?], or provide a mean lease
> for the helpe of his wife and children it is accompted greedy
> covetousness and mistrust in the providence of God.[109]

When they sought to safeguard the wellbeing of their wives and
children, standards were applied to them which were not adopted by
the gentry and courtiers who criticized them. This double standard
was one which underlay the ideals of the period for the gentleman
and the lady, and embraced far more than sexual ethics. As Ruth
Kelso has pointed out, the values by which the gentleman lived were
pagan, while those of the lady were Christian.[110] The gentleman
valued self-expansion and self-realization, and cultivated all that
raised him above the crowd and enhanced his authority. The feminine
ideal was one of obedience, selflessness, chastity, patience and
humility. On the one hand the bishop was expected, in bearing the
port of a bishop and in exercising a princely hospitality, to uphold the
ideal for the gentleman, but he was also criticized for failing to comply
with the queen's demands for leases and advowsons for her favourites
at the expense of their sees and to exercise a suicidally Christian
submissiveness, which was quite out of character in a gentleman. The
bishop as the compliant prop of the establishment was being moulded.
But if bishops were expected to assume otherworldly 'feminine'
virtues, what of their wives? The wife who sought to protect her
husband's interests (and her own through him) was not to be tolerated,
for she was taking on a 'masculine' role. When Bishop Cox, strong
man though he was, sought to oppose the granting of over-favourable
leases to Lord North at the Queen's behest, Lord North saw Mrs
Cox's hand in it, and wrote menacingly to Cox:

> Yo[r] wife hath also counselled you to be a Latimer in theis daies,
> gloryinge as it were to stand against yo[r] naturall prince. Well, my
> L. let not your wives shallowe experience carie you to farr, leaste
> she laye yo[r] honoure and credite agrownde and haply makes a
> Shippwarke of the whole.[111]

The myth of Mrs Proudie was already taking shape.

Yet the bishop's wife had remarkably little power in the Elizabethan episcopal palace, which continued to be run very much on the medieval pattern, with a large retinue of servants and episcopal officials, who were often jealous of any trespass by the wife within their traditional spheres. According to one official, wives should have nothing to do with the order, rule or government of the episcopal household or family (that is, the *familia*) apart from their children, maidservants and maidens. They should limit themselves to godly exercises and good works. They must not intrude in the worldly affairs of the palace.[112] Although we have no diaries to give an account of the day-to-day life of an Elizabethan bishop's wife, it is possible to build up some sort of picture of the better-off bishops' wives from their wills. Unfortunately we learn more of their widowhood than of their married life. Seventeen widows left wills.[113] Those of bishops in wealthy sees left most: eight wills come from the three wealthy sees of York, Durham and Winchester. Canterbury is not represented. Although Archbishop Parker outlived his wife, and Strype speaks of her will, none survives. The other archbishops were unmarried.

Some of the widows continued to live in the cathedral town of their husband's diocese, as did Mrs Younge and Mrs Mathew, but more commonly they lived near a favourite palace in the country. Thus three widows of former Bishops of Lincoln clustered near Buckden in Huntingdonshire: Amy Cooper at Buckden itself, Catharine Chaderton at Holywell, Anthonina Wykeham at Alconbury. Elizabeth Scory and Alice Pilkington may have moved to London to be near their families, while Cicely Sandys lived at Edwins Hall at Woodham Ferrars in Essex, a property that had belonged to the family of her husband's first wife, a distant cousin, which was perhaps being established as a family seat.

Many of the wills show a wide generosity, with legacies to friends, servants, cousins of all sorts, as well as their own children. Only a few tell us much about their households. The wills of Amy Cooper and Cicely Sandys are unusually full of detail. Amy Cooper, who styled herself a 'gentlewoman', leased the parsonage of Buckden and ran a working farm. Her will mentions various carts and horses, hoggets and wethers. Her brother Robert Royce may have helped her with it. 'Thomas Lea, gent.', lived in the house, perhaps acting as a steward. The servants included one Elias Riley, probably a nephew. Her main beneficiaries were her daughter Elizabeth Belley and son-in-law John Belley, DCL chancellor of the diocese of Lincoln, who lived in a neighbouring village. The will ends with a schedule of her silver plate.

Cicely Sandys shared her house with her son Miles and left a legacy to her granddaughter Bridget who waited on her. A bequest was set aside for her son George, the poet, should he ever return from his travels. Money was allocated for gowns for mourners for her funeral including 'my sons children which I have brought up'. Two Geneva Bibles, one the present of her brother Francis Wilsford, were given to daughters, and £200 was to be spent on the funeral. There was, however, more of the great lady than the widow of the godly superintendent about Cicely Sandys. Although her husband had been a Marian exile, he was one of the bishops most active in establishing his family.[114]

As Amy Cooper's husband had pointed out, such households had to be maintained by the investments of the bishops in leases and advowsons, with a certain amount of readily realizable assets in the form of plate. With landholding came the associated pack of values, the obsession with keeping an estate together and the apparatus for passing it on: primogeniture, marriage settlements, even the buying of a wardship in the case of Sandys, as his will showed.

It cannot be claimed that the recrudescence of sacerdotalism in the late Elizabethan church occurred entirely because the more well-to-do bishops had become gentrified and had inserted their families into the hierarchy of the landed gentry. Theology must play some part. The idea of the priesthood of all believers was fading, as had that of the bishop as the godly superintendent. So also were the other egalitarian influences which seemed so much more meaningful in a city-state than under a monarchy. The position of the Church of England as a conservative force supporting the secular establishment subtly moulded people's thought. The idea of the equality of men and women before God was difficult to assimilate in a country in which hierarchy was fundamental to its sense of order, and the Anglican Church increasingly dissociated itself from radical Protestant beliefs. Women had no place in its hierarchy. Sacerdotalism prevailed, and, as in the past, in a sexist form.

Something of this can be seen expressed in stone, if we compare the tombs of two bishops who had been Marian exiles, Bishop Bentham and Archbishop Sandys. Bishop Bentham had, it will be remembered, married a fellow exile, Mawde Fawcon. He seems to have adhered more closely to the Protestantism of the exile than many other bishops.[115] The bishop's tomb is now consigned to a dark corner in a dark vestry in the parish church at Eccleshall, the village in which the bishop's castle lay. On the top of the stone is incised a rather crude likeness of the bishop, but on its side the bishop may be seen kneeling in prayer with his wife and children in descending order behind him, his wife in a plain dress and hat. There is still order in the family, but its members exist on the same plane. Artistically the tomb cannot be compared with the splendid memorial to that thrusting and proud prelate Archbishop Sandys in Southwell Minster. His effigy is very grand. He lies on his tomb, richly robed, at prayer, attended by angels, whilst below his wife and children kneel also at prayer. Beruffed and accomplished figures they may be, but they exist on a lowlier plane. The tomb of Bishop Bentham illustrates the nearest approach to spiritual equality a bishop's wife could achieve, in marriage to a godly superintendent; that of Archbishop Sandys the sacerdotalism that was almost unconsciously overtaking even the first Elizabethan bishops. Not surprisingly Mrs Sandys was to have a monument to herself at Woodham Ferrars, stately in her widow's weeds, in a bower of roses.

It is a paradox that those who first instituted clerical marriage recognized a new dignity in the married state, not recognized in the medieval church, but the wives of the bishops themselves were socially and legally disadvantaged compared with other women, and rendered all but invisible in public life. The status of women in the church remained low, as it still does. For a more egalitarian tradition it is necessary to look to the Puritanism which succumbed to the forces of conservatism under Elizabeth, the tradition of such women as Jane Wilkinson and Anne and Agnes Warcup, which was to run underground until the Civil War.

NOTES

[1] Steven Ozment, *The Age of Reform, 1250–1550* (New Haven, Conn., and London, 1980), p. 383; Owen Chadwick, *The Reformation 1250–1550* (Harmondsworth, 1976), p. 409.

[2] A. G. Dickens, *The Counter Reformation* (London, 1968), pp. 124–7.

[3] James Atkinson (ed.), 'The Judgement of Martin Luther on Monastic Vows', in *Luther's Works*, ed. J. Pelikan and H. Lehman, 55 vols (St Louis, Mo., 1958–67), XLIV, pp. 252–329.

[4] Ruth Kelso, *Doctrine for the Lady of the Renaissance* (Urbana, Ill., 1956), pp. 5–13, discusses this literature.

[5] Walter I. Brundt (ed.), 'The Estate of Marriage', in *Luther's Works*, XLV, p. 39.

[6] Gereth M. Spriggs, 'Good Man Joseph, his place in the Christmas story', *Country Life* (30 November 1972), pp. 1434–7.

[7] 'On the Seven Deadly Sins', in Thomas Arnold (ed.), *Select English Works of John Wyclif*, III (Oxford, 1871), pp. 162–6; 'Of Weddid Men and Wifis and of here Children also', ibid., pp. 190–1; 'Of the Leaven of the Pharisees', in F. O. Mathew (ed.), *The English Works of Wyclif hitherto unpublished*, EETS, LXXIV (1880), pp. 6–10.

[8] Claire Cross, *Church and People, 1450–1660* (Fontana, 1979 edn), pp. 9–52.

[9] Sir Thomas More, *The Confutacyon of Tyndales Answere* (London, 1532), I, p. ccliiii.

[10] William Tyndale, *An Answere to Sir Thomas More's Dialogue*, Henry Walter (ed.), PS (1850), p. 18.

[11] Christopher Hill, 'Clarissa Harlowe and her Times', in *Puritanism and Revolution* (London, 1958), pp. 386–91.

[12] Alice Clark, *Working Life of Women in the Seventeenth Century* (first edn, 1919; new impr., London, 1968), pp. 6–8.

[13] Christopher Hill, *Economic Problems of the Church* (Oxford, 1956), pp. 200–11; Felicity Heal, *Of Prelates and Princes: a study of the economic and social problems of the Tudor episcopate* (Cambridge, 1980).

[14] Miriam U. Chrisman, 'Lay Response to the Protestant Reformation in Germany, 1520–1528', in Peter Newman Brooks (ed.), *Reformation Principle and Practice* (London, 1980), pp. 42–3. This discusses a pamphlet attacking convent life, almost certainly by a woman.

[15] Gottfried G. Krodel (ed.), *Letters*, II & III (*Luther's Works*, XLIX, L), *passim*, and especially II, 234 and III, 277. Sherrin M. Wyntjes, 'Women in the Reformation Era', in R. Bridenthal and C. Coonz (eds), *Becoming Visible: Women in European History* (Boston, Mass., 1977), pp. 174–5.

[16] Roland H. Bainton, *Women of the Reformation in Germany and Italy* (Minneapolis, Minn., 1971), pp. 55–76. For a bibliography of her works see p. 75.

[17] Ibid., p. 56; Ozment, op. cit., pp. 381–8.

[18] Bainton, op. cit., pp. 79–95.

[19] *Correspondence of Matthew Parker*, ed. John Bruce, PS (1853), pp. 41–2.

[20] A. G. Dickens, *The English Reformation* (1964, 8th impr., London, 1976), pp. 166–9; W. F. Hook, *Lives of the Archbishops of Canterbury*, NS II (London, 1868), pp. 27–8; 25 Henry VIII c. 21, clauses iii, vi, viii.

[21] R. E. Chester Waters, *Genealogical Memoirs of the Extinct Family of Chester of Chicheley* (London, 1878), II, pp. 396–7, 448–9; P. H. Hembry, *The Bishops of Bath and Wells 1540–1640* (London, 1967), pp. 83–9. Dr Hembry does not consider this possibility.

[22] *Miscellaneous Writings and Letters of Thomas Cranmer*, ed. J. E. Cox, PS (1846), p. 467; Hook, op. cit., pp. 25–30.

[23] *LP Henry VIII*, XVI, 733, 737; Heal, op. cit., p. 121.

[24] James Sawtrey, *The Defence of the Mariage of Preistes, Against Steven Gardiner* (London, 1541), sig. Aiii^v–iv, gives a brief account of the plight of

priests' wives after the passing of the Act of Six Articles (31 Henry VIII c. 14).

[25] Jasper Ridley, *Thomas Cranmer* (Oxford, 1962), pp. 147–8.

[26] Marina Warner, *Alone of All Her Sex* (New York, 1978), pp. 50–67.

[27] Robert Crowley, *The Confutation of XIII Articles Whereunto Nicolas Shaxton, Late Byshop of Salisburye Subscribed* (London, 1548), sig. Aii–[iii].

[28] Heal, op. cit., pp. 128–9.

[29] A. G. Dickens, *Lollards and Protestants in the Diocese of York* (Hull, 1959), p. 185.

[30] Hastings Robinson (ed.), *Original Letters Relative to the English Reformation 1537–1558*, I, PS (1846), p. 75; for Robert Ferrar and his son see Foxe, *A & M*, VII, pp. 8–9, 15.

[31] Foxe, *A & M*, VI, p. 637; *Original Letters*, I, pp. 107–15; I would like to thank Fraulein Ruth Greminger for checking the Staatsarchiv des Kantons Zurich for letters from Anne Hooper to Mrs Bullinger. None have survived.

[32] John Hooker, *The Ancient History and Description of the City of Exeter with a Calalogue of all the Bishops of Exeter* (Exeter, n.d.), pp. 280–1.

[33] Foxe, *A & M*, VI, pp. 644–5.

[34] *Original Letters*, I, p. 109.

[35] Barbara Wentworth, Holgate's wife, came from a Yorkshire gentry family (A. G. Dickens, 'The Marriage and Character of Archbishop Holgate', *EHR*, LII (1937), p. 430); Edith Ashley, wife of Paul Bushe, came of Somerset gentry stock (*CPR, P & M*, III, p. 410); her brother, Henry, married Katharine Bassett, daughter of Honor, Lady Lisle (*The Lisle Letters*, ed. Muriel St John Byrne, 6 vols (Chicago and London, 1981), VI, p. 276).

[36] E. J. Payne, 'The Montforts, the Wellesbournes, and the Hughenden Effigies', *Records of Buckinghamshire*, VII (1896), pp. 393–4; Claire Cross, ' "Great Reasoners in Scripture": Women Lollards 1386–1530', in Derek Baker (ed.), *Medieval Women* (Oxford, 1978), p. 368.

[37] Peter Clark, *English Provincial Society: Religion, Politics and Society in Kent 1500–1640* (Hassocks, 1977), p. 52.

[38] Nicholas Harpsfield, *A Treatise on the Pretended Divorce Between Henry VIII and Catharine of Aragon*, CS, NS XXI (1878), pp. 275–6, p. 291; Myles Hogarde, *The Displaying of the Protestantes* (London, 1556), ff. 73–5.

[39] *The Diary of Henry Machyn*, ed. John Gough Nichols, CS, (1848), p. 8; *Chronicle of the Grey Friars of London*, ed. John Nichols, CS, (1852), p. 70; N. Saunders, *Rise and growth of the Anglican Schism* (1582), trans. David Lewis (London, 1877), pp. 208–9.

[40] *Collectanea Topographica et Genealogica*, IV (1837), p. 91; *The Visitation of Kent 1619–21*, HS (1898), XLII, p. 185; A. G. Dickens, 'Holgate', *EHR*, LII (1937), 432.

[41] Dickens, *Lollards and Protestants*, pp. 185–7.

[42] J. F. Davis, 'Lollard Survival and the Textile Industry in the South-East of England', *Studies in Church History*, III (1966), pp. 191–201; Cross, op. cit., pp. 9–42.

[43] For example, Chaucer's 'Millers Tale' and the 'pretty jest of the friar' in V.

de Sola Pinto and A. E. Rodway, *The Common Muse* (Harmondsworth, 1965), pp. 463–5.

44 P. Tyler, 'The Status of the Elizabethan Parish Clergy', *Studies in Church History*, IV (1967), pp. 87–8; Keith Thomas, *Religion and the Decline of Magic* (Harmondsworth, 1973), p. 37. Although it was firm Catholic teaching that the unworthy minister did not invalidate the sacrament, this was not necessarily the popular view, as Cranmer's visitation articles for Canterbury show: W. H. Frere (ed.), *Visitation Articles and Injunctions of the period of the Reformation*, II (1536–1558), Alcuin Club Colls., XV, p. 189.

45 Frere, ibid., pp. 292–3.

46 5 & 6 Ed. VI, c. 12.

47 Henry King, 'To my honourd friend Mr. George Sandys', appeared first in 1638.

48 1 Mary, Session II, c. 2.

49 *The Letter Book of John Parkhurst, Bishop of Norwich*, ed. R. A. Houlbrooke, Norfolk Record Soc., XLIII (1974–5), p. 77.

50 Dickens, *English Reformation*, p. 381

51 *CPR, Ed. VI*, V, p. 298; York Minster Library, Wb.*f.* 101. I owe this last reference to Felicity Heal.

52 *CPR, P & M*, III, p. 410.

53 Peter Leversage and John Taylor, *An Illustrated History of Bristol Cathedral* (Clifton, *c.* 1888), p. 84; Timothy Kendall (ed.), *Flowers and Epigrammes* (1577), Spencer Society, XV (1874), p. 216.

54 *Visitation of Kent, 1619*, p. 185; Christina Hallowell Garrett, *The Marian Exiles* (Cambridge, 1938), p. 183; PROB 11/85/31.

55 *DNB*.

56 Already imprisoned in Mary's reign (*DNB*).

57 *The Autobiography of Sir John Bramston, KB*, [ed. Lord Braybrooke], CS, XXXII (1845), pp. 9–13; Maria Dowling and Joy Shakespeare, 'Religion and Politics in Mid-Tudor England Through the Eyes of an English Protestant Woman: The Recollections of Rose Hickman', *Bulletin of the Institute of Historical Research*, LV (1982), pp. 100–1.

58 Foxe, *A & M*, VII, pp. 190–2.

59 Peter Clark, op. cit., p. 100.

60 Dickens, *English Reformation*, pp. 374–7.

61 Garrett, op. cit., gives an inadequate and unreliable account of this lady under the entry for one Rowland Wilkinson. PROB 11/42B/29; *DNB* (Edward North).

62 *Sermons & Remains of Hugh Latimer*, ed. G. E. Corrie, PS (1845), p. 444.

63 *Original Letters*, I, pp. 113–14; R. Jung, *Die Englische Flüchtlings–Gemeinde in Frankfurt am Main 1554–1559* (Frankfurt am Main, 1910), pp. 52, 57. The inventory of Anne Hooper mentioned here was destroyed by bombing during the Second World War. I am grateful to Dr Kaspar von

Greyerz for his inquiry on my behalf; T. Vetter, *Relations between England and Zurich During the Reformation* (London, 1904), p. 42.

[64] Garrett, op. cit., pp. 187, 242.

[65] PROB 11/42B/29; PROB 11/53/44.

[66] Quoted in Gordon Rupp, *The Righteousness of God: Luther Studies* (London, 1953), p. 314.

[67] PROB 11/53/44.

[68] E. A. McArthur, 'Women Petitioners and the Long Parliament', *EHR*, XXIV (1909), pp. 698–709; K. V. Thomas, 'Women and the Civil War Sects', *P & P*, XIII (1958); Ivy Pinchbeck, *Women Workers and the Industrial Revolution 1750–1850* (1930; repr. London, 1977), pp. 62–3.

[69] Garrett, op. cit., p. 87 (under Bentham). Women are listed under males of the same surname even if the males, as with Margaret Cranmer and Anne Hooper, are children, or not certainly known to be related. See also 'Livre des Anglois' in J. S. Burn, *The History of Parish Registers* (1862; repr. East Ardsley, Wakefield, 1976), p. 285; Cross, *Church and People*, p. 97.

[70] Garrett, op. cit., pp. 332–3; Patrick Collinson, 'Cranbrook and the Fletchers' in Brooks (ed.), *Ref. Prins.*, pp. 175–6; *DNB* (Wilsford); *Visitation of Kent, 1619*, pp. 53, 104 (the two pedigrees are inconsistent).

[71] PROB 11/63/24; PROB 11/53/44; PROB 11/38/12; PROB 11/85/25; *Visitation of Hants*, HS, LXIV (1913), p. 3 (incomplete); J. E. Neale, *Elizabeth and her Parliaments, 1559–1581* (London, 1953), p. 90.

[72] J. Fines, 'An Incident of the Reformation in Shropshire', *Transactions of the Shropshire Archaeological Society*, LVII (1966), pp. 166–70; *DNB*.

[73] Dowling and Shakespeare, op. cit., pp. 94–102; Bramston, op. cit., pp. 9–13; Roland H. Bainton, *Women of the Reformation from Spain to Scandinavia* (Minneapolis, Minn., 1977), pp. 89–94; Patrick Collinson, 'The Role of Women in the English Reformation Illustrated by the Life and Friendship of Anne Locke', *Studies in Church History*, II, (1965); PROB 11/53/14; PROB 11/85/31; Garrett, op. cit., pp. 292–3; PROB 11/59/16. The kinsmen of Jane Locke née Wilkinson included Richard Springham, the sustainer and Ralph Hetherington, son-in-law of the Puritan author Thomas Wood. Wood's son and namesake probably married the daughter of Maria Ponet (PROB 11/85/31).

[74] Cambridge University Library, Archdeaconry Court of Ely, George Alder (*sic*) (1545); M. M. Knappen, *Tudor Puritanism* (1939; repr., Chicago, 1970), pp. 59–60; C. E. Raven, *English Naturalists from Neckham to Ray* (Cambridge, 1974), pp. 48–137; William Turner, *Libellus de Re Herbaria Novus* (1538), ed. B. D. Jackson (London, 1877), pp. i–x; for his controversy with Gardiner on clerical marriage see *The Huntyng and Fynding out of the Romishe Fox* (Basle, 1543); Gardiner's reply, 'The Examination of a Proud Presumptious Hunter', is given in Turner's *The Seconde Course of the Hunter at the Romish Fox and Hys Advocate*, ([Zurich?], 1545); *DNB* (William Turner, Peter Turner); Patrick Collinson, *The Elizabethan Puritan Movement* (London, 1967), pp. 286–7, 291, 296–7.

[75] *CPR, P & M*, III, p. 483; PRO C3/169/6.

[76] Hook, op. cit., II, pp. 108–9.

[77] *DNB* for Wolfe and Whitchurch; for Whitchurch's publications see also *STC* entries for *Bible*, Liturgies: *Book of Common Prayer*, etc.

[78] PRO C3/170/81; *DNB* for Norton.

[79] C3/217/30.

[80] BI, HC CP 1575/1; BI Prob. Reg. 19B/804. The Prerogative Court of Canterbury's copy, PROB 11/56/42, has been tampered with.

[81] C3/217/30, quotation slightly abbreviated and modernized.

[82] It was restored under James I (1 Jac. I, c. 25, clauses viii, 1).

[83] John Strype, *Annals of the Reformation*, 3 vols (London, 1709), I, p. 81.

[84] C. W. Foster, *The State of the Church in the Reigns of Elizabeth and James I as Illustrated by Documents Relating to the Diocese of Lincoln*, I, Lincoln Record Society, XXIII (1926), xxi–xxii; Paul L. Hughes and James F. Larkin (eds), *Tudor Royal Proclamations*, II (New Haven, Conn., and London, 1969), pp. 125–6.

[85] Maria Lynn Cioni, 'Women and Law in Elizabethan England with Particular Reference to the Court of Chancery', unpublished Cambridge Ph.D. thesis 1974, pp. 1–25.

[86] William Leonard, *The Third Part of the Reports of Several Excellent Cases of Law, from the First to the Five and Thirtieth Yeare of her Reign* (London, 1686), No. XXVI (Simonds Case, 8 Eliz.).

[87] J. H. Baker, *An Introduction to English Legal History* (London, 1971), pp. 146–7; David Marcombe, 'The Dean and Chapter of Durham, 1558–1603', unpublished Durham Ph.D. thesis (1973), p. 25.

[88] Joel Berlatsky, 'Marriage and Family in a Tudor Élite: Familial Patterns of Elizabethan Bishops', *Journal of Family History*, III (1978), p. 8. Dr Berlatsky was able to identify fifty-five bishops as certainly married (omitting Sodor and Man). Three more can now be added: Curteys (Sir Henry Ellis, 'Notices of Richard Curteys, Bishop of Chichester, 1570–1582', *Sussex Archaeological Colls.*, X (1852), p. 58); Berkeley (*Parkhurst*, ed. Houlbrooke, p. 143); Bennett (PROB 11/130/122, codicil. He asked to be buried 'beyond the seate of my wife erected for herself'. Box pews were just coming in).

[89] Heal, op. cit., p. 253.

[90] Ibid., pp. 290–1.

[91] Ibid., pp. 245–6.

[92] Christopher Haigh, 'Finance and Administration in a New Diocese: Chester 1541–1641', in Rosemary O'Day and Felicity Heal (eds), *Continuity and Change* (Leicester, 1976), p. 156.

[93] Sir John Harington, *A Briefe View of the State of the Church in England, to the Year 1608* (London, 1653), p. 94.

[94] For Hutton, *The Correspondence of Dr Matthew Hutton, Archbishop of York*, ed. James Raine, Surtees Society, XVII (1843), pp. 178–9, and D. M. Palliser, *Tudor York* (Oxford, 1979), p. 228; for Mathew, *Proceedings of the Society of Antiquaries of Newcastle upon Tyne*, 4th ser., I (1923), p. 132.

[95] Corpus Christi College Library, Cambridge, 114A, p. 109.

[96] John Selden, *Table Talk*, ed. Sir F. Pollock (London, 1927), p. 139; see also William Cavendish, Duke of Newcastle, *The Triumphant Widow* (London, 1677), I, ii. I owe these references to Sara Mendelson and Barbara Todd, respectively.

[97] Heal, op. cit., p. 240; PRO SP 12/20/12.

[98] Harington, op. cit., pp. 120–1.

[99] PRO REQ 2/51/45; *CSPD* 1598–1601, p. 178; Harington, op. cit., 156.

[100] Those marrying twice were Barnes*, Blethin, N. Bullingham, H. Cotton*, Cox, Fletcher, Godwin, Middleton, Overton, Sandys, Still, Younge. Goldesborough* and Hutton married thrice. Asterisks indicate those not listed by Berlatsky, op. cit., p. 10.

[101] For her own family see Gifford, *Visitation of Hants*, HS, LXIV, p. 16; *DNB* (see Sir John Baker and also Sir Richard Baker, i.e. the namesake and nephew of her husband). The Bakers lived at Sissinghurst in the parish of Cranbrook, where Fletcher's father was the minister. After Bishop Fletcher's death she married Sir Stephen Thornehurst (*Visitation of Kent, 1619*, pp. 63–4), and there is a monument to her in St Michael's chapel, Canterbury Cathedral, which makes no mention of her marriage to Fletcher.

[102] See for instance, Marcombe, op. cit.

[103] *OED*, 'annate', 'ann'.

[104] Heal, op. cit., pp. 299–303. Cases between bishops were dealt with by the Court of Arches and Delegates, whose records for this period do not survive. The accounts of the estate of Archbishop Younge (who died in 1568), which were drawn up for his widow, show that she had to pay Grindal, her husband's successor, £910, and her legal and other expenses amounted to £113. 6s. 8d. Thomas Younge's estate was not fully administered by 1623 when a grant of administration *de bonis non* was made by the Consistory Court of York.

[105] PRO, C2 Jas. I/C11/50, Katharine Chaderton *v.* Joan Barlow.

[106] Heal, op. cit., p. 316.

[107] PRO E 178/2082.

[108] Hill, *Economic Problems of the Church*, pp. 200–1; Heal, op. cit., *passim*.

[109] Thomas Cooper, *An Admonition to the People of England* (1589), ed. Edward Arber (Birmingham, 1883), pp. 113–15.

[110] Ruth Kelso, *Doctrine for the Lady of the Renaissance*, (Urbana, Ill., 1956), pp. 23–37.

[111] Quoted by George L. Blackman, 'The Career and Influence of Bishop Richard Cox 1547–1581', unpublished Cambridge Ph.D. thesis (1953), pp. 218, 294.

[112] PRO SP 15/24/8.

[113] Judith Aylmer (PROB 11/133/14); Jane Barnes, later Pilkington (BI Prob. Reg., vol. 31, f. 99); Elizabeth Best (PROB 11/56/42); Anne Blethin (PROB 11/113/18); Catharine Chaderton (PROB 11/136/102, PROB 11/137/12); Amy Cooper (PROB 11/107/24); Mary Cotton, widow of William

(PROB 11/157/14); Jane Cox (PROB 11/73/5); Margaret Holland alias Davies, widow of Thomas (PROB 11/58/36); Frances Hutton (BI Prob. Reg. 35/495); Frances Mathew (BI Prob. Reg. 40/397); Alice Pilkington (PROB 11/85/25); Cicely Sandys (PROB 11/117/15); Elizabeth Scory (PROB 11/81/26); Jane Still (PROB 11/113/33); Anthonina Wykeham (PROB 11/91/54); Jane Younge (BI Prob. Reg. 32/651).

[114] BI R Bp. 28/12 'Patents of Offices and Leases granted by the late Archbishop Sandys'; *North Country Wills*, Surtees Society, CXXI (1912), pp. 135–8; but see also W. J. Sheils, 'Profit, Patronage, or Pastoral Care: The Rectory Estates of the Archbishopric of York, 1540–1640' in Rosemary O'Day and Felicity Heal (eds), *Princes and Paupers in the English Church, 1500–1800* (Cambridge, 1980), pp. 91–109, for a defence of archiepiscopal policy on the letting of rectory estates.

[115] 'The Letter-Book of Thomas Bentham, Bishop of Coventry and Lichfield, 1560–1561', ed. Rosemary O'Day and Joel Berlatsky, in *Camden Miscellany* XXVII, CS, 4th ser., XXII (1979). His humility in the face of criticism from fellow exiles who had not become bishops shows his anti-hierarchic view of the church. See especially pp. 189–90.

Recusant women
5   1560–1640

MARIE B. ROWLANDS

The women of English recusant[1] families from 1560 to 1640 formed a distinct group. The state found it necessary to attempt to devise special measures to control them, and their church recognized their special role in the evolution of Catholicism in England. They are probably better documented than other women of the period, but the documentation available relates almost entirely to those who internalized the teachings of their religion and whose behaviour was rooted in, and sustained by, that assent. Even the documentation in public records arises from the attempts of the state to control those who refused to compromise. Thus the evidence is biased to reveal those women who were vigorous, active and capable of making an impression. No doubt such women were a minority within the overall spectrum of Catholic women of the period, but a study of this special group of the committed nevertheless reveals something of the attitudes of the state and of the Roman Catholic Church to women in general.

In the period of the Counter-Reformation, rulers throughout Europe found themselves faced with substantial minorities of religious dissidents. These groups were often partly composed of influential and respectable people with an established place in the social framework. The existence of such groups raised fundamental issues – as, for example, the nature and limits of state authority, of the right to resist, and of civil and religious obedience. In the particular case before us a further problem arose – namely, how far a woman who broke the law was responsible for her own actions.

RECUSANT WOMEN AND THE LAW

Church attendance

From 1559 attendance at the Book of Common Prayer service was the means by which individuals were required to express obedience to the church established by law.[2] By authority of the Act of Uniformity (1559) the penalty of a fine of twelve pence was to be levied by the churchwardens of the parish. The duty of enforcing the law lay primarily with the ecclesiastical courts, the bishops and the Ecclesiastical Commissions. However, the Act also empowered the Queen's Justices to deal with refusal to attend upon an indictment for trespass. Thus both the church authorities and the civil authorities were associated in the attempt to secure conformity, even though no person could be punished by both courts for the same offence.[3]

Women – spinsters, wives and widows – figured prominently in the lists of those who refused to attend. Spinsters of competent age and widows were held responsible for their own actions and could be indicted, fined and if necessary imprisoned.[4] The problem lay in obtaining the conformity of married women. While on the one hand a husband could not be held responsible for his wife's criminal acts,[5] on the other hand society was very strongly convinced that the duty of ensuring the proper religious behaviour of the family lay with the paterfamilias.

In the north of England from 1575 onwards the Northern High Commission under the presidency of the Earl of Huntingdon was very active indeed in attempting to secure religious conformity, and looked to the local ecclesiastical and secular authorities for co-operation.[6] The proceedings at York provide a useful insight into the attitudes both of the recusant wives and of the authorities. In York by 1575 there had emerged a hard core of about forty recusant families who were articulate, vigorous and determined. The husbands were butchers, tailors, drapers – some of whom were, or aspired to be, members of the city's government.[7]

The wives were well able to speak for themselves when required to do so. Fifty-one were questioned in November 1576 and asked their reasons for refusing to attend church. Ellen Wilkinson said there was neither priest nor altar nor sacrifice. Isabel Bowman said that her conscience would not allow her to attend; 'the sacrament was not hung up nor other things as they had been aforetime'. Anne Brierley said that if she went to church she would damn her own soul. Jane

Geldart said her conscience would not allow her to go and that there was no greater cause than conscience. Janet Strychett said that the bread and wine were not consecrated. Jane West said it was 'not the right church'.[8] The other women gave similar replies with individual variations. Between them they covered most of the doctrinal matters at issue.

The Northern Court of High Commission looked to the husbands of these women to overcome their resistance. Some claimed that they had tried to carry out their responsibilities. Christopher Kinchingman had dragged his wife to church by force on one occasion, and George Hall had beaten his wife. Some husbands undertook to pay their wives' fines and forfeitures but could not compel their attendance. Several began by resisting but after a period of fines and imprisonments submitted. Lord Mayor Dinley, whose wife was to prove one of the most obstinate, was in a particularly embarrassing position and was formally lectured on the disgrace of a man set to govern a city who could not govern his household.[9]

Most of the husbands, however, were themselves determined recusants, and the couples concerned – the Geldarts, Teshes, Wellards and others – entered into a long conflict with the authorities. After a time a husband was released on bond, and pressure was brought to bear to make him pay fines and forfeitures for both of them. The wives were released on bond from time to time, at Christmas or for child-bearing, and then returned to prison. In several cases the sequence of imprisonments, releases, arrests and rearrests, fines and forfeitures, bonds entered into and bonds defaulted upon, was to continue for many years.[10]

From other parts of the country came similar accounts. John Goldsmith was in Manchester prison because he could not control his wife in these matters, and Privy Council considered that it should be 'laid to her own carcase', and that he should be released.[11]

In the 1580s the ideological pressures became more acute, in anticipation of the war with Spain. In 1581 the 'Act to retain the Queen's Majesty's subjects in their due obedience'[12] made Justices of the Peace responsible for enforcing religious conformity. This Act – described by Bossy as the 'heavy footed intervention of a Puritan led House of Commons'[13] – brought home for the first time to every Justice of the Peace in the shires and to every village constable the intractability of the problem of recusant wives. A clause aimed at controlling them had been considered when the Act was under discussion, but significantly it had been dropped. The justices were left to struggle with the situation that, although wives could indeed be indicted and convicted, they could not be fined, and forfeiture could not be made nor distraints levied upon them during the husband's lifetime, since the wife had no property of her own to distrain. If he died first, two-thirds of her jointure could be immediately seized, and the Exchequer roll of 1593–4 recorded sixty such cases among 450 forfeitures. However, future and uncertain fines were no answer to present disobedience.[14]

In practice the only punishment available for married women was imprisonment, and many women were sent to gaol. Poor women in particular were likely to find themselves in prison for failure to pay fines, resistance to distraint or refusal to confer with Church of England ministers. In 1594 it was reported that eleven women had died in Ousebridge gaol, York, out of thirty imprisoned there over a period of fourteen years.[15] In 1598 there were twenty-five recusant prisoners in the same prison, eleven of whom were women.[16] However, the imprisonment of recusants who could not pay for their keep was too expensive. In Cheshire in 1582 many poor men and women were for this reason released on bond.[17]

Evasion of the statute was widely practised by both men and women. The simplest method was to be absent when sought and ensure that the constable made a return of 'not found in my bailiwick'. This provoked a succession of writs and these too were ignored. Only in a minority of cases of recusants presented did an indictment follow. Even if the recusant was indicted, the ultimate penalty for refusing to appear was outlawry, and this could not be imposed in the case of a married woman. She had no property or civil rights and could only be 'waived'.[18]

The returns to both the civil and the ecclesiastical authorities give the impression that Catholic women, in particular, were always just disappearing over the horizon. There was Mrs Brudiman of Toddington in Bedfordshire who, when the bishop served process, 'slipped out of my diocese'.[19] Mrs Hancorne of Warwickshire fled out of the parish at the time of her presentment.[20] Margaret Attwood was a fugitive who moved from place to place. Mrs Phillips 'departed from us about 4 or 5 years since and as we suppose is now at Evesham', and Mrs Jeffries 'hath flytted out of town and is now at Stratford'.[21] In 1592 it was said that Mrs Bridget Strange of Badgington, Gloucestershire, had not been to church for thirty years. She heard some pursuivants were coming to her house in Warwickshire whereupon she fled and carried off with her the altar vessels and vestments.[22]

Gentlemen in the provinces charged with the duty of maintaining the law sent a succession of queries to Privy Council asking for clarification, support and guidance in this matter of recusant women, and of the men who 'go to church themselves but have Mass at home for their wives'.[23] In Hampshire the 'most obstinate' sister of Nicholas Sanders was imprisoned, and the bishop begged that she might be kept there, since her return to Winchester 'would do more harm than ten sermons do good'.[24] In the year of the Armada, 1588, the Sheriff of Cambridge begged to know how to proceed against women recusants 'whom he dare not presume to apprehend without advice',[25] and the Sheriff of Leicester and the Earl of Kent wrote to the same effect.[26]

Meanwhile, in 1586, a further Act had attempted an extensive clarification of procedures for prosecuting recusants and collecting penalties.[27] It did not, however, resolve the problem of how to control recusant wives effectively. Between 1591 and 1593 there was sustained agitation and debate on this issue. By this time the attitude of the professional administrators of the law had hardened. Men like Lord Burghley, the Earl of Huntingdon, Chief Justice Popham and Recorder Fleetwood of London knew that the root of their difficulties lay with the failure to enforce the law against obstinate and influential wives 'in respect that by their example whole families refuse to resort to Church and continue in recusance'.[28]

Chief Justice Popham reported on behalf of the judges in 1593, advocating much more direct and stringent measures: women should be imprisoned, children should be removed from recusant families, and Catholics living in London should be required to report regularly to the authorities.[29] Richard Topcliffe,[30] the vigorous prosecutor of papists, also submitted a memorandum urging strong measures against recusant wives. As early as 1590, on taking up the secretaryship after the death of Walsingham, Lord Burghley had listed among his priorities in matters of religion measures to ensure that recusant wives should be indicted, condemned and imprisoned and that their husbands should pay their fines.[31]

The attitude of Privy Council was more equivocal. The Earl of Derby was told that he should indict all recusants 'as well women as the rest'.[32] In September 1593 the commissioners of Dorset were told to forbear until the judge's opinion had been taken.[32] The Bishop of Sarum was told to commit women of good position and influence to prison,[33] yet ordered to release on compassionate grounds the wife of John Searle.[34]

There was much activity in the north. Six gentlewomen in Northamptonshire, and sixteen Lancashire gentlewomen were arrested.[35] The Earl of Huntingdon committed twenty-three women of quality, including Lady Constable, Mrs Metham, Mrs Ingleby, Mrs Babthorpe and Katherine Radcliffe. The husbands of these women were wealthy and influential and brought pressure to bear. Letters for their release were sent in June, but the earl delayed and was actually praised for his delay, Privy Council claiming that the former letters should have been recalled. Eventually the women were released after fourteen months in prison.[36] Other women were put into the custody of Protestant leaders. Margaret Throckmorton, for example, was put in the care of the Dean of Gloucester and her mother into the house of Thomas Denys of Gloucester.[37]

It was against the background of renewed fears of Spanish invasion that Parliament, meeting in February 1593, was called upon to consider two bills concerning recusants. One bill, in the Lords, proposed that recusants should be confined to within five miles of their home; the other, in the Commons, included substantial measures to deal with recusant wives. A recusant heiress was to lose two-thirds of her inheritance, a woman marrying a recusant could lose her dower or jointure, and children were to be taken from their parents at the age of 7. Heads of households would pay £10 a head for every member of the household not attending church.[38]

An intercepted letter from England to an exiled Catholic described the Commons bill as 'not much liked',[39] and indeed the debate opened with Francis Craddock from Stafford who supported the bill but asked for moderation of the clauses relating to family life. Mr Wroth of Liverpool opposed the fining of a husband for his wife's recusancy. The Commons, though prepared for the most vigorous action against Jesuits and seminary priests, felt threatened and uncertain when it came to an intrusion by the state into the family. There were members who 'had a special eye to the statutes of recusancy, that no such thing might be inserted which might wind them within such a penance', for many had recusant women relatives.[40]

The Commons bill was dropped altogether and was replaced by a new statute which confined itself to enforcing the five-mile restriction, and the £10 fine on heads of households for every member of their family not attending church.[41] However, the judges were not satisfied and, by means of a neat manœuvre behind the scenes, obtained the insertion of a clause (clause x) into the Act against seditious sectaries. This clause, 'technically precise, yet obscure enough to arouse no suspicions', allowed a husband to be sued jointly with his wife and enabled the courts to enforce forfeitures against a married couple jointly. Immediately after the Act became law, there was a rush of recusancy prosecutions of this kind,[42] and in August the Privy Council ordered bishops to conduct a special inquiry into the matter of recusant wives.[43]

Although the administrators had gained their object, the government had also been made to realize that the family 'was a sensitive area into which the government entered at its peril'.[44] Even Lord Burghley kept a wary eye on public opinion. In ordering the imprisonment of all men with recusant wives in March 1594, he wished it to be understood that this was only a precaution in case of invasion and stressed that they must be 'restrained of their liberty ... in all convenient condition for health and sustenance'.[45]

Between 1597 and 1604 there was some relaxation of pressure against recusants, but during 1605 tension again mounted, culminating in November 1605 in the crisis of the Gunpowder Plot. The Parliament that followed debated further measures to root out popery. However, even in the atmosphere of crisis, when it came to the question of whether a married man should pay for his wife's recusancy there was 'much dispute' and it was resolved that there should be 'further consideration'.[46]

By the 'Act for the better discovery of Popish Recusants' of that year,[47] Catholics became liable to imprisonment and forfeiture of property for refusing an oath of allegiance which was couched in terms designed to distinguish the 'loyal' from the 'disloyal'. This oath was to be tendered to all popish recusants convicted, to all who were merely indicted, to those who had refused the sacrament under the Anglican rite, and to all strangers who refused to deny that they were popish recusants.[48] This very broad category included married women. The penalty for married women refusing the oath was imprisonment without bail until the oath was taken. For all other persons refusing – men, single women and widows – the penalty was loss of all goods and imprisonment for life.

In 1610 the Commons again discussed whether the oath should be tendered to married women. Eighty-eight members voted against the measure but ninety-one were in favour, and the clause was duly included in the 'Act for the Administration of the Oath of Allegiance and the Reformation of Married Women Recusants'. In the ensuing ten years there were numerous indictments and imprisonments of women for refusing the oath.

The Act continued to require attendance at church and sought to devise a process that could be legally enforceable against married women. If a married woman who was already a convicted popish recusant failed to reform, then she was to be imprisoned without the option of bail. However, her husband could secure her release by paying £10 a month or one-third of his estate.[49] These measures were part of a wide range of penalties on papists. The husband of a popish wife was forbidden to exercise public office. He was liable to a £100 fine for any of his family who were baptized or buried otherwise than according to the rites of the established church. He could be fined £10 for any servants or guests in his household or children over 9 years who refused to attend church. Recusant widows were further penalized. At her husband's death a widow lost two-thirds of her dower or her jointure. She could forfeit all share in her late husband's goods and could be disqualified from acting as his executor or administrator.[50] This marks the high point of the English government's attempts to find means of enforcing the church attendance of married women by means of fines and imprisonments. From 1620 onwards the incidence of prosecution for recusancy declined sharply. The oath of allegiance continued to be tendered, but mainly to priests, gentlemen and persons already charged with other offences. Increasingly the pointlessness of trying to enforce fines against the poor and against married women who had no goods to distrain was recognized. Governments turned instead to compounding with Catholic landowners who could produce revenue for the Crown.[51]

The state thus never solved the problem of dealing with married women recusants; instead it withdrew from an inconclusive engagement.

Harbouring priests

Another illegal activity in which women were prominent was the harbouring of priests. Under the statute of 1585 against Jesuit and seminary priests, all priests ordained abroad were liable to prosecution when they returned to England. All who harboured them were liable to be prosecuted for a capital felony.[52]

The traditional picture of the harbouring of priests was derived in the main from colourful Jesuit narratives and biographies, and the names of Margaret Clitherow, Dorothy Lawson, Anne Vaux and her sister and perhaps half a dozen other women were familiar in Catholic hagiography.[53] Recent writing has tended to stress that these narratives described atypical cases and that few homes at this date had a resident priest.[54] This revisionist approach, while salutary, should not be allowed to distract attention from the size and nature of the infrastructure that enabled priests to operate in England at all.

Every priest in England needed a safe home, discreet friends and a network of communication. The numbers requiring such provision were considerable. Between 1558 and 1603, 815 English priests were ordained abroad, and a further 925 between 1603 and 1659. Not all these priests returned to England but the great majority did so, if only for a time. Some were able to live with relatives, keep a low profile and avoid trouble. Some lived in lodgings in London or other towns, some in twos and threes in rented or borrowed houses. Many moved frequently from place to place. The risks in this period were real. Of the 1740 priests ordained, 152 were executed – 123 in the reign of Elizabeth, and 20 in the first half of the seventeenth century. Many others were imprisoned for varying periods and with varying degrees of severity, many were exiled, and some died in prison.[55]

Women were necessarily prominent in the felonious activity of harbouring them. Widows with their own houses and incomes were especially well placed to receive priests. Priests in lodgings usually placed confidence in their Catholic housekeepers or landladies. In cases where a married couple provided the priest with a home, it was still the wife rather than the husband who made the arrangements, controlled the curiosity of children and servants, and ensured secrecy. The women were more usually at home when the pursuivants arrived. They exploited their supposed frailty and innocence; they provided searchers with meals which distracted their attention; they pleaded bodily infirmity. Husbands kept out of the way and concentrated on preserving public respectability. Hundreds of women were involved in receiving priests into the house for a few hours or a few days at a time so that they could say mass for a small gathering. The wife of Ralph Sheldon of Worcestershire was probably typical of many. She 'sent for a priest to come to her at Strensham which he did accordingly, and at his coming being so requested by her did say Mass, finding at Strensham such vestments and other things as are usually occupied in the celebration of Mass.'[56]

It was not only gentlewomen who harboured priests. Alice Tully, wife of Henry Tully, yeoman of Forebridge, near Stafford, was 'a continual recetter' of one Perton and one Barclay, both being 'old [i.e. Marian] priests'.[57] Mrs Williams of the Swan in Oxford received priests, to the embarrassment of her husband, a JP and alderman.[58]

Dorothy Vavasour, a doctor's wife, was harbouring at York in August 1578, and mass was celebrated in her house.[59]

Against the background of the many women who received priests occasionally, under the disguise of stewards, tutors or relatives, there were a few women who can be described as 'professionals' – women who made the harbouring of priests a full-time occupation. Anne Line, a widow, maintained three adjoining houses in London – her own house where she educated children, a small detached house for the priests and a third which was used as a rest house for the Jesuits. She continued this work for eight years before she was arrested.[60]

Anne Vaux, a spinster, and her widowed sister gave twenty years of active service and support to the Jesuit Henry Garnet. They began harbouring in the 1580s at Shoby in Northamptonshire, where they learned to cope with searchers. By 1591 they were renting the manor house of Baddesley Clinton in Warwickshire, using it as a priests' residence and meeting place for retreats and the renewal of vows. When the house was searched in 1591, five Jesuits and two secular priests were concealed in the house. By 1601 Anne Vaux was responsible for Garnet's London house and when this became untenable she and her sister took White Webbs at Enfield. Here as many as eight Jesuits would sometimes gather.[61]

Women who harboured priests rarely paid the full legal penalty for their defiance of the law. Only three women were executed as against twenty-seven men. Margaret Clitherow, executed at York in 1586, was the first woman to die. She was not, however, executed for harbouring but, having refused to plead, died under *peine forte et dure*.[62] Similarly, Jane Wiseman, tried for harbouring in 1598, also refused to plead, and she too was condemned to *peine forte et dure* but was eventually pardoned, though kept in prison until 1603.[63]

The question of why these two refused to plead is of some interest. As felons they could not speak to defend themselves. However, they would certainly have been called upon under oath to answer questions about the movements of priests. Margaret Clitherow had been very active, maintaining three hiding places and protecting priests on the move. Jane Wiseman harboured priests and visited the priests' special prison at Wisbech. Margaret Clitherow's own explanation of her refusal to plead was that she was protecting her children from having to give evidence and her judges from the sin of condemning her. It seems probable that both women may also have been determined to avoid having to reveal what they knew of the names and whereabouts of priests.

Anne Line was also prosecuted after eight years of making harbouring and assisting priests her main business. She did plead, but in her case she was arrested at a time when the priest had left the house and there was reason to believe that the prosecution would not have grounds to prove her guilt. However, Lord Chief Justice Popham gave clear directions to the jury and she was hanged on 27 February 1601.[64]

Only one other woman was executed – Margaret Ward, a widow from Congleton, Cheshire. She was executed for helping a priest to escape from prison. Her execution took place at the height of the purge of papists in the summer of 1588 when six priests and seventy-one laymen were executed in two months. In the same crisis period a number of women who had been convicted of harbouring died in prison. Mrs Anne Lauder, after having been in prison at York and Hull, was transferred to the Clink, where she died in 1589. Mrs Phillip Lowe died in the White Lion Prison in 1588 and Mrs Ursula Forster in Shrewsbury gaol in 1590 after severe ill treatment.[65] Catherine Bellamy, who had harboured many Jesuits including Robert Parsons, died in the Tower under sentence of death in 1586. The list could be considerably extended.[66]

However, in the seventeenth century, when the crisis years passed, English Catholics were increasingly able to protect themselves from the penalties of their dissidence by knowing and managing the law to their advantage. Some lawyers and conveyancers specialized in helping papists in their difficulties. The documentation relating to Jane Vaughan of Cleiro in Gloucestershire reveals how a woman who was both well advised and well protected could escape the law. In the 'no popery' excitement of 1641 she was imprisoned in Gloucester Castle for harbouring John Broughton (*vere* Crowther), OSB. He had been residing on her manor of Ruarden for some years and acted as her steward. He was arrested in 1641 and tried in London for his priesthood. Meanwhile Jane was summoned to the assizes at Gloucester and tried to avoid trial by the classic method of failing to appear. This manœuvre was insufficient, and she was imprisoned and expected to be tried. Counsel's instructions to her on how to plead have survived, and internal evidence suggests that the copy was made by Jane herself.

As was usual, the anticipated questions of the court were set out, together with the answers the defendant was advised to give. She must admit nothing and throw the onus of proof on the court. To be successful, the prosecution must prove that Broughton was an ordained priest at the time he was in her house, that she knew he was a priest, that she knew him to be born in England, and that she had been present when he said mass some time in the previous three years. Even if all this were proved, she was advised: 'we are not in fault though we harboured him, for if they fail to prove anything fully, they prove no thing.' In the event, the matter was not put to the question. Her son, John, petitioned Charles I, and the warrant for the arrest was recalled under the royal seal on 26 July 1641. However, it was a narrow escape and cost money; as a later note puts it, 'the charge of her Gloucester troubles was paid out of her jewels and plate, pawned by herself.'[67]

From the 1620s the nature of the conflict between the state and Catholics changed. The state was interested less in securing the conversion and conformity of individuals than in obtaining a regular revenue from an irreducible minority and controlling its political influence. From time to time, as in 1641 and 1678, 'no popery' became politically significant, and again the prisons were full of recusants, and again priests and laymen were executed. At such times women were again prominent.

Increasingly the pressures on Catholics were legal, political and financial, exercised in the public rather than the private domain. In these circumstances, women were less conspicuous, retreating again into comparative invisibility in the records. During the period of conflict a considerable number of women had had to commit themselves to acts of defiance and to sustain publicly the consequences of their individual actions. Some of them at least had shown themselves articulate, obstinate in resistance and resourceful in expedients. The state had been hampered in controlling them by the countervailing need to maintain the co-operation of the gentry and burgesses who were not prepared to allow the state to invade the integrity and unity of the family, or to override their rights as husbands and fathers. To make a wife, as an individual, responsible for her conscientious resistance was to go beyond the bounds of acceptable public policy.

RECUSANT WOMEN AND THE ROMAN CATHOLIC CHURCH

It was not only the state which was faced with new circumstances and new problems in the post-Reformation period. The Roman Catholic

Church was operating in a very different context from that of the Middle Ages – a context of a divided Christendom and a 'New World'.[68] In the particular circumstances of England it was the church of a penalized minority, relying heavily upon the adhesion of individuals supported by networks of family and influence. As a result, the role of women assumed a particular importance in the transmission of culture and maintenance of facilities. In a significant number of households the ruling Catholic influence was feminine. Rowse commented in characteristic fashion on aggressive and domineering recusant wives dragging their husbands into trouble with the law,[69] and Bossy saw women as playing an 'abnormally large part' in the early history of the English Catholic community.[70] In a recent study, Aveling has shown that 200 of the 300 Catholic households of Yorkshire can be classified as matriarchal in this sense.[71] These households comprised a range of types. There were those where the head of the household was a widow, usually supported by daughters and servants. In other households the husband was a church papist and the wife provided the religious leadership with or without his connivance and support. There were even a few households where the husband was a Protestant. In Worcester diocese in 1595/6 it was reported that the wealthier recusants consisted of twenty-two gentlemen, Lady Waldegrave and her retinue, eleven gentlewomen who refused to attend church although their husbands did not, two widows and four spinsters. The writer added that in addition to the wealthier sort there were ninety households where the man, or the wife, or both were recusants, besides children and servants.[72]

A variety of explanations have been offered for the predominance of matriarchal households. Bossy suggested that Catholic nonconformity 'appealed especially to English gentlewomen who felt deprived of their functions by the reformation and who reacted against a religion in which literacy was a significant element and which moreover deprived them of a useful ally in the family priest.'[73] Keith Thomas, writing more generally of women as religious dissidents, suggested that 'women had more time for piety; they were less used to saving themselves by their own exertions and their experience of childbirth made them far more conscious of the imminence of death.'[74]

However, the predominance of women can also be linked with the daily tension for English Catholic families between compromise and resistance.[75] In their various circumstances and degrees, all English Catholic families constantly sought accommodations with the ruling powers, whether by means of representations to officials or through the use of local contacts and connections. This led them daily into friendly relations with Protestants and to the acceptance of many norms and conventions of public behaviour and civil obedience. At the same time, they were engaged in resistance, in perpetuating forbidden beliefs and practices, in protecting forbidden persons, in supporting forbidden organizations. As with many other dissident groups in other times and other places, it was in the private domain of the home that such resistance could be carried on. The paterfamilias maintained a public stance of accommodation, ensuring not only the survival of Catholicism but its continuing social status. The women – precisely because they had no public role and were protected to some extent by public opinion – were able to engage in resistance. Thus the Catholic family held the two divergent tendencies of accommodation and resistance in tension. When the head of the family was a woman, then the balance could swing towards resistance.

In England, moreover, heads of households, whether men or women, carried more responsibility for the day-to-day development of religious life than was normal in the Catholic Church. Between 1559 and 1623, and again from 1631 to 1686, there was no English Catholic bishop in England, and it was not until after 1625 that the secular clergy began to organize themselves into regular districts and accumulate their own funds. The Jesuits developed local organizations from 1620 and met for retreats and renewal of vows, but their numbers never exceeded 185. Members of the Benedictine, Franciscan, Dominican and Carmelite orders had some degree of organization, but their members usually lived in isolation from each other and came together only for short periods. The absence of structures of clerical authority encouraged a sense of individual responsibility among Catholic heads of households.

Recusant women at home

The lives of a number of widows and wives who carried out the role of a Catholic head of a household to the admiration of their contemporaries were written and circulated shortly after their deaths. These *vies édifiantes* can be supplemented by fifty or so vignettes of Catholic family life drawn from convent annals and also from the 'lives' of priests and martyrs.[76] The purpose of these records was to edify; all jarring notes of conflict and failure were eliminated. The information provided is thus factually true but idealized. To the modern historian, therefore, they offer an insight into what was regarded as the best practice – the ideal which very few could achieve but towards which all, according to their capacity, should aspire and strive.

In these households the full liturgical cycle was celebrated. There were permanent chapels and priests living in the house. The chapels were elaborately furnished. Lady Montague had a stone altar with three stone steps, altar rails, pulpit and choir. Dorothy Lawson's Tyneside chapel of St Antony's cost £500. Elaborate vestments were embroidered, and there was a wealth of altar vessels, candlesticks and 'church stuff'. The full rituals of Holy Week and the vigils, fasts, feasts, ember and rogation days were observed, and on special feasts mass was celebrated with priest, deacon and sub-deacon, and sung by trained musicians. Morning and evening devotions were led by the priest for the whole household. The ladies organized their days round a demanding programme of private prayer. Even Margaret Clitherow, who was not free from the butcher's shop and the housework until after 4 p.m., managed two hours of devotions and prayer every day as well as mass and evensong. Mary Gifford, a gentlewoman of Cosford, Staffordshire, sat up until ten or eleven at night to pray, even when travelling and staying at inns. She spent so much time in prayer that she had to have patches on her dresses where they were worn at the knees.[77] They meditated daily, fasted regularly, and used physical mortifications such as the hair shirt and the discipline. They examined their consciences systematically and daily. They went to confession and communion frequently – even daily.

There is much in all this that was common to general Christian practice, and also to pre-Reformation Catholicism. Nevertheless, there is a distinctly post-Tridentine emphasis. For women, as for men and for children, the need was to confront the devil, the world and the flesh with disciplined belief and ordered practice. The issue to be faced was death, judgement, hell or heaven for ever. The response was the surrender of self to the all-redeeming sacrifice of Jesus Christ, his love being mediated to all on earth through the mass, the sacraments and the teaching of the one true church.[78] Hence the emphasis in the 'lives' on the mass and the liturgical cycle, on prayer and meditation on the Passion of Christ. Encouragement of frequent communion was one of the main issues of the period, especially where Jesuit influence was predominant. Regular individual participation in the mass and the sacraments by laypeople instructed in the underlying dogma was a leading pastoral concern on the continent at this time, and is reflected in these 'lives'.[79] The prayers recommended for use during mass were emotional and personal. There was great emphasis on the reality of the presence of Christ in the Blessed Sacrament and upon the visual and physical aspects of the passion and death of Christ. Although personal, emotional religion was encouraged, it was to be firmly controlled by reason and authority. Very few of the women are described as having experienced private revelations, and even when visions are recounted they were usually invitations to practical action or, alternatively, were kept very private. There was great emphasis on the humility and obedience which the women rendered to their spiritual directors – priests trained, ordained and authorized to exercise control over the possible dangers and excesses of individual piety.

The emphasis on reason and authority did not, of course, exclude the miraculous. The all-protecting hand of providence is made evident in the narratives in many accounts of narrow escapes, fortunate encounters and unforeseen turns of events. On the other hand, the irrational – magic, superstition, the invoking of charms, omens and dreams – was utterly rejected as sinful and dangerous in the extreme. This rejection was the more vigorous, no doubt, in view of the prevalence of such practices in popular culture.[80]

The 'lives' place much emphasis on corporal and spiritual works of mercy. Mary Gifford had special surgical skills which she placed at the service of the poor women of South Staffordshire. Mrs Elizabeth Skinner was a forceful lady. Even during her Protestant husband's lifetime, she made her children fast and pray, and after his death she lived in great poverty in London 'by the work of her hands' – presumably by sewing. She sent her daughter to an aunt, but remained in London to look after plague victims and orphans and to visit the sick in Bedlam. She died of the plague while nursing. It was recorded that she was 'naturally choleric' in temper and to overcome this wore the hair shirt.[81]

Many of the women were described as having assisted poor women in childbirth. On one particularly dramatic occasion, the Countess of Arundel was called out to help a poor vagrant woman giving birth in the public cage or crib in the main street leading from Hammersmith to London,[82] and most of the narratives describe the giving of such assistance as a frequent occurrence, though not usually in so public a place. This corporal work of mercy had an important spiritual side. Newborn babies were at risk and if they died unbaptized they were excluded from heaven for ever. Thus all concerned with the real welfare of the child would wish to ensure that he or she was baptized quickly and properly.[83]

There was much emphasis on the systematic teaching of the elements of faith and practice. The women catechized their servants daily and taught neighbours and tenants' children the Pater, the Ave, the Creed, and the Commandments of God and the church. Sister Dorothea, a member of a religious institute living in England, described how she tried to teach the 'simple and vulgar sort' their prayers and catechism and observed:

> that they seldom or never go to the heretical churches and abhor receiving their profane communion, that they leave to offend God in any great matter, and seldom to sin, and so little by little I endeavour to root out the custom of swearing, drinking etc. ...[84]

The emphasis on catechizing within the Catholic community can be compared both with the movement on the continent to develop parochial catechizing and with the spread of catechetical instruction in the Church of England in the same period.[85] In all three cases the emphasis was on individual learning by heart of authorized statements of belief, and unequivocal directives for behaviour. Among Catholics, if the application of these norms proved difficult, then the matter was referred to the authority of the priest trained in the application of church teachings to particular cases of conscience and to the particular circumstances in England.

In marriage the first duty was the procreation of children and the educating and rearing of them in the true faith. Women were, however, saved not merely by bearing children but also by educating, disciplining and training them to piety. Their part in this process was intellectual and spiritual as well as physical. Married women were subject to their husbands but were to be treated with respect. Eve was made from the side of Adam as his companion, not from his head to rule, nor the foot to be trodden on.[86] However, there was no doubt that spiritual duties took precedence over natural duties, even those towards husbands and children. Henry Garnet wrote to women, 'your husbands over your soul have no authority and over your bodies but limited power'.[87]

Margaret Clitherow asked her confessor whether she might receive priests and serve God without her husband's consent. She was told that the less he knew the better, and that nothing could override her duty to serve God by receiving God's priests.[88] Priests in the seminaries were taught that it was proper for wives of conforming or careless husbands to spend their husbands' money on providing priests to administer the sacraments, for they were doing it on behalf of their husbands.[89] Even so, there is nothing in the 'lives' and annals to encourage women to turn the world upside-down, still less to encroach upon the role of priests in holy orders or of their husbands. The whole emphasis was upon order, with every relationship and duty understood with respect to its due place above or below other relationships and duties. Even conflict with the state was legitimated as the restoration of true order. Sometimes, it was understood, inferiors in England had to perform actions beyond their normal station because of the difficulties of the times – as, for example, women answering mass – but it was also clear that these were temporary aberrations and unsatisfactory expedients.

The ideal delineated in these narratives did nevertheless offer a contrast to the traditional clerical platitudes about the frailty of women which continued to appear in some recusant writing of the period.[90] The older image of woman represented her as the root of all evil, the temptation of man and the bringer of discord.[91] The narratives show us women who were vigorous, capable of quick thinking and practical organization. They served the church intelligently and faithfully, they prayed systematically, and in all things they were subject to proper authorities.

These two images could be brought into a single focus by emphasizing that the weaker the woman's nature the greater the spiritual achievement under proper direction, and, indeed, this is implicit in much of the Jesuit writing. On the other hand, in the convent annals written by women for women, it is the men who often appear faint-hearted. Be that as it may, the image of the capable, lively woman of faith and good works was a powerful and attractive one, and remained influential within the private domain of the English Catholic community long after 'normal' conditions returned in the later seventeenth century.

English recusant women as nuns

Although much was written about the great value of a religious life in the world, most spiritual directors believed that the fullness of the religious life was possible only if the secular world was put aside. Moreover, although the married state was holy, virginity was angelical, a holier state of life. The pursuit of perfection demanded the whole mind, the whole will and the harnessing of all the passions.

The century of the Counter-Reformation saw an extraordinary proliferation of religious communities, and hundreds of houses were established in Europe for men and for women by all the main religious orders. English women participated in this foundation movement, uninhibited by the particular circumstances of England. Between 1597 and 1642 seventeen houses of English women belonging to eight orders were established on the continent. At least 300 young women went to join these communities.[92]

Most of the girls were from families where both parents were Catholics and where there was already a well-established pattern of Catholic life. They were usually in their late teens and early twenties, though very occasionally younger girls or older widows were admitted. Many of them had aunts or sisters who had preceded them to the continent. An extreme case was the family of Francis and Katherine Bedingfield (*née* Fortescue). Ten of their eleven daughters and two of their grand-daughters became nuns. Nevertheless, the transition from England to the convent could be difficult. There were men and priests who made a business of getting girls out of England secretly, but the journey was rarely uneventful. There was frequently a difficult and unhappy experience awaiting the girl on her arrival in the Low Countries. She was often inadequately informed about the way of life and the places available. She might find the convent of her choice unsuitable, in great poverty, racked by internal dissensions or oppressed by local wars. There was much unseemly rivalry for good, well-endowed candidates, and some over-zealous spiritual directors were only too ready to send promising young women from wealthy families to houses they favoured. After a novitiate of at least a year the girl was professed and would live out her life in that community. She was unlikely to move unless she was sent to found a daughter house, or unless the convent was disturbed by war.

Almost all the choir sisters came from aristocratic and gentry families, for they had to have a substantial dowry. The lay sisters were a group apart, often drawn from superior servants or towns-women, and their duties were domestic work and nursing sick sisters. They were respected for the loyalty of their service. The aristocratic ethos of the convent was reinforced by the presence within the enclosure of young girls from wealthy families sent over for education, and by the visits to the convent of their travelling relatives. The ethos of the community was also influenced by the fact that in the first sixty years most of the nuns came from families with personal experience of persecution. Fathers, mothers and brothers who had suffered forfeitures, imprisonments or even death were lovingly remembered, the details of their sufferings recorded, and their relics and portraits collected. So the collective image of devotion and self-denial was strengthened, and the bonding of the Catholic community was reinforced.

Many of the nuns lived to a considerable age and, when a sister died, the annals dwelt upon her virtues, stressing particularly prayer, heroic self-denial and humility. The endurance of physical pain, the deliberate seeking of opportunities for petty humiliation and self-imposed additional penances were recorded with admiration, but the annals also stress the even greater virtues of obedience to authority, respect for and dedication to the admonitions of the convent's spiritual director and the regular performance of appointed duties. The model presented was one in which the deepest possible personal commitment was held in due discipline by the regularity and order of convent life and the advice of a properly authorized and trained spiritual director. In view of the importance of the spiritual director in this scheme, it is not surprising that these same convents were frequently racked by bitter dissensions and internal feuds concerning the choice of director, leading in some cases to permanent divisions within the orders.[93]

There was scope for individual women to develop their character and intellect to the fullest extent, and some achieved distinction for heroic sanctity, for intellectual and spiritual leadership, or for carrying responsibility well beyond the normal demands. Such were the mystic Dame Gertrude More,[94] the scholar Margaret Clement, and the foundress of the first convent abroad, Lady Mary Percy.[95] But all were firmly contained within the controlling hand of the church as a whole, subject to the authority of the ordained ministers, and in an essentially private setting. All were subject to the rules of enclosure, and all their work, including the education of young girls, took place within the walls of the convent.

It was a very different matter when women aspired to live an independent and public life in the service of God and the church. In the early years of the Counter-Reformation there were many major initiatives to create communities of women living under the vows of the religious life, but working in the wider community as teachers, nurses or servants of the poor and outcast.[96] At first these orders were not enclosed, but all eventually had to submit to a limitation of their work by accepting enclosure. The experience of one such group – usually known as the 'English Ladies' – demonstrates how abhorrent was the idea of a public and independent role for women in the Counter-Reformation church, even when the women concerned were of unimpeachably respectable Catholic families of admitted holiness and integrity.

Mary Ward (1585–1645)[97] and her companions set out their motives and intentions in 1616 in a memorial to Pope Paul V:

> As the sadly afflicted state of England, our native country stands greatly in need of spiritual labourers, and as priests both religious and secular, work assiduously as apostles in this harvest, it seems that the female sex should and can in like manner undertake something more than ordinary in this same common spiritual necessity ... we also desire ... to embrace the religious state and at the same time to devote ourselves according to our slender capacity to the performance of those works of Christian charity towards our neighbour that cannot be undertaken in convents. We therefore propose to follow a mixed kind of life, such a life as we hold Christ our Lord and Master to have taught his disciples; such a life as his Blessed Mother seems to have led ... and many holy virgins and widows; and especially at this time when the Church is sorely oppressed in our country that by this means we more easily instruct virgins and young girls from their earliest years in piety, Christian morals and the liberal arts that they may afterwards according to their respective vocations profitably embrace either the secular or the religious state.[98]

The memorandum went on to outline a plan for an institute of religious women bound by vows to a life of prayer and perfection and the education of girls. They asked to live as a community but without enclosure, to elect their own chief mother superior and to be subject, not to the diocesan bishop, but directly and solely to the jurisdiction of the Pope. Provisional pontifical approbation was given to this plan and the Institute of the Blessed Virgin Mary was founded on 10 April 1616. It had been developing since 1609, when Mary Ward and ten companions had begun to live together in Saint-Omer and to teach without payment English and Flemish children in the town. They lived openly as laywomen, and went with their pupils to mass and the sacraments in the public churches.

They attracted many recruits, not only from England, but also from countries throughout western Europe. The Institute soon became a very extensive enterprise indeed. New houses, each with their own free public schools, were established at Liège (1616), Cologne (1620), Trier (1620), Rome (1622), Naples (1623), Munich (1627), Vienna (1628) and Prague (1628). A separate novitiate house was founded at Liège. Most important of all in the eyes of Mary Ward, a group of sisters maintained an active community life of teaching and missionary work in England. By 1631 there were in all some 300 members of the Institute, and some of their free public schools claimed over 500 pupils.[99] Their teaching work was consciously professional, with emphasis on the need for sound academic knowledge on the part of the teachers. They taught religion, Latin, Greek, French and the local languages, mathematics, geography and astronomy, needlework and music, both vocal and instrumental. The girls were taken for country walks and gave public performances of Latin plays. In the free schools poor children were taught reading, writing and the catechism and taken to daily mass. In Rome and Naples the street children were taught a trade.[100]

The working day of the members of the Institute was carefully regulated. They awoke at 4 a.m. and meditated and prayed privately. They then heard mass, said the office together and engaged in spiritual reading. They then went to their daily work. At 10.30 a.m. there was a break for examination of conscience, and this was followed by dinner, recreation and more reading. The afternoon was taken up with work until 5 p.m. and the evening was occupied with prayer, supper, recreation and meditation.

The administrative work of establishing and maintaining the ten houses and their schools was enormous. Mary Ward had secured first the support of the Bishop of Saint-Omer, the Bishop of Ypres and the Abbot of Saint-Bertin, then the town authorities of Saint-Omer. She was able to gain the active, personal and persevering support of Archduke Albert and Archduchess Isabella of the Netherlands at Brussels. As the network spread, so did the number and status of the personages with whom she had to negotiate. At Liège she gained the support of the Prince Bishop, and the support and financial aid of the Emperor Maximilian of the Holy Roman Empire that later enabled her to establish houses at Munich and Vienna. Pope Paul V (1616), Gregory XV (1622) and Urban VIII (1624) all expressed approbation and materially assisted the work. In all these contacts, Mary Ward engaged personally and directly in the meetings and business required. Only in her first approach to the Pope in 1616 did she go through 'normal channels' and make use of a clerical agent. Thereafter she spoke on her own behalf. She travelled constantly. She went to Rome in 1621 mainly on foot, crossing the St Gotthard Pass in winter and taking only two months over a journey of over 500 miles. She went to Naples, to Munich and to Vienna. She went by boat down the Danube to Prague. She and her sisters engaged in endless correspondence, much of it of a technical nature, memorializing cardinals, princes, nuncios and town authorities, as well as corresponding with the superiors of the ten houses and even with the sisters in England. She made four visits to England and in 1619 was arrested there – though released by the influence of friends in high places. Members of the community who could write speedy and effective Latin were in demand, and most of the sisters were forced by circumstances to learn several European languages. They had to master protocol and, while living in extreme poverty themselves, cultivated wealthy patrons and raised huge sums of money for their work.

Such activity carried out in the full light of courts, public capitals and centres of Catholic resort aroused as much horror and opposition as it did admiration and support. Mary Ward had been subject to attacks upon her personal integrity ever since, at the age of 20, she had left the Poor Clares on finding the order wholly unsuited to her vocation. The Institute she eventually developed was all too obviously a female counterpart of the work of the Jesuits, and this fact alone was more than enough to arouse bitter opposition from secular clergy and other religious orders. Mary Ward did not go about to disarm criticism and her actions and manners, especially in England, were seen as likely to provoke the attentions of the law. The great success of the new Institute in recruiting able and well endowed girls appeared as a threat to the other religious orders. Her foreign houses and her acceptance of Irish, French, German, Hungarian and Italian sisters laid her open to suspicion among English Catholics.

These, however, were not the real causes of hostility to the Institute. The new organization was offensive and disturbing because although they were women they proposed to retain responsibility for their own work, and to do it in the public domain. They had seen from the beginning that in order to achieve this, they would have to remain unenclosed, free from diocesan control and responsible directly to the Pope through their own elected Mother Superior General. The Jesuits had succeeded in establishing these conditions for their work and in the process had aroused great hostility. In trying to establish a similar but separate organization Mary Ward and her sisters challenged the traditional concept of the religious life for women, and the traditional structures of order and authority, but they also raised the even more emotional issue of how far women could be trusted with responsibility. This was especially threatening in a church led and organized by celibate men, and in the English context where so much depended on retaining the support of the respectable.

Great pressure was put upon the Institute to accept enclosure. All the similar communities which had been founded in the sixteenth century had capitulated: the Visitation nuns in 1610; the Ursulines in 1612 and the Notre Dame sisters in 1615.

The position of the Jesuit order was difficult. Individual Jesuits helped the Institute in its early days and gave support and approval to the founding of schools. Even the Rector General Vitelleschi had recommended the work. A good friend in the early days had been John Gerard, perhaps rendered more sympathetic in view of his own experience of the work of English gentlewomen when he had been on the English mission himself. However, the Jesuit order had from the beginning set its face against having any responsibility for women or for women's houses, and to this they now adhered. The English Jesuits – and in particular their provincial, Blount – were among the most bitter opponents of Mary Ward. John Gerard was even forced to resign his rectorship of Liège College as a result of his support for the Institute.[101]

Not all the opposition was irresponsible or irrational. There were sound reasons why prudent administrators would hesitate to endorse the Institute. The organization was all too clearly over-extended. Mary Ward never had any difficulty in attracting recruits, but it was apparent by 1628 that she was finding it difficult to provide sufficient superiors and leaders, and she was forced to move trusted assistants from house to house far too often. There were serious dissensions within the older communities, especially the house at Liège, and some of the disaffected were ready to publish 'evidence' against Mary Ward to her opponents. To the public scandal of women ruling themselves was now apparently added the further scandal of their doing it badly.

In 1631 ten houses were ordered to be closed, the schools were dismissed, and the 300 sisters were sent home to their families. Mary herself was imprisoned in a convent in Munich by the Holy Office (the Inquisition). In prison, in the best tradition of English recusants, Mary Ward established a secret correspondence – written in orange juice – with her sisters, who secured her release. She returned to Rome and by sheer determination was able to obtain from Pope Urban VIII permission to continue to live together with her most loyal sisters and to continue to teach. The work in Munich also struggled on under the support of the Elector of Bavaria.[102] In 1638 Mary Ward returned to England and renewed the work there, living near London until forced by the outbreak of Civil War to take refuge in Yorkshire – the scene of her childhood.[103]

Mary Ward knew that she and her companions offered a profound challenge to the clerical authority of the church she sought to serve. Her most explicit statements of the role of women in the church were the three important discourses given to her community at Saint-Omer in 1617. She insisted that there 'is no such difference between men and women that women may not do great things as we have seen by the example of many saints'. The will to achieve and the ability to know and serve God are given equally to men and to women. The women must have confidence in themselves and concentrate on the *Veritas Domini* and the work that lay before them. She acknowledged that 'wives are to be subject to their husbands and that men are the head of the church, women are not to administer the sacraments nor preach in a public church', but in all other work they were the equal of men. She recognized that what they were attempting was 'a course never thought of before' but encouraged her hearers to prove to their critics that 'all the world can be bettered by us'.[104]

In spite of this claim to equality and an independent role, it would be misleading to see the conflict between the 'English Ladies' and the church as only a feminist issue. Bossy described Mary Ward as 'the victim of a patriarchal backlash',[105] but this backlash was itself part of an even deeper and more fundamental conflict in the Counter-Reformation church.

On the one hand was the centrifugal missionary dynamic which sent priests to America and Asia and Africa, involving them in dangerous relations with 'heretics' and pagans, confronting other cultures and alien religions. This brought with it the need to adapt, to improvise, to create new structures and to imbibe new ideas. On the other hand there was the countervailing drive towards centralization, regulation and control. This required that the teachings of the church should be defined and safeguarded in the hands of properly accredited professionals; proper procedures should be followed and authority supported. In the end, where women were concerned, the church in the seventeenth century settled for control. The women's orders were all enclosed and no nuns were sent to the foreign missions.

In England the divergent tendencies were translated into compromise and resistance, and it is relevant to note that the most vitriolic opposition to Mary Ward came from the English Jesuits and the English secular clergy. In their situation of anxiety and real danger, the prospect of such dynamic innovation was especially disturbing; moreover, the debate was made even more emotional by the similarity between the Institute and the Jesuit order. This touched a nerve made sensitive by a long history of conflict between secular priests and Jesuits.[106]

The Catholic Church was successful in containing women within the private domain. So long as they remained within a family, the church offered women demanding spiritual, intellectual and practical goals and gave recognition to those who achieved them, but any public role was entirely unacceptable.

CATHOLIC, ANGLICAN AND PURITAN WOMEN

It remains to be seen whether the experience of English Catholic women in the early seventeenth century was similar to that of other women in devout households.

It is well established that in seventeenth-century England religious observance, education and culture were increasingly concentrated in the family – whether it was the Puritan family, the Anglican family or the Roman Catholic family. It has also been observed that this shift tended to enhance the role of the paterfamilias.[107] In Roman Catholic families this consequence may have been less marked. The father, like every other member of the family, was subject to the extrinsic authority of the church exercised through the priests. More than ever in this period, priests were trained in the seminaries to apply the 'teachings of the church', through defined formulas and the models of casuistry, to specific situations. The catechisms and books of pastoral theology provided regulations for eating and drinking, for behaviour of husbands towards wives and fathers towards daughters, and for wages and labour.[108] The actual visits of the priests may have been fleeting and erratic, but their right to intervene, to advise and correct was very real and readily exercised. Furthermore, the Catholic father was not in a position to act as the 'interpreter of scripture' to his family: the layman had no more authority in this field than the laywoman.

The position of the Catholic woman differed somewhat from that of Anglican and Puritan women in that the option of the religious life remained open to her, especially if she was well endowed. As we have seen, this meant the private world of enclosed nuns, but it was a respected alternative to marriage and, indeed, the life itself conferred status on even its least effective practitioners. In theory, there was a third alternative – that in which a group of widows and single women lived together under temporary vows. A very unrealistic sketch of such a life does exist,[109] but evidence of actual communities of this kind in England in the early seventeenth century is still lacking. The only possible example was the household of the Spanish noblewoman Luisa de Carvajal[110] in London in the 1620s – an exceptional and extraordinary case.

One of the most conspicuous distinctions between the devout Anglican or Puritan household on the one hand and Catholic household on the other was that, whereas the former centred on the Bible and family prayer, the Catholic household continued to emphasize the mass and the feasts and fasts of the liturgical year. If it is true that the importance of the written word disadvantaged women in Protestant households, then it seems to follow that the visual and affective appeal of the mass and the liturgy would encourage women to feel they had an important role. This, however, is to belittle the level of participation and to trivialize the issue. It is probably more important to note that women as well as men were defined as 'rational creatures of God',[111] and that the ability to learn, expound and teach religious knowledge was encouraged. Episodes in which women successfully debated with 'heretics' were recounted with approbation. The level of knowledge and intellectual activity expected in religious matters of laypeople remained low, but this was the case for both men and women.

From the 1580s onwards the Catholic Church in England collected memorials of its experience of persecution. These memorials were reinforced by the written and oral traditions of convents, by the family histories of the gentry and by local cults among yeomen and tradesmen. Together the stories of martyrdoms, miracles and human courage created a timeless collective memory – a myth comparable to Fox's *Book of Martyrs*, or the later Quaker *Sufferings*. Within this developing mythology the ideal Catholic woman appeared as capable, energetic and humorous. She was shown as quick-witted in crisis and persevering under difficulties. She was a woman of prayer, and of deeply felt religious emotions, yet rational and self-controlled. She was capable of heroic self-denial but was subject in all things to the overruling authority of the church. She was humble, obedient and chaste but never weak or foolish.

This image – idealized as it is – may be the most distinctive contribution of English Catholics to the overall understanding of women in the seventeenth century. How much it may have in common with images of other women in crisis – as, for example, the Protestant women who helped the Protestant divines in Mary's reign – goes beyond the scope of this chapter.

NOTES

[1] A recusant was one who refused to attend the services of the Church of England on Sundays and Holy Days, according to the Act of Uniformity. In 1593 (35 Elizabeth, c. 1 & 2) the term 'popish recusant' was introduced to distinguish Catholic from other absentees. When 'recusant' is used without qualification, the word is usually taken to mean papist and has been so used in this paper.

[2] 1 Eliz., c. 2.

[3] H. Bowler (ed.), *Recusant Roll No. 2, 1593–4*, CRS, LVII (1965), p. xii; F. X. Walker, 'Implementation of the Statutes concerning Recusancy in the Reign of Elizabeth', unpublished London Ph.D. thesis (1961), *passim*.

[4] M. M. C. Calthrop (ed.), *Recusant Roll No. 1, 1592–3*, CRS, XVIII (1916), pp. xvi–xix.

[5] W. R. Trimble, *The Catholic Laity in the Reign of Elizabeth 1558–1603* (Cambridge, Mass., 1964), p. 153.

[6] C. Cross, *The Puritan Earl* (London, 1966), pp. 228–34.

[7] J. C. H. Aveling, *Catholic Recusancy in the City of York, 1558–1791*, CRS monograph, ser. 2 (1970), pp. 60–6.

[8] A. Raine (ed.), *York Civic Records*, VII, Yorkshire Archaeological Society Record, ser. CXV (1950), pp. 130–1. Some women confronted with the same questions took refuge behind their femininity, as did Mrs Elizabeth Moninge of Kent in 1591. When examined by the bishop, she replied that it was 'a harsh question never asked of a woman before and as a wife under subjection she had no ability to give an answer': J. N. McGurke, 'Lieutenancy and Catholic Recusants in Elizabethan Kent', *Recusant History*, XII (1973–4), p. 161.

[9] Raine, (ed.), op. cit., VII, pp. 150–1.

[10] Aveling, op. cit., p. 187.

[11] *APC*, XII, 1580–1, p. 332.

[12] 'An Act to retain the Queen's Majesty's subjects in their due obedience', 23 Eliz., c. 1 (1581).

[13] J. Bossy, *English Catholic Community 1570–1850* (London, 1975), p. 154.

[14] Bowler (ed.), op. cit., p. xxxiv.

[15] 'Notes by a Prisoner in Ousebridge Kidcote', in J. Morris (ed.), *Troubles of our Catholic Forefathers Related by Themselves*, ser. III (1872), p. 302.

[16] In ibid., III, p. 283.

[17] K. R. Wark, *Elizabethan Recusancy in Cheshire*, Chetham Society, 3rd ser., XIX (1971), p. 19.

[18] S. A. H. Burne (ed.), *Staffordshire Quarter Session Rolls, I: 1581–89*, SHC, LIII (1929), p. xxxiv.

[19] 'Diocesan Returns of Recusants for England and Wales, 1577', in *Miscellanea*, xii, CRS, XXII (1921), pp. 21–2.

[20] M. Hodgetts, 'A Certificate of Warwickshire Recusants 1592', *Worcester Recusant*, V (1965), pt 1, p. 31.

[21] J. Tobias, 'New Light on Recusancy in Warwickshire 1952', *Worcester Recusant*, XXXVI (1980), pp. 21–2.

[22] A. G. Petti (ed.), *Recusant Documents from Ellesmere Manuscripts*, CRS, LX (1968), p. 74.

[23] *CSPD*, CLXXV, p. 214, 21 November 1584.

[24] *CSPD*, CLXXV, p. 291, 10 December 1585.

[25] *CSPD*, CCVIII, p. 462, 8 February 1588.

[26] *CSPD*, CCVIII, p. 463, 10 February 1588.

[27] 'Act for the more speedy execution of certain branches of the statute made in the 23rd year of the Queen Majesty's reign', 28 Eliz., c. 6.

[28] *APC*, XXIII, 1592, p. 193.

[29] BL Lansdowne MS 72/41, 27 June 1592, Popham to Waade.

[30] BL Lansdowne MS 72/48, undated and unsigned but attributed on the manuscript to Richard Topcliffe and filed under June 1592. Richard Topcliffe never held an official position but was active in the prosecution of Jesuits and other papists and notorious for his cruelties, having a rack in his own house: *DNB*.

[31] A. Conyers Read, *Lord Burghley and Queen Elizabeth* (London, 1960), p. 469.

[32] *APC*, XXIII, 1592, p. 164, 2 September and also 1592–3, pp. 26–7.

[33] *APC*, XXIII, 1592, p. 182, 10 September. Judge's opinion was requested, May 1593, p. 234.

[34] *APC*, XXIII, 1592, pp. 215–16, 30 September and 5 October.

[35] *CSPD*, CCXI, p. 108. Walker, op. cit., pp. 320–1.

[36] Cross, op. cit., p. 234; *APC*, XXIV, 1592–3, pp. 317–18, 335, 421.

[37] *APC*, XXIV, 1592–3, pp. 279–80.

[38] J. Neale, *Queen Elizabeth and her Parliaments*, II (London, 1957), pp. 281, 293–4.

[39] *CSPD*, CCXVII, p. 328.

[40] Neale, op. cit., II, p. 297.

[41] 'Act to restrain the Queen's Majesty's subjects in their allegiance', 35 Eliz., c. 2; Act against seditious sectaries, 35 Eliz., c. 1.

[42] Bowler (ed.), op. cit., pp. xlvii–ix.

[43] *APC*, XXV, 1595–6, p. 513.

[44] Bossy, op. cit., pp. 155–7.

[45] *CSPD*, CCXLVIII, p. 454, 6 March 1594.

[46] *House of Commons Journals*, I, p. 263, 1 February 1606.

[47] 3 & 4 Jac. I, c. 4.

[48] J. A. Williams, *Catholic Recusancy in Wiltshire 1660–1791*, CRS monograph, ser. 1 (1968), pp. 7–8.

[49] 'Act to prevent the dangers that may grow from popish recusants', 7 & 8 Jac. I, c. 6, clause v. For the canonical and legal difficulties of the marriages

of Catholics, see J. C. H. Aveling, 'The Marriages of Catholic Recusants 1559–1642', *Journal of Ecclesiastical History*, XIV (1963), pp. 68–83.

50 Williams, op. cit., p. 7.

51 J. Bossy, 'The English Catholic Community 1603–25', in A. G. R. Smith (ed.), *The Reign of James VI and I* (London, 1973), pp. 91–106.

52 27 Eliz., c. 2.

53 P. Caraman (ed.), *John Gerard, the Autobiography of an Elizabethan* (London, 1951); P. Caraman (ed.), *William Weston, the Autobiography of an Elizabethan* (London, 1955); J. D. Hanlon, 'They be but Women', in C. H. Carter (ed.), *Renaissance to Counter-Reformation: Essays presented to Gerard Mattingley* (London, 1966), pp. 367–93.

54 J. C. H. Aveling, 'Catholic Households in Yorkshire, 1580–1603', *Northern History*, XVI (1980), pp. 85–101.

55 G. Anstruther, *Seminary Priests: A Dictionary of the Secular Clergy, 1558–1850* (Ware, 1968–76), I and II, *passim*; E. I. Watkin, *Roman Catholicism in England* (London, 1957), pp. 42, 64, 84, 93, 96.

56 M. Hodgetts, 'Elizabethan Recusancy in Worcestershire: I', *Transactions of the Worcestershire Archaeological Society*, ser. 3, I (1965–7), p. 73.

57 Burne (ed.), *Staffordshire Quarter Sessions Rolls II: 1590–93*, SHC (1930), p. 255.

58 A. G. Petti, *Roman Catholicism in Elizabethan and Jacobean Staffordshire*, SHC, 4th ser., IX (1979), pp. 56, 66.

59 Aveling, *Catholic Recusancy in the City of York*, p. 221.

60 H. Foley, *Records of the English Province of the Society of Jesus*, ser. 1 (1888), I, p. 4141.

61 P. Caraman, *Henry Garnet 1555–1606 and the Gunpowder Plot* (London, 1964), *passim*, especially pp. 133–5, 349–50 and 367–71.

62 'Mr John Mush's Life of Margaret Clitherow', in Morris (ed.), op. cit., III, pp. 331–433.

63 H. Pollen, *Unpublished Documents Relating to the English Martyrs*, CRS, V (1908), pp. 364, 367.

64 Caraman, *Henry Garnet*, pp. 72, 78.

65 Morris (ed.), op. cit., III, pp. 35–7.

66 Caraman (ed.), *William Weston*, p. 8.

67 J. H. Matthews (ed.), 'Papers from the Courtfield Muniments', in *Miscellanea*, viii, CRS, XIII (1913), pp. 150–9.

68 J. Delumeau, *Catholicism between Luther and Voltaire* (London, 1977), p. 6.

69 A. L. Rowse, *England of Elizabeth* (London, 1950), pp. 430, 558.

70 Bossy, *English Catholic Community*, p. 158.

71 Aveling, 'Catholic Households in Yorkshire', pp. 85–101.

72 Clare Talbot (ed.), *Miscellanea: Recusant Records*, CRS, LIII (1961), p. 129.

73 Bossy, 'The English Catholic Community', p. 158.

74 K. V. Thomas, 'Women and the Civil War Sects', *P & P*, XIII (1958),

p. 45. These and other possible reasons for the association of women and religious dissidence are discussed in the French context by N. Z. Davis, *Society and Culture in Early Modern France* (1965), pp. 65–70.

[75] P. Holmes, *Resistance and Compromise* (Cambridge, 1982), pp. 83–4, 113–15.

[76] For contemporary lives, see W. Palmes (ed.), *Life of Mrs Dorothy Lawson of St Antony's near New Castle on Tyne* (Newcastle upon Tyne, 1851); *Philip Howard, Earl of Arundel, and Anne Dacre, his Wife* (London, 1857). For Magdalen, Viscountess Montague, see A. C. Southern (ed.), *An Elizabethan Recusant House* (London, 1950). For Margaret Clitherow, Morris (ed.), op. cit., III, pp. 331–443. For Isabel Lander and others, ibid., III, p. 469.

[77] A. Hamilton, *Chronicle of the English Augustinian Canonesses of St Monica's at Louvaine, 1548–1644* (Edinburgh, 1904), I, p. 28.

[78] The summary of the teachings of the church based on the Scriptures and the decrees of the Council. First authorized in 1565, it was the basis of all pastoral instruction.

[79] Delumeau, op. cit., pp. 194–6.

[80] K. Thomas, *Religion and the Decline of Magic* (London, 1971), pp. 147, 582–3, 560–7.

[81] Hamilton, op. cit., I, p. 54.

[82] *Philip Howard, Earl of Arundel, and Anne Dacre, his Wife*, p. 309.

[83] If there was immediate danger of death, the midwife or a layperson could baptize. On the continent the ecclesiastical authorities trained and examined midwives in this important matter.

[84] H. Coleridge (ed.), 'Sister Dorothea's Narrative', in M. C. Chambers, *Life of Mary Ward*, 2 vols (1882–7), II, p. 29.

[85] L. Stone, *Family, Sex and Marriage in England, 1500–1800* (London, 1976), pp. 140–1. In 1565, Lawrence Vaux published *A Catechism or Christian Doctrine Necessary for Children and Ignorant People*, based on the Catechismus ad Parochos. This went through many editions and was widely used in England: T. G. Law (ed.), *A Catechisme, or Christian Doctrine, by Laurence Vaux, B. D.*, Chetham Society, NS, IV, (1885).

[86] *Catechismus ad Parochos* (Louvaine, 1682), pp. 300–1.

[87] Henry Garnet,'Treatise on Christian Renunciation', quoted by Holmes, op. cit., pp. 109–10.

[88] Morris (ed.), op. cit., III, pp. 381–2.

[89] P. Holmes, *Elizabethan Casuistry*, CRS, LXVII (1581), p. 29.

[90] As, for example, Cardinal J. Bona, *Guide to Heaven* (Roan, 1673).

[91] G. H. Tavard, *Women in the Christian Tradition* (Indiana, 1973), pp. 131–49; R. Ruether and E. McLauchlin, *Women of Spirit: Female Leadership in the Jewish and Christian Traditions* (New York, 1979), p. 132.

[92] Hamilton, op. cit., *passim*; J. Gillow (ed.), 'Records of the English Benedictine Nuns at Cambrai, 1620–1793', in *Miscellanea*, viii, CRS, XIII (1912), pp. 1–85; J. Gillow (ed.), 'Registers of the English Poor Clares at Gravelines 1608–1837', *Miscellanea*, ix, CRS, XIV (1914), pp. 25–173; J. S.

Hansom (ed.), 'The Register Book of Professions, etc., of the English Benedictine Nuns at Brussels and Winchester, 1598–1856', in *Miscellanea*, ix, CRS, XIV (1914), pp. 174–99; 'Obituary Notices of the Nuns of the English Benedictine Abbey of Ghent, 1627–1811', in *Miscellanea*, xi, CRS, XIX (1917), pp. 1–88; R. Trappes-Lomax (ed.), *English Franciscan Nuns, 1619–1821*, CRS, XXIV (1925), pp. 1–94, 123–34, 177–258.

[93] P. Guilday, *English Catholic Refugees on the Continent* (London, 1914), pp. 261, 298; J. C. H. Aveling, *The Handle and the Axe* (London, 1976), pp. 92–4.

[94] M. Norman, 'Dame Gertrude More and the English Mystical Tradition', *Recusant History*, XIII (1975–6), p. 196.

[95] J. Gillow, *A Literary of Biographical History or Dictionary of English Catholics*, 5 vols (1885–1902), I, p. 500; ibid., V, p. 264.

[96] For example, the Ursulines, the Visitation nuns, the Daughters of Charity, the Oblates of Torre da Specchi. See also H. O. Everitt, 'The New Orders', *New Cambridge Modern History* (Cambridge, 1958), IX, pp. 289–90.

[97] Chambers, op. cit.; Guilday, op. cit., pp. 163–4; I. Wilkes, 'Mary Ward and her Apostolic Vocation', *The Way*, supplement, no. 17 (1972), pp. 130–1.

[98] Chambers, op. cit., I, p. 375.

[99] Ibid., I, pp. 357–71, 462–77; ibid., II, pp. 21–39, 81–257.

[100] M. Norman, 'Eve's Daughters at School', *Atlantis* (Spring 1978), pp. 66–81; Chambers, op. cit., I, p. 369.

[101] The reports and memoranda were published by Chambers, op. cit., II, pp. 40, 65, 183; and in M. A. Tierney (ed.), *Dodd's Church History of England*, 5 vols (1839–43), IV, p. ccxxvii. Tierney also gives a selection of the scandalous reports of Mrs Mary Alcock and of Bennet's correspondence on the subject.

[102] Chambers, op. cit., II, pp. 93–100.

[103] Mary Ward died in 1645. The Institute was eventually recommended and was approved by Clement XI in 1703 with the words *Lasciate gubernare le donne dalle donne* and the decree *Inscrutabilae Diviniae Providentiae*. In 1980 the Institute had 3742 members in 178 houses in five continents.

[104] Chambers, op. cit., I, pp. 408–12.

[105] Bossy, *English Catholic Community*, pp. 160, 282.

[106] Delumeau, op. cit., p. 81; Holmes, *Resistance and Compromise*, pp. 81–98.

[107] Stone, op. cit., pp. 154–7; L. L. Schücking, *The Puritan Family* (London, 1969), pp. 33–5.

[108] P. J. Holmes, *Elizabethan Casuistry*, CRS, LXVII (1981), pp. 15–42.

[109] Stonyhurst College, Blackburn, Lancashire, Stonyhurst MSS Anglia VI, No. 53.

[110] G. F., *Life of Luisa de Carvajal* (London, 1873), App. II, pp. 295–8.

[111] L. Vaux, *Catechism* (Roan, 1605), p. 8.

6 Stuart women's diaries and occasional memoirs

SARA HELLER MENDELSON

Sources that offer a direct record of women's everyday experience for the Stuart period are neither abundant nor easy to find.[1] To be sure, there is plenty of contemporary material *about* women. Sermons and conduct books, plays and pamphlets all claimed to delineate women's true nature and prescribe their ideal role. But, although these works tell us a good deal about contemporary attitudes towards the female sex, they rarely address themselves to women's own sensibilities or the *minutiae* of their daily lives. In order to learn about women from the female point of view, we must turn to the diaries and occasional memoirs that were written by women themselves.

The present study is based on the works of the twenty-three Stuart women who left diaries, occasional memoirs or other serial personal memoranda which it has been possible to locate.[2] Although the number is small, it contains a surprisingly heterogeneous group of diarists and diaries. In age the women range from Lady Elizabeth Delaval, who first began to record her meditations when she was 14 years old, to Sarah Savage, who was still keeping a diary at over 80 years of age. Every matrimonial status is represented: unmarried women, wives and widows, once and twice married, with or without children. The diarists also differed greatly in temperament and in their motivation for keeping personal memoranda. Celia Fiennes described her extensive travels, Joyce Jeffreys kept detailed business accounts, and other women chronicled local or national happenings in addition to their own spiritual and material concerns.

In their literary form, journals and memoirs varied as much as the women who composed them. Seventeenth-century memoirs had not yet crystallized into their modern-day forms, the diary and the auto-biography. Instead, they represent a continuum from one genre to the other, ranging from the daily journal to a variety of sporadic memoranda. In part, this stylistic diversity can be attributed to the protean quality of feminine writing. Quite a number of women left a hodgepodge of miscellaneous manuscripts, including diaries, occasional meditations, instructions for their children, autobiographical reminiscences, extemporaneous prayers, rules for living, notes and commentaries on the Bible, and unclassifiable memoranda.[3] Some women attempted to keep a daily journal and then gave it up in favour of the less taxing occasional memoir.[4] Others began to record their spiritual meditations but found their egos intruding in the form of autobiographical asides.[5] Several women appear to have reworked their original diaries into a more continuous narrative, sometimes providing a preface, a table of contents, or other products of hindsight.[6]

For the purposes of this study, the self-conscious autobiography – that is, an entire life recollected from a particular point in time – has been ignored. The sources chosen consist of diaries and other personal memoirs written in serial form through a succession of moments in time.[7] Hence some of the best-known female autobiographers, such as the Duchess of Newcastle and Mrs Hutchinson, have been excluded. Of course, this distinction cannot be maintained in its pristine purity. Most of the writings included here were subject to tampering after their original composition, whether by their own authors or by later editors. In any case, even an immediate record of the day's experience is always subject to selective processes. None the less, even if we cannot hope to find raw experience conveyed in neat daily bundles, there is much to be learned from these occasional memoranda about the *minutiae* of women's daily lives and their feelings about the events they set down.

A major disadvantage presented by this material is that it is not representative of women as a whole but only that élite minority who had learned to write. One undisputed attribute of the seventeenth-century female population is its overwhelming illiteracy with respect to writing skills. Although there was a considerable rise in female literacy in London towards the end of the seventeenth century, all the literacy tests indicate that, for most of the century, few women throughout England were able even to sign their names.[8] This finding does not necessarily imply that the majority of women were unable to read. In fact it was a widespread practice to teach girls to read but not to write, and the actual extent of female illiteracy with respect to reading ability remains a matter of controversy among historians.[9] In any case, it seems clear that most women were disqualified from the start from composing memoranda of their experiences.

Women of the lower ranks were rarely literate. No example has survived of a female diary below the level of the middle class.[10] It should not be assumed, however, that all female authors were gentle-women. Elizabeth Walker, for example, was described by her husband as a 'plain private Woman, and conversed only with obscure Persons of low Degree.'[11] Anne Bathurst's journal of mystical visions reveals her to have been on the very edge of illiteracy.[12] In all, six of the women can be ranked as middle class.[13] Of the remainder, thirteen came from various degrees of the gentry, and four belonged to the aristocracy by birth or marriage.

Although female illiteracy accounts in part for the small number of diaries below the gentry level, there is reason to suspect that accidents of survival played a role as well. Several autobiographical fragments have been preserved which were written by women of the servant and labouring classes.[14] Such autobiographical memoirs were printed verbatim by contemporaries and were consequently saved for posterity. Some women from the lower ranks of society even managed to break the literacy barrier by narrating their experiences to others who saw to their publication.[15] Journals, in contrast, usually required a heroic editing job because of their sheer bulk and repetitious quality. As Samuel Bury commented on his wife's diary:

> It has been one of the greatest Difficulties to me ... to leave out at least Nine Parts in Ten of what I thought was truly Valuable ... yet ... it was absolute'ly necessary, or else the Volume must have swell'd to such a Bigness, as to have been Useless ...[16]

Moreover, there was a fundamental difference of intention between the autobiography and the diary. The autobiographical memoir was written with a public audience in mind, whether that audience included all posterity or was limited to the author's own children.[17] Although some mixed motives are evident among female diarists,[18] their journals were generally intended for their own private use, not for publication. In fact, most diarists took active steps to conceal their writings from all other eyes. A common and effective method was to employ a personal shorthand.[19] Of course, Samuel Pepys is the most well-known exemplar of the practice, but women often acquired shorthand in order to take sermon notes,[20] and there is no knowing how many female diaries are now lost to us because family members were unable to break the code. Elizabeth Bury kept her spiritual diary in shorthand for the first twenty or thirty years. As her husband lamented after her death, 'her accounts ... cannot be recovered by me, nor, I believe, by any other, because of many peculiar characters and Abbreviations of her own.'[21] Mrs Elizabeth Dunton took double measures to prevent the posthumous disclosure of her journal:

> Mrs. Dunton had ... kept a Diary for near on Twenty Years, and made a great many Reflections, both on the state of her own soul, and on other things. ... But she was so far from Vain-Glory, or Affectation of being talkt of after Death, that she desired that all those large Papers might be burnt, though ... much of what she writ was in a short-hand of her own Invention.[22]

Several of her contemporaries also destroyed their own manuscripts when the dangers of childbirth or a serious illness made them apprehensive of a posthumous discovery.[23]

Some women were apparently diffident about attempting a journal at all because they had no means of keeping it secret. Sarah Savage had been discouraged from beginning a diary for a long time partly for lack of 'the advantage of writing characters'. Finally she decided to use longhand but to 'endeavour to keep it private'.[24] Katharine Austen, a widow at the time she began her miscellaneous diary, prefixed a warning to the casual reader:

> Who so ever shal look in these papers ... wil easily discerne it concerned none but my self & was a private exercise directed to my self.... The singularity of these conceptions doth not advantage any.[25]

Other women had to rely on the discretion of their husbands. When Elizabeth Walker was caught red-handed by her husband in the act of writing, she extracted a promise from him that he would never look at her papers so long as she lived, a vow he 'most faithfully made good'.[26] Elizabeth Pepys was less prudent. During a quarrel, she read aloud to Samuel Pepys an unflattering memoir she had composed about her situation. As he remarked in his diary, it was

> so picquant, and wrote in English and most of it true, of the retirednesse of her life and how unpleasant it was, that being writ in English and so in danger of being met with and read by others, I was vexed at it and desired her and then commanded her to teare it ...[27]

No doubt many diaries and memoirs were lost, like other women's manuscripts, because family members or heirs who were able to decipher them at all were liable to find them either embarrassing or irrelevant.[28]

It is impossible to estimate how many diaries and occasional memoirs were either saved or destroyed because of the nature of their subject matter. It is probably no accident that three-quarters of the works in the present sample contain considerable devotional content.[29] Feminine piety always reflected well upon the family, and any tangible display of it might be considered sufficiently edifying to preserve or even print. Of course, to some extent this profusion of devotional literature reflects the real importance of religion in the lives of seventeenth-century women. Indeed, the female sex was thought to exceed the male in that particular virtue. 'The weaker sexe, to piety more prone', wrote the Earl of Stirling, voicing a common sentiment of the time.[30] On the other hand, it is clear that a large number of women's diaries would never have been undertaken in the first place if their authors had not been goaded on by religious fervour. Over half the diaries and occasional memoirs included in this study appear to have been initiated for spiritual purposes of one sort or another. In fact, the need to enforce a devotional regime was the reason most commonly supplied by women for beginning a daily journal. Elizabeth Bury had

> often advised with herself and others, upon the properest and most effectual Means to promote and carry on her spiritual and pious Designs; and at last determin'd upon this one, *To keep a daily Memorial of what she did*; which should be *a Witness betwixt God and her own Soul*.[31]

A similar motive impelled Sarah Savage, who hoped her diary might be 'a means to make me the more watchful of the frame of my heart when it must be kept on record.'[32] Among the pious, successful diarists were likely to be drawn from the more fanatical end of the spectrum. In his guide to diary-keeping, *The Journal or Diary of a Thankful Christian* (1656), John Beadle admitted that the practice was regarded as an extraordinary duty rather than a normal one: '*But what needs this waste*, may some say, *of time and paines? it's too strict and precise a practise ... a duty too legall for Gospel liberty*.'[33]

Since religious discipline usually supplied the driving force behind spiritual journals, it is not surprising to find in many of these works the family likeness of a genre. It is not known exactly how or when the practice of keeping a spiritual ledger in diary form became wide-spread. Lady Hoby began her journal in 1599, more than half a century before John Beadle published his manual for diary-keeping in 1656. In any case it is evident that the model behind these early works was the Puritan duty of pious self-examination. Richard Rogers, one of the earliest spiritual diarists, was also the author of a popular guide to the art of godly self-examination.[34] Scores of such guides were published throughout the century, some of them directed specifically towards women.[35] One of these, John Featley's *A Fountain of Tears* (1646), includes a list of thirty-eight questions for women to ask themselves each night before going to sleep, in order to scrutinize every aspect of the day's activities.

1. At what time ... did I arise from my bed?
2. What first did I?
3. How devoutly prayed I?
4. What Scripture read I?

The catechism continues through the day's household business, dinner, company, recreation ('Was it not affected with too much delight?'), to the final evening prayers.[36] When we look at actual female spiritual diaries, we can watch their authors ticking off these points one by one.[37]

Thus the spiritual journal helped women to fit the day's activities into a godly straitjacket, and it is not surprising to find that a common trait displayed by female diarists was the urge to impose some comprehensible order upon the fortuitous incidents that made up their lives. Elizabeth Bury, for example, 'would often say, That were it not for her *diary*, she should neither know what she *was*, or what she *did*.'[38] Indeed, this interpretative function of the diary was one of its main *raisons d'être*, as John Beadle explained to his readers: 'Take great notice of the singular peculiar excellency of all Gods dispensations towards you above the world. ... Every passage of providence towards you, if you be the Lords, hath something more speciall in it.'[39]

The providential interpretation of life's accidents which moulded contemporary spiritual diaries offered a coherent and satisfying explanation of world-historical events.[40] It could also transform an outwardly dull and unhappy life into scenes of high drama, punctuated by hairbreadth escapes from death or damnation. Perhaps more important, the habit of looking for patterns in chance circumstances helped women get through life from day to day. Writers often noted that they had read through old volumes of their diaries to give them insight into current problems.[41] As Mrs Bury expressed it, 'the review of former experience was an Extraordinary Help to future Confidence.'[42] Many of these daily balance sheets seem to have had a cathartic as well as an interpretative function. Elizabeth Mordaunt believed that by recording and then repudiating her sins she could 'Laye me doune and rest in pece, with a full ashuranc, that they shall never more be layde to my charge.'[43] Sometimes this confessional purpose of the diary could lead to exaggerated expressions of guilt for minute lapses, so that the author could be sure she had settled her spiritual account for the day.[44]

The introspective purpose of spiritual diaries was apt to influence their mood as well as their contents. The Countess of Warwick's journal exhibits so many expressions of despairing self-reproach that we might infer she was continually depressed. Yet her chaplain described her cheerful temper as the 'sweetest ... in the world'.[45] Presumably her devotional exercises, which included the duty of reviling herself daily for her sins, imparted their peculiar tone to many of her diary entries. In other cases, this excessive rigour seems to have been associated with a special emotional make-up. One anonymous diarist voiced her suspicions that her own religious impulses were merely the product of her neurotic personality: 'I fere to[o] much of my zele was ockashoned by the naturall sadness and pevisness of my temper which is apt to ca[u]se a meltingness of hartt to[o] oft mistaken for zele.'[46]

Another highly influential genre which helped to shape both form and content of female reminiscences was the narrative of God's mercies to the author. A typical example of the genre is found in the memoirs of Alice Thornton, who justified her occasional memoranda by prefacing them with the following observation:

> it is the dutie of every true Christian to remember and take notice of Allmighty God our Heavenly Father's gracious acts of Providence over them, and mercifull dealings with them, even from the wombe, untill the grave bury them in silence, as also to keepe perticuler remembrances of His favours, both spirituall and temporall, together with His remarkable deliverances of theire soules and bodies ... [47]

The genre produced all sorts of sporadic memoirs: occasional meditations, intermittent chronicles, lists of providences, prayers and miscellaneous memoranda. These occasional reminiscences selected the high and low points of life and omitted the uneventful jog-trot of domesticity. Since they recorded notable happenings, whether good or bad, they tend to convey an atmosphere of crisis. Although there are grounds for suspecting that seventeenth-century life was considerably more crisis-ridden than its modern equivalent, we should allow for the influence of contemporary models in suggesting some of the contents of occasional memoirs. 'Put into your Journal all deliverances from dangers, vouchsafed to you or yours', John Beadle instructed his readers.[48] This practice was certainly followed, sometimes with more enthusiasm than judgement. Among many remarkable escapes listed in her memoirs, Mrs Thornton expressed her indebtedness to God for a deliverance from a surfeit of lobster, Richmond, 1643.[49] Dame Sarah Cowper noted in her diary that her husband had been thrown into the river during a coach ride without her, and added, 'I believe Providence directed me to avoid a fright and danger'.[50] Such lists of nearly averted disasters found in most memoirs of the period seem to have served a practical purpose. Those who had been spared for the present could hope to ward off future harm by recording their gratitude that they were still alive and well. The petitionary prayers and occasional meditations that women produced in abundance at this time are another variation on the same theme. They tend to be selective in their subject matter, partly because women were apt to record their private prayers and meditations chiefly during periods of anxiety or despair. Entries describing the pleasures of everyday life are comparatively few, although they are not entirely absent from occasional memoirs.

Although spiritual memoirs account for a large proportion of the feminine manuscripts that have been preserved, it is impossible to estimate how much secular material failed to survive or was deleted by editors of manuscripts that were subsequently printed. There are reasons for suspecting that a substantial amount of non-devotional writing may have disappeared in this manner, because editors from the seventeenth to the nineteenth centuries exhibited a marked preference for female piety. This preference is evident in their editorial prefaces, which usually single out their subject's religious fervour as an especially praiseworthy attribute.[51] It is also evident in their selection of diary passages best calculated to display the saintliness of their authoress. In many cases in which the original manuscript still exists, comparison with the printed version reveals that personal and secular matters or lapses from spiritual perfection were systematically omitted.[52] To add to these selective effects, it should be noted that a high proportion of female diarists were the wives, daughters or patronesses of clergymen. Of the six middle-class women in the sample, three were wives of clergymen and a fourth was the daughter of a famous Nonconformist preacher.[53] Clergymen's families, like clergymen themselves, were more literate than the average for their social class, and the wife's facility in self-expression was apt to be matched by her husband's ability to edit and publish her manuscripts. Clerical editorial principles placed a high priority on the spiritual edification of the reader.[54]

Among the various types of personal writing, devotional diaries offer the most detailed picture of the domestic routine. Although incidents recorded in spiritual journals are apt to be distorted by the religious lens through which they are viewed, we can nevertheless glimpse women's daily round. Naturally, since their chief concern was spiritual, these diaries devote a good deal of space to recording the performance of religious duties. Most of those who noted their pious endeavours appear to have followed contemporary guides to devotion with few deviations into originality. These standard exercises, usually performed two or three times daily, included private prayer, reading a portion of Scripture and books of devotion, several hours of divine meditation, and the confession of sin.[55] This was a time-consuming routine which in some women took on the dimensions of a career. In his devotional guide *The Heart's Ease* (1660), Simon Patrick admonished those who took an exaggerated view of their spiritual requirements, 'as those do, who think they must alwayes be at prayer, or hearing Sermons, or reading spiritual books.'[56] But quite a number of women recorded slack or indifferent performance of their duties, and there are grounds for suspecting that they often found the practice of piety tedious. The diaries and meditations are filled with confessions of dullness and coldness in prayer and wandering thoughts in divine meditation, even from those women who were renowned in their day as paragons of piety.[57]

Many diarists also recorded their domestic routine. It is noteworthy in this connection that early rising was reckoned as one of the spiritual graces. For example, Elizabeth Walker generally rose at four o'clock, winter and summer, and Elizabeth Delaval resolved to make do with only '6 houer's slepe in the 24' as part of her spiritual discipline.[58] This spiritual impetus behind early rising helps explain how Stuart women managed to get through such a heavy load of secular responsibilities. After devotions and family prayers were finished, much of the day was devoted to housework, even among upper-class women. Although servants performed the menial and heavy work, their activities were subjected to continual supervision by the mistress of the household. The Countess of Warwick directed all the domestic affairs of her Essex manor, keeping a close eye on subsidiary concerns like the dairy and henhouse. She was also involved in the business side of estate management, for it was she who checked the annual accounts. Elizabeth Walker not only supervised the farm labourers and household servants in their tasks, but shared some of the work herself, especially in exacting enterprises such as dairying and brewing.[59] Most women occupied their spare hours with needlework, the great feminine time-filler. Some also noted their reading. Although the spiritual journals indicate that contemporary devotional guides made up women's staple reading, some diarists lamented their wicked youth which had been wasted reading plays, poetry and romances.[60] The most commonly recorded leisure activity was social visiting – the favourite diversion of both sexes, and of the middle as well as the upper classes. Women's immense enjoyment of social gatherings was the source of a great many confessions of guilt among the pious, often expressed in their diaries as a condemnation of their own 'vain and frothy discourse' on these occasions.[61] Hospitality could lead to other sins as well. After friends from Whitchurch had visited Sarah Savage, she noted in her diary how 'the desire to entertain them handsomely easily degenerates into Pride'.[62] In Stuart England, as in other pre-industrial cultures, hospitality was not only the expression of obligatory reciprocity, but also an opportunity for conspicuous display. The overall impression that emerges from the diaries is that women took an equal share and derived equal honour from the rites and exchanges entailed by hospitality.

It is interesting to note that the diaries reveal fewer class variations in women's daily round of activities than might have been expected. For example, the aristocratic Countess of Warwick and her middle-class neighbour Elizabeth Walker performed similar tasks and indulged in similar recreations. Both spent their day running the household, educating their children, supervising servants, sewing and reading, entertaining friends and relations, visiting the neighbouring poor, and performing a lengthy devotional routine. The differences appear to lie more in the scale of their responsibilities than in the essential nature of their duties. The most conspicuous variations found in female occupations arose not from social rank so much as from age and matrimonial status. No doubt a different picture would emerge if we were to include lower-class women, who do not appear directly in the diaries. But among those women who left personal memoirs, gender was apparently more important than class in shaping the basic pattern of their lives.

Contemporary modes of thought divided female life into three distinct stages: virginity, marriage and widowhood. The conduct books employed this tripartite scheme in their description of feminine duties and privileges,[63] and women themselves appear to have been very self-conscious about passing through each condition in turn. For example, in beginning her narrative of 'the first yeare of my widdowed condition', Mrs Thornton commented:

> I haveing now passed through the two stages of my life of my virgin estate, and that of the honrable estate of marriage as St. Paull tearmes it (tho' with much troubles in the flesh), the same has had its comforts alaied to me ...[64]

Nor was the concept an artificial one. Women's diaries and memoirs illustrate the notion of three modes of feminine existence, each with its appropriate deportment, duties and concerns.

Although unmarried young women comprise the smallest group of diarists, it seems clear that, despite continual subordination to parents or guardians, maidenhood represented the most carefree and enjoyable of the three female conditions. Indeed, most of the anxieties expressed by the youngest writers in the group stemmed from their guilt at taking too much pleasure in life. In her earliest meditations Elizabeth Delaval noted her repentance for flirting shamelessly with suitors, running up debts at court, mounting a production of *Il Pastor Fido* with a cast of Lincolnshire yokels, and over-indulging in fruit.[65] At the age of 23, Sarah Henry, who came from a deeply religious background, appears to have been extremely happy living in the bosom of her family. Her most serious worry before she became engaged to be married was her habit of sleeping through the sabbath service.[66]

Once marriage was in prospect, however, young women often entered a tense and anxious period. Sarah Henry noted herself 'much perplexed with thoughts about the changing of my condicōn'.[67] Other diarists noted their unwillingness to abandon their liberty. Alice Thornton recalled, 'For my owne perticuler, I was not hastie to change my free estate without much consideration ... wherein none could be more sattisfied.'[68] Mary Boyle, although her father was besieged with offers for her hand, 'still continued to have an aversion to maridge, liveing so much at my ease that I was unwilling to change my condition.'[69] Marriage could represent a major trauma for women, and various sources reveal that they regarded it as the crucial turning-point in life. Their hopes and fears about matrimony are symbolized by a common female superstition concerning the wedding-day – the belief that the state of the weather on that occasion would foretell their future happiness or unhappiness with their husbands. Obviously this was an unfortunate superstition to hold in England. Elizabeth Walker felt that she had good grounds for her optimism when providence caused the sun to shine literally as well as figuratively upon her nuptials.[70] Elizabeth Freke's experience was less propitious. She noted in her diary: 'I was maryed 14 of November 1671, to Mr Percy Frek, withoutt my deer Fathers Consentt or knowledg, In a most dreadfull Raynie day, A presager of all my sorrows & Misfortuns to mee.'[71]

Marriage initiated a number of significant changes in feminine behaviour, as social pressures combined with religious precepts to mould wives' deportment towards their husbands, their in-laws and the world at large. Soon after her marriage, Elizabeth Delaval noted that

> in every change off our life we have reason to set a new watch upon our selves; for the same actions are not alike inocent in every condition ... the gayety of my humour and the harmelesse mirth in my conversation was pleaseing to those I formerly kept company withall, and what was estimed by them to be wit ... is look'd upon to be a gidynesse unbecomeing a wife ...[72]

Newly married Mrs Mordaunt reproached herself in her diary for feuding with her mother-in-law, and for gazing at a former suitor 'when it might renue his pashon for me, which being marryed was unlafull'.[73] Sarah Savage prayed on her wedding night for 'a new heart for my new condition, & help mee to discharge ye duties of it, as a wife, a Mother, & a daughter in law'.[74]

As for the success or failure of these unions, the diaries vividly portray a diversity of connubial relations, from uxorious bliss to bitter enmity and desertion. Some women did not conceal the failure of their marriages. On the contrary, they appear to have derived a gloomy satisfaction from recording their husbands' shortcomings and their own undeserved martyrdom. Elizabeth Freke's diary, suggestively titled 'Som few remembrances of my misfortuns which have atended me in my unhappy life since I were marryed', is a catalogue of personal and financial disasters which she attributed to

Mr Freke and his relations. Lady Anne Clifford commended God for taking her side in her running battles with her husband.[75] Dame Sarah Cowper filled her diary with rancorous complaints against her husband Sir William, whom she described as 'the most difficult humour to live at Ease with this world ever afforded'. Elsewhere she commented, 'since it is not possible for me to redress these Domestick greivances, I wou'd notice them to no other purpose, but to find by what means to sustain and bear them well.'[76] On the other hand, a number of extremely happy unions were recorded. Sarah Savage wrote on her wedding anniversary, 'my greatest fear this last month ... is lest our love to each other would exceed – tis hard to keep the mean'.[77] Others left similar expressions of wedded bliss.[78]

One anonymous female diarist agreed with certain modern historians that married love was 'a thing very rare',[79] but evidence derived from such diaries and memoirs as survive does not bear out her opinion. By counting the number of successful and unsuccessful unions among the diarists, it is possible to give some precision to vague impressions about the distribution of matrimonial happiness. Of the twenty-three women, two remained spinsters. (Incidentally, to all appearances, both were perfectly happy in their maiden state.)[80] Of the twenty-one women who married, four of them married twice, making a total of twenty-five unions. Four of these marriages do not offer sufficient information for our purposes. Among the twenty-one remaining ones, there were fifteen loving and companionable marriages, and six unsatisfactory marriages.[81] Although it might appear that the numbers are biased in favour of happy unions because loving husbands would have preserved their wives' manuscripts, this tendency is sufficiently balanced by those disgruntled wives who wrote their memoirs in order to vilify their husbands. There does not seem to be an obvious explanation for the high proportion of happy unions. In thirteen of the twenty-one marriages, however, there is some information about the circumstances in which these unions were contracted. Eight happy marriages included the following patterns: two love matches in which parents were displeased but finally gave consent; three cases of free choice (two were second marriages); two arranged marriages with a clear veto allowed to the bride; one arranged marriage in which the bride was only 13.[82] Five unhappy unions included the following circumstances: one elopement; two forced marriages; the two marriages of Lady Anne Clifford, of which the first was arranged, and the second her own choice.[83] If any conclusion can be drawn from these examples, it is the importance that contemporaries attached to giving all parties the opportunity to consent to the union. In the two extremes of elopement and forced marriage in which parents or children withheld their consent, the union was more liable to founder. Arranged marriage did not necessarily lead to unhappy unions, so long as children were offered a reasonable chance to express their own inclinations.[84]

One pattern exhibited in both happy and unhappy marriages is the role played by contemporary religious teaching in reinforcing wifely obedience. Those diarists who took their piety seriously felt obliged to confess and repudiate all manifestations of marital insubordination. Thus an anonymous diarist deplored 'some litell frowardness and unbecoming pevishnes to my Husband which tho I aproved not I did not strive enouf against'.[85] The most exhaustive illustration of this pattern is found in the Countess of Warwick's mammoth diary. From 1666, when she first began to keep a journal, until the Earl of Warwick's death in 1673, there are frequent entries detailing her continual struggle to repress her own strong will in conformity with her biblical notions of wifely subjection. Occasionally the urge for self-expression got the better of her, as on one evening when she returned late from a visit:

> my lord fell, without any occasion given by me, into a great pasion with me, which troubled me so much that I fell into a dispute with him wherin I was very pationately affected, and wepte much, and spake unadvisedly ...

Afterwards, ashamed of this lapse of self-control, she begged God's pardon 'for my shedding so many teares for anything but my sinnes, and for not being content with what his providence was pleased to order for me'.[86]

If piety was apt to buttress traditional social roles in the married state, we can also see some women turning to the religious life to compensate for the inadequacies of wedlock. For a summary of contemporary thinking on this subject, we can turn to a little essay on marriage found among the Countess of Bridgewater's occasional meditations. She pointed out that, in the case of a truly intolerable union, the practice of piety offered the wife what amounted to an alternative spouse:

> if he [the husband] be fickle and various, not careing much to be with his wife at home, then thus may the wife make her own happinesse, for then she may give her self up in prayer ... and thus, in his absence, she is as much God's as a virgine ...[87]

This species of displacement to a heavenly object was strongly encouraged by the devotional literature of the time. In sermons and tracts, divines quoted the Song of Songs in advising women to take Christ as their spouse.[88] But what we find in some women's diaries is an emotional involvement with God which goes far beyond the allegorical relationship that clerics presumably had in mind. Among certain women with no husband or an extremely unsatisfactory one, some sort of erotic transference seems to have taken place. During periods of her husband's most outrageous behaviour, the Countess of Warwick recorded numerous experiences of the passionate 'warmth' and 'fire' of God's love. She seems to have recognized an earthly tincture to her more rapturous expressions, since she crossed them all out at a later date.[89] The widow Anne Bathurst recorded mystical visions which carried the notion of a heavenly spouse to the most extravagant lengths. On one occasion she 'desyred often in the day his return of Love, and hoped at night yt I might ly in his arms as I had done the night before'. A few days later, Christ seemed to her 'to kiss me with the kisses of his mouth'. Although admittedly an extreme case, she was not an isolated example.[90]

One of the most significant features of women's private memoranda is their expressive portrayal of the biological cycle of married life. Most species of feminine writings tend to reiterate similar concerns, which were much the same as those that obsess demographers of the present day: marriage, conception, birth, illness and death. But, unlike demographers, seventeenth-century women were interested in the personal rather than the statistical application of these patterns. The more arduous aspects of married women's biological and social role were ably summarized by the Duchess of Newcastle, herself childless:

> all the time of their lives is ensnared with troubles, what in breeding and bearing children, what in taking and turning away servants, directing and ordering their family ... and if they have children, what troubles and griefs do ensue? Troubled with their forwardnesse and untowardnesse, the care for their well being, the fear for their ill doing, their grief for their sicknesse, and their unsufferable sorrow for their death ...[91]

In diaries such as that of Sarah Savage we can follow every stage of this process. In the early years of marriage she recorded her anxiety each month that she would never become pregnant. Eventually she succeeded, but her first pregnancy ended in miscarriage, and she was soon apprehensive about the possibility of another. Having finally succeeded in bearing a son at full term, she watched him die when he was a few days old. By the end of her life she had borne nine children, of whom four were to survive her.[92]

Women's anxieties about pregnancy and childbirth form a leitmotif which appears in various guises throughout their diaries and memoirs. They expressed their apprehensions about the pain of labour; the Countess of Bridgewater periodically beseeched the Lord to 'have compassion on me in the great paine I am to fele in the bringing forth of this my child … lay no more on me then thou wilt enable me to beare.'[93] Many voiced their expectation of dying in childbirth. There was also concern about the child to come, especially the oft-expressed worry that it might be born misshapen. A deformed infant represented not only a physical but a moral reflection on the parents, since contemporary superstition held that an infant's malformation was a direct punishment for the sins of the parents. Thus Lady Bridgewater begged that her child might be 'borne without any deformity, so that I and its father may not be punisht for our sinnes, in the deformity of our Babe'.[94] Lady Mordaunt requested a similar favour during her pregnancy. She also asked, 'if it be thy blessed will let it be a boy', a common appeal by prospective parents of both sexes.[95]

As for the lying-in itself, some women provided full obstetric details of their labours. Alice Thornton offered the following account of the breech birth of her fifth child. After three days in labour, she fell into 'exceeding sharp travill' so that the midwife thought she was ready to deliver.

> But loe! … the child staied in the birth, and came crosse with his feet first … at which time I was upon the racke in bearing my child with such exquisitt torment, as if each limbe weare divided from other, for the space of two houres; when … beeing speechless and breathlesse, I was … in great mercy delivered.[96]

Unfortunately her labour was so prolonged that the child was 'half-strangled' and lived only half an hour. Mrs Thornton left similarly gruesome accounts of her other eight labours. Her descriptions convey not only the great terror she felt at the prospect of childbirth, but pride in her strength and fortitude in surviving the ordeal.

Women's diaries also illustrate the degree to which childbirth was a communal event rather than a purely individual trauma. Diarists often left accounts of those labours of relatives and friends whose lyings-in they were duty-bound to attend. The Countess of Warwick described her niece's ordeal:

my Lady Barringtons being in labor ... I went directly thiether. ...
I stayde with her all night she haveing a most terable sharpe labor I
was excidingly afraide of her and with much earnestnes and many
teares begde a safe dealivery for her ...[97]

Sarah Savage offered a much lengthier narrative of her daughter's
labour and subsequent illness.[98] Not only did most women run the
gauntlet themselves many times, but they were continually called
upon to witness their friends' agonies in like circumstances. And so
these sociable childbed gatherings – which were intended to provide
maximum support for the woman in labour – became a means of
equitably distributing her terror to the rest of her female acquaintance.

Once a woman had borne a child, it was no easy matter keeping it
alive. Lady Isabella Twysden was exceptionally fortunate in bearing
six children who each survived to adulthood.[99] At the other extreme,
Elizabeth Walker was the mother of eleven children, all of whom
predeceased her.[100] Most of the women diarists' experiences were
somewhere in the middle, and their prayers and occasional meditations
are filled with desperate appeals to heaven for the recovery of their
sick children, and with moving elegies on their deaths. Usually these
maternal laments represented an attempt to bear the loss with Christian
fortitude. Women tried to assure themselves that their own sins were
to blame and that in any case their innocent children had attained the
joys of eternal life. One of Anne Bathurst's mystical visions was of
her dead children rising to heaven:

> as they came up, I remembered Two little children, died
> one at fourteen weeks, the other at fourteen days end, and ime-
> diatly as soon as I began to desire it, they came like two Bright
> Sparks, one after another, and entred into this great Light and
> became one with it ...[101]

The Countess of Warwick kept the anniversary of her son's death as a
fast day each year, noting in her diary the assurances she had obtained
that he was in heaven, and reckoning up her own sins which had
caused him to be taken from her.[102]

Lady Warwick was heroically successful in her efforts to put a
stoical face upon her grief. As her chaplain Anthony Walker recalled,
'her behaviour was so submiss, serene, and calm, I confess I cannot
but judge it scarce imitable.'[103] But many women betrayed an internal
struggle between the irresistible urge to mourn their loss and the
compulsion to behave in conformity with contemporary religious

orthodoxy. When Mrs Thornton grieved excessively for the death of her baby son, she received a lecture from her 4-year-old daughter:

> 'My deare mother, why doe you morne and weepe soe much for my brother Willy? doe you not thinke he is gon to heaven ... wher he has noe sickness, but lives in happines? ... be patient, and God can give you annother son to live with you and my father ...'

At this speech Mrs Thornton did 'much condemne' herself and begged patience from the Lord, who 'had putt such words into the mouth of soe young a child to reprove my immoderate sorrow'.[104] In one of the Countess of Bridgewater's occasional meditations entitled 'upon occasion of the death of my boy Henry', she struggled against 'heathenish' impulses:

> let me not fall to wish I never had borne it, rather than to part with it, Lose it I cannot say, if I be a christian ... in the knowledge of all this, why should I wish my Babe had not beene, rather then to dye?[105]

After the death of Elizabeth Walker's eleventh and last child, she fell into a prolonged atheistic depression.[106]

While female meditations and prayers tend to be dominated by the crises of child-bearing and child-rearing, daily journals offer a glimpse of the rewarding side of the maternal role. Mary Woodforde proudly chronicled her family's comings and goings, noting her sons' progress at school and college.[107] Lady Clifford's satisfaction in one of the lesser *rites de passage* of her little daughter is evident from her diary:

> May 1617. Upon the 1st I cut the Child's strings off from her coats and made her use the togs alone, so as she had two or three falls at first but had no hurt with them.[108]

Widowhood was the third 'estate' of womankind. Of the twenty-one diarists who married, thirteen are known to have been widowed at some point in life. Eleven of these composed some portion of their memoranda during widowhood.[109] The diarists display a wide variety of reactions to their widowed estate, ranging from almost suicidal mourning to barely disguised relief. Out of this diversity of experience, two contrasting patterns are especially noteworthy. First, some women apparently came into their own when the toils of child-bearing and the rigours of wifely subordination were over. They had earned the independence and resources to do as they pleased, and they derived comfort and respect from a web of social relations centred on children and dependants. This matriarchal model is found particularly among aristocratic dowagers like the Countess of Pembroke and the Countess of Warwick, each of whom enjoyed the status of monarch in her own local world.[110] Women of minor gentry status might also behave in this fashion, albeit on a smaller scale. Elizabeth Freke took pleasure in building a comfortable little fortune from her farming activities, once she had been freed from the burden of her feckless husband.

For other women, widowhood not only deprived them of a beloved companion but plunged them into a sea of economic difficulties. In her miscellaneous diary, Katherine Austen continually bemoaned the sad state of her financial affairs since her widowhood, railing at the treachery of friends and relations who took advantage of her naïve lack of business acumen.[111] The widowed Mrs Thornton also found herself in a financial morass which she attributed to her husband's mismanagement during his lifetime. Attempting to salvage an estate heavily encumbered with debts, she was obliged to borrow from numerous friends and relations, and bitterly remarked:

> it was a very pinching consideration to me that I was forced to enter the first conserne of my widdowed condition with bonds, debts, and ingagements for others, whereas I brought soe considerable a fortune, and never knew what debt was ... but what I had bin servicable to many in necessity to lend for charity ...[112]

The fact that women's diaries tend to illustrate sharply defined life stages – the periods before, during and after marriage and child-bearing – distinguishes them from contemporary male diaries, where the most obvious variations relate to class and occupation. There is also a discernible difference in atmosphere. Women's diaries are more apt to be centred around the household and its personnel. The prevailing picture of everyday life evoked in their writings is of women going about their domestic tasks, retreating to their closets to perform their devotions, entertaining and being entertained in each other's houses. Men's diaries exude more of the atmosphere of public life: occupations outside the home, social gatherings in alehouses, political gossip interwoven with narratives of local affairs. Of course, this divergence between male and female perspectives does not preclude a good deal of overlap. Men often wrote about their wives in their diaries; they also recorded the illnesses and deaths of children. In some memoirs men even narrated their wives' childbirth experiences.[113] When diarists of either sex wrote of domestic life, they described the same world, although they looked at it from different angles. However, a number of works convey a sense of the separation of masculine and feminine realms, much as they were set forth in early seventeenth-century conduct books. Men were supposed to 'travel, seek a living ... deal with many men ... dispatch all things outdoor'. Their wives should 'keep the house ... oversee and give order within'.[114]

Nevertheless, some important exceptions to this generalization should be noted. First of all, the picture would be much altered if diaries existed for women from the lower ranks of society. We should be able to see them working in the fields, selling their wares at markets and from door to door, travelling long distances without their husbands to find work, and participating in an alehouse culture of their own.[115] Secondly, exceptional circumstances might cause a middle- or upper-class woman to take on a 'male' role, whether permanently or on a temporary basis. The necessity to fight a lawsuit or serve as the executor of a will could force a widow to journey to London with newly acquired expertise in the masculine realms of legal stratagems, high finance and parliamentary procedure.[116] Thirdly, certain periods of national crisis appear to have captured the imagination of female diarists, provoking them to take a consuming interest in political affairs. A good example is the Civil War diary of Lady Isabella Twysden, much of which is devoted to recording current events of national significance.[117] Other major crises like the invasion of William of Orange were noted by many female diarists who ordinarily said little or nothing about current events.[118]

Finally, it is possible to discern the vague outlines of a trend away from feminine domesticity from the late sixteenth to the late seventeenth centuries. In her Jacobean diary, Lady Anne Clifford noted her boredom and resentment at being marooned in the country while her husband enjoyed himself in the capital:

> All this time my Lord was in London where he had all and infinite great resort coming to him. He went much abroad to Cocking, to Bowling Alleys, to Plays and Horse Races. ... I stayed in the country having many times a sorrowful and heavy heart ... so as I may truly say, I am like an owl in the desert.[119]

But, despite her exceptionally stubborn spirit, she was unable to move unless her husband sent for her.[120] Writing almost a century later, Dame Sarah Cowper appears to exemplify a change in mores. Her diary combines the pious introspection of an earlier age with a lively commentary on the intellectual and political currents of the time. Like Lady Clifford, she was on bad terms with her husband; indeed, they rarely spoke to each other except in order to quarrel. Yet when Sir William went to London for the season his wife assumed as a matter of course that she would accompany him.[121] Perhaps the most suggestive symptom of a new outlook on female potentialities is not a memoir at all but the travel diary of Celia Fiennes. Having concluded her heroic series of journeys throughout the length and breadth of England, she prefaced her account of them with advice to the rest of her sex to expand their horizons in like manner:

> with a hearty wish and recommendation to all, but especially to my own Sex, the studdy of those things which tends to improve the mind and makes our lives pleasant and comfortable as well as proffitable in all Stages and Stations ... and render Suffering and Age supportable and Death less formidable and a future State more happy.[122]

Women's journals were ready to shift their attention from the inward contemplation of the soul to a lively appreciation of the world at large.

APPENDIX: ANNOTATED LIST OF DIARISTS AND DIARIES

Names marked with an asterisk are not found in W. Matthews, *British Diaries* (Berkeley, Cal., 1950).

[ANON.-a relative of Cromwell (b. 1654)]. Autobiographical and occasional memoirs, *c.* 1687–1702. BL Add. MS 5858, ff. 213–21.

[ANON.]. Daily spiritual diary, *c.* 1679–81. Bodl. MS Rawlinson Q.e. 26–7.

AUSTEN, Katherine (b. 1628).* Miscellaneous diary, *c.* 1664–6. BL Add. MS 4454.

BATHURST, Anne (b. 1647).* Autobiographical memoirs and spiritual diary, chiefly of mystical visions, 1679 *et seq.* Bodl. MS Rawl. D. 1262–3 (contemporary transcript; fragment of original is Bodl. MS Rawl. Q.e. 28).

BRIDGEWATER, Elizabeth Egerton, Countess of (1626–63), of Little Gaddesden, Hertfordshire.* Occasional meditations and prayers, *c.* 1648–63. BL MS Egerton 607.

BURY, Elizabeth (1644–1720), of Clare, Suffolk. Extracts from her daily spiritual diary, *c.* 1690–1720. In S. Bury, *An Account of the Life and Death of Mrs Elizabeth Bury* (Bristol, 1720).

CLIFFORD, Lady Anne, Countess of Pembroke (1590–1676), of Westmorland. Autobiographical preface (1603) and diary for 1616–17, 1619. *The Diary of Lady Anne Clifford*, ed. V. Sack-ville-West (London, 1923).

COWPER, Dame Sarah (1644–1720), of Hertford.* Daily diary, 1700–16. Hertfordshire RO, Panshanger MSS, D/EP/F29–35.

DELAVAL, Lady Elizabeth (b. 1649), of Seaton Delaval.* Occasional meditations and prayers interspersed with autobiographical memoirs, c. 1653–71. *The Meditations of Lady Elizabeth Delaval*, ed. D. G. Greene, Surtees Society, CXC (1975). Printed from Bodl. MS Rawl. D. 78.

FIENNES, Celia (1662–1741), of Newton Toney and London. Travel journals, c. 1685–1703. *The Journeys of Celia Fiennes*, ed. C. Morris (London, 1947).

FREKE, Elizabeth (1641–1714), of County Cork. Occasional memoirs, 1671–1714. 'Mrs Elizabeth Freke her Diary, 1671–1714', *Journal of the Cork Historical and Archaeological Society*, XVI–XIX (1910–13). Printed from BL Add. MSS 45718–19.

HARCOURT, Lady Anne, of Stanton Harcourt, Oxfordshire. Occasional memoirs, prayers and lists of mercies, c. 1649–61. Extracts in *The Harcourt Papers*, ed. E. W. Harcourt (Oxford, 1876), I, pp. 169–99.

HOBY, Lady Margaret (1570–1633), of Hackness, Yorkshire. Daily diary, August 1599–July 1605. *The Diary of Lady Margaret Hoby*, ed. D. M. Meads (Boston, Mass., 1930). Printed from BL MS Egerton 2614.

JEFFREYS, Joyce (c. 1570–1650), of Ham Castle, Worcestershire. Business diary, 1638–48. BL MS Egerton 3054. Extracts in R. G. Griffiths, 'Joyce Jeffreys of Ham Castle', *Transactions of the Worcestershire Archaeological Society*, NS, X–XII (1933–5).

MILDMAY, Lady Grace (1552–1620), of Apethorpe, Northamptonshire. Autobiographical and occasional memoirs, 1570–1617. Extracts in R. Weigall, 'The Journal of Lady Mildmay', *Quarterly Review*, CCXV (1911), pp. 119–38.

MORDAUNT, Elizabeth, Viscountess (1633–79), of Middlesex. Daily spiritual diary, 1656–7, and occasional memoirs, 1657–78. *The Private Diarie of Elizabeth Viscountess Mordaunt* (Duncairn, 1856).

PAKINGTON, Lady Dorothy (d. 1679), of Westwood, Worcestershire.* Prayers and meditations, *temp.* Charles II. Bodl. MS Add. B. 58.

SAVAGE, Sarah (1664–1745), of Broad Oak, Flintshire. Spiritual diary, 1686–8 and 1714–23. CCRO D/Basten/8 (1686–8), and Bodl. MS Eng. Misc. e. 331 (1714–23). Diary, 1694–1732. Extracts in J. B. Williams, *The Life of Mrs Savage* (London, 1848).

THORNTON, Alice (1627–1707), of East Newton, Yorkshire. Occasional memoirs, 1629–67. *The Autobiography of Mrs Alice Thornton*, ed. C. Jackson, Surtees Society, LXII (1875).

TWYSDEN, Lady Isabella (1605–57), of East Peckam, Kent. Occasional public and personal memoranda, 1645–51. 'The Diary of Isabella, Wife of Sir Roger Twysden, Baronet', *Archaeologia Cantiana*, LI (1939), pp. 113–36. Printed from BL Add. MSS 34169–72.

WALKER, Elizabeth (1623–90), of Essex. Autobiographical and occasional memoirs, *c.* 1635–90. Extracts in A. Walker, *The Holy Life of Mrs Elizabeth Walker* (London, 1690).

WARWICK, Mary Rich, Countess of (1624–78), of Leighs, Essex. Daily spiritual diary and occasional meditations, 1666–78. BL Add. MSS 27351–6.

WOODFORDE, Mary, of Winchester. Diary, 1684–90. In *Woodforde Papers and Diaries*, ed. D. H. Woodforde (London, 1932), pp. 12–15.

NOTES

[1] For the relative paucity of sources on women's everyday life at the local level, see A. Macfarlane, *Reconstructing Historical Communities* (Cambridge, 1977), p. 207; K. Wrightson and D. Levine, *Poverty and Piety in an English Village* (New York, 1979), pp. 21–2.

[2] See Appendix.

[3] For examples, see N. Parkhurst, *The Faithful and Diligent Christian* (London, 1684), pp. 81–3; J. Evelyn, *The Diary of John Evelyn*, ed. E. S. de Beer, 6 vols (Oxford, 1955), IV, p. 431; 'S.C.', *The Life of the Lady Halket* (Edinburgh, 1701), appendix listing manuscript 'Books written by the Lady Halket'; A. Walker, *The Holy Life of Mrs Elizabeth Walker* (London, 1690), pp. 5–8.

[4] E. Mordaunt, *The Private Diarie of Elizabeth Viscountess Mordaunt* (Duncairn, 1856); M. Hoby, *The Diary of Lady Margaret Hoby*, ed. D. M. Meads (Boston, Mass., 1930).

[5] E. Delaval, *The Meditations of Lady Elizabeth Delaval*, ed. D. G. Greene, Surtees Society, CXC (1975), pp. 18–19; Katherine Austen, Diary, BL MS Sloane 4454.

[6] [Anon.], BL Add. MS 5858; Anne Bathurst, Diary, Bodl. MS Rawl. D. 1262–3; Sarah Cowper, Diary, Hertfordshire RO, Panshanger MSS, D/EP/F29.

[7] See R. Pascal, *Design and Truth in Autobiography* (Cambridge, Mass., 1960), pp. 3–4.

[8] D. Cressy, *Literacy and the Social Order* (Cambridge, 1980), pp. 106, 112–13, 115, 119–21, 128–9, 144–7. Samples ranged from 84 to 98 per cent illiterate, apart from London, where there was a dramatic fall to 52 per cent illiteracy by the 1690s.

[9] M. Spufford, *Small Books and Pleasant Histories* (London, 1981), pp. 25,

34–6, 43–5; T. C. Smout, 'New Evidence on Popular Religion and Literacy in Eighteenth-century Scotland', *P & P*, XCVII (1982), p. 121.

[10] For males there are diaries lower down the social scale; for example, R. Lowe, *The Diary of Roger Lowe*, ed. W. L. Sachse (New Haven, Conn., 1938).

[11] Walker, *Holy Life*, sig. A3.

[12] A fragment of her original manuscript has survived as Bodl. MS Rawl. Q.e.28 (miscatalogued as part of what is in fact a different diary, Bodl. MS Rawl. Q.e.26–7). The contemporary transcript by several other hands is Bodl. MS Rawl. D. 1262–3.

[13] The six are Anne Bathurst, Elizabeth Bury, Sarah Savage, Elizabeth Walker, Mary Woodforde, and the anonymous author of BL Add. MS 5858.

[14] For autobiographical narratives or fragments by women of lower rank than the female diarists, see A. Beaumont, *The Singular Experience and Great Sufferings of Mrs Agnes Beaumont* (London, 1822); A. Hayes, *A Legacy or Widow's Mite Left by Alice Hayes* (London, 1723); B. Blaugdone, *An Account of the Travels and Sufferings ... of Barbara Blaugdone* (London, 1691); J. Turner, *Choice Experiences* (London, 1653). The last work appears to have been based on a diary which has disappeared. Quakers and other Nonconformist groups played an important role in printing narratives by women below the level of the gentry.

[15] Some narrated lives are T. Brooks, *The Legacy of a Dying Mother ... Being the Experiences of Mrs Susanna Bell* (London, 1673), pp. 44–61; C. Wordsworth, 'The Conversion of Mary Hurl, Lace Maker's Apprentice', *Wiltshire Archaeological and Natural History Magazine*, XXXV (1907), pp. 103–13.

[16] S. Bury, *An Account of the Life and Death of Mrs Elizabeth Bury* (Bristol, 1720), sig. A3.

[17] Women often began autobiographies or biographies with a preface to their children. See, for example, *The Memoirs of Anne, Lady Halkett and Ann, Lady Fanshawe*, ed. J. Loftis (Oxford, 1979), pp. 101–2.

[18] Dame Sarah Cowper commented before her diary, 'Books generally begin with a preface which draws in the Reader to go on. But upon review of my manuscripts I think the beginning will forbid any further reading.' Cowper, *Diary*.

[19] Women as well as men invented new forms of shorthand. Mrs Bathsua Makin invented a new shorthand which she called 'radiography'. See R. C. Alston (ed.), *A Bibliography of the English Language from the Invention of Printing to the Year 1800*, VIII (Leeds, 1966), p. 1602. (I am indebted to Dr Vivian Salmon for this reference.)

[20] D. Gardiner, *English Girlhood at School* (Oxford, 1929), p. 269.

[21] Bury, *Account*, pp. 9–10.

[22] T. Rogers, *The Character of a Good Woman* (London, 1697), sig. e 5.

[23] J. Evelyn, *The Life of Margaret Godolphin* (London, 1904), p. 110.

[24] Sarah Savage, Diary (1686 *et seq.*), CCRO, D/Basten/8, f. 1.

[25] Austen, *Diary*, f. 4ᵛ.

[26] Walker, *Holy Life*, p. 5.

[27] Samuel Pepys, *The Diary of Samuel Pepys*, ed. R. C. Latham and W. Matthews, 11 vols (London, 1970–83), IV, p. 9.

[28] A number of diaries mentioned by contemporaries are now lost. See, for example, E. Burnet, *A Method of Devotion*, 3rd edn (London, 1713), p. xvi; S. Clarke, *The Lives of Sundry Eminent Persons* (London, 1683), pp. 152–8; F. Atterbury, *A Discourse Occasioned by the Death of ... Lady Cutts* (London, 1698), p. 14; Rogers, op. cit., sig. e 5; E. Staunton, *A Funerall Sermon Preacht ... At the Funerall of ... Elizabeth Wilkinson* (Oxford, 1659), p. 24.

[29] Even diaries which are not primarily devotional tend to be filled with providential language, like those of Mary Woodforde and Elizabeth Freke.

[30] Earl of Stirling, *Recreations with the Muses* (London, 1637), p. 107 (*Doomsday*, Hour 5, stanza 55).

[31] Bury, *Account*, p. 9.

[32] Savage, Diary (CCRO), f. 1.

[33] J. Beadle, *The Journal or Diary of a Thankful Christian* (London, 1656), sig. b 4.

[34] R. Rogers, *Seven Treatises* (London, 1603), pp. 294–404. For his diary, see W. Knappen, *Two Elizabethan Diaries* (Chicago, Ill., 1933).

[35] Several were written by women: for example, Burnet, op. cit.; [Susanna Hopton], *Daily Devotions* (London, 1673); *The Countess of Morton's Daily Exercise* (Dublin, 1723). For the Puritan practice of self-examination, see O. Watkins, *The Puritan Experience* (London, 1972), pp. 9–20.

[36] J. Featley, *A Fountain of Tears* (London, 1646), pp. 90–1.

[37] Bodl. MS Rawl. Q.e.26–7; Countess of Warwick, Diary, BL Add. MSS 27351–5.

[38] Bury, *Account*, p. 11.

[39] Beadle, op. cit., p. 109.

[40] K. Thomas, *Religion and the Decline of Magic* (Harmondsworth, 1973), pp. 90–132.

[41] For example, H. Allen, *Satan His Methods and Malice Baffled* (London, 1683), p. 8; Warwick, Diary, 26 July 1667 and 20 September 1671; Lady Anne Clifford, *The Diary of Lady Anne Clifford*, ed. V. Sackville-West (London, 1923), p. 56.

[42] Bury, *Account*, p. 11.

[43] Mordaunt, *Private Diarie*, p. 6.

[44] The Countess of Warwick was especially prone to this tendency; nearly all her confessions of sin are expressed in exaggerated language.

[45] A. Walker, *Eureka, or, The Virtuous Woman Found* (London, 1678), p. 71. Men's spiritual diaries could also present a distorted view of their temperament. See W. Haller, *The Rise of Puritanism* (New York, 1938), pp. 38–9.

[46] Bodl. MS Rawl. Q.e.26, f. 22.

47 A. Thornton, *The Autobiography of Mrs Alice Thornton*, ed. C. Jackson, Surtees Society, LXII (1875), p. 1.

48 Beadle, op. cit., p. 55.

49 Thornton, *Autobiography*, p. 39.

50 Cowper, Diary, p. 6.

51 For contemporary examples, see Bury, *Account*; Walker, *Holy Life*. For Victorian examples, see prefaces to J. B. Williams, *The Life of Mrs Savage* (London, 1848); Thornton, *Autobiography*; Countess of Warwick, *The Autobiography of Mary, Countess of Warwick*, ed. T. C. Croker, Percy Society, XXII (1848).

52 For example, the Reverend Thomas Woodroofe's editorial selections are marked on the Countess of Warwick's MS diary, BL Add. MSS 27351-5. He clearly chose passages for their saintly character.

53 The diarists are, respectively, Elizabeth Bury, Elizabeth Walker, Mary Woodforde and Sarah Savage. Mrs Savage was also the sister of Matthew Henry, the well-known biblical commentator.

54 Spiritual edification was the commonest reason cited by contemporaries for publishing individual lives. See Clarke, op. cit., sig. a3ᵛ, cited in Watkins, op. cit., p. 1. Many diarists read biographies, especially those of their own sex, for this purpose. See, for example, Bodl. MS Rawl. Q.e.26, ff. 13, 36.

55 Funeral sermons give a good idea of female devotional practice. See S. Ford, *A Christian's Acquiescence* (London, 1665); J. Collinges, *Par Nobile* (London, 1669); W. Typing, *The Remarkable Life and Death of the Lady Apollina Hall* (London, 1647); S. Denison, *The Monument or Tomb-stone* (London, 1620); J. Prude, *A Sermon at the Funeral of ... Mrs Ann Baynard* (London, 1697).

56 S. Patrick, *The Heart's Ease* (London, 1660), p. 35. He may have been thinking of women like Elizabeth Juxon, who allegedly heard nine or ten sermons a week. See Denison, op. cit., p. 86.

57 Bodl. MS Rawl. Q.e.26, ff. 5ᵛ, 6, 8; Mordaunt, *Private Diarie*, pp. 226-31; Bodl. MS Add. B. 58, ff. 14ᵛ, 18ᵛ, Warwick, Diary, January 1673; Delaval, *Meditations*, p. 40.

58 Walker, *Holy Life*, p. 33; Delaval, *Meditations*, p. 118. See also Bodl. MS Rawl. Q.e.26, May–June 1680.

59 Walker, *Holy Life*, pp. 34-5.

60 Favourites mentioned by diarists include Baxter's works, Henry Hammond's *A Paraphrase and Annotations upon All the Books of the New Testament* (1653), St Augustine's *Confessions*, Foxe's *Book of Martyrs*, Bishop Hall's *Meditations*, contemporary books of sermons, and 'lives' of pious women. For regrets about reading plays and romances, see Warwick, Diary, 6 December 1671; Delaval, *Meditations*, p. 32; Mordaunt, *Private Diarie*, p. 227.

61 For example, Bodl. MS Rawl. Q.e.26, ff. 11, 19ᵛ; Mordaunt, *Private Diarie*, pp. 226, 232; Delaval, *Meditations*, pp. 83, 118-19; Warwick, Diary,

21 and 29 August and 6 October 1671; Savage, Diary (CCRO), ff. 4ᵛ, 7, 9, 11; Cowper, Diary, pp. 9, 16, 23.

[62] Savage, Diary (CCRO), f. 8ᵛ.

[63] [R. Allestree], *The Ladies Calling* (Oxford, 1673), p. 144.

[64] Thornton, *Autobiography*, p. 234.

[65] Delaval, *Meditations*, pp. 40, 68–9, 75, 155.

[66] Savage, Diary (CCRO), 5ᵛ, 7ᵛ, 8.

[67] Ibid., 5ᵛ. Finally parting with her relations to be alone with her husband, she called it 'ye saddest day yt ever came over my head'. While preparations were being made for Elizabeth Delaval's marriage, she entered a prolonged depression (Delaval, *Meditations*, pp. 177–9, 185–6).

[68] Thornton, *Autobiography*, p. 76.

[69] BL Add. MS 27357, f. 4ᵛ. See also Evelyn, *Diary*, IV, p. 426.

[70] Walker, *Holy Life*, pp. 27–8.

[71] E. Freke, 'Mrs Elizabeth Freke her Diary, 1671–1714', *Journal of the Cork Historical and Archaeological Society*, XVII (1911), p. 1.

[72] Delaval, *Meditations*, pp. 207–8.

[73] Mordaunt, *Private Diarie*, p. 225.

[74] Savage, Diary (CCRO), f. 12.

[75] Clifford, *Diary*, pp. 20, 54, 56, 61.

[76] Cowper, Diary, pp. 1, 19.

[77] Savage, Diary (CCRO), 33ᵛ.

[78] For example, see the Countess of Bridgewater, Meditations, BL MS Egerton 607, ff. 111ᵛ–112; Thornton, *Autobiography*, pp. 234–5; Austen, Diary, f. 23; Bury, *Account*, pp. 21–2; Walker, *Holy Life*, pp. 28–9, 40.

[79] Bodl. MS Rawl. Q.e.26, f. 24ᵛ.

[80] The travel journal of Celia Fiennes so overflows with the joy of life that it is difficult to imagine she was unhappy with her condition (C. Fiennes, *The Journeys of Celia Fiennes*, ed. C. Morris (London, 1947)). For personal details which can be gleaned from the business accounts of Joyce Jeffreys, see R. G. Griffiths, 'Joyce Jeffreys of Ham Castle', *Transactions of the Worcestershire Archaeological Society*, NS, X (1933), pp. 1–32.

[81] The fifteen are Austen, Bridgewater, Bury (two marriages), Harcourt (second), Hoby, Mordaunt, Pakington, Savage, Thornton, Twysden, Walker, Warwick, Woodforde and the anonymous author of BL Add. MS 5858. The six are Clifford (two), Cowper, Freke, Delaval (first) and Mildmay.

[82] The eight cases are, respectively, Twysden, Warwick, Walker, Bury, Harcourt, Thornton, Savage and Bridgewater.

[83] The five cases are Freke, Mildmay, Delaval and Clifford (two marriages).

[84] For a good example, see Alice Thornton's negotiations prior to her marriage, in *Autobiography*, pp. 75–81.

[85] Bodl. MS Rawl. Q.e.26, f. 7ᵛ.

[86] Warwick, Diary, 26 November 1667. For the importance of 'relationes duties', see ibid., 24 December 1675, and Savage, Diary (CCRO), f. 31.

[87] Bridgewater, Meditations, f. 82^v.

[88] N. Ranew, *Solitude Improved by Divine Meditation* (London, 1670), p. 110.

[89] Warwick, Diary, 18 December 1668, 11 March and 24 December 1669, 22 August 1670.

[90] Bathurst, Diary, p. 45. The role of 'bride of Christ' is a familiar one for Roman Catholic mystics in the tradition of St Teresa of Avila but is less expected in a seventeenth-century Protestant context. For more on Protestant symbolism, see D. N. Maltz, 'The Bride of Christ is Filled with His Spirit', in J. Hoch-Smith and A. Spring (eds), *Women in Ritual and Symbolic Roles* (New York, 1978), cited in P. Mack, 'Women as Prophets During the Civil War', *Feminist Studies* VIII (1982), p. 39, note 5. For another example of erotic symbolism, see Beaumont, op. cit., pp. 12, 21.

[91] Margaret Cavendish, Duchess of Newcastle, *Playes* (London, 1662), p. 160.

[92] Savage, Diary (CCRO), ff. 28, 40, 40^v, 41, 44; P. M. Crawford, 'Attitudes to Pregnancy from a Woman's Spiritual Diary, 1687–8', *LPS*, XXI (1978), pp. 43–5; Williams, *Life of Mrs Savage*, pp. 60–4.

[93] Bridgewater, Meditations, f. 25^v.

[94] Ibid., f. 33. This fear was particularly associated with breaking the contemporary taboo on intercourse at the time of the woman's menstrual period. See P. M. Crawford, 'Attitudes to Menstruation in Seventeenth-Century England', *P & P*, XCI (1981), p. 62.

[95] Mordaunt, *Private Diarie*, pp. 14–15, 235.

[96] Thornton, *Autobiography*, p. 95.

[97] Warwick, Diary, 24 August 1667.

[98] Sarah Savage, Diary (1714 *et seq.*), Bodl. MS Eng. Misc. e.331, p. 19.

[99] F. Jessop, *Sir Roger Twysden* (London, 1965), p. 28.

[100] Walker, *Holy Life*, pp. 61–4, 99.

[101] Bathurst, Diary, p. 13.

[102] Warwick, Diary, entries for 16 May 1667, 1668, 1671, 1672, 1673, 1675, 1676 and 1677. (Some parts of the diary are missing.)

[103] Walker, *Eureka*, p. 49.

[104] Thornton, *Autobiography*, p. 126. Mrs Thornton was later lectured by her 6-year-old son for grieving excessively over her husband's death; ibid., pp. 261–3.

[105] Bridgewater, Meditations, 114^v–115.

[106] Walker, *Holy Life*, p. 116.

[107] *Woodforde Papers and Diaries*, ed. D. H. Woodforde (London, 1932), pp. 14–17, 21–3.

[108] Clifford, *Diary*, p. 16.

[109] The eleven are Austen, Bathurst, Bury, Clifford, Freke, Mildmay, Mordaunt, Warwick, Savage, Thornton and the author of BL Add. MS 5858.

[110] M. Holmes, *Proud Northern Lady* (London, 1975), pp. 132–75; S. Mendelson, 'Women in Seventeenth-Century England: Three Studies',

unpublished Oxford D.Phil. thesis (1981), pp. 205–13. For another example of the type, Lady Joan Barrington, see A. Searle, *Barrington Family Letters, 1628–1632*, CS, 4th ser., XXVIII (1983), pp. 16–21.

[111]   Austen, Diary, ff. 35–40, 45, 57, 68^v.

[112]   Thornton, *Autobiography*, p. 261.

[113]   G. Holles, *Memorialls of the Holles Family*, ed. A. C. Wood, CS, 3rd ser., LV (1937), pp. 230–4; A. Boate, *The Character of a Trulie Vertuous and Pious Woman ... Margaret Dungan* (Paris, 1651), sigs A5–B4.

[114]   For an excellent discussion of these ideals, see Kathleen Davies, 'Continuity and Change in Literary Advice on Marriage', in R. Outhwaite (ed.), *Marriage and Society* (New York, 1981), pp. 58–80.

[115]   A. Clark, *Working Life of Women in the Seventeenth Century*, ed. M. Chaytor and J. Lewis (London, 1982), pp. 62–4, 87–92; P. Clark, 'The Migrant in Kentish Towns 1580–1640', in P. Clark and P. Slack, *Crisis and Order in English Towns 1500–1700* (Oxford, 1976), pp. 142–4; Spufford, op. cit., pp. 53, 77 n. 28; [anon.], *The Women's Fegaries* (London, [1675]); R. Gough, *The History of Myddle*, ed. D. Hey (Harmondsworth, 1981), p. 109.

[116]   Joyce Jeffreys, who was a talented businesswoman, seems to have been a rarity for her social class. For the Countess of Warwick's temporary 'male' role as executor, see Mendelson, op. cit., pp. 206–10.

[117]   This was one aspect of women's greater involvement in public affairs during the Civil War. For other aspects, see K. V. Thomas, 'Women in the Civil War Sects', *P & P*, XIII (1958), pp. 42–62; Mack, op. cit.

[118]   Freke, 'Diary', 15 November 1688; Woodforde, *Woodforde Papers*, pp. 13, 17, 21.

[119]   Clifford, *Diary*, p. 28.

[120]   Ibid., p. 23.

[121]   Cowper, Diary, p. 19.

[122]   Fiennes, *Journeys*, p. 1.

7 Women's published writings 1600–1700

PATRICIA CRAWFORD

1

The first English printed books appeared in the fifteenth century. While some women's writings were published in the sixteenth century, up to 1640 few women wrote for publication, and those who did were conscious of behaving in an unusual way. During the Civil Wars and Interregnum, women published in increasing numbers, and they continued to write after some setback at the Restoration.

Much of this publication by women in seventeenth-century England was ignored by their contemporaries. Subsequently, some works were forgotten, others reascribed to male authors.[1] Anne Conway's treatise, for example, *Opuscula Philosophica*, published in 1690, was ascribed to van Helmont, who had simply translated it into Latin.[2] Cataloguing practices have further obscured women's activity.[3] More recently, women's writings have attracted attention,[4] and part of the purpose of this study is to make visible the substantial body of women's writing published during the seventeenth century. In addition, it explores the impact of contemporary ideas about women upon those who wrote for publication. Although writing for publication was not a socially approved activity, women both wrote and tried to justify themselves. We may need to modify our views of the extent to which all women accepted their society's canons of behaviour. As we shall see, some women could both accept ideals about good women and their proper place in the world yet use these to behave in different ways. Finally, women's reasons for their writing are discussed. Although it has been argued that women in the seventeenth century were not sufficiently conscious of themselves ever to write or speak for themselves as women,[5] their own statements suggest that they were forced to write for publication because they knew that their experiences as women were different from those of men.

In 1616 when Dorothy Leigh's book of maternal advice was published, she said that this was something 'unusual among us'.[6] She was right. From an analysis of the material in the check-list, (Appendix 1), which is discussed in Appendix 2, it is possible to calculate half-decade totals of women's publications.[7] As Table 7.1 shows, in the half-decade 1616–20, the total number of new publications by women was a mere eight. Reissues and further editions added only four. By comparison, the total number of works published in that half-decade catalogued in Pollard and Redgrave's *Short-Title Catalogue* was around 2240. That is, women's publications amounted to only 0.5 per cent of all publications in that decade (see Appendix 2, Figure 7.2). As Figure 7.1 shows, before the Civil Wars the quantity of publications by women was very small.

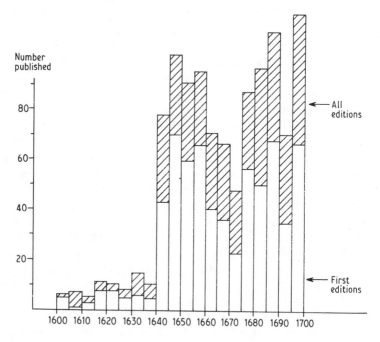

Figure 7.1 Frequency distribution of first editions and all editions of women's works published by half-decades

The impact of the Civil Wars and Interregnum upon women's publications was remarkable. The quantity of publication increased, as Table 7.1 shows, to sixty-nine new editions in the half-decade 1646–50, which was the greatest number of women's first editions in any half-decade of the century. In addition, after 1640 there was an expansion of the range of women's publications. They began to publish in political controversy, and wrote prose fictions. Increasingly, women wrote of their personal experiences and published lives and letters. Quaker women began to write in the 1650s. Their work amounted to about 20 per cent of women's output for the whole century, a disproportionate share given their numbers in society. Prophetic writings were also more numerous after 1640. Much of this was the work of a few women, such as Eleanor Douglas, Anna Trapnel, Eleanor James and Jane Lead. Despite the general trend against religious enthusiasm after 1660, women continued to publish visions. Practical advice, recipes and cures became a steady part of women's publications after 1640, and after 1670 women medical practitioners and others found that a printed advertisement was a suitable way of making themselves known.[8]

The Civil Wars and Interregnum were the high points of women's publication. They were a time of change for women's writings as for so much else. Two things were important. First, the Wars forced women to act in a number of unaccustomed roles. With husbands, fathers and sons away fighting or in exile, women were defenders of their homes, petitioners for estates and generally responsible for their families' survival. Secondly, in order to debate political issues, they had to engage in controversy. The experience of opposition and hostility forced them to refine and sharpen their arguments, and so led to further publications. This can most clearly be seen in the petitions that women published for the release of the imprisoned Leveller leaders in April and May of 1649. When they presented the first petition, the Sergeant-at-Arms told them that they had no place in public affairs:

> That the matter you petition about, is of an higher concernment than you understand. That the House gave an answer to your husbands; and therefore that you are desired to goe home, and looke after your owne businesse, and meddle with your huswifery.[9]

The women refused to accept their dismissal and returned with an even more strongly worded petition the week after. Katherine Chidley, who was probably the author,[10] was a different kind of woman from those before the Wars who had modestly and self-effacingly offered their ideas or translated those of others. She argued forcefully and confidently about political issues.

Women who wrote for publication in the seventeenth century were a small group. Approximately 231 named women wrote most of the 653 first editions. Of these, twenty-two women account for nearly half the total number, while the majority of women had only one or two publications to their names (see Appendix 2, Figure 7.3). Not surprisingly, women of aristocratic and gentry origin published out of proportion to their numbers in the society. There were differences in the circumstances of publication. The women of higher social rank could pay for their works to be published, unlike Aphra Behn who sought to make a living by her writing. The poems of aristocratic women might circulate in manuscript until they were finally published, perhaps by an admiring male relative. Anne Bradstreet's poetry, for example, was published without her consent and with an extravagant title: *The tenth muse lately sprung up in America*.[11] At the other end of the social scale, a poor and illiterate woman, Elinor Channel, was assisted in publishing her message by Arise Evans.[12] The women authors were not a homogeneous group. Even those literary women who wrote plays, poems and prose fiction increasingly lacked access to the literary world, and were not themselves numerous enough to constitute an alternative literary society. Nevertheless, women wrote with increasing self-confidence and in growing numbers during the seventeenth century, a remarkable achievement in the face of intense social opposition.

2

In the seventeenth-century, it was generally believed that women belonged to a separate sphere. Their place was the household. Ideally, a good woman was modest and silent, although there was a large literature and folklore on the supposed garrulity of women.[13] Good women knew that they should be self-effacing. Elizabeth Joceline, for example, advised her unborn child that, if she should be a daughter, 'remember thou art a Maid, and such ought thy modesty to bee, that thou shouldst scarce speak, but when thou answerest'.[14]

Books were claimed as 'part of man's prerogative' so that women writing were conscious that they invaded territory that men had defined as their own. Anne Finch's observation on a woman writing poetry is well known.

Alas! A woman that attempts the pen,
Such an intruder on the rights of men.[15]

Margaret Cavendish was told to take up her sewing:

Work *Lady* work, let writing *Books* alone
For surely *wiser Women* nere wrote one.[16]

Women did write on a variety of subjects, but their range was restricted by their lack of education, which excluded them from the language of particular learned groups. Virtually all women were ignorant of Latin, the language of professional and theological discourses.[17] Educated men did not expect women to participate in their discussions. When Elizabeth Bury, who was interested in medicine, stated 'the most nice and difficult cases' in such proper terms as might be expected only from men of their own profession, medical men were surprised.[18] When Mary Wortley Montague spoke Latin, her husband-to-be was amazed, 'as if he had heard a piece of wax work talk'.[19] James I, however, was unimpressed with a 'learned maid' who was presented to him because she could speak and write in Latin, Greek and Hebrew: 'but can shee spin?' he enquired.[20] Part of the explanation of why women published very little in areas such as science, geography, genealogy and economics was their lack of schooling.[21] Other women excused themselves because of their limited education. The dramatist Aphra Behn, writing an apology for a woman speaker in a dialogue about Copernicus, could defend him only 'as far as a woman's learning can go'. For her own work, she claimed that a woman 'is not supposed to be well versed in the terms of Philosophy.'[22] Margaret Cavendish apologized, in her life of her husband the Duke of Newcastle, for her ignorance, 'of the Rules of Writing Historie'.[23] Weakness in words, especially in debate with the learned, was also pleaded by Susanna Parr in 1659 in her controversy with the minister Lewis Stuckley. She wanted him to cease printing his angry books against 'weake women (who are not able to speak for themselves in *Print* ... so well as men, especially Schollers).'[24]

Women were aware that there were certain rules for different kinds of discourse, and they felt uneasy at not knowing them. Even in the religious sects, where inspiration was to replace formal learning, women resented their exclusion from university education. The time is coming, said Mary Cary in 1651, when 'not onely men but women shall prophesie; ... not onely those that have University-learning but those who have it not; even servants and handmaids'.[25] Anna Trapnel, a prophet in the late 1640s, declared that Christ will come and 'deep speech gathered up and fetcht from both *Cambridge* and *Oxford* Universities shal not affright the Lords flock, though they stammer, they shal be understood'. Trapnel rejected the 'deep subtile speeches, though they be brought forth with a Latine tongue, and in Greek expressions.'[26]

Women's access to education had important consequences for them as authors and for their relationship with their audience. Studies of literacy suggest that the bulk of those who could read in seventeenth-century England were male. David Cressy, basing his calculations on the ability to sign one's name, argues that the male literacy rate may have been 30 per cent and the female 10 per cent in the 1640s at the time of the Civil Wars, rising to 45 per cent for males in the early eighteenth century and 30 per cent for females.[27] This may underestimate literacy, for, as Margaret Spufford has shown, writing was a skill taught separately from and later than reading.[28] Even if female literacy was higher than Cressy calculates, and was increasing faster than the male rate, the proportion of male to female readers remained greater. Any woman who wrote for publication was therefore uneasily aware that she was addressing herself to a largely male audience. Many tried to direct their work to their own sex. There was a female audience for godly publications, for, although some men joked about women reading nothing but recipes and romances, much of their reading was of religious works.[29] Women who wrote works of piety knew that they had an audience among their own sex.

In writing for publication, women risked their reputations. In seventeenth-century England, modesty was strongly linked with sexual morality: an immodest woman was an unchaste one. A woman's air of freedom might disgrace her whole family: 'a daughter that is bold dishonoureth both hir father, and hir husband.'[30] Silence was an essential component of modesty. A preacher commended Anne Baynard for 'her great Modesty. ... For her Words were very few.'[31] Women who wished to speak publicly knew that they risked their honour. Elizabeth Warren was conscious of changing 'the shape of my silent modestie' by writing, but declared that a message of grace could not deprive a woman of her virtue. She left her vindication to the Lord.[32] Playwrights faced particular problems, for ideas about propriety restricted their choice of subjects and of words. The whole female sex could be impugned by their boldness. John Dryden advised an aspiring woman poet to avoid the licence of style which

Aphra Behn allowed herself, for this gave 'some scandall to the modesty of her sex'.[33] Susannah Centlivre, the playwright, asked her readers' pardon for her 'bluntness'. Modest language, she said, 'from the truly Vertuous is expected', but in seeking to expose the vices of the seeming religious she created some unvirtuous characters.[34] In writing of sin for a conventional moralizing piece, Elizabeth Major, in 1656, answered the anticipated criticism:

> it may be some will say, There are sins named, that your blushing Sex should want confidence to mention. To this I answer, Sure I am, that fewer ever writ against them than committed them: ... therefore I desire to put on a holy confidence, and not to blush to declare the hatred of my soul against any of them.[35]

Many women knew that as they defied the canons of ideal behaviour by publishing, they would be attacked. Elizabeth Poole admitted that people might be surprised that she should hold up her head any more after the criticisms made of her message.[36] Other women were aware of the disapproval of their friends and relations: 'the frownes and strange speeches of those who were my familiar freinds' were enough to deter Mary Pope for a time.[37] Sometimes the reactions survive, so that we can see that the women were not imagining hostility where none existed. Elizabeth Avery published a work of Scriptural prophecy in 1647, 'not fearing any thing in way of opposition from the creature', but was attacked in print by her brother in 1650: 'your printing of a Book, beyond the custom of your Sex, doth rankly smell.' He described it as 'an attempt above your gifts and Sex'; 'What will you make your self to be?'[38] Anne Docwra, a Quaker, was attacked by Francis Bugg as 'the old Woman with her Incoherent Fables'. He taunted her by imagining critical responses: 'Your Brother, Giles Barnardiston, would have scorned to have dipt his Pen in such muddy Ink as you have done'.[39] Individual responses to hostility varied, but some who published displayed courage. Although Mary Cary was attacked in print in 1649 – 'a pity that a woman of her parts should build with so much confidence upon so rotten a foundation' – she was unabashed. She delayed the publication of *New Jerusalem's Glory* until 1651 because she considered that the world was not ready for it earlier. In order to disarm her critics, her preface contained statements by three ministers praising her message.[40] Elizabeth Tipper forced herself to be brave: 'to rebuke Vice boldly, requires more courage than our Sex usually pretend to'.[41]

Not all women were criticized for publishing. Margaret Cavendish, Duchess of Newcastle, had the approval of her husband, and other aristocratic women had an admiring male coterie.[42] In the previous century, Queen Elizabeth was extravagantly lauded in *The Art of English Poesie* (1589): her 'learned, delicate and noble muse, easily surmounteth all the rest that have been written before her time or since.'[43] Alice Sutcliffe's work was prefaced by men's poems praising her, and Elizabeth Warren was said to be 'The Phoenix of this Age', 'the envy and glory of her sex'.[44] But even commendation was difficult for women to enjoy, for they feared that they were being praised for their social rank and for their sex, and that men spoke out of politeness and gallantry rather than truth.[45] Women suspected references to their gender.

Some women feared that, if their writing were good, men would refuse to believe that it was their own. As Hugh Peter, in his laudatory preface to Mary Cary's prophecies observed, she wrote so well 'that you might easily think she plow'd with anothers Heifer'.[46] In 1634 George Withers pointed out that men were either over-critical of women's work 'or doubting whether from themselves it came'.[47] Could it be possible, enquired the publisher of Anne Bradstreet's poems, that they were truly her work?[48] Two Quaker women taunted Elizabeth Atkinson, who had written critically of the Friends: 'Who did help thee to compose and word thy lying Pamphlet?'[49] Doubts about Elizabeth Warren's authorship led George Jenny to ask her to authenticate her work.[50] The denial of women's intellectual abilities which prompted questions about their authorship posed further problems for women writers.

Another difficulty that women faced was men's unwillingness to take their words seriously. Since men believed that women were inferior, knew little and lacked self-control, what they had to say was not worth heeding. Not surprisingly, a woman who had something urgent to say reiterated her statement, talked harder and gained a reputation for loquacity. This may be illustrated by the account of an attempt by Katherine Chidley who preached as well as published to argue a theological issue with the Independent minister, William Greenhill, in 1645. Greenhill

> laboured to reduced to a short head all she had spoke ... she would not hold to the stating of the question ... but in stead of being satisfied or giving any answer, shee was so talkative and clamorous, wearying him with her words, that he was glad to goe away, and so left her.[51]

It was difficult for women to write when they expected that men would either ignore their words or not take them seriously.

So far I have discussed the social climate in which women wrote, and some of the negative attitudes and hostility that they anticipated and in some cases actually confronted. The ways in which women responded to this negative climate varied. First, some adopted the values of their opponents and used their gender as an excuse. They pleaded the ideology that made them inferior as an apology for their inadequacies. Late in the sixteenth century, Anne Dowriche begged her mother to excuse any faults in her work because it was 'a woman's doing'.[52] At the end of the seventeenth century, Amey Hayward was apologizing for her 'weak poems' because she was one of 'the weaker sex'.[53] This argument of female weakness was, of course, a two-edged sword, and invited readers not to take the work seriously. The preface to Dorcas Bennet's moral advice of 1670 explained that no man could quarrel with what she had to say, for 'they will get little by the victory, because they contended with one of the weakest [sic] Sex'.[54] Some women also reminded their readers that since they were, as good women, concerned with affairs of the household, this must serve as an apology for the deficiencies of their work. As Elizabeth Warren explained, 'The condition of my appointed Station puts mee continually upon such imployments, as straitens my leisure in affaires of this nature'.[55] Women neither commanded their own time nor felt that their writing was important enough to merit neglecting their usual tasks. Dorcas Bennet studied for her writing 'while others slept'.[56] 'Family cares unfit me for publication', said Susanna Parr, while Rachel Speght wrote her defence of women in such time as she could spare 'from affaires befitting my Sex'.[57]

Secondly, women responded to negative attitudes to their writing by showing anxiety about their sexual identity. Some believed that by acting in ways not sanctioned by the ideology they risked their femininity. Elizabeth Cellier, a Roman Catholic midwife who was tried for high treason in 1680, feared that her bold attempts to justify herself 'may be thought too Masculine'.[58] Womanliness and certain abilities seemed incompatible: Aphra Behn labelled her poetic gifts as 'my Masculine Part the Poet in me'.[59] Eleanor James, on the other hand, wanted to be male: 'O that I were but a Man', she wrote in at least two of her pamphlets. She was convinced that James II would have heeded a man's warnings about his Roman Catholicism.[60] Women who published anonymously may betray ambivalence about their sexual identity, suppressing their gender in order that their words might be taken seriously. Eleanor Douglas published *A Warning to the Dragon* anonymously in 1625: 'to maske my name with boldnesse to unmaske Error I craue no Pardon'.[61] Bathsua Makin, in *An essay to revive the antient education of gentlewomen* published in 1673, went to the lengths of saying in the preface 'I am a Man my self, that would not suggest a thing prejudicial to our Sex'.[62] Catherine Cockburn's defence of Locke was anonymous in 1702. Her reason, explained in a later edition, was her belief 'that the name of a woman would be a prejudice against a work of that nature'.[63] Mary Astell published anonymously, knowing 'that when a woman appears in Print, she must certainly run the gauntlet'.[64] Contemporary comment on her work and her gender suggest that her assessment was correct. Dean Atterbury commended her observations on his sermons as containing 'not an expression that carries the least air of her sex from the beginning to the end of it.'[65]

Thirdly, hostility to their writing encouraged other women to escape criticism by writing specifically for their own sex. Slightly more of their works were dedicated to women than to men.[66] This seems particularly significant if we remember that one of the purposes of dedication was to secure a patron, and that women had less money to dispose of than men. Dedicatory statements show that women felt more comfortable in addressing members of their own sex: Mary Cary dedicated her work to Elizabeth Cromwell, Bridget Ireton and Margaret Roll, 'being of your own sex'.[67] Elizabeth Richardson addressed her book of prayers to her daughters and daughters-in-law, not including her sons, 'lest being men, they misconstrue my well-meaning; yet I presume that you my daughters will not refuse your Mothers teaching'.[68] Even if women did not present their works to women, many addressed their own sex. Dorothy Partridge, a midwife who published an almanac, claimed that her work was 'adapted to the Capacity of the Female Sex'.[69] Jane Owen, a Catholic, wrote a treatise on purgatory for all English Catholics, but towards the end she addressed women directly, saying that to other women she felt 'the more bold to speake freely'.[70] However, by the early eighteenth century, women playwrights and scholars knew that they could not rely on other women to support them against the 'Critick Men'.[71] Elizabeth Elstob, the Anglo-Saxonist, was bitter about members of her own sex who declared that 'they hated any woman that knew more than themselves'.[72] Thus, as a last resort, some authors defied all audience response: 'I matter not how I appear to Man' were the opening words of Susannah Bateman's work.[73] 'Tis for our Selves, not them, we *Write*,' said Anne Finch the poet.[74]

Fourthly, by choosing a subject deemed appropriate for women, writers could both conform to social norms and publish without too much conflict. Religious writing of various kinds was the most important area of publication for seventeenth-century women. Nearly half their output consisted of works of piety, prayers, meditations, godly advice, prophecies and Quaker warnings, admonitions and lamentations.[75] Religion was always important to women. After the Reformation, ministers encouraged women to take responsibility for their own salvation, so here women had an area of freedom. As Katherine Chidley said, a husband had authority over bodily and civil things, but not over a wife's conscience.[76] Further, Keith Thomas has shown how the multiplication of religious sects during the 1640s gave many women the opportunity to participate directly in religious life.[77]

The Bible provided women with a number of justifications for publication. Women cited the parable of the talents. Everyone, explained Rachel Speght in 1621 and Anne Halkett in 1701, was expected to give an account, even if only of one talent. Elizabeth Bathurst, a Quaker, spelt out that this applied to women as well as men.[78] The parable of the poor widow led women to conclude that each must contribute her mite.[79] Quaker women used the Bible to justify their testimony. No one could hide her light under a bushel.[80] The Bible also provided role models. The women petitioners of 1642, 1649 and 1653 cited Deborah, Jael and Esther.[81] Mary Pope begged the members of Parliament in 1647 to listen to her, just as King David had listened to the woman of Tekoah (2 Samuel 14:12).[82] The title of a book sometimes echoed a Biblical model, as did *Susanna's apologie against the elders. Or, a vindication of Susanna Parr*.

The Protestant church set store by religious experience, and this indirectly encouraged publication. Women began by keeping records of their spiritual lives. Some of their accounts were published post-humously. Anne Venn's book of meditations was not found until after her death, and was then published.[83] Susanna Bell wanted her experiences published after her death, as they were in 1673.[84] However, Jane Turner published her own account, after initial hesitation: 'I thought I might seem to walk in an untrodden path, having never seen anything written before in this manner and method'.[85] Her work appeared in 1653, and in the same year Vavasor Powell published a collection of religious experiences which included several spiritual autobiographies by women.[86]

Maternity offered another subject on which women could publish without implicitly attacking conventional values, and this was an important area of publication earlier in the century. A group of five mothers published chiefly before the Civil Wars.[87] In 1622 the Countess of Lincoln wrote specifically to persuade mothers to breastfeed their babies.[88] The more general advice books of Elizabeth Grymeston, Dorothy Leigh and Elizabeth Joceline were published posthumously in 1604, 1616 and 1624 respectively. The only maternal advice printed during the period 1640–60 was that of Elizabeth Richardson, appearing in 1645.[89] These women were of impeccable social background: they were all gentlewomen. One was a countess, another a bishop's grand-daughter and another the wife of a Chief Justice. They took their maternity seriously and expected their contemporaries to do the same.[90] Their advice was conventional. Although Leigh's *Mothers blessing* was published posthumously, she intended publication. She knew that to show her writing publicly might provoke censure, but 'motherly affection' and wifely duty overrode all scruples. A mother's love for her children, she claimed, was beyond the bounds of reason: to save her children's souls, 'a Mother will venture to offend the world'. She offered the customary advice about salvation, but directed it to girls as well as boys. Both sexes needed to read the Bible.[91]

Elizabeth Richardson's chief excuse to those who condemned her 'boldness' in publishing was that her legacy to her daughters was simply one of 'devotions or prayers'.[92] While the material published was conventional, the fact of publishing was not. Another group of mothers who published collectively later in the century were Quaker women. Less inhibited, they offered their advice on the basis of their own maternal experiences: 'for we which have been Mothers of Children and Antient Women in Our Families, do know in the Wisdom of God, what will do in Families'.[93] The general tenor of their admonitions was conservative. The York Women's Meeting of 1692, for example, urged women to be 'good examples to your Children and Servants'.[94] Nevertheless, the use of conservative arguments should not blind us to the radicalism of these women's actions in publishing their ideas.

Finally, some were prepared to criticize aspects of their society. Many of these women belonged to religious sects. Because the sects allowed women a much more active role in religion, many of the publications in the 1640s and 1650s were by women with sectarian backgrounds. Quaker women, in particular, published extensively,[95] as did women prophets. The sects offered women the chance to prophecy. As a religious experience which required no learned background, prophecy gave women the opportunity to be taken seriously.[96] As prophets, women were heeded differently from those who had reached their conclusions in more orthodox ways. For example, while the members of Parliament told the women petitioners to go home and be quiet, the Army Council – admittedly a body more open to spiritual infiltration – spent two days examining Elizabeth Poole about her prophecy. The Lord had directed her that the Army could put the King on trial but not execute him. Her prophecy was listened to, published, and written about in the newsbooks, but silence greeted Mary Pope's publication arguing against the Army Remonstrance which stated that the King should be tried. Pope's argument was based on a reasoning from Scriptural texts, but no one answered her or even mentioned her pamphlet.[97] Sometimes the prophecies or visions of women in a state of trance were published by men, such as those of Sara Wight or Anna Trapnel during the 1640s and 1650s.[98] After the Restoration, religious enthusiasm was suspect, so that although women continued to publish prophecies by the end of the century they were less heeded. Charles I had imprisoned Eleanor Douglas for her prophetic activities, but at the court of Charles II, Elinor James was a figure of fun.[99]

From 1641, women participated in public political activity, and on several occasions during the 1640s and 1650s they joined together to present petitions to Parliament. In so doing, they were forced to argue that women possessed political rights. Those who petitioned in February 1642 disclaimed any desire for equality with men, but offered 'several Reasons why their sex ought thus to petition as well as the men'. Political activity was, they said, part of 'that duty we owe to God, and the cause of the Church'.[100] At that date, on the eve of the Civil Wars, the members of Parliament thanked them and expressed their concern for the women.[101] Later, when women petitioned on behalf of the imprisoned Leveller leaders in April and May of 1649, the members of Parliament were less receptive, for not only were the women involved in the general radical campaign, but their petitions made some of the most extreme claims about women's social role of any in the seventeenth century. When the women delivered their first petition to the House of Commons, they were told to go home;[102] but the women were neither abashed nor silenced. They returned with a second document which, thanks to this opposition, was even more forcefully and cogently argued than the first. The claims the women made were grounded in Scripture but they were developed into a far-reaching doctrine of political rights.

That since we are assured of our Creation in the image of God, and of an interest in Christ, equal unto men, as also of a proportionable share in the Freedoms of this Commonwealth, we cannot but wonder and grieve that we should appear so despicable in your eyes, as to be thought unworthy to Petition or represent our Grievances to this Honourable House. ... And are we Christians, and yet must we sit still and keep at home ... and shall we shew no sence of their sufferings? ... Let it be accounted folly, presumption, madness, or whatsoever in us, whilst we have life and breath, we will never leave them.[103]

In 1653 Katherine Chidley led a group of women presenting a petition to Parliament which was said to be signed by 6000 women.[104] The women argued that it was their right to have their petition heard because God received petitions from all, and the ancient laws of England were not contrary to the word of God. Their petition included an attack on the members for their luxurious lifestyle.[105] By the 1690s the printer Elizabeth Johnson could use the language of political rights to make a feminist point: the male claims to monopolize sense were 'Violations on the *Liberties of Free-born English Women*'.[106] During the century, some women had gained a way of conceptualizing political rights and roles, and were learning how conservative ideas could be put to radical purposes.

3

Obviously not all women took society's advice to be quiet. An examination of their statements about why they wrote for publication reveals various kinds of compulsion.

'The word of the Lord came unto me, saying write, and again I say write': thus began Dorothy White, a Quaker, in 1659, under the irresistible command of God.[107] Quaker women felt freer than others to publish their works, as they knew that the Society of Friends recognized neither male nor female in the Lord.[108] They, as other Friends, were guided by the spirit of the Lord: 'I am moved in the everlasting Spirit of Truth' was a common statement.[109] Some were directly ordered to write. Priscilla Cotton doubted whether her words would be heeded, but the Lord had told her, 'Whether they will hear or forbear, publish it.'[110] Susannah Blandford was 'incouraged by the Immortal God to Print this'.[111] Many of the Quaker women's publications were warnings, admonitions or lamentations. Most were a woman's sole venture into print, and show a strong sense of duress. 'This Warning and Reproof ... I dare not with hold from this my Native Land,' wrote Elizabeth Redford.[112] Some women could neither rest nor eat until they had published.[113] Their message was a burden to them until it was in print: 'in true love to your Immortal Souls, have I cleared my Conscience'.[114] They feared the sin of blood guilt which would lead to their punishment from the Lord. The 7000 women who petitioned Parliament against tithes in 1659 did so 'not to be guilty of innocent blood'.[115] The supposedly divine origin of their messages gave Quaker women authority and pride. Dorothea Gotherson told King Charles II that what the Lord had put into her heart to write was not beneath the dignity of a king to read, 'which many think above me to write, in respect of my sex'.[116] 'Take this Counsel, though from a woman', the widowed Joan Whitrowe told King William: 'The Lord is no respecter of persons.'[117] More mundanely, many Quaker women said that they wrote to help others, or to declare their experiences 'for the benefit of those that are passing through'.[118] The women's meetings offered advice particularly to young people.

A desire for justice impelled some women to publish. While many of their printed petitions were formal documents,[119] others were personal pleas. For example, two sisters of a murdered gentleman asked for justice, 'obliged thereunto by the Bonds of common nature, as well as those of the strictest affection'.[120] Mary Blaithwaite addressed her complaint to the Lord Protector, Oliver Cromwell, in 1654. She had worn out her friends 'to get justice', but as they were ineffective, she was compelled to make herself 'a foole in Print'.[121] Other women published for personal vindication. 'I was forced to print', wrote the midwife Hester Shaw, in order to right the world's view.[122] So, too, wrote Susanna Parr after she was excommunicated in 1654. Her good name, she claimed, was 'worth more than riches, and the next in esteeme to life it self'. Although she pleaded female and personal weakness, she was determined to resist the charges against her.[123] In addition to these formal and personal documents, the women's petitions of the 1640s and 1650s complained of the subject's deprivation of liberty and rights.[124]

Some women jeopardized their marriages in order to write. Lady Eleanor Davis was furious with her husband, Sir John, for burning her prophecies. She predicted his death within three years. (Her reputation as a prophet was enhanced when he died a week later.)[125] Eleanor lived on to publish more single titles than any other woman in the century.[126] Anne Wentworth left her husband because he hindered her work. She was willing to return 'provided I may have my just and necessary liberty to attend a more then ordinary call and command of God to publish things which concern the peace of my own Soul, and of the whole Nation.'[127] Obviously she took her writing seriously, and so too did other women, some of whom spoke of it as their child. 'Tis my Childe', said Margaret Cavendish, herself childless.[128] Of her meditations Elizabeth Major wrote that, 'though I was not ambitious of a beautiful babe, yet I confess I would gladly have had it appear comely'.[129] 'This naked Child' was the description of Sarah Jones, a dyer's wife.[130] The language of a woman in labour was used by Elizabeth Poole, whose message was 'the Babe Jesus in mee'. She said that in writing 'The pangs of a travelling [travailing] woman were upon me'.[131]

Many women's publications betray a compulsion to write. Although Anne Finch knew that the courtiers would laugh at a versifying maid of honour, 'an irresistible impulse' drove her to poetry.[132] Mary Pope found 'God over-powring my spirit, and as it were forcing me on'.[133] Mary Cary wrote because the saints, like Luther, could not be silent.[134] Elizabeth Warren was conscious of 'sex-deficiency', but her words were wrung out of her, just as the dumb son of Croesus spoke when his father was in danger.[135] Women knew that their actions put them outside the normal boundaries. 'I walk alone as a woman foresaken', declared Joan Whitrowe after she had left her family to walk 200 miles to deliver her message from the Lord.[136]

In seventeenth-century England, women knew that their ideas were not so highly valued as those of men of the same social rank. Nevertheless, because some knew that their experiences as women were dissimilar from those of men, they wrote to bear witness to their own different reality. They knew, for example, that marriage was a loss of freedom. Jane Barker exalted the single life for women.[137] Jane Owen, a Catholic, wrote of marriage as a subjection to a man, and widowhood as the time 'your states are in your owne disposall'.[138] Women were aware of the bonds of marriage in a way that they knew men were not, as Anne Finch in one of her manuscript poems, 'The Unequal Fetters', poignantly shows:

> Marriage does but slightly tye Men
> Whil'st close Pris'ners we remain
> They the larger Slaves of Hymen

Still are begging Love again
At the full length of all their chain.[139]

Motherhood was a unique experience which led not just to advice
books for children but also to publications in other areas. Mary Pope
published her views about civil power in 1647: 'God having made me
a Mother in Israel, I thought it my duty to put [out] my helping hand,
having good warrant out of Gods word so to doe.'[140] Strength of
maternal feeling could even contribute to a vision of an ideal world
which was unique. While men published treatises of utopias and
devised constitutional schemes for better government, women envisaged a different perfection. Mary Cary, a Fifth Monarchist, published
her *Mappe of the New Jerusalem* in 1651. It came directly from her
experiences as a woman and a mother: there would be no deaths of
children and dear relations. With such a vision, Mary Cary could not
be silent. She had no alternative but to write for publication:

> So that this is clear, No infant of days shall die; none shall die
> while they are young: all shall come to a good old age. They shall
> not be afflicted for the loss of their children.[141]

Knowing that the female perspective was different, some wrote
advice for their own sex. Hannah Wolley counselled girls about their
choice of employment. If they wanted to be nursemaids, then they
must love young children, for the nurse's life was not easy. Her
emphasis differed from that of the physicians who advised people to
choose a nurse on criteria such as the colour of her complexion or the
quality of milk, rather than her attitude to the child.[142] Another
woman anonymously suggested that girls should learn to keep
accounts rather than to embroider.[143] Jane Sharp was the only
woman to write a handbook to help midwives aid their own sex.[144]
Men might be learned, she observed, but in childbirth 'It is not hard
words that perform the work, as if none understood the Art that
cannot understand Greek'.[145] Mary Trye and the almanac writers,
Sarah Jinner and Mary Holden, tried to meet women's need for
gynaecological advice and medical information. On such matters
women looked to each other: 'Women have a more knowne simpathy
& feeling of one anothers paines & perills,' wrote the pseudonymous
author of *The womens sharpe revenge*.[146]

Gender could act as an incentive to publication. Because women
were weak, they claimed that the Lord had chosen them as instruments.
The women who petitioned against tithes in 1659 knew that their
action was unusual: 'it may seem strange to some that women should

appear in so public a manner as this of tithes.' This, Mary Forster blandly observed, was 'the work of the Lord'.[147] Women petitioners to the Parliament in 1653 claimed that the very weakness of women was the reason why the Lord used them: 'nothing is more manifest then that God is pleased often times to raise up the weakest means to work the mightiest effects.'[148]

While women in seventeenth-century England implicitly challenged existing ideas about their roles by the mere act of writing, some delivered an explicit challenge. These women believed that women suffered from systematic social injustice because of their sex. For this they may be termed feminists.[149] Many showed feminist sentiments without arguing a case at length. For example, in 1611 Aemilia Lanyer contested some of the contemporary wisdom about women, arguing that the Fall was the fault of Adam not Eve: 'We know right well he did discretion lack.' Men ought to abandon their false claims to superiority:

> Then let vs haue our Libertie againe,
> And challendge to your selues no Sou'raigntie;
> You came not in the world without our paine,
> Make that a barre against your crueltie.[150]

The author of *Triumphs of female wit*, published in 1683, made a feminist protest in rejecting the destiny of 'needles and puddings' for women.[151] Margaret Cavendish echoed the conventional ideas about women in many prefaces, but in her imaginative fictions she painted a very different picture of their roles. Women as well as men, she wrote, had souls to be cultivated, but out of custom they were given only 'low imployments' which stunted their development, 'so as we are become like worms that only live in the dull earth of ignorance'. 'We are kept like birds in cages to hop up and down in our houses',

> we are never imployed either in civil nor marshall affaires, our counsels are despised, and laught at, the best of our actions are troden down with scorn, by the over-weaning conceit men have of themselves and through a dispisement of us.[152]

Feminists were social determinists. Nature had divided humanity into two sexes without intending any great difference in intellect, said Hannah Wolley.[153] Many feminists subscribed to conspiracy theories: men had sought 'to make us more weake by our Nurture'.[154] The complaint was reiterated by Sarah Jinner in 1658,[155] and again anonymously in 1683. Men's power depended upon keeping women ignorant.

> For should we understand as much as they,
> They fear their Empire might decay.[156]

Because women's inferior social position was ascribed to custom and lack of education, several gentlewomen published pleas for improved schooling.[157] The work of the German scholar, Anna Maria Schurman, was translated into English in 1659 as a moderate demand for better education and was in turn cited by Bathsua Makin. Makin denied that she was arguing for equality, much less the superiority of women over men. Women should be trained in their housewifely roles first. Further education would make them better wives and mothers, for ignorant mothers would breed their children as 'a generation of baboons'.[158] Although Makin used conservative arguments and appealed to precedents of learned women in the past, the radical potential was there: if women were educated in Greek and Latin, how could their thoughts be confined? Latin and Greek may not have made men radical, but they were marked out as male territory. If women could secure the right to education, they could gain other rights. 'We covet Learning,' said the woman who found a life of sewing and cooking unsatisfactory.[159] Even Hannah Wolley, who believed that the purpose of life was usefulness, sought a higher destiny for women than breeding and cleaning: 'Vain man is apt to think we were meerly intended for the Worlds propagation, and to keep its humane inhabitants sweet and clean.'[160] The household was not an attractive sphere to all women: 'the dull mannage of a servile house', Anne Finch called it.[161]

Some feminist publications belong to the literary debate about the nature of woman, a debate with a long history and a rhetoric of its own. There were a number of treatises on the subject published in the sixteenth and seventeenth centuries, many of which used similar arguments, such as that women were part of God's creation, and that men should remember that women were their mothers. The earliest published contribution by a woman to this debate in England appeared in 1589 under the pseudonym of Jane Anger.[162] Around 1617 the publication of a violently misogynist piece, *The Arraignment of Lewd, Idle and Unproductive Women*, by Joseph Swetnam, provoked three replies under women's names. Constantia Munda and Esther Sowernam were obvious pseudonyms, and the former may not even have been a woman.[163] The third, Rachel Speght, later published another treatise on a religious subject.[164] All three claimed that women were men's equals, and Sowernam even hinted at female superiority. Both Speght and Sowernam used the creation story to demonstrate that woman was created from Adam's side to be his equal, not out of his foot to be crushed.[165]

In 1640 *The womens sharpe revenge*, published under two pseudonyms, Mary Tattlewell and Joane Hit-Him-Home, showed deep suspicion of men.[166] The author deployed the familiar arguments about the meaning of the creation story, the gratitude men owed to their mothers, and the moral superiority of women. In addition, she protested at the double standard of sexual morality which made a man who got a maid with child 'a nine days wonder', while the woman was irredeemable.[167] No woman was a whore 'but there must bee a Whoore-master to make her so'. She rebutted men's standard accusations against women's sexuality, arguing that they had sexual relations only so that they might have children, rather 'than for any carnall delight or pleasure they had to accompany with men; ... they had more joy in being Mothers than in being Wives.'[168] Suspicion of male sexuality permeated her work. Some feminists thus differed from men who defended women, for they revealed dislike of and even contempt for the male sex. While none expressed the same virulence as male misogynists, some women were extremely hostile to men.

In the 1690s Mary Astell's anonymous publications offered the most sustained arguments of the century for a reassessment of women's place in society. Briefly, Astell argued, as a social determinist, that men could not prove their rights to dominance. Women were subject simply because of custom and their lack of education. Their incapacity was acquired, not natural. While Astell used these traditional arguments, she added that there was no justification for all men being born free, all women slaves. Her feminism has attracted recent discussion. Joan Kinnaird has shown that despite her reassessment of women's roles, Astell was deeply conservative, developing a 'separate spheres' argument for men and women which left women in the home in possession of moral superiority. This may be so, yet in the 1690s, what other sphere apart from the household was there for women? In another account, Ruth Perry has pointed to Astell's 'sexual disaffection, a rejection of physiological womanhood, and a satiric dismissal of men as a class'.[169]

Although women shared many of the values of men in seventeenth-century English society, there were some differences in their experiences, ideals and attitudes. They accepted that they were inferior to men, but not all saw themselves as powerless. As the Catholic Jane Owen wrote in 1634, 'though you be weake in Nature, yet know your owne strength'.[170] During the century, women developed confidence in their ability to write. After the collapse of censorship of the press in 1641, they shared with men in the greater freedom to publish. Cautiously, they began to write in different areas. Sarah Jinner, publishing an almanac in 1658, knew that she was breaking new ground: 'You may wonder to see one of our Sex in print, especially in the Celestial Sciences.'[171] By 1675, when Mary Trye published a book of medical advice for women, she found 'it is little of Novelty to see a Woman in print'.[172] There was a growing awareness that women could write for publication, and women gained a sense of their own developing literary tradition. Many of the names in their tradition are unfamiliar today, but among the poets it began with those of Greece and Rome and came up to more recent times with Anne Bradstreet and Katherine Philips.[173] By the end of the century the names of Aphra Behn and Anna Maria Schurman were added,[174] and women writers recommended works by their own sex to their readers.[175]

Women's writing was a small proportion of total publications during the seventeenth century. Much of it was for their own sex, although during the Civil Wars and Interregnum they commented on national issues for a wider audience. A hostile environment may have silenced some women, but others were undeterred. By 1700 it was no longer a wonder that a woman should write for publication. While their writing was not greatly heeded at the time, nor has it been accorded a significant place in either literary or historical traditions, a substantial body of material survives which depicts women growing in self-confidence. Vividly and directly, women's publications tell of the ideas and experiences of women in seventeenth-century England. Valuing themselves, these women could not be silent. They had no alternative but to write for publication.

APPENDIX 1: PROVISIONAL CHECKLIST OF WOMEN'S
PUBLISHED WRITINGS 1600–1700

PATRICIA CRAWFORD

This checklist is based chiefly upon the following catalogues and library searches. *STC* and Wing conventions of capitalization and punctuation have been followed.

POLLARD, A. F., and REDGRAVE, F. W. *A Short-Title Catalogue of Books Printed in England, Scotland, and Ireland ... 1475–1640*. London, 1926.
—— *A Short-Title Catalogue ... 1475–1640*. 2nd edn. vol. II only. Revised by W. A. Jackson, F. S. Ferguson and Katharine F. Pantzer. London, 1976.
WING, Donald. *Short-Title Catalogue of Books Printed in England, Scotland, Ireland, Wales, and British America and of English Books Printed in Other Countries 1641–1700*. 3 vols. New York, 1945–51.
—— *Short-Title Catalogue ... 1641–1700*. 2nd edn. Vols. I and II only. (Vol. II revised and edited by Timothy J. Crist.) New York, 1972–82.

ALDEN, John. *Wing Addenda and Corrigenda*. (Reproduced from typescript.) Charlottesville, Virginia, 1958.
ALLISON, A. F., and ROGERS, D. M. 'A Catalogue of Catholic Books in English Printed Abroad or Secretly in England, 1558–1640'. *Biographical Studies*, III, nos 3 and 4 (1956).
ARBER, Edward. *A Transcript of the Registers of the Company of Stationers, 1554–1640*. 5 vols. London, 1875–94.
—— *The Term Catalogues, 1668–1709* A.D.: *with a Number for Easter Term, 1711* A.D. 3 vols. London, 1903–6.

GARTENBERG, Patricia, and WITTEMORE, Nena. 'A Checklist of English Women in Print, 1475–1640'. *Bulletin of Bibliography and Magazine Notes*, XXXIV (1977), pp. 1–13.

SMITH, Joseph. *A Descriptive Catalogue of Friends' Books*. 2 vols. London, 1867.

WHITING, John. *Catalogue of Friends' Books*. London, 1708.

Works not found in *STC* or Wing are listed as such, and a location given according to the appropriate convention. I am grateful to the Bibliographical Society for allowing me to consult proof copy of *STC*, Vol. I.

Immensely useful as the above catalogues are, there are difficulties in using them as a guide to women's published writings. Cataloguing practices obscure joint authors, and on many occasions the cataloguer, faced with a joint publication by a man and a women, lists the man only.[176] Wing's practice of making all works anonymous unless the names are on the title-page is misleading, particularly for the vast body of Quaker literature in which there is no attempt to hide identity.

Another problem is that of anonymity, for which women may have special reasons.[177] In some cases, the author indicated that she was a woman. Some authors were subsequently identified, but presumably many women's writings remain successfully hidden.

The checklist is organized as follows:

1 Works known to be by women.
    This includes any works published by women, or containing part by a woman. The latter category is obviously incomplete and would require a search of the entire body of seventeenth-century publications. Quaker testimonies, in particular, would repay a systematic search. Included also are petitions (although some are merely formal legal documents while others are the product of organized effort by a number of women), speeches of queens, and other such official publications. Some works by English women in foreign languages have been listed, but this category too is incomplete. While these incomplete categories have not been included in the computer analysis, I have listed them here to assist those seeking to follow up publications by individual women.

2 Sixteenth-century works reprinted 1600–1700.

3 Advertisements.

4 Works which may be by women, but for which there is no clear evidence.

5 Works attributed to women, but which are now doubted.

6 Satires or spoofs purporting to be by women.

7 Brief checklist of works about rather than by women.

1 WORKS KNOWN TO BE BY WOMEN

ABBOTT, Margaret. *A testimony against the false teachers.* [1650], A70B.

ADAMS, Mary. *A warning to the inhabitants of England.* 1676, A489.

[ALLEINE, Mrs Theodosia]. *The life and death of Mr. Joseph Alleine.* 1671, A1011; anr edn, 1672, A1012; anr edn, 1672, A1013; anr edn, 1672, A1013A; anr edn, 1673, A1014; anr edn, 1677, A1015; anr edn, 1693, A1016.

ALLEN, Hannah. *Satan his methods and malice baffled.* 1683, A1025.

ANDERDON, Mary. *A word to the world.* [1662], A3084A.

ANNA OF MEDAN. *XII visions of Stephen Melish.* 1663 (trans. fr. German), not in Wing (LF).

ANNE, Queen of England. *The Princess Anne of Denmark's letter to the queen.* [1688], A3224.

ANONYMOUS. *Advice to the women and maidens of London by one of that sex.* 1678, A664; anr edn in Stephen Monteage, *Debtor and creditor ... made easie* [1682], M2488.

—— *An essay in defence of the female-sex.* 1696, A4058; anr edn, 1696, A4059; anr edn, 1697, A4060. (Maybe Mary Astell, or maybe Judith Drake, see Smith, *Mary Astell*, Appendix II.)

—— *The gentlewoman's cabinet unlocked.* 1673, G523bA; anr edn, 1675, G523A; anr edn, [1686–88], G523cA.

—— *The gentlewoman's delight in cookery.* [1690?], G523eA.

—— *The humble petition of many hundreds of distressed women.* 1642 (previously H3470, currently awaiting Wing Vol. 3).

—— *The ladies of London's petition.* [1684–8], L157.

—— *Letters of love and gallantry,* 1693, L1784, 'all written by ladies', T C, II. 466, including Catherine Cockburn.

—— Vol II, 1694, L1785.

—— *The mother's blessing,* 1685, M2937.

—— J.B., *Severall petitions presented to the Honourable Houses of Parliament. I. The humble petition of many thousands of courtiers, citizens, gentlemen, and trades-mens wives ... concerning the staying of the Queenes intended voyage.* 1641[2], B124.

—— *Spirituall experiences of sundry believers. Held forth by them at several solemne meetings, and conferences.* Ed. Vavasor, Powell 1653, P3095.

—— *To the Parliament. The humble petition of diuers afflicted women, in behalf of M. John Lilburn.* [29 July 1653], T1585.

—— *To the right honourable the house of Peers ... the humble petition of many thousands of courtiers, citizens, gentlemens and tradesmens wives.* 1641, T1628; reprinted, B124.

—— *To the supreme authority of the Commonwealth.* [August 1650], T1734.

—— *To the supreme authority of England the Commons ... the humble petition of divers well-affected women.* [24 April] 1649, T1724.

—— *To the supreme authority of the nation, the Commons ... the humble petition of divers well-affected persons of ... London.* [1649], T1730.

—— *A true copy of the petition of the gentlewomen, and tradesmenswives, in and about the City of London.* 4 February 1641 [1642], T2656; anr edn, 1642, T2657; anr edn, 1642, T2657A; anr edn, Edinburgh, 1642, T2657ᴿ.

—— *Triumphs of female wit, in some Pindaric odes.* [1683], T2295.

—— *Unto every individual member of Parliament, the humble representation.* [29 July 1653], U99.

—— *The womens petition to ... General Cromwell.* 30 October 1651, W3332.

—— Translation of Georges Scudéry, *Manzini his exquisite academicall discourses.* 1654, M557; anr edn, 1655, M558.

ARDEN, Alice. *The complaint and lamentation of.* [1633?], 732.

ARNOLD, Elizabeth (translator). Thomas Tuke, *A treatise against painting.* 1616, 24316.

[ASTELL, Mary]. *A farther essay relating to the female sex.* 1696, A4061.

—— *A serious proposal to the ladies.* 1694, A4062; anr edn, 1695, A4063; anr edn, 1696, A4064; anr edn, 1697, A4065; part II, 1697, A4065A.

—— *Six familiar essays upon marriage.* 1696, A4066.

—— *Some reflections upon marriage.* 1700, A4067.

—— and NORRIS, John

—— *Letters concerning the love of God.* 1695, N1254.

ATKINSON, Elizabeth. *A breif and plain discovery of the labourers in mistery.* 1699, A4129A.

—— *Weapons of the People called Quakers.* 1669, A4129B.

AUDELEY, Eleanor (see also DOUGLAS, Lady Eleanor). *All the kings of the earth shall prayse thee.* Amsterdam, 1633, 903.5.

—— *A warning to the dragon and all his angels.* 1625, 904.

—— *Woe to the house.* Amsterdam, 1633 (not in *STC*).

AUDLAND, Anne. *A true declaration of the suffering of the innocent.* 1655, A4195.

—— *The saints testimony finishing through suffering.* 1655, S365. (Audland one of several authors.)

—— and CAMM, Thomas. *The admirable and glorious appearance.* 1684, C394.

AULNOY, Marie Catherine la Mothe, Comtesse d'. *The ingenious and diverting letters.* 1691, A4217A; anr edn, 1692, A4217B; anr edn, 1697, A4217C.

—— *The memoirs of.* 1699, A4218.

—— *Memoirs of the court of France.* 1692, A4218A.

—— *Memoirs of the court of France relating to the amours of the Duke of Maine.* 1697, A4219.

—— *Memoirs of the court of Spain.* 1692, A4220.

—— *The novels of Elizabeth queen of England.* 1680, A4221.

—— *The novels of Elizabeth queen of England, the last part.* 1681, A4222.

—— *The present court of Spain.* 1693, A4223.

—— *The second part of the ingenious … letters.* 1692, A4223A.

—— *The third and last part of the ingenious … letters.* 1692, A4223B.

AVERY, Elizabeth. *Scripture-prophecies opened.* 1647, A4272.

—— *Spiritual autobiography* by her in John Rogers, [Hebrew] *Ohel or Beth–Shemesh*, 1653, R1813.

BARKER, Mrs Jane. *Poetical recreations.* 1688, B770.

BARWICK, Grace. *To all present rulers.* 1659, B1007A.

BASTWICK, Susannah. *To the high court of Parliament.* [1654], B1073.

BATEMAN, Susannah. *I matter not how I appear to man.* [1657], B1097.

BATHURST, Elizabeth. *An expostulatory appeal to the professors.* [1680?], B1135A.

—— *The sayings of women*. 1683, B1135B.

—— *Truth vindicated*. 1691, B1135C; anr edn, 1695, B1136.

—— *Truth's vindication*. 1679, B1137; anr edn, 1683, B1138; anr edn, 1683, B1139.

BECK, Margaret. *The reward of oppression*. 1655, B1648; anr edn, 1656, B1649.

BECKWITH, Elizabeth and Marmaduke. *A true relation of the life & death of Sarah Beckwith*. 1692, B1655B.

BEHN, Aphra. *The histories and novels of*. 1696, B1711.

—— *Histories, novels and translations*. 1700, B1711A.

—— *All the histories and novels*. 1698, B1712; anr edn, 1699, B1713; anr edn, 1700, B1714.

—— *Abdelazar*. 1677, B1715; anr edn, 1693, B1716.

—— *Aesops fables*. 1687, A703.

—— *The amorous prince*. 1671, B1717.

—— *The amours of Philander and Silvia*. 1687, B1718.

—— *The city-heiress*. 1682, B1719; anr edn, 1698, B1719A; anr edn, 1698, B1720.

—— *A congratulatory poem to her ... Majesty*. 1688, B1721; anr edn, 1688, B1722.

—— *A congratulatory poem to ... Queen Mary*. 1689, B1723.

—— *A congratulatory poem to the king's ... on the happy birth of the Prince of Wales*. 1688, B1724.

—— *The counterfeit bridegroom*. 1677, M1893.

—— *Covent Garden drollery*. 1672, C6624.

—— *The debauchee*. 1677, B1677.

—— *The Dutch lover*. 1673, B1726.

—— *The emperor of the moon*. 1687, B1727; anr edn, 1688, B1728.

—— *The fair jilt*. 1688, B1729.

—— *The false count*. 1682, B1730; anr edn, 1682, B1732; anr edn, 1697, B1731.

—— *The feign'd curtizans*. 1679, B1733.

—— *The forc'd marriage*. 1671, B1734; anr edn, 1688, B1735; anr edn, 1690, B1736.

—— *The history of the nun*. 1689, B1737.

—— *The lady's looking-glass*. 1697, B1738.

—— *The lives of sundry notorious villains*. 1678, B1739.

—— *Love letters between a noble-man and his sister*. 1684, B1740; anr edn, 1693, B1741; anr edn, 1694, B1742.

—— *Love letters between Polydorus the Gothick king*. 1689, B1689.

—— *Love letters from a nobleman ... second part*. 1693, B1743A.

—— *The luckey chance*. 1687, B1744.

—— *The lucky mistake*. 1689, B1745.

—— *Lycidus: ... together with a miscellany of new poems*. 1668, T129.

—— *Memoirs of the court of the King at Bantam*. 1697, B1746.

—— *A new song sung in Abdelazar*. [1695], B1747.

—— *Oronooko*. 1688, B1749.

—— *A pindarick on the death of our late sovereign*. 1685, B1750; anr edn, 1685, B1751; anr edn [1685?], B1752.

—— *A pindarick poem on the happy coronation*. 1685, B1753.

—— *A pindaric poem to the reverend Doctor Burnet*. 1689, B1754.

—— *A poem humbly dedicated to the great patern of piety ... Catherine*. 1685, B1755.

—— *A poem to Sir Roger L'Estrange*. 1688. B1756.

—— *Poems upon several occasions*. 1684, B1757; anr edn, 1697, B1758.

—— *A prologue by ... to her new play, called Like father*. 1682, B1759.

—— *Prologue spoken by Mrs Cook*. [1684], B1759A.

—— *Prologue to Romulus*. 1682, B1760.

—— *The Roundheads*. 1682, B1761; anr edn, 1698, B1762.

—— *The rover*. 1677, B1763; anr edn, 1697, B1764.

—— *The second part of The rover*. 1681, B1765.

—— *Sir Patient Fancy*. 1678, B1766.

—— *Three histories*. 1688, B1766A.

—— *To poet Bavius*. 1688, B1767.

—— *To the most illustrious Prince Christopher*. 1687, B1768.

—— *The town-fopp*. 1677, B1769; anr edn, 1699, B1770.

—— *The town raves. A song*. [1696], B1770A.

—— *Two congratulatory poems*. 1688, B1771.

—— *The unfortunate bride*. 1698, B1772; anr edn, 1700, B1773.

—— *The wandring beauty*. 1698, B1773A; anr edn, 1700, B1773B.

—— *The widdow ranter*. 1690, B1774.

—— *The woman turn'd bully*. 1675, W3322.

—— *Young Jemmy*. [c. 1681], B1775.

—— *The young king*. 1683, B1776; anr edn, 1698, B1777.

—— *The younger brother*. 1696, B1778.

BEHN, Aphra (translator). J. B. de Brilhac, *Agnes de Castro*. 1688, B4693A.

—— Bernard le Bovier Fontenelle, *A discovery of new worlds*. 1688, F1412; *The History of Oracles*, 1688, F1413.

BELL, Susanna. *The legacy of a dying mother*. 1673, B1802.

BENNET, Dorcas. *Good and seasonable counsel.* 1670, B1883A.

[BENTLEY, Catharine], Sister Magdalene Augustine (translator). Luke Wadding, *The history of the angelicall virgin glorious S. Clare.* Douay, 1635, 24924.

[BERNARD, Catherine]. *The Count of Amboise.* 1689, B1983.

—— *The female prince.* 1682, B1984.

BETTRIS, Jeane. *A lamentation for the deceived people of the world.* 1657, B2085.

—— *Spiritual discoveries.* 1657, B2086.

BIDDLE, Hester. *Oh! wo, wo, from the Lord.* 1659, B2864C.

—— *To the inhabitants of the town of Dartmouth.* 1659, B2864D.

—— *The trumpet of the Lord God.* 1662, B2864E.

—— *The trumpet of the Lord sounded.* 1662, B2865.

—— *A warning from the Lord God of life.* 1660, B2866.

—— *Wo to the towne of Cambridge.* [166–?], A2866A.

—— *Wo to thee city of Oxford.* [1655], B2867.

BLACKBORROW, Sarah. *Herein is held forth the gift and good-will of God.* 1659, B3063.

—— *The just and equal ballance discovered.* 1660, B3064.

—— *The oppressed prisoners complaint.* [1662], B3064A.

—— *A visit to the spirit in prison.* 1658, B3065.

BLAITHWAITE, Mary. *The complaint of Mary Blaithwaite, widow.* [1654], B3129.

BLANDFORD, Susannah. *A small account given forth.* 1698, B3163A.

—— *A small treatise writ by one of the true Christian faith.* 1700, B3163B.

BLAUGDONE, Barbara. *An account of the travels, sufferings... of.* 1691, A410.

BLEMING, Jone. *The new prayers for K. William and Q. Mary.* 1693, B3187A.

BLOUNT, Lady Amy. *To the honourable assembly of the Commons house. The humble complaint of.* [1621?], 3134.5.

BOOTH, Mary. Preface to James Naylor, *Milk for babes.* 1661, N299.

BOOTHBY, Frances. *Marcelia: or the treacherous friend. A tragicomedy.* 1670, B3742.

BOREMAN, Mary, and PENNYMAN, John. *The ark is begun to be opened.* 1671, P1403.

BOULBIE, Judith. *A few words to the rulers of the nation.* [1673], B3827A.

—— *A testimony for truth against all hireling priests.* [1665], B3828.

—— *To all justices of the peace, or other magistrates.* [1667], B3828A.

—— *A warning and lamentation over England.* 1679, B3828B.

[BOURIGNON, Antoinette]. *An admirable treatise of solid virtue* (trans.). 1698, B3840; anr edn, 1699, B3841.

—— *The light of the world.* 1696, B3842.

—— *The second part of The light of the world.* 1696, B3842A.

BRADSTREET, Anne. *Several poems...by a gentlewoman in New England.* 1678, B4166.

—— *The tenth muse.* 1650, B4167.

BRAIDLEY, Margaret, and TAYLOR, Christopher. *Certain papers which is the word of God.* [1655], T260.

BROOKSOP, Jone. *An invitation of love.* [1662], B4983.

BURCH, Dorothy. *A catechisme of the several heads of Christian religion.* 1646, B5612.

CALDWELL, Elizabeth. Letter by her in Gilbert Dugdale, *A true discourse of the practises of Elizabeth Caldwell on the parson of T. Caldwell.* 1604, 7293.

CARTWRIGHT, Joanna. *The petition of the Jewes.* 1649, C695.

CAREW, or CARY, Lady Elizabeth. *The tragedie of Mariam, the faire queene of Jewry.* 1613, 4613.

—— Translator, Jacques Davy du Perron, *The reply of the Cardinal of Perron, to the answeare of the King of Great Britaine.* 1630, 6385.

CARY, Mary. *The little horns doom.* 1651, C736. Part of this work is entitled *A new and more exact mappe...of New Jerusalem's glory.*

—— *The resurrection of the witness.* 1648, C737; anr edn, entitled [*Twelve new*] *proposals.* 1653, C738. Wing also lists as R51.

—— *A word in season.* 1647, C739.

CELLIER, Elizabeth. *Maddam Celliers answer to the Popes letter.* 1680, C1659.

—— *The ladies answer to that busie body.* 1670, C1660.

—— *Mistriss Celliers lamentation.* 1681, C1660A.

—— *Malice defeated.* 1680, C1661.

—— *The matchless rogue.* 1680, C1662.

—— *To Dr —— an answer to his queries.* [1688], C1663.

—— *A true copy of a letter of consolation.* 1681, C1663A.

[CENTLIVRE, Mrs Susannah]. *The perjur'd husband.* 1700, C1671.

CHANNEL, Elinor. *A message from God...to his Highness.* 1653, C1936.

CHEEVERS, Sarah, and EVANS, Katherine. *To all the people upon the face of the earth.* 1663, C3776A.

CHIDLEY, Katherine. *Good counsel, to the petitioners for Presbyterian government.* [1645], C3831.

—— *The ivstification of the independant churches of Christ.* 1641, C3832.

—— *A New-Yeares-gift, or a brief exhortation to Mr Thomas Edwards.* 1645, C3833.

CHRISTINA, Queen of Sweden. *A declaration of...concerning Prince Charles.* 1649, C3963.

[CHUDLEIGH, Lady Mary]. *The female advocate.* 1700, C3984.

CLARK, Frances. *A briefe reply to the narration of Don Pantaleon Sa.* [1653], C4439.

CLARK, Margret. *The true confession of.* 1680, C4482; repr. in *Warning for servants,* 1680, C4483.

CLAYTON, Anne. *A letter to the King.* [1660], C4609.

CLAYTON, Prudence. *John Clayton, executor of Dame Mary Clayton...Prudence Clayton Respondent.* [1699], C4614.

CLIPSHAM, Margery, and ELLWOOD, Mary. *The spirit that works abomination.* [1685], C4716A; anr edn, 1685, C4716B.

[COCKBURN, Mrs Catherine]. *Agnes de Castro.* 1696, C4801.

—— *Fatal friendship; a tragedy.* 1698, C4802.

COLE, Mary, see COTTON, Priscilla

COLEMAN, Elizabeth, and TRAVERS, Anne. *A back-slider reproved.* 1669, C6925.

COLLINS, Anne. *Divine songs and meditacions.* 1653, C5355.

[CONTI, Louise Marguerite, Princesse de]. *Intrigues of love.* 1689, C5955.

[CONWAY, Anne Finch]. *Opuscula Philosophica.* Amsterdam, 1690.

—— *The principles of the most ancient and modern philosophy.* 1692, C5989.

COOKE, Frances. *Mris Cooke's Meditations.* [1650], C6008.

C[OTTON], P[riscilla]. *A briefe description by way of supposition.* [1659], C6473B.

—— *A testimony of truth to all Friends.* N.d., not in Wing (LF).

—— *A visitation of love unto all people.* 1661, C6475.

—— *As I was in the prison house.* 1656, not in Wing (LF).

—— and COLE, Mary. *To the priests and people of England, we discharge our consciences.* 1655, C6474.

CRASHAWE, Elizabeth. *The honour of vertue.* [1620], 6030.

CURWEN, Alice. *A relation of...Alice Curwen.* 1680, M857, (includes some of her letters and a relation by her.)

DALE, Lady Elizabeth. *A briefe of the Lady Dales petition to the Parliament.* [1624], 6191.5.

D'ANVERS, Alicia. *Academia; or, the humours of the University of Oxford*. 1691, D220.

—— *A poem upon His Sacred Majesty, his voyage for Holland*. 1691, D221.

DARCIE, Lady Grace. *To the honourable assembly of the Commons house in Parliament. The humble petition of*. [1624], 6273.7.

DAVIS, Eleanor, see AUDELEY, Eleanor, and DOUGLAS, Lady Eleanor

DAVY, Sarah. *Heaven realiz'd*. 1670, D444.

[DESJARDINS, Marie Catherine Hortense de, Madame de Villedieu]. *The amours of the Count de Dunois*. 1675, D1187.

—— *The annals of love*. 1672, D1187A.

—— *The disorders of love*. 1677, D1188.

—— *The husband forced to be jealous*. 1668, D1188A.

—— *Love's journal*. 1671, D1189.

—— *The loves of sundry philosophers*. 1673, D1190.

—— *The memoires of the life, and rare adventures of Henrietta Sylvia Moliere*. 1672, D1191.

—— *The memoires...The II,...last parts*. 1677, D1192.

—— *The unfortunate heroes*. 1679, D1193.

DIRRECKS, Geertruyde Niessen. *An epistle to be communicated to Friends*. [1677], D1558.

DOCWRA, Anne. *An apostate conscience exposed*. 1699, D1777.

—— *A brief discovery of the work of the enemy*. 1683, D1777A.

—— *An epistle of love and good advice*. [1683], D1778.

—— *A looking-glass for the recorder*. [1682], D1779.

—— *The second part of an apostate-conscience exposed*. 1700, D1780.

—— *Spiritual community, vindicated*. [1687], D1781.

DOLE, Dorcas. *Once more a warning*. 1683, D1834; anr edn, 1684, D1834A.

—— *A salutation and seasonable exhortation*. 1683, D1835; anr edn, 1700, D1835A.

—— and STIRREDGE, Elizabeth. *A salutation of my endeared love*. [1683], S5685A; anr edn, 1685, D1836; anr edn, [1685?], D1836A.

[DOUGLAS, Lady Eleanor] (see also AUDELEY, Eleanor). *Amend, amend; Gods kingdome is at hand*. [1643], D1967.

—— *And without proving what we say*. [1648?], D1968.

—— *Apocalyps, chp 11. Its accomplishment*. [164-?], D1969.

—— *Apocalypsis Jesu Christi*. 1644, D1970.

—— *The Lady Eleanor, her appeale*. 1646, D1971.

—— *The Lady Eleanor her appeal.* 1646, D1972.

—— *The appearance.* 1650, D1972A.

—— *The arraignment.* 1650, D1972B.

—— *As not unknowne, this petition.* [1645], D1973.

—— *Before the Lords second coming.* 1650, D1974.

—— *The benediction.* 1651, D1975.

—— *The benediction. I have an errand.* 1651, D1976.

—— *The benidiction. I have an errand.* 1651, D1977.

—— *Bethlehem signifying the house of bread.* 1652, D1978.

—— *The bill of excommunication.* 1649, D1979.

—— *The blasphemous charge against Her.* 1649, D1980; anr edn, 1649, D1981.

—— *The brides preparation.* 1645, D1982.

—— *The crying charge. Ezekiel. 22.* 1649, D1982A.

—— *The day of ivdgements modell.* 1646, D1983.

—— *The dragons blasphemous charge.* 1651, D1984.

—— *Elijah the Tishbite's supplication.* 1650, D1985.

—— *The everlasting gospel.* 1649, D1986.

—— *The excommunication out of paradice.* 1647, D1987.

—— *Ezekiel, Cap. 2.* [164-?], D1988.

—— *Ezekiel the prophet explained.* [1679], D1988A.

—— *For the blessed feast of Easter.* 1646, D1989.

—— *For the most honorable states.* 1649, D1989A.

—— *For the right noble, Sir Balthazar Gerbier.* 1649, D1989B.

—— *For Whitsun Tyds last feast.* 1645, D1990.

—— *From the Lady Eleanor, her blessing.* 1644, D1991.

—— *The gatehouse salutation from.* 1646, D1991A.

—— *Given to the Elector Prince Charles of the Rhyne.* Amsterdam, [1648], D1992; anr edn, [1651], D1993.

—— *Great Brittains visitation.* 1645, D1994.

—— *Hells destruction.* 1651, D1995.

—— *I am the first, and the last.* [1645], D1996.

—— *Je le tien. The general restitution.* 1646, D1996A.

—— *The Lady Eleanor Douglas, dowager, her iubilees.* [1659], D1996B.

—— *The mystery of general redemption.* 1647, D1996C.

—— *The new Jerusalem at hand.* 1649, D1997.

—— *The new proclamation, in answer.* 1649, D1998.

—— *Of errors ioyned with Gods word.* 1645, D1999.

—— *Of the general great days approach.* 1648, D1999A.

—— *Of times and seasons.* 1651, D2000.

—— *A prayer or petition for peace*. 1644, D2001; anr edn, 1645, D2002; anr edn, 164[7], D2003.

—— *A prophesie of the last day*. 1645, D2004.

—— *Prophetia de die*. 1644, D2005.

—— *Reader, the heavy hour*. 1648, D2005A.

—— *The Lady Eleanor her remonstrance*. 1648, D2006.

—— *The restitution of prophecy*. 1651, D2007.

—— *The restitvtion of reprobates*. 1644, D2008.

—— *The revelation interpreted*. 1646, D2009.

—— *Samsons fall*. [1649], D2010.

—— *Samsons legacie*. [1642], D2011.

—— *The [Second] co[mming of Our] Lo[rd]*. 1645, D2012.

—— *The serpents excommunication*. 1651, D2012A.

—— *A sign given them*. 1644, D2012AA.

—— *Sions lamentation*. 1649, D2012B.

—— *The star to the wise*. 1643, D2013.

—— *Strange and vvonderful prophesies*. 1649, D2014.

—— *To the most honorable the High Covrt of Parliament assembled &c My Lords; ther's a time*. [1643], D2015.

—— *Tobits book; a lesson*. 1652, D2016.

—— *Wherefore to prove the thing*. [1648], D2017.

—— *The vvord of God*. 1644, D2018.

—— *The writ of restitution*. 1648, D2019.

—— *Zach. 12. And they shall look*. [1649?], D2020.

[EGERTON, Sarah]. *The female advocate*. 1681, E251A; anr edn, 1687, E251B.

ELIZABETH, Queen of England. *Her majesties most princelie answere, delivered at Whitehall*. 1601, 7578; anr version, [c. 1628], 7579.

—— *The golden speech of* [1659]; anr edn, 1698, E528A.

—— *Injunctions given by the Queenes Majestie*. 1641, E529.

—— *The last speech and thanks of*. 1671, E530.

—— *A most excellent and remarkabl speech*. 1643, E531.

—— *Queen Elizabeth's opinion concerning transubstantiation*. 1688, E532.

—— *A speech made by*. 1688, E533.

—— *Queene Elizabeths last speech to her last Parliament*. [1642], E534; anr edn, 1648, E535.

ELSON, Mary, and others. *A tender and Christian testimony to young people*. [1685], E642 (see also WHITEHEAD, Ann).

ELLWOOD, Mary. See CLIPSHAM, Margery and ELLWOOD, Mary

EVANS, Katherine. *A brief discovery of God's eternal truth*. 1663, E3453 (see also CHEEVERS, Sarah).

[EVELYN, Mary]. *The picture of the Princesse Henrietta*. 1660, E3523A (lost).

EVERARD, Margaret. *An epistle of*. 1699, E3535.

FAGE, Mary. *Fames roule*. 1637, 10667.

FAIRMAN, Lydia. *A few lines given forth*. 1659, F257.

FEARON, Mrs Jane. *Universal redemption*. 1698, F576A.

FEATHERSTON, Sarah, and BROWNE, Thomas. *Living testimonies*. 1689, F576B.

FELL, Lydia. *A testimony and warning given forth in the love of truth*. [1676], F625.

FELL, Margaret. *A call to the universall seed of God*. 1665, F625A.

—— *A call unto the seed of Israel*. [1668?], F626.

—— *The citie of London reprov'd*. [1660], F626A.

—— *Concerning ministers made by the will of man*. 1659, F626B.

—— *The daughter of Sion awakened*. 1677, F627.

—— *A declaration and an information from us*. 1660, F628.

—— *An evident demonstration to Gods elect*. 1660, F629; anr edn, 1660, F630.

—— *False prophets, anticrists* [sic.]. 1655, F631.

—— *For Manasseth Ben Israel. The call of the Jewes*. 1656, F632.

—— *A Letter sent to the King from*. [1666], F633.

—— *A loving salutation to the seed of Abraham*. 1656, F634; anr edn, 1660, F634aA.

—— *A paper concerning such as are made ministers*. 1659, F634A.

—— *The standard of the Lord revealed*. 1667, F635.

—— *A testimonie of the touchstone*. 1656, F636.

—— *This is to the clergy*. 1660, F637.

—— *This was given to Major Generall Harrison*. 1660, F638.

—— *To the general councill of officers of the English army*. [1659], F638A.

—— *To the general council of officers. The representation*. 1659, F638B.

—— *To the general council*. 1659, F638C.

—— *To the magistrates and people of England*. 1664, F638D.

—— *A touch-stone, or, a perfect tryal*. 1667, F639.

—— *A true testimony from the people of God*. 1660, F640.

—— *Two general epistles to the flock of God*. 1664, F641.

—— *Women's speaking justified*. 1666, F642; anr edn, 1667, F643.

FINCH, Anne, see WINCHILSEA, Anne Finch, Countess of

FISHER, Abigail. *An epistle in the love of God*. 1696, F984A.

—— *A few lines in true love*. 1694, F984B; anr edn, 1694, F984C; anr edn, 1696, F985.

—— *A salutation of true love.* 1690, F986.

[FLETCHER, Elizabeth]. *A few words in season to all.* 1660, F1328.

FORSTER, Mary. *A declaration of the bountifull loving-kindness.* 1669, F1603; anr edn, 1693, F1603A.

—— *Some seasonable considerations to the young men and women.* 1684, F1604.

—— Preface to Thomas Forster, *A guide to the blind.* 1671, F1607; anr edn, 1671, F1608; anr edn, 1676, F1609.

—— and others. *A living testimony from the power and spirit of our Lord Jesus Christ.* [1685], L2598A.

—— and 7000 Hand-maids of the Lord. *These several papers was sent to the Parliament.* 1659, F1605.

GAINSBOROUGH, Katherine, Countess of. *Baptist, earl of Gainsborough...Appellants. Katherine countess dowager of Gainsborough, respondent. The respondents case.* [1693], G131A.

GARGILL, Ann. *A brief discovery of that which is called the Popish religion.* 1656, G258.

—— *A warning to all the world.* 1656, G259.

GAUNT, Elizabeth. *Last speech.* [1685], G381A.

GETHIN, Grace Norton, Lady. *Misery's virtues whetstone. Reliquiae Gethinianae.* 1699, G625; anr edn, 1700, G626.

GILMAN, Anne. *An epistle to friends.* 1662, G768.

—— *To the inhabitants of the earth.* 1669, G768A.

GOODENOUGH, Mary. Letter by her in *An account of the trial, condemnation of.* 1692, (not in Wing).

GOTHERSON, Dorothea. *To all that are unregenerated. A call.* 1661, G1352.

GOULD, Ann. *An epistle to all the Christian magistrates.* 1659, G1414.

GREENBURY, Catherine (Sister Francis) (translator). F. Paludanus, *A short relation, of the life, of S. Elizabeth.* Brussels, 1628, 19167.

GREENWAY, Margaret. *A lamentation against the professing priest and people of Oxford.* [c.1657], G1861.

GREY, Alexia (translator). *The rule of the most blissed father Saint Benedict.* [1632], 1860.

GRYMESTON, Elizabeth. *Miscelanea. Meditations. Memoratives.* 1604, 12407; anr edn, [1608], 12407.5; anr edn, [1606?], 12408; anr edn, [1618?], 12410.

HALL, Anne. *A brief representation and discovery.* 1649, H324.

HAMILTON, Elizabeth. *To the Parliament of the Common-wealth of England, the humble petition of.* [1651], H477A.

HAMILTON, Margaret, Baroness. *Unto His Grace, His Majesty's High Commissioner...the humble petition of.* [1695], H485A.

HATT, Hannah, see ALLEN, Hannah.

HATT, Martha. *To the right honourable the Commons...the humble petition of.* 1660, H1141A.

—— *To the right honour:ble the Lords...the humble petition of.* [1660], H1141B.

HATTON, Lady Elizabeth. *A true coppy of a letter from.* 1642, H1149.

HAYWARD, Amey. *The females legacy.* 1699, H1227.

HENDRICKS, Elizabeth. *An epistle to Friends in England.* 1672, H1447.

—— *Een brief aen Vrienden.* Amsterdam, 1671 (LF).

HENRIETTA MARIA, Queen of England. *De boodtschap ende brief van de.* 1642, H1455.

—— *A copie of the Queen's letter.* 1642, H1456.

—— *The Queens Majesties declaration and desires to the States of Holland.* 1642, H1457. (Cancelled 2 edn.)

—— *The Queens Maiesties gracious answer to the Lord Digbies letter.* [1642], H1458.

—— *The Queens letter from Holland.* [1643], H1459; anr edn, [1642], H1463.

—— *The Queens majesties letter to the Parliament.* [1649], H1461.

—— *The Queens majesties message and declaration.* [1649], H1462.

—— *The Queenes majesties propositions to the States of Holland.* 1642, H1465.

—— *The protestation of.* 1643, H1466.

—— *The Queens speech.* 1641, H1467; anr edn, [1641], H1467A.

HENSHAW, Anne. *To the Parliament of the commonwealth...the humble petition of.* [1654], H1477.

HERRING, Anne. *The case of.* 1678, H1600A.

HEWITT, Mary. *To the...Parliament the...petition of.* [1660], H1640.

HIGGES, Susan. *A true relation of one S. Higges.* [1635?], 13441.

HINCKS, Elizabeth. *The poor widow's mite.* 1671, H2050.

HOLDEN, Mary. *The woman's almanack for...1688.* 1688, A1827.

—— *The woman's almanack for 1689.* 1689, A1827A.

HOMEL, Anne. *French cruelty.* [1689], H2536B.

HOOTON, Elizabeth. *To the King and both Houses of Parliament.* [1670], H2710A.

—— Testimony by her in *A short relation concerning the life and death of ... William Simpson.* 1671, S3618.

—— and ALDAM, Thomas, HOLMES, Jane, FISHER, Mary, and others. *False prophets and their false teachers described.* [1652], A894BA.

[HOPTON, Susannah]. *Daily devotions*. 1673, H2761.

HOWGILL, Mary. *A remarkable letter of*. 1657, H3191.

—— *The vision of the Lord of hosts*. 1662, H3192.

HUME, Anne (translator). Petrarch, *The triumphs of love*. 1644, P1873.

IVY, Lady. [Claim to lands], [1696], L166C.

JAMES, Elinor. *Mrs James's advice to the citizens of London*. [1688], J415.

—— *Mrs Jame's apology*. [1694], J415A.

—— *Mrs James's application to the...Commons*. [1695], J415B.

—— *The case between a father and his children*. 1682, J416.

—— *Dear soveraign*. [1687], J416A.

—— *Mrs James's defence of the Church of England*. 1687, J417.

—— *Mrs James's humble letter*. [1699], J417aA.

—— *I can assure your honours...East-India-Company*. [1699?], J417bA.

—— *An injur'd prince vindicated*. [1688], J417A.

—— *May it please your honours,...East India Company*. [1699?], J417B.

—— *May it please your Majesty, to accept my Thanks*. [1689], J417AC.

—— *May it please your most sacred Majesty, seriously to consider my great zeal*. [1685], J417B.

—— *Most dear Soveraign, I cannot but love*. [1689], J417C.

—— *My Lord, I thought it my bound duty*. [1687], J418.

—— *My Lords, I can assure*. [1688], J419.

—— *My Lords, I did not think*. [1690], J419A.

—— *My Lords, you can't but be sensible*. [1688], J419B.

—— *Mrs James her new answer to a speech*. [1681], J420.

—— *Sir, my Lord Major*. [1690?], J421.

—— *This being your Majesty's birth-day*. [1690], J421aA.

—— *To the honourable convention, Gentlemen, you seem*. [1688], J421A.

—— *To the honourable House of Commons*. [1685], J421B.

—— *To the honourable House of Commons*. [East India Co.]. [1699], J421C.

—— *To the honourable the House of Commons...I am very sorry*. [1696], J422.

—— *To the Kings most excellent majesty*. [1685], J422aA.

—— *To the right honourable Convention. Gentlemen, though you have a new name*. [1688], J422bA.

—— *To the right honourable the House of Lords. My lords*. [1688], J422A.

—— *To the right honourable, the Lord Mayor...and all the rest of the loyal citizens.* [1683], J422B.

—— *Mrs James's vindication of the Church of England.* 1687, J423.

JERMYN, Lady Rebecca. *A true state of the right and claime of...to the Registers office in Chancery.* [1655], J681bA.

JEVON, Rachel. *Exultationis carmen.* 1660, J730.

—— Translation of *Carmen.* 1660, J729.

JINNER, Sarah. *An almanack or prognostication for...1658.* [1658], A1844.

—— *Almanack.* [1659], A1845.

—— *Almanack.* [1660], A1846.

—— *Almanack.* 1664, A1847.

—— *The woman's almanack.* 1659, A1848.

JOCELINE, Elizabeth. *The mothers legacie to her unborne child.* 1624, 14624; anr imp., 1624, 14624.5; anr imp., 1625, 14625; anr imp., 1632, 14625.5; anr imp., 1635, 14625.7; anr edn, 1684, J756.

J[ONES], Mrs S[arah], 'a diars wife'. *To Sions lovers.* 1644, J990.

JONES, Mrs Sarah. *This is the light's appearance.* [1650], J989.

K[EMP], Mrs A[nne]. *A contemplation on Bassets down-hill.* [1658?], K257.

KENT, Elizabeth Grey, Countess of. *A choice manuall, or rare and select secrets,* published by W.J., gent. 1653, K310; anr edn, 1653, K310A; anr edn, 1653, K310B; anr edn, 1653, K311; anr edn, 1654, K312; anr edn, 1655, K312A; anr edn, 1656, K312B; anr edn, 1659, K313; anr edn, 1659, K313A; anr edn, 1661, K313B; anr edn, 1663, K314; anr edn, 1664, K315; anr edn, 1667, K315A; anr edn, 1671, K315B; anr edn, 1682, K316; anr edn, 1687, K317.

—— *A true gentlewomans delight.* 1653, K317A; anr edn, 1653, K317B; anr edn, 1671, K317C; anr edn, 1687, K317D.

KILLIGREW, Anne. *Poems.* 1686, K442.

KILLIN, Margaret. *A warning from the Lord to the teachers.* 1656, K473.

L., Elizabeth. *Short remains of a dead gentlewoman.* [1690?], L17A.

[LA FAYETTE, Marie Madeline de La Vergne, Comtesse de]. *The Princess of Cleves.* 1679, L169; anr edn, 1688, L170.

—— *The Princess of Montpensier.* 1666, L171.

—— *Zayde, a Spanish history.* 1678, L172; anr edn, 1678, L172A; anr edn, 1690, L173.

—— *Zayde...Second and last part.* 1678, L173A.

LAMB, Catharine. *A full discovery of the false evidence.* 1688, L205C.

LANYER, Mrs Aemilia. *Salve deus rex Iudaeorum. Containing, the passion of Christ.* 1611, 15227; anr issue, 15227.5.

[LA ROCHE-GUILHEM, Mlle Anne de]. *Almanzor and Almanzaida.* 1678, L446.

—— *Asteria and Tamberlain.* 1677, L447.

—— *Rare en tout. Comedie.* 1677, L448.

—— *Royal lovers: or, the unhappy prince. A novel.* 1680, L449.

—— *Taxila, or love prefer'd.* 1692, L449A.

—— *Zingis: a Tartarian history.* 1692, L450.

LA VALLIÈRE, Louise Françoise, Duchesse de. *The penitent lady.* 1684, L623G; anr edn, 1685, L623H.

[LEAD, Jane]. *The ascent to the mount of vision.* 1699, L782.

—— *The Enochian walks with God.* 1694, L783.

—— *A fountain of gardens.* 1696, L783aA; anr edn, 1697, L783bA; anr edn, 1697, L783A.

—— *A fountain of gardens.* Vol II. 1697, L783B.

—— *A fountain of gardens.* Vol. III, pt i. 1700, L784.

—— *The heavenly cloud.* 1681, L785.

—— *The laws of paradise.* 1695, L786.

—— *A message to the Philadelphian Society.* 1696, L787.

—— *A messenger of an universal peace.* 1698, L788.

—— *The revelation of revelations.* 1683, L789.

—— *A revelation of the everlasting gospel-message.* 1697, L789A.

—— *The signs of the times.* 1699, L790.

—— *The tree of faith.* 1696, L791.

—— *The wars of David.* 1700, L791A.

—— *The wonders of God's creation manifested.* [1695?], L792.

LEIGH, Dorothy. *The mothers blessing. Or the godly counsaile of a gentle woman.* 1616, 15402; anr edn, 1607, 15402.5; anr edn, 1618, 15403; anr edn, 1618, 15403a; anr edn, 1621, 15404; anr edn, 1627, 15405; anr edn, 1629, 15405.5; anr edn, 1630, 15406; anr edn, 1633, 15407; anr edn, 1634, 15407.3; anr edn, 1636, 15407.5; anr edn, 1640, 15408; anr edn, 1656, L980; anr edn, 1663, L981; anr edn, 1667, L981A; anr edn, 1674, L982.

LEVINGSTON, Mrs Anne. *The state of the case in brief, between the Countess of Sterlin, and.* [1654], L1824.

—— *A true narrative of the case.* [1655?], L1825.

LILBURNE, Elizabeth. *To the chosen and betrusted knights,…the humble petition of.* [1646], L2077.

LILBURNE, Elizabeth (*fl.* 1696). *Elizabeth Lilburne…against William Carr…The case.* [1696], L2077aA.

LINCOLN, Elizabeth Clinton, Countess of. *The Countesse of Lincolnes nurserie.* 1622, 5432.

LIVINGSTON, Helen, Countess of Linlithgow. *The confession and conversion of my lady C[ountess] of L[inlithgow].* 1629, 16610.

LOVE, Mrs. *Loves name lives.* 1651, L3141; anr edn, 1663, L3142.

LYNAM, Margaret. *The controversie of the Lord.* 1676, L3564.

—— *For the Parliament sitting at Westminster.* [1659], L3564aA.

M., A. *Queen Elizabeth closset of physical secrets.* 1652, M5A; anr edn, 1656, M5B.

—— *A rich closet of physical secrets.* 1652, M7; anr edn, 1653, M7A; anr edn, [1653], M7B.

M., M. *The womens advocate.* 1683, M813EA; anr edn, 1687, M813EB; anr edn, M813F. (Wing attributes this work by M.M. to M. Marsin. If this is correct, then at least sixteen other works are by this same woman.)

M., W. *The Queens closet opened.* 1665, M96; anr edn, 1656, M97; anr edn, 1658, M98; anr edn, 1659, M99; anr edn, 1661, M99A; anr edn, 1662, M100; anr edn, 1662, M100A; anr edn, 1664, M100B; anr edn, 1668, M100C; anr edn, 1671, M101; anr edn, 1674, M102; anr edn, 1679, M103; anr edn, 1683, M104; anr edn, 1684, M104A; anr edn, 1696, M105; anr edn, 1696, M105A; anr edn, 1698, M106.

MAJOR, Elizabeth. *Honey on the rod.* 1656, M305.

[MAKIN, Mrs Bathsua]. *An essay to revive the antient education of gentlewomen.* 1673, M309.

MAN, Judith (translator). John Barclay, *An epitome of the history of faire Argenis and Polyarchus.* 1640, 1396.

MANLEY, Mrs Mary de la Rivière. *Letters written by.* 1696, M434.

—— *The lost lover.* 1696, M435.

—— *The royal mischief.* 1696, M436.

MARKHAM, Jane. *An account of the life and death of...Thomas Markham.* 1695, not in Wing (LF).

MARTEL, Margaret. *A true copy of the paper delivered by.* [1697], M817A.

—— *A true translation of a paper...delivered by.* 1697, M817B.

MARTINDALE, Anne, and others. *A relation of the labour, travail and suffering of...Alice Curwen.* 1680, M857.

[MASHAM, Damaris], Lady. *A discourse concerning the love of God.* 1696, M905; anr edn, 1697, M905A.

MEDICI, Mary de'. *Declaration de la reyne.* 1638, 17553; translation of, 1639, 17554.

—— *The Remonstrance made by the queene-mother of France*. 1619, 17555.

MELVILLE, Elizabeth. *Ane godlie dreame*. [1603], 17811; anr edn, [1604?], 17812; anr edn, 1606, 17813; anr edn, 1620, 17814; anr edn, 1644, M1649; anr edn [1686], M1649A; anr edn, 1698, M1650.

[MONTPENSIER, Anne Marie Louise d'Orleans]. *The characters or pourtraicts of the present court of France*. 1668, M2507.

[MOORE, Mary]. *Wonderfull news from the North. Or, a true relation*. 1650, M2581.

MORE, Agnes (translator). Saint Francis of Sales, *Delicious entertainment of the soule*. 1632, 11316.

MORE, Gertrude. *The holy practises*. 1657, M2631A.

—— *The spiritval exercises*. 1658, M2632.

MORTON, Anne Douglas, Countess of. *The Countess of Mortons daily exercise*. 1666, M2817; anr edn, 1679, M2817A; anr edn, 1689, M2818; anr edn, 1692, M2818A; anr edn, 1696, M2819.

MOSS, Elizabeth. Parts by, in Samuel Watson, *An Epistle by way of testimony*. 1695, W1096, and *A narrative and testimony Concerning Grace Watson*. 1690, N167.

M[UDD], A[nn]. *A cry, a cry: a sensible cry*. 1678, M3037.

MUNDA, Constantia (pseud.). *The worming of a mad dogge: or, a soppe for Cerberus*. 1617, 18257.

MURRAY, Janet. *Unto the lords of the council and session, the petition of*. [1700], M3107.

NEWCASTLE, Margaret Cavendish, Duchess of. *De vita et rebus gestis*. 1668, N848.

—— *Description of a new world*. 1666, N849; anr edn, 1668, N850.

—— *Grounds of natural philosophy*. 1668, N851.

—— *The life of...William Cavendishe*. 1667, N853; anr edn, 1675, N854.

—— *Natures pictures*. 1656, N855; anr edn, 1671, N856.

—— *Observations upon experimental philosophy*. 1666, N857; anr edn, 1668, N858.

—— *Orations of divers sorts*. 1662, N859; anr edn, 1662, N860; anr edn, 1663, N861; anr edn, 1668, N862.

—— *The philosophical and physical opinions*. 1655, N863; anr edn, 1663, N864.

—— *Philosophicall fancies*. 1653, N865.

—— *Philosophical letters*. 1664, N866.

—— *Plays, never before printed*. 1668, N867.

—— *Playes written*. 1662, N868.

—— *Poems, and fancies*. 1653, N869; anr edn, 1664, N870; anr edn, 1668, N871.

—— *CCXI sociable letters*. 1664, N872.

—— *The worlds olio*. 1655, N873; anr edn, 1671, N874.

[NORTHUMBERLAND, Elizabeth Percy, Countess of]. *Meditations and prayers*. 1682, N1308; anr edn, 1687, N1308A; anr edn, 1693, N1309; anr edn, 1700, N1309A.

OVERTON, Mary. *To the right honourable, the knights...the humble appeale*. [1647], O617.

OWEN, Jane. *An antidote against purgatory*. 1634, 18984.

P., Mrs T. Letter by her in Abiezer Coppe, *Some sweet sips of spirituall wine*. 1649, C6093.

—— Letter by her in POOLE, Elizabeth, *A prophecie*.

PAGET, Briget. Preface to John Paget, *Meditations of Death*. 1639, 19099.

PARR, Susanna. *Susanna's apologie against the elders*. 1659, P551.

PARTRIDGE, Dorothy. *The woman's almanack for...1694, adapted to the capacity of the female sex*. 1694, A2016.

PEMBROKE, Mary Sidney, Countess of. Poems in Francis Davison, *A poetical rapsody*. 1602, 6373.

—— Translator of Philippe de Mornay, *Six excellent treatises of life and death*. 1607, 18155.

PENNYMAN, Mary. *Something formerly writ*. 1676, P1429.

—— and John. *The ark is begun to be opened*. 1671, P1403.

PERROT, Lucy. *An account of several observable speeches of*. 1679, P1643.

PETITIONS, see ANONYMOUS

PETTUS, Katherine. *Katherine Pettus, plaintiffe Margaret Bancroft defendent in Chancery*. [1654], P1913.

[PHILIPS, Mrs Joan]. *Advice to his Grace*. [c.1681–2], P2029.

—— *Female poems on several occasions. Written by Ephelia*. 1679, P2030; anr edn, 1682, P2031.

P[HILIPS], Mrs K[atherine]. *Poems*. 1664, P2032; anr edn, 1667, P2033; anr edn, 1669, P2034; anr edn, 1678, P2035.

PHOENIX, Anne. *The saints legacies*. 1631, 10635; anr edn, 1633, 10635.3; anr edn, 1640, 10636.

PINDER, Bridget, and HOPPER, Elizabeth. *A lively testimony*. 1676, J514.

PIX, Mary. *Alass! When charming Sylvia's son*. [1697], P2325.

—— *The beau defeated*. [1700], P2326.

—— *The deceiver deceived*. 1698, P2327.

—— *The false friend*. 1699, P2328.

—— *Ibrahim*. 1696, P2329.

—— *The innocent mistress*. 1697, P2330.

—— *Queen Catharine*. 1698, P2331.

—— *The Spanish wives*. 1696, P2332.

—— *To the right honourable the earl of Kent,...this poem*. [1700?], P2332A.

—— *When I languish'd...song in the innocent Mrs*. [1697?], P2333.

POOLE, Elizabeth. *An alarum of war*. 1649, P2808; anr edn, 1649, P2809.

—— *A prophecie touching the death of King Charles*. 1649, P2809A.

—— *A vision*. 164[9], P2810.

POPE, Mrs Mary. *Behold, here is a word*. 1649, P2903.

—— *A treatise of magistracy*. 1647, P2904.

[POWYS, Elizabeth, Marchioness]. *A ballad upon the Popish plot*. [1679–80], P3118.

[PRICE, Elizabeth]. *The countess of Banburies case*. 1696, not in Wing (L).

PRIMROSE, Diana. *A chaine of pearle. Or a memoriall of queene Elizabeth*. 1630, 20388.

QUAKER WOMEN (see also FORSTER, Mary, and others). *From our half-years meeting in Dublin*. [1691], F2239A.

—— *From our women's meeting held at York*. [1692], F2239B.

—— *From our womens yearly meeting held at York*. [1698], F2239C.

—— *From our womens yearly meeting held at York*. [1700], F2240.

—— *From our yearly meeting at York*. [1690], F2240A.

REDFORD, Elizabeth. *The love of God is to gather the seasons*. [1690], R660A.

—— *A warning, a warning from the Lord*. [1696], R661.

—— *A warning from the Lord to the City and nation, in mercy to the people*. [1695], not in Wing (L).

—— *The widow's mite*. [1690?], R662.

RICHARDSON, Mrs Elizabeth. *A ladies legacy*. 1645, R1382.

ROLPH, Alice. *To the chosen and betrusted knights...the humble petition of*. [1648], R1889.

[RONE, Elizabeth]. *A reproof to those church-men*. 1688, R1914A.

[ROWE, Mrs Elizabeth Singer]. *Poems on several occasions*. 1696, R2062.

ROWLANDSON, Mrs Mary. *The soveraignty & goodness of God*. 1682, R2093.

—— *A true history of the captivity & restoration of*. 1682, R2094.

RUSSELL, Lady Elizabeth (translator). John Poynet, *A way of reconciliation of a good and learned man, touching the nature of the sacrament*. 1605, 21456.

SANDILANDS, Mary. *A tender salutation of endeared love*. 1696, S654.

SCAIFE, Barbara. *A short relation of some words*. 1686, S806.

SCHURMAN, Anna Maria van. *The learned maid*. 1659, S902.

SCUDÉRY, Madeleine de. *Almahide*. 1677, S2142.

—— *Amaryllis to Tityrus*. 1681, S2145.

—— *Artamenes or the grand Cyrus*. 1653, S2144; anr edn, 1691, S2143.

—— *Clelia*. 1655, S2151.

—— *Clelia*. Vol. II. 1656, S2152.

—— *Clelia*. Vol. III. 1658, S2153.

—— *Clelia*. Vol. IV. 1660, S2154.

—— *Clelia*. Vol. V. 1661, S2155.

—— *Clelia*. Five parts. 1678, S2156.

—— *Conversations upon several subjects*. 1683, S2157.

—— *Les femmes illustres or the heroick harrangues*. 1681, S2158; anr edn, 1693, S2159.

—— *Ibrahim*. 1652, S2160; anr edn, 1674, S2161.

—— *The third volume of Artamenes*. 1654, S2162.

—— *A triumphant arch erected*. 1656, S2163.

—— *Zelinda*. 1676, S2164.

SHARP, Jane. *The midwives book*. 1671, not in Wing (L).

SHAW, Hester. *Mrs Shaw's innocency restored*. 1653, S3018; anr edn, 1653, M2286.

—— *A plaine relation of my sufferings*. 1653, S3019.

SIMMONDS, Martha. *A lamentation for the lost sheep*. 1655, S3791; anr edn, 1656, S3792.

—— *O England; thy time is come*. [1656–65], S3793.

—— *When the Lord Jesus came*. [1655], S3794.

SIMPSON, Mary. *Faith and experience*. 1649, S3818.

SMITH, Mary. *These few lines are to all*. 1667, [1665, LF edn], S4130.

S[MITH], R[ebecca]. *The foundation of true preaching*. 1687, S4150.

SMYTH, Anne. *The case of*. [1650], S4358.

SOPHIA AMELIA, Queen of Denmark. *The Queen of Denmark's letter to the Scots*. 1651, S4689.

SOWERNAM, Ester (pseud.). *Ester hath hang'd Haman: or an answere to a lewde pamphlet*. 1617, 22974.

SPEGHT, Rachel. *Mortalities memorandum, with a dreame prefixed.* 1621, 23057.

—— *A mouzell for Melastomus, the cynical bayter of Evahs sex.* 1617, 23058.

STIRLING, Mary Alexander, Countess of. *The state of the case in brief.* [1654], S5685.

STIRREDGE, Elizabeth (see also DOLE, Dorcas). *A faithful warning to all the inhabitants of England.* [1689], not in Wing (LF).

STONE, Katherine. *To the High Court of Parliament...the humble petition of.* [1654], S5731.

STRONG, Mrs. *Having seen a paper printed.* [1655], S5988.

SUTCLIFFE, Alice. *Meditations of man's mortalitie. Or, a way to true blessednesse.* 1634, 23447.

SUTTON, Katherine. *A Christian woman's experience.* 1668, S6212.

TATTLEWELL, Mary, and HIT-HIM-HOME, Joane (pseud.). *The womens sharpe revenge: or an answer to sir Seldome Sober.* 1640, 23706.

THERESA, Mother. *The lyf of the Mother Teresa of Jesus.* 1611, 23948.5.

TICKELL, Dorothy. Part by her in *Some testimonies concerning the life and death of Hugh Tickell.* 1690, S4622.

TILLINGHAST, Mary. *Rare and excellent receipts.* 1678, T1182; anr edn, 1690, T1183.

TIPPER, Elizabeth. *The pilgrim's viaticum.* 1698, not in Wing (L); anr edn, 1698, T1305.

TOWNSEND, Theophila. *An epistle of love to friends.* [1680], T1987A.

—— *An epistle of tender love.* 1690, T1988.

—— *A testimony concerning the life and death of Jane Whitehead.* 1676, T1989.

—— *A word of counsel.* [1687], T1990.

—— Testimony by her in Charles Marshall, *Some testimonies of the life, death and sufferings of Amariah Drewet.* 1687, M743.

TRAPNEL, Anna. *The cry of a stone.* 1654, T2031.

—— *A legacy for saints.* 1654, T2032.

—— *Anna Trapnel's report.* 1654, T2033.

—— *Strange and wonderful news from White-Hall.* 1654, T2034 (about her).

—— [A] *Voice for the king of saints.* 1658, T2035.

—— [Poem, untitled, Bodl. S.1.42.Th]. N.d., not in Wing.

TRAVERS, Anne, see COLEMAN, Elizabeth.

TRAVERS, Rebeckah. *For those that meet to worship.* 1659, T2059.

—— *Of that eternal breath.* [1659], T2060.

—— *A testimony concerning the light.* 1653, T2061.

—— *A testimony for God's everlasting truth.* 1669, T2062.

—— *This is for all or any.* 1664, T2063.

—— *This is for any of that generation.* 1659, T2064.

—— Parts by her in WHITROWE, *The work of God*

—— and RIGGE, Ambrose. *The good old way.* 1669, R1483.

—— *A collection of the several writings of... William Bayley.* 1676, W1517.

TRYE, Mrs Mary. *Medicatrix, or the woman-physician.* 1675, T3174.

TURNER, Jane. *Choice experiences.* 1653, T3294.

VENN, Anne. *A wise virgins lamp burning.* 1658, V190.

VOKINS, Mrs Joan. *God's mighty power magnified.* 1691, V685.

—— *A loving advertisement.* [1670], V686.

—— *A tender invitation.* 1687, V687.

W., Ez. *The answere of a mother unto hir seduced sonnes letter.* 1627, 24903; anr edn, 1627, 24903.5.

WAILS, Isabel. *A warning to the inhabitants of Leeds.* 1685, W221.

WAITE, Mary. *A warning to all Friends who professeth.* [1679], W224.

WALKER, Mrs Elizabeth. Letters and an autobiography by her in Anthony Walker, *The holy life of Mrs Elizabeth Walker.* 1690, W305.

WALKER, Mary. *The case of.* [1650], W395.

WARREN, Elizabeth. *The old and good way vindicated.* 1646, W958; anr edn, 1646, W959.

—— *Spiritual thrift.* 1647, W960.

—— *A warning-peece from heaven.* 1649, W961.

WATERS, Margaret. *A warning from the Lord.* [1670], W1058.

W[EAMYS], A[nna]. *A continuation of Sir Philip Sydney's Arcadia.* 1651, W1189.

WEBB, Mary. *I being moved of the Lord.* 1659, W1205.

WELLS, Mary. *A divine poem.* 1684, W1296.

WENTWORTH, Anne. *Englands spiritual pill.* [1678?], not in Wing (EU).

—— *The revelation of Jesus Christ.* 1679, W1355.

—— *A vindication of.* 1677, W1356.

WESTON, Elizabeth Jane. *Parthenicon Elisabethae Joanne Westoniae virginibus nobilissimae.* Prague, [1605].

—— *Poemata.* Frankfurt, 1602.

WHARTON, Mrs. Poems by her in *The temple of death, a poem.* 1695, T663.

WHITE, Dorothy. *An alarum sounded forth from.* 1662, W1744.

—— *An alarum sounded to Englands inhabitants.* 1661, W1745.

—— *A call from God out of Egypt.* 1662, W1746.

—— *The day dawned.* 1684, W1747.

—— *A diligent search.* [1659], W1747A.

—— *An epistle of love, and of consolation.* 1661, W1748.

—— *Friends. You that are of the Parliament.* [1662], W1749.

—— *Greetings of pure peace.* [1662], W1750.

—— *A lamentation unto this nation.* [1660], W1751.

—— *A salutation of love to all the tender-hearted.* [1684], W1752.

—— *This to be delivered.* 1659, W1753.

—— *To all those that worship.* [1663], W1754.

—— *A trumpet of the Lord.* 1662, W1755.

—— *Universal love to the lost.* [1684], W1756.

—— *Unto all Gods host in England.* [1660], W1757.

—— *Upon the 22nd day of the 8th month, 1659, the word.* 1659, W1758.

—— *A visitation of heavenly love.* 1660, W1759.

—— *A visitation of love.* 1684, W1760.

—— *The voice of the Lord.* 1662, W1761.

WHITE, Elizabeth. *The experiences of God's gracious dealing with.* 1696, W1762.

WHITEHEAD, Anne, and 35 women, *For the King and both Houses.* [1670], W1884.

—— Part by her in *Piety promoted.* 1686, W1885.

—— and ELSON, Mary. *An epistle for true love.* 1680, W1882; anr edn, [1680?], W1883.

WHITROWE, Joan. *Faithful warnings.* 1697, W2032A.

—— *The humble address of.* 1689, W2033.

—— *The humble salutation.* [1690], W2034.

—— *The widow Whitrows humble thanksgiving.* 1694, W2035.

—— *To King William and Queen Mary.* 1692, W2036.

—— *To Queen Mary.* 1690, W2037.

—— *To the king and both houses of Parliament.* 1696, W2038.

—— *The work of God in a dying maid.* 1677, W2039.

WHITTON, Katharine. *An epistle to Friends.* 1681, W2050.

—— *A testimony for the Lord and his truth.* [1688], W2051.

WIGHT, Sara. *The exceeding riches of grace advanced by the spirit of grace in an empty nothing creature.* 1647, J687; anr edn, 1647, J688; anr edn, 1648, J689; anr edn, 1648, J690; anr edn, 1652, J691; anr edn, 1658, J692; anr edn, 1658, J692A; anr edn, 1666, J692B.

—— Dreams of hers in Henry Jessey, *A wonderful plesant and profitable letter*. 1656, W2106.

WIGINGTON, Letitia. *The confession and execution of*. [1681], W2110.

WILKS, Judith. *The confession of*. 1689, W2257.

[WINCHILSEA, Anne Finch, Countess of]. *The prerogatives of love*. [1695], W2966.

WOLLEY, Hannah. *The accomplished ladies' delight*. 1675, W3268; anr edn, 1677, W3269; anr edn, 1677, not in Wing (L); anr edn, 1683, W3270; anr edn, 1684, W3271; anr edn, 1685, W3272; anr edn, 1696, W3273.

—— *The compleat servant-maid*. 1677, not in Wing (City of London Poly.); anr edn, 1683, not in Wing (L); anr edn, 1685, W3274; anr edn, 1691, W3275; anr edn, 1700, not in Wing (L).

—— *The cook's guide*. 1664, W3276.

—— *The gentlewoman's companion*. 1675, W3277; anr edn, 1682, W3278.

—— *The ladies delight*. 1672, W3279.

—— *The ladies directory*. 1661, W3280; anr edn, 1662, W3281.

—— *The queen-like closet*. 1670, W3282; anr edn, 1672, W3283; anr edn, 1675, W3284; anr edn, 1681, W3285; anr edn, 1684, W3286.

—— *A supplement to the queen-like closet*. 1674, W3287; anr edn, 1684, W3288.

WORCESTER, Margaret Somerset, Countess of. *To the Parliament of the Commonwealth...the humble petition of*. [1654], W3537.

WROTH, Lady Mary. *The countesse of Mountgomeries Urania*. [1621], 26051.

WYNDHAM, Anne. *Claustrum regale reservatum*. 1667, W3772.

YEAMANS, Isabel. *An invitation of love*. 1679, Y20.

YORK, Anne Hyde, Duchess of. *A copy of a paper written by the late Duchess of York*. [1670], Y46.

—— *Reasons of her leaving the communion*. [1670], Y47.

—— and CHARLES II. *Copies of two papers*. 1686, C2943; anr edn, 1686, C2944; anr edn, 1686, C2945; anr edn, 1686, C2946; anr edn, 1687, C2946A.

ZINS-PENNICK, Judith. *Een erstige berispinge*. Amsterdam, 1660.

—— *Some Worthy Proverbs*. 1663, Z13.

2 SIXTEENTH-CENTURY WORKS REPRINTED 1600–1700

ASKEW, Anne. *An Askew, Intituled, I am a woman poor and blind*.

[1635?], 853; anr edn, [1670–89], A3211; anr edn, [1670–90], A3212; anr edn, [1670–90], A3213; anr edn, [1680–90], A3214.

DUDLEY, Lady Jane. Part by her in *The life, death and actions of*. 1615, 7281.

DU VERGERE, Susan (translator). Bishop Jean Pierre Camus, *Admirable events*. 1639, 4549; anr issue, 1639, 4550.

HILGARD, nun. *A strange prophecie against bishops*. 1641, H1983.

MARGUERITE DE NAVARRE. *Heptameron, or*. 1654, M593.

MARGUERITE DE VALOIS. *The works of*. 1642, M593aA.

—— *The grand cabinet-counsels unlocked*. 1656, M593bA; anr edn, 1658, M593cA; anr edn, 1660, M593dA.

—— *The history of*. 1649, M593A; anr edn, 1650, M594; anr edn, 1653, M594A; anr edn, 1654, M594B.

—— *The history or memorials of*. 1648, M594C.

—— *The memorialls of*. 1641, M595; anr edn, 1645, M596; anr edn, 1647, M596A; anr edn, 1662, M596B; anr edn, 1664, M596C; anr edn, 1665, M597.

PROWSE, Anne (translator). Jean Taffin, *Of the markes of the children of God*. (First, 1590), 1608, 23653; anr edn, 1609, 23654; anr edn, 1615, 23655; anr edn, 1634, 23656.

STUBBES, Katherine. Spiritual account in Philip Stubbes, *A christal glasse for christian women*. 1600, 23382.3; and 22 subsequent editions.

3 ADVERTISEMENTS

ANONYMOUS. *The gentlewoman who lived in Red-Lyon-Court ... hath a most excellent wash to beautifie the face*. [1690?], G523aA.

BROWNING, Mrs Mercy. *A catalogue of theological...Books*. [1680], B5187A.

CLARK, Mary. *The great and wonderful success*. [c.1685], C4483A.

GARWAY, Mrs. *The incomparable neck-laces of Major Choke...sold only by Mrs Garway*. [1690–1700], G278A.

—— *A most excellent cephalick-water ... sold only by*. [1695–1700], G278B.

GILL, Mrs. *At the sign of the Blew-Ball...liveth*. [1690?], G741B.

GOODIN, Madam. *By his majesty's authority...is to be seen two monsters*. [1696], G1099A.

GREEN, Mrs Mary. *Mrs Mary Green, living at a haberdasher of hats*. [1693], G1811.

HEUSE, Sarah Cornelius de. *Loving reader...secret arts for to cure...dangerous accidents.* [1670?], H1627A.

INGLISH, Isabella. *At the Hand and Pen...true Scots pills.* [1690], I187B.

LAVERENST, Anne. *In Holbourn...liveth,* [1700?], L626A.

—— *To ladies,...cure any distemper incident to woman-kind.* [1700?], in Wing, 2nd edn, but not assigned a number.

MARIS, Elizabeth. *At the Blew-Ball...liveth.* [1700?], M602A.

[OLIVER, Elizabeth]. *Catalogue of valuable books.* 1689, O274.

4 WORKS WHICH MAY BE BY WOMEN, BUT FOR WHICH THERE IS NO CLEAR EVIDENCE

ANONYMOUS. *The ladies cabinet opened.* 1639, 15119.

—— *The ladies companion, or, a table furnished with sundry sorts of pies and tarts.* 1654, L152.

—— *The ladies delight.* [1659–63], L153; anr edn, [1670–77], L154.

—— *The ladies invention.* [1698], L154A.

—— *The Lady Isabella's tragedy.* [1664?], L165A; anr edn, [1672–96], L166; anr edn, [1700], L166B.

—— *The married wives complaint of her unkind husband.* [1680?], M713.

B., M. *The ladies cabinet enlarged and opened.* 1654, B135; anr edn, 1655, B136; anr edn, 1667, B137.

H., N. *Ladies dictionary.* 1694, H99.

I., W. *A true gentlewoman's delight.* 1653, I20.

M., W. *The compleat cook.* 1671, M88.

5 WORKS ATTRIBUTED TO WOMEN, BUT WHICH ARE NOW DOUBTED

[ALCOFORADO, Marianna d']. *Five-love-letters from a nun.* 1678, A889; anr edn, 1680, A890; anr edn, 1686, A891; anr edn, 1693, A892.

—— *Seven Portuguese Letters.* 1681, A893. (Charles C. Mish, *Restoration Prose Fiction 1666–1700: An Anthology of Representative Pieces (Lincoln, Neb., 1970), pp. 37_8, doubts this attribution.)*

(Lincoln, Neb., 1970), pp. 37–8, doubts this attribution.)

—— *Seven love letters*. 1693, A894.

BRADMORE, Mrs Sarah. *Mrs Sarah Bradmores Prophecy of the wonders*. 1686, B4139.

CARLETON, Mary. *The case of* 1663, C586A.

—— *An historical narrative of the German princess. Written by her self*. 1663, H2106.

—— *A true account of the tryal of, published for her own vindication, at her own request*. 1663, not in Wing (O).

(See C. F. Main, 'The German Princess; or, Mary Carleton in fact and fiction', *Harvard Library Bulletin*, X (1956), pp. 166–85.)

CARY, Lady Elizabeth. *The history of the life, reign and death of Edward II*. 1680, F313. (Wing catalogues to Henry Cary, 1st Viscount Falkland. Has also been attributed to Elizabeth. Daniel Woolf, in an unpublished paper, suggests that it may be a forgery of the exclusion crisis period.)

[EVELYN, Mary]. *The ladies dressing-room unlock'd*. 1700, E3520. (This and other editions *BMC* attributes to John Evelyn.)

[EYRE, Mrs Elizabeth (Packington)]. *A letter from a person of quality in the North*. 1689, E3940.

—— *The ladies companion*. 1654, L152.

LA MUSSE, Margaret. *Triumphs of love*. 1687. (Wing, 2nd edn, cancels and catalogues under title.)

MAZARIN, Hortense Mancini, Duchesse de. *The memoirs of*. 1676, M1538, and subsequent editions. (Wing, 2nd edn, cancels and attributes to César Vischard de Saint-Réal.)

PAGE, Mrs Ulalia. *The lamentation of Master Pages wife of Plimmouth*. [1640?], 6557.4. (*STC* now attributes to Thomas Deloney.)

The petition of the weamen of Middlesex. 1641, P1838.

R., M. *The mothers counsell, or, live within compasse*. 163[0], 20583.

SHINKIN ap Shone. *Her prognostication for...1654*, 1654, A2385.

TURNER, Anne. *Mistris Turners farewell to all women*. [1615], 24341.5.

WITH, Elizabeth. *Elizabeth fools warning*. 1659, W3139.

6 SATIRES, OR SPOOFS, PURPORTING TO BE BY WOMEN

A., E. [a sister]. *The Presbiterian brother and sister*. [1 November 1645], A6.

ANONYMOUS. *A declaration of the maids of the City of London*. [1659], D710.

—— *The ladies remonstrance*. Imprinted at London for Virgin Want; to be sold by John Satisfie. [1659], L160.

—— *The mid-wives just petition*. 1643, M2005.

—— *The petition of the widows*. For the use of the Wide-O's of London, 1693, P1839.

—— *The poor whores complaint*. 1672, (not in Wing).

—— *The virgins complaint*. 31 January, 1642, V640.

—— *The whores petition to the London prentices*. 1668, W2067.

—— *The widowes lamentation*. 1643, W2093.

—— *The women's petition against coffee*. 1674, W3331.

B., J. *Mrs Wardens observations upon her husbands reverend speech*. [1642], B114.

B., M. *A letter from a matron of rank quality*. 1682, B139.

CRESWELL, Lady (pseud.). *A letter from the Lady Cresswell to Madam C. the Midwife*. [1680], L1529.

[CLEVELAND, Barbara Palmer, Countess of]. *The gracious answer of*. [1668], C4653.

JESSERSON, Mrs Susanna. *A bargain for bachelors*. 1675, J686.

LAMBERT, Lady. *To His Excellency General Monck*. [1660], L230. (Wing cancels 2nd edn.)

MASON, Margery, spinster (pseud.). *The tickler tickled: or, the observations upon the late tryals of Sir George Wakeman*. 1679, T1159.

STIFF, Mary. *The good womens cryes*, 1650, S5551.

7 BRIEF CHECKLIST OF WORKS WHICH *STC* AND WING CATALOGUE TO WOMEN, BUT WHICH ARE *ABOUT* RATHER THAN *BY* THEM.

(The second edition of Wing has corrected a number of these entries.)

Abbot, Elizabeth 23.

Adams, Mary A488.

Bertie, Catharine 1971.

Browne, Agnes 3907.

Clark, Margaret C4482.

Cromwell, Elizabeth C7063.

Davis, Alice 6367.

Dell, Annis 6552.

Fanshaw, Mrs F617 (cancelled Wing, 2nd edn).

Ferneseede, Margaret 10826.

Fetherstone, Maria 10838.

Flower, Joane 11106.
Frith, Mary L2005.
Goodwin, Meg 12032.
Griselda 12383.
Hester, Queen 13251.
Scarborow, Ann S821.
Shipton, Ursula 3442.
Skinker, Tannakin 22627.
Taets, Elizabeth 13525.
Vincent, Margaret 24757.
Wellington, Alice 25232.

APPENDIX 2: STATISTICAL ANALYSIS OF WOMEN'S PRINTED
WRITINGS 1600–1700

RICHARD BELL AND
PATRICIA CRAWFORD

The following data were prepared from an analysis of material in the
checklist (Appendix 1). Works were coded by author, date, edition
number and genre. The data were too sparse to permit analysis by
single years. Half-decades were generally chosen because analysis by
full decades obscured trends. The coded data were analysed using the
Statistical Package for the Social Sciences.

Table 7.1 Women's publications, by half-decades

	First editions	*All editions*
1600–5	6	7
1606–10	1	8
1611–15	3	6
1616–20	8	12
1621–5	8	11
1626–30	5	9
1631–5	6	15
1636–40	5	11
1641–5	43	57
1646–50	69	80
1651–5	59	69
1656–60	65	74
1661–5	40	50
1666–70	36	46
1671–5	23	37
1676–80	56	66
1681–5	50	75
1686–90	67	89
1691–5	35	49
1696–1700	66	96
Total	651	867

Figure 7.2 Women's writings, by half-decade, as a percentage of estimated total published material 1600–1700

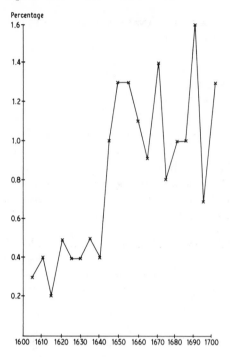

This figure shows that women's publications vary to some extent independently of general publication trends.

Details of total publications 1600–40 for the letters I–Z are available: see Philip Rider, *A Chronological Index to the Revised Edition of Poland and Redgrave, Short-Title Catalogue, 1475–1640* (Northern Illinois University, 1978). These have been multiplied by two to give a rough estimate of total publications per half-decade. This information is not available for the works catalogued by Wing in his *Short-Title Catalogue*. The total count of around 70,000 is based on the addition of the numbers per letter of the alphabet, an underestimate, since the second edition has added in a number of extra works, and furthermore Wing excluded all newsbook items. A random sample of 900 works was catalogued by half-decades for purposes of comparison. Overall, from 1640 to 1700, women's publications amounted to 1.2 per cent of the total publications, which more than doubled their pre-Civil-War contribution of around 0.5 per cent.

Table 7.2   Women's publications (all editions) per half-decade as a percentage of total women's publications 1600–1700*

	Women's publications
1600–5	0.8
1606–10	0.9
1611–15	0.7
1616–20	1.4
1621–5	1.3
1626–30	1.0
1631–5	1.7
1636–40	1.3
1641–5	6.6
1646–50	9.2
1651–5	8.0
1656–60	8.5
1661–5	5.8
1666–70	5.3
1671–5	4.3
1676–80	7.6
1681–5	8.7
1686–90	10.3
1691–5	5.7
1696–1700	11.1
Missing	0.8
Total	100.0

* Sample size was 867 and covered all editions.

Note
This table shows that in the half-decade 1696–1700 there were more publications by women than in any other half-decade. The next most important were 1686–90, and 1646–50.

Table 7.3   First editions and all editions by genre, per decade

This table compares several broad categories of women's writings over the century. Works were catalogued according to one of forty labels, but, since the numbers were small, categories have been grouped for comparative purposes. Where works belong to more than one genre, the one that seems more important has been chosen. For example, a prophetic poem could be catalogued as either a poem or a prophecy. In most cases I have categorized such poems as prophecy, especially in the case of Anna Trapnel, where this rather than the verse is important. Since the numbers were too small to make half-decades useful, full decades have been compared.

The categories are grouped as follows:

1 Prophecy
   Includes prophetic poems, but not Quaker literature. Quaker warnings and visions have been grouped with Quaker literature.

2 Prayers
   Includes collections of prayers, religious exhortations, Christian expositions and general moral advice.

3 Quaker
   Includes all works written by women known to be Friends.

4 Literature
   Plays, poems, ballads, songs.

5 Translations
   Works translated by women.

6 Prose
   Fictions, including foreign works in translation, essays, collections of letters.

7 Political
   Includes pamphlets of political significance, feminist works, educational discussion and petitions by groups of women, and serious philosophy.

8 Advice: Practical
   Almanacs, cookery books, mixtures of medical cures and recipes, and medical works.

9 Mother's advice

10 Lives
   Autobiographies, personal justifications, confessions, dying words of women including criminals.

11 Advertisements

12 Miscellaneous
   Includes more formal documents such as legal petitions, speeches of queens, prefaces.

Table 7.3 First editions and all editions by genre, per decade

	1600 1610	1611 1620	1621 1630	1631 1640	1641 1650	1651 1660	1661 1670	1671 1680	1681 1690	1691 1700	Totals
Prophecy	1 (2)	–	1 (1)	– (2)	56 (60)	16 (17)	3 (3)	5 (5)	3 (4)	7 (9)	92 (103)
Prayers	–	– (1)	–	3 (5)	4 (4)	3 (4)	1 (1)	1 (2)	1 (4)	5 (9)	18 (30)
Quaker	–	–	–	–	1 (1)	55 (57)	38 (38)	20 (21)	37 (42)	26 (30)	177 (189)
Literature	–	2 (3)	3 (3)	1 (2)	1 (1)	2 (2)	4 (8)	9 (11)	22 (30)	24 (35)	68 (95)
Translation	2 (4)	1 (2)	1 (1)	5 (8)	1 (1)	1 (2)	–	–	4 (4)	1 (1)	16 (23)
Prose	1 (1)	–	–	–	1 (1)	11 (13)	7 (14)	5 (9)	11 (12)	15 (26)	51 (76)
Political	–	3 (3)	–	1 (1)	21 (30)	12 (13)	8 (9)	4 (4)	17 (19)	2 (3)	68 (82)
Advice practical	–	–	–	–	3 (3)	3 (8)	3 (6)	8 (12)	3 (15)	1 (4)	21 (48)
Mothers	1 (5)	1 (4)	3 (10)	– (6)	1 (1)	– (1)	– (1)	– (1)	–	1 (1)	7 (31)
Lives	–	1 (1)	–	–	4 (11)	8 (11)	5 (7)	4 (11)	5 (8)	3 (4)	30 (53)
Advertisements	–	–	–	–	–	–	–	1 (1)	3 (3)	10 (10)	14 (14)
Miscellaneous	2 (2)	1 (1)	4 (6)	1 (2)	16 (21)	10 (12)	3 (3)	8 (10)	6 (13)	7 (8)	58 (78)
All genres	7 (14)	9 (15)	12 (21)	11 (26)	109 (134)	121 (140)	72 (90)	65 (87)	112 (155)	102 (140)	620 (822)

Note
All editions are given in parentheses

Figure 7.3   Distribution of number of works per author

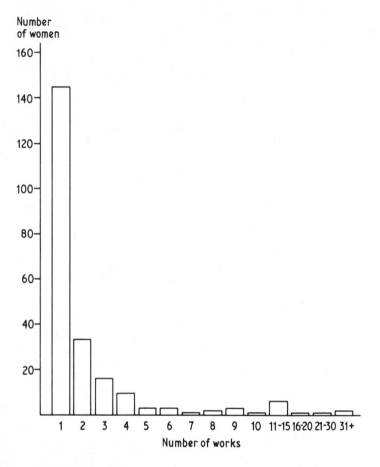

Total first editions 1600–1700 was 653. Total works analysed here, 637 first editions. 22 women who wrote 5 or more works published a total of 318, amounting to 49.9 per cent of the total analysed (or 48.6 per cent of 653). 209 named women wrote 4 or less works. 16 first editions were anonymous. These anonymous works have been included in the calculations of percentage of those who wrote 4 or less works but are not represented in the figure. Together, 209 women and the authors of 16 anonymous works wrote 319 works, or 50.1% of the total analysed.

Tables 7.4 to 7.6

These tables compare the pattern of publication of the women who were prolific authors with those who wrote less than five works. Before the Civil War there was only one woman who wrote more than four works. Table 7.4 analyses the patterns of publication of the two groups of women by genre. Table 7.5 shows that for prolific authors the 1640s were important, when 24.2 per cent of their work was published. For women who wrote less than five works, the 1650s were significant, as 20.8 per cent of their work was published then. Table 7.6 shows that prophecy, literature and prose fictions were the areas in which the more prolific writers mainly published. For women who wrote less than five works, apart from Quaker women, the publication of controversial works was significant.

Table 7.4 also shows the way in which women expanded the number of genres in which they published over the century.

For a discussion of the genres, see note on Table 7.3, p. 268.

Table 7.4 Comparison of publications by genre and by decades of women who wrote more than four works and those who wrote fewer than five

	1600–10	1611–20	1621–30	1631–40	1641–50	1651–60	1661–70	1671–80	1681–90	1691–1700	Total
Prophecy											
More than 4	—	—	1	—	52	12	1	3	2	7	78
Fewer than 5	1	—	—	—	4	4	2	2	1	—	14
Prayers											
More than 4	—	—	—	—	—	—	—	—	1	—	1
Fewer than 5	—	—	—	3	4	3	1	1	1	4	17
Quaker											
More than 4	—	—	—	—	—	28	22	5	13	11	79
Fewer than 5	—	—	—	—	1	27	16	15	24	15	98
Literature											
More than 4	—	—	—	—	—	1	2	6	19	15	43
Fewer than 5	—	2	3	1	1	1	2	3	3	9	25
Translations											
More than 4	—	—	—	—	—	1	—	—	4	1	6
Fewer than 5	2	1	1	5	1	—	—	—	—	—	10
Prose											
More than 4	—	—	—	—	—	10	6	4	8	10	38
Fewer than 5	1	—	—	—	1	1	1	1	3	5	13

Political										
More than 4	—	—	—	9	4	1	1	14	1	30
Fewer than 5	3	—	1	12	8	7	3	3	1	38
Advice: practical										
More than 4	—	—	—	3	2	3	6	1	—	15
Fewer than 5	—	—	—	—	1	—	2	2	1	6
Mothers' advice										
More than 4	1	—	—	—	—	—	—	—	—	1
Fewer than 5	1	3	—	—	—	1	—	—	1	6
Lives										
More than 4	—	—	—	—	3	1	—	—	—	4
Fewer than 5	1	—	—	4	5	4	4	5	3	26
Miscellaneous										
More than 4	—	3	—	13	—	—	4	2	1	23
Fewer than 5	2	1	1	3	10	3	4	4	6	35
Total										
More than 4										318
Fewer than 5										288
Missing observations										47

Note

Anonymous works are in the 'more than 4' category

Table 7.5 Comparison of percentages of first editions per decade by women who wrote more than four and fewer than five

	More than four	Fewer than five		More than four	Fewer than five
1600–10	—	2.4	1651–60	19.2	20.8
1611–20	—	3.1	1661–70	11.6	12.5
1621–30	1.3	2.8	1671–80	9.1	12.2
1631–40	—	3.8	1681–90	19.8	15.9
1641–50	24.2	10.8	1691–1700	14.8	15.7
			Total	100.0	100.0

Table 7.6 Comparison of patterns of publication, by genre, of women who wrote fewer than five works and those who wrote more than four works (percentage)

	Fewer than five	More than four
Prophecy	4.9	24.5
Prayers	5.9	0.3
Quaker	34.0	24.8
Literature	8.7	13.5
Translations	3.5	1.9
Prose	4.5	11.9
Political	13.2	9.4
Advice: practical	2.1	4.7
Mothers' advice	2.1	0.3
Lives	9.0	1.3
Miscellaneous	12.1	7.4
Total	100.0	100.0
Sample size	288	318

NOTES

[1] For example, A. S. P. Woodhouse, *Puritanism and Liberty: Being the Army Debates (1647–9)* (London, 1938), p. 367, doubted women's authorship of the two petitions of 1649 discussed below in note 10.

[2] Conway's work was translated into English in 1692. Carolyn Merchant, *The Death of Nature: Women, Ecology, and the Scientific Revolution* (New York, 1980), pp. 251–8.

[3] Wing lists one author of a work only, usually the male, which obscures female contributions; for example, C394 by Thomas Camm only. Sometimes he catalogues by title only, obscuring women; for example, *An account of the travels* (A410) is a spiritual autobiography by Barbara Blaugdone, and *A lively testimony* (J514) is by several women, and about, not by, Robert Jeckell. The entry for *STC 24316* does not mention that the translation was by a woman, Elizabeth Arnold.

[4] Bridget MacCarthy, *Women Writers: Their Contribution to the English Novel, 1621–1744* (Cork, 1944); Mary Mahl and H. Koon, *The Female Spectator: English Women Writers before 1800* (Bloomington, Ind., 1977); Sandra Gilbert and Susan Gubar, *Shakespeare's Sisters: Feminist Essays on Women Poets* (Bloomington, Ind., 1979); Betty Travitsky, *The Paradise of Women: Writings by Englishwomen of the Renaissance* (Westport, Conn., 1981).

[5] Richard Vann, 'Towards a New Life Style: Women in Pre-Industrial Capitalism', in R. Bridenthal and C. Koonz (eds), *Becoming Visible: Women in European History* (Boston, Mass., 1977), p. 210.

[6] Leigh, *The mothers blessing*, p. 4. Full references to the women's works are to be found in the checklist, (Appendix 1).

[7] Information in the checklist was coded with respect to date, edition number, author's social status and religious affiliation, and genre. Richard Bell analysed these data using the statistical package for the social sciences. For method of analysis, see Appendices 1 and 2.

[8] For an analysis, see Appendix 2, Table 7.3.

[9] *Perfect Occurrences*, 20–27 April 1649, TTE. 529.21, 998.

[10] For authorship, see H. N. Brailsford, *The Levellers and the English Revolution* (London, 1961), p. 318, n. 8; Patricia Higgins, 'The Reactions of Women, with Special Reference to Women Petitioners', in B. Manning (ed.), *Politics, Religion and the English Civil War* (London, 1973), p. 218; Ian Gentles, 'London Levellers in the English Revolution: The Chidleys and Their Circle', *Journal of Ecclesiastical History*, XXIX (1978), p. 293.

[11] [Bradstreet], *The tenth muse* (1650); *Several Poems*, sig. a3^v.

[12] Channel, *A message from God*, pp. 1–7.

[13] For example, see J. Ray, *A collection of English proverbs* (London, 1670); J. W. Spargo, *Juridicial Folklore in England: Illustrated by the Cucking-Stool* (Durham, NC, 1944).

[14] Joceline, *The mothers legacie*, p. 69.

[15] Anne Finch, 'The Introduction', *The Poems of Anne Finch, Countess of Winchelsea*, ed. Myra Reynolds (Chicago, Ill., 1903), p. 4.

[16] Newcastle, *Poems, and Fancies*, sig. A3ᵛ.

[17] For women's education, see Myra Reynolds, *The Learned Lady in England 1650–1760* (New York, 1920); D. Gardiner, *English Girlhood at School: A Study of Women's Education through Twelve Centuries* (London, 1929); Walter Ong, 'Latin Language Study as a Renaissance Puberty Rite', in *Rhetoric, Romance and Technology* (Ithaca, NY, 1971).

[18] George Ballard, *Memoirs of Several Ladies of Great Britain* (Oxford, 1752), p. 424.

[19] Quoted in Reynolds, *Learned Lady*, p. 196.

[20] W. J. Thoms (ed.), *Anecdotes and Traditions*, CS (1839), V, p. 125.

[21] Cf. Edith L. Klotz, 'A Subject Analysis of English Imprints for Every Tenth Year from 1480 to 1640', *Huntingdon Library Quarterly*, I (1937–8), pp. 417–19.

[22] Behn (trans.), *A discovery of new worlds*, Preface.

[23] Newcastle, *The life of … William Cavendishe*, sig. b[1].

[24] Parr, *Susanna's apologie against the elders*, p. 114.

[25] Cary, *The little horns doom*, p. 238.

[26] Trapnel, *Anna Trapnel's report*, p. 55.

[27] David Cressy, *Literacy and the Social Order* (Cambridge, 1980), p. 176. Cressy argues that the experience of London women diverged dramatically from that of women in country districts in the late seventeenth century. In the 1670s in London 78 per cent of women were unable to sign their names, in the 1680s 64 per cent, and in the 1690s 52 per cent; ibid., p. 147.

[28] Margaret Spufford, 'First Steps in Literacy: The Reading and Writing Experiences of the Humblest Seventeenth-Century Spiritual Autobiographers', *Social History*, IV (1979), pp. 407–35.

[29] S. W. Hull, *Chaste, Silent and Obedient: English Books for Women 1475–1640* (San Marino, Calif. 1982); *Petition of the Ladies of London and Westminster … for Husbands* (1693), in *Harleian Miscellany*, X (1810), p. 168; *Rare verities. The cabinet of Venus unlocked* (1658).

[30] Thomas Bentley, *The monument of matrones; Conteining seuen seuerall lamps of virginitie* (1582), III, p. 35 (*STC* 1892).

[31] John Prude, *A sermon at the funeral of … Mrs Anne Baynard* (1697), Preface, sig. [A3].

[32] Warren, *The Old and Good Way Vindicated*, sig. A3ᵛ.

[33] *The Works of John Dryden*, ed. W. Scott and G. Saintsbury, XVIII (1893), p. 166.

[34] Centlivre, *The perjur'd husband*, sig. A3.

[35] Major, *Honey on the rod*, 'Sin and Mercy', sig. h3.

[36] Poole, *A prophecie*, sig. A2.

[37] Pope, *Behold, here is a word*, p. 32.

[38] Avery, *Scripture-prophecies opened*, Preface; *The copy of a letter written by Mr Thomas Parker … to his sister, Mrs Elizabeth Avery* (London, 1650), pp. 13, 17, 5.

39 Francis Bugg, *Jezabel withstood* (London, 1699), pp. 2, 8.

40 *The Account Audited*, [London, 13 April], 1649, p. 2; Cary, *The little horns doom*, sig. A7 (*New Jerusalem* was part of this).

41 Tipper, *The pilgrim's viaticum*, sig. A2.

42 Men may not be snobs, Virginia Woolf observes, but they appreciate for the most part 'the efforts of a countess to write verse'; *A Room of One's Own*, new edn (London, 1931), p. 87.

43 L. G. Black, 'A Lost Poem by Queen Elizabeth I', *TLS*, 23 May 1968, p. 535.

44 Sutcliffe, *Meditations*; Warren, *Spiritual thrift*, sig. [A2ᵛ].

45 W[eamys], *A Continuation of Sir Philip Sydney's Arcadia*, sig. [q6]. Any woman offered praise might doubt whether it came from her ability rather than male gallantry. Matthew Prior wrote a preface to a woman's play in 1717, arguing that a woman's sex should defend her from all criticism:

> The Female Author who recites to Day
> Trusts to her Sex the Merit of her Play.

See *The Literary Works of Matthew Prior*, ed. H. B. Wright and M. K. Spears, 2 vols (Oxford, 1959), I, p. 437.

46 Cary, *The little horns doom*, sig. a2.

47 Sutcliffe, *Meditations*, sig. [7ᵛ].

48 [Bradstreet], *The tenth muse*.

49 Coleman and Travers, *A back-slider reproved*, p. 22.

50 Warren, *The old and good way vindicated*, sig. F3–[F4ᵛ], p. 38.

51 Thomas Edwards, *Gangraena* (1646; repr. Exeter, 1977), I, pp. 79–80. Edwards was critical of Greenhill's response.

52 Anne Dowriche, *The French historie* (1589), Preface (*STC* 7158).

53 Hayward, *The females legacy*, Preface, sig. [6] and p. 93; see also Elizabeth Cary (trans.), Davy du Perron, *The reply*.

54 Bennet, *Good and seasonable counsel*.

55 Warren, *The old and good way vindicated*, 2nd edn, sig. F3–3ᵛ.

56 Bennet, *Good and seasonable counsel*, Preface.

57 Parr, *Susanna's apologie*, sig. A3; Speght, *A mouzell for Melastomus*, sig. F.

58 Cellier, *Malice defeated*, p. 32.

59 Behn, *The luckey chance*, sig. a.

60 James, *Mrs James's vindication of the Church of England*, Preface [p. 2]; *Mrs James's thanks to the Lords and Commons for their sincerity to King George*, brs (1715).

61 [Audeley], *A warning to the dragon*, sig. a iiᵛ.

62 [Makin], *An essay to revive the antient education of gentlewomen*, p. 5.

63 *The Works of Mrs Catharine Cockburn*, ed. Thomas Birch, 2 vols (London, 1751), I, p. xv.

64 [Astell], *Six familiar essays*, sig. A2.

65 Florence Smith, *Mary Astell* (New York, 1916), p. 116.

66 Others were to men and women, to the royal family in general, and to institutions.

[67] Cary, *The little horns doom*, sig. A5.
[68] Richardson, *A ladies legacy*, sig. A3^{v}.
[69] Partridge, *The woman's almanack* (1694).
[70] Owen, *An antidote against purgatory*, sig. 2, pp. 178–9.
[71] [Susannah Centlivre], *The Platonick Lady* (1707), sig. A2^{v}.
[72] Elizabeth Elstob, *An English-Saxon Homily on the Birth-Day of St Gregory* (London, 1709), p. iv. Since the social position of women in general was precarious and could be lost by their behaviour, individuals were no doubt anxious to affirm their position by conforming to the dominant values.
[73] Bateman, *I Matter Not*, p. 1.
[74] [Anne Finch], 'Mercury and the Elephant', *Miscellany Poems* (1713), p. 3.
[75] See Appendix 2, Table 7.3.
[76] Chidley, *The ivstification of the independant churches*, p. 26.
[77] Keith Thomas, 'Women and the Civil War Sects', in T. Aston (ed.), *Crisis in Europe 1560–1660* (London, 1965).
[78] Speght, *Mortalities memorandum*, p. 5; [Anne Halkett], *Meditations on the twenty and fifth Psalm* (Edinburgh, 1701), Preface; Bathurst, *The sayings of women*, pp. 23 and *passim*. See also Pope, *A treatise of magistracy*, sig. C2^{v}.
[79] See, for example, Hincks, *The poor widow's mite*.
[80] Forster and others, *A living testimony*, p. 2.
[81] Anon., *To the supreme authority of England*, [24 April] 1649, p. 5; Anon., *Unto every individual member* [1653].
[82] Pope, *A treatise of magistracy*, sig. 6.
[83] Venn, *A wise virgins lamp burning*.
[84] Bell, *The legacy of a dying mother*, p. 38.
[85] Turner, *Choice experiences*, sig. [B8].
[86] Vavasor Powell, *Choice experiences of sundry believers* (1653).
[87] There are other publications which purport to be advice by mothers, but which seem to be written by men. For example, M.R., *The mothers counsell, or live within compasse* (163[0?]), *STC* 20583, was probably issued with *STC* 14900, *Keepe within compasse: or, The worthy legacy of a wise father to his beloved sonne*. M.R.'s counsel, with its extensive discussion of the need for chastity, and the dangers of lust and women's tongues, seems similar in patterns of thought to many works by men. I see no reason to argue that M.R. was a woman.
[88] Lincoln, *The Countesse of Lincolnes nurserie*. For further discussion of contemporary recognition of the strength of maternal feeling, see Michael Macdonald, *Mystical Bedlam: Madness, Anxiety and Healing in Seventeenth-Century England* (Cambridge, 1981), pp. 80–5.
[89] Lincoln, *The Countesse of Lincolnes nurserie*; Leigh, *The mothers blessing*; Joceline, *The mothers legacie*; Grymeston, *Miscelanea. Meditations. Memoratives*. See Ruth Hughey and P. Hereford, 'Elizabeth Grymeston and her *Miscellanea*', *The Library*, XV (1934), pp. 61–91.
[90] Richardson, *A ladies legacy*.
[91] Leigh, *The mothers blessing* (1618), sig. [A6], pp. 3–5, 24.

92 Richardson, *A ladies legacy*, sig. A2.

93 Forster and others, *A living testimony*, pp. 2–3.

94 [Quaker, women's meetings], *From our womens yearly meeting held at York*, p. 4.

95 See L. M. Wright, *The Literary Life of the Early Friends, 1650–1725* (1932), (New York, 1966).

96 Phyllis Mack, 'Women as Prophets During the English Civil War', *Feminist Studies*, VIII (1982), p. 28.

97 For Poole, see *The Clarke Papers*, ed. C. H. Firth, CS, NS, LIV (1894), pp. 150–4, 167–9; Pope, *Behold, here is a word*.

98 Trapnel, *Cry of a Stone; Legacy for Saints; Voice for the King of Saints*, also, a huge untitled poem, lacking any publication details in the Bodleian library S.1.42 Th; see also C. Burrage, 'Anna Trapnel's Prophecies', *EHR*, xxvi (1911), pp. 526–35; Wight, *Exceeding Riches of Grace*.

99 See her own account, James, *Mrs. James's reasons* (1715), p. 5. For Eleanor Douglas, see T. Spencer, 'The History of an Unfortunate Lady', *Harvard Studies and Notes in Philology and Literature*, 20 (1938), pp. 43–59; introduction to Rota Edition of *The Restitution of Prophecy* (1651), (Exeter, 1978).

100 *A true copy of the petition*, T 2656.

101 *Commons Journals*, II, p. 413.

102 *Perfect Occurrences*, (20–27 Apr. 1649), TTE 529.21, p. 998.

103 *To the supreme authority*, [5 May 1649].

104 Bodl., Clarendon MS 46, f.130v.

105 *To the Parliament the humble petition*, T 1585; *Unto every individual member of Parliament; The true and perfect diurnall*, (19–26 July 1653), TTE 707.6, pp. 11–14.

106 Rowe, *Poems*, Preface, sig. A3.

107 White, *A diligent search*, p. 1. This is a standard formulation; see also Braidley and Taylor, *Certain papers*, pp. 4, 7, 10.

108 Evans, *A brief discovery*, pp. 35–6; Docwra, *An epistle*, p. 3; Fell, *Women's speaking justified, passim*. The Quakers were aware of the importance of the press as a means of publicizing their views and countering those of their opponents; see T. P. O'Malley, 'The Press and the Quakers, 1653–1659', *Journal of the Friends' Historical Society*, LIV (1979), pp. 169–84.

109 Blackborrow, *Herein is held forth*, p. 7; Fell, *A declaration*, p. 8; Audland, *A true declaration*, p. 2; B[landford], *A small account*, p. 40; Wails, *A warning*, p. 3.

110 C[otton], *As I was in the prison house*.

111 Blandford, *A small account*, p. 40.

112 Redford, *A warning*, p. 2 (Wing R661).

113 Whitton, *An epistle*, p. 10; Wails, *A warning*, p. 9.

114 Dole, *Once more a warning*, p. 19.

115 Patricia Crawford, 'Charles Stuart, that Man of Blood', *Journal of British*

Studies, XVI (1977), pp. 41–61; [Forster], *These several papers*, p. 3. See also Jane Fearon, *Absolute predestination not Scriptural* (1705), sig. A3.

[116]   Gotherson, *To all*, sig. A2ᵛ.

[117]   Whitrowe, *The humble salutation*, p. 14.

[118]   Blaugdone, *An account of the travels*, p. 7.

[119]   For example, Worcester, *To the Parliament*; Levingston, *The State of the case*.

[120]   Frances [Clark], *A briefe reply*, p. 1.

[121]   Blaithwaite, *The complaint*, pp. 2, 6.

[122]   Shaw, *Mrs Shaw's innocency restored*, p. 4; see also, Ann Hughes (ed.), *Biographical Dictionary of British Women* (forthcoming) my entry for Hester Shaw.

[123]   Parr, *Susanna's apologie*, sig. A2, [A5].

[124]   See checklist (Appendix 1).

[125]   Douglas, *The Lady Eleanor, her appeal*; Spencer, 'An Unfortunate Lady' pp. 43–59.

[126]   Eleanor Audeley wrote sixty-six works, Aphra Behn fifty and Margaret Fox twenty-four. For further information on numbers of works, see Appendix 2, Table 7.3.

[127]   Wentworth, *A vindication*, p. 6.

[128]   Newcastle, *Poems*, sig. [A8ᵛ].

[129]   Major, *Honey on the rod*, 'Sin and Mercy', sig. h[3ᵛ].

[130]   Jones, *To Sions lovers*, Preface.

[131]   Poole, *A prophecie*, sig. [A3].

[132]   Finch, (unpublished MS), *Poems*, ed. Reynolds, p. 9.

[133]   Pope, *A treatise of magistracy*, sig. C2ᵛ.

[134]   Cary, *The resurrection*, p. 20.

[135]   Warren, *The old and good way vindicated*, sig. A3ᵛ.

[136]   Whitrowe, *The humble address*, p. 9.

[137]   Barker, *Poetical recreations*, pp. 12–13.

[138]   Owen, *An antidote against purgatory*, p. 185.

[139]   Finch, 'The Unequal Fetters', *Poems*, ed. Reynolds, p. 151.

[140]   Pope, *A treatise of magistracy*, sig. C2ᵛ.

[141]   Cary, *The little horns doom*, pp. 289–90.

[142]   Wolley, *The gentlewoman's companion* (1675), pp. 208–9; Wolley, *The compleat servant-maid*, pp. 110–13.

[143]   Anon., *Advice to the women*, pp. 1–3.

[144]   Sharp, *The midwives book*. *TC*, II, p. 316, lists another edition of Sharp's work for 1690.

[145]   Sharp, *The midwives book*, pp. 3–4.

[146]   Tattlewell and Hit-Him-Home, *The womens sharpe revenge*, pp. 75–6.

[147]   Forster, *These several papers was sent to the Parliament*, Preface to the reader.

[148]   Anon., *To the Parliament: The humble petition* (1653).

[149] Janet Richards, *The Sceptical Feminist: A Philosophical Enquiry* (London, 1980), p. 13. For another discussion of the term 'feminist', see I. Maclean, *Women Triumphant: Feminism in French Literature 1610–1652* (Oxford, 1977), p. 1.

[150] Lanyer, *Salve deus*, sig. D^v, D2.

[151] Anon., *Triumphs of female wit*, sig. [A3].

[152] For a discussion of Margaret Cavendish, Duchess of Newcastle, see Sara Mendelson, 'Women in Seventeenth-Century England: Three Studies', D.Phil. thesis (Oxford, 1982). Newcastle, *The philosophical and physical opinions*, sig. B2^v.

[153] Wolley, *The gentlewoman's companion*, sig. [A6], pp. 1, 29.

[154] Tattlewell and Hit-Him-Home, *The womens sharpe revenge*, p. 42.

[155] Jinner, *An Almanack* [1658], sig. B. As early as 1578 Margaret Tyler, who translated Ortunez's *The Mirrour of Princely Deeds*, criticized the poor education of women. See E. D. Mackerness, 'Margaret Tyler: An Elizabethan Feminist', *Notes and Queries* (1946), pp. 112–13.

[156] Anon., *Triumphs of female wit*, sig. [B3^v].

[157] Finch, *Poems*, ed. Reynolds, p. 6 (from MS, *c.* 1689); [Masham], *A Discourse*, p. 58; [Mary Chudleigh], *The Ladies Defence* (1701), sig. a[2].

[158] Makin, *An essay to revive the antient education of gentlewomen*, pp. 16, 32 and *passim*.

[159] Anon., *Triumphs of female wit*.

[160] Wolley, *The gentlewoman's companion*, sig. [A6], pp. 1, 29.

[161] Finch, *Poems*, ed. Reynolds, p. 5 ('The Introduction').

[162] Jane Anger, *Jane Anger her protection for women by Ja. A. Gent* (1589), *STC* 644.

[163] The language of Constantia Munda's *The worming of a mad dogge* (1617) differs from that of other pamphlets by known women. Explicit discussion of whores, doxies and prostitutes may be a reason for a woman to conceal her identity, or may indicate a man's authorship.

[164] Speght, *Mortalities memorandum* (1621).

[165] Speght, *A mouzell for Melastomus*, sig. B2^v, p. 10; Sowernam, *Ester hath hang'd Haman*, pp. 1–4, 6, 21.

[166] *STC* (2nd edn) suggests that *The womens sharpe revenge* may have been written by John Taylor, the water poet, author of several misogynist works. S. Halkett and J. Laing, *A Dictionary of Anonymous and Pseudonymous Publications in the English Language 1475–1640*, 3rd edn ed. John Horden, (1980), accept this attribution. The evidence cited in Halkett and Laing is that the work was entered in the Stationer's Register on the same day (24 April 1639) as Taylor's *Divers Crabtree Lectures*. This is not conclusive. Halkett and Laing also cite the unpublished Harvard Ph.D. thesis of R. B. Dow, 'Life and Times of John Taylor the Water Poet' (1930), II, p. 107, but he offers no further evidence. Stylistic evidence, also cited, seems to me to be clear evidence of a female author.

[167] A similar argument was used earlier by Sowernam, *Ester hath Hang'd Haman*, p. 24.

[168] Tattlewell and Hit-Him-Home, *The womens sharpe revenge*, pp. 88, 120, 133–4.

[169] Joan Kinnaird, 'Mary Astell and the Conservative Contribution to English Feminism', *Journal of British Studies* (1979), pp. 53–75. Ruth Perry, 'The Veil of Chastity: Mary Astell's Feminism', in Roseann Runte (ed.), *Studies in Eighteenth-Century Culture*, Wisconsin, IX (1979), pp. 25–43.

[170] Owen, *An antidote against purgatory*, p. 179.

[171] Jinner, *An almanack* [1658], sig. B.

[172] Trye, *Medicatrix*, Preface, sig. A2.

[173] [Makin], *An essay to revive the antient education of gentlewomen*, pp. 16–21; Wolley, *The gentlewoman's companion* (1675), pp. 29–30.

[174] Rowe, *Poems*, Preface, sig. A3ᵛ.

[175] Wolley, *The gentlewoman's companion*, p. 5; Jinner, *An almanack* [1658], sig. B.

[176] For example, Thomas Camm only is listed as the author of his joint publication with Anne Audland, Stephen Crisp as the author of a pamphlet by Elizabeth Coleman and Anne Travers, Christopher Taylor of a joint work with Margaret Braidley, and John Norris of his joint publication with Mary Astell. Sometimes no author is mentioned, as, for example, *An Account of the Travels, Sufferings and Persecutions of Barbara Blaugdone*, which is a spiritual autobiography by her. The testimonies of many Quakers are catalogued to one person only; for example, *A Lively Testimony*, which is signed by Bridget Pinder and Elizabeth Hopper, is catalogued to the dead man, Robert Jeckell. Elizabeth Arnold is not mentioned as the translator of Thomas Tuke. For further details, see the checklist (Appendix 1). Given the difficulties of locating women's works, it is a pity that the Eighteenth-Century Short-Title Catalogue has chosen not to catalogue for gender.

[177] Margaret, Duchess of Newcastle, feared that, since no *gentleman* would dare appear in print against a lady, she would be criticized by a man using a woman's identity: *Conway Letters*, ed. M. Nicholson (London, 1930), p. 237. George Hicks thought that a daughter would be more influenced by a mother, another reason for adopting a female identity (quoted in Smith, *Mary Astell*, p. 75). The bio-bibliography which Elaine Hobby is preparing should provide solutions to some of these puzzles.

Index

Abingdon, Berkshire: almshouses 79; Christ's Hospital 57, 79; economy of 77–9; life expectation in 63; mortality 63; parish registers of 57; St Helen's parish 57, 59, 61, 79; St Nicholas's parish 57; poor relief 79; population 57
abortion 22
abstention, sexual 22
Acton, Sir John 28
Acts of Parliament 111, 122, 123, 126, 150, 151, 153, 155–6
adaptability, women's 16–17, 96
age: see fertility, age-specific; marriage, age of
agriculture, women in 13
Aldenham 30
ale-house keeping 70–1
Allworth, Lady 54
amenorrhoea: of lactation 23, 25, 48–9; of malnutrition 23, 25
America 82
Amey, Mrs 113
Anger, Jane 229
ann or annate 136
Ann ******, Oxford milliner 112
Anstey, Thomas Chisholm 93
anti-feminist attitudes to women writers 218–20, 229–31; and their response 220–2, 229–31
apprentices 9–10, 102, 111; parish apprentices 103–4, 105
apprenticeships 100, 103–10
Arundell, Catharine 43
Arundell, Sir John 43
Ashley, Sir Henry 127
Askew, Anne 123
Astell, Mary 220, 230
Atkinson, Elizabeth 218
Atterbury, Dean 220
Austen, Katherine 76–7, 184, 199
authority, clerical 173
Avery, Elizabeth 217
Awder, George 131

Bacon, Nathaniel 111
Baker, Lady see Fletcher
Banbury, women trading in 113
Baptists 76
Barker, Jane 226
Barlow, Agatha (née Wellesbourne) 122, 125
Barlow, William, Bishop of St Asaph, St David's, Bath and Wells, Chichester 122, 125, 127, 136; for his daughters see Day, Matthew, Overton, Westfaling, Wykeham
Barwick, Judith (née Best) 132

bastards, bastardy 29, 77, 133–4
Bateman, Susannah 220
Bathurst, Anne 183, 195, 197
Bathurst, Elizabeth 221, 236
Baynard, Anne 216
Becon, Thomas 80
Bedingfield family 167
Behn, Aphra 214, 215, 217, 219, 231
Bell, Susanna 221
Bellamy, Catherine 159
Bennet, Dorcas 219
Bentham, Mawde 130, 137, 140
Bentham, Thomas, Bishop of Coventry and Lichfield 130, 134, 140–1
Bernard, Richard 80
Best, Elizabeth 132, 134
Best, Judith see Barwick
Best, Richard, Bishop of Carlisle 132
Bible, The 24, 80, 124, 182, 221, 223
Birde, John, Bishop of Chester, and his wife 125, 127
Birmingham 108
birth/death/birth intervals 39–42
birth intervals 23–6, 33, 35–7, 39–43; of wet nurses 33, 35
bishops: see celibacy, children, clerical marriage, divorce, double standards, intermarriage, marriage settlements, martyrs, nepotism, remarriage, repudiation of wives
Blackacre, Widow 55–6, 75
Blaithwaite, Mary 225
Blandford, Susannah 224
Blethin, Anne 136
Bodleian Library 3
Boleyn, Anne 122
borough custom: governing married women owning property for trade 103; governing trading of Oxford freemen and their widows 103; governing remarriage of freemen's widows in Abingdon 89 (n. 24)
Bossy, J. 151, 173
Bowes, Martin 134; Sir Martin Bowes 134

Boyle, Mary 191–2; see also Warwick, Countess of
Bradstreet, Anne 214, 218
breastfeeding 23, 24–9, 38, 45–6, 50; demand feeding 24, 25, 26; non-exclusive 23, 25; of adults 29; patterns of 25; writers on 27–9, 222; scheduled 24; see also amenorrhoea; fertility; lactation; wet-nurses
Bridgewater, Countess of 194, 196, 198
British Museum 3
Bucer, Elizabeth (née Silberstein) 121
Bucer, Martin 121
Bucer, Wibrandis 121, 131
Buckinghamshire 23, 33, 36
Bugg, Francis 217
Bullinger, Henry 124, 129
Bullingham, Elizabeth (née Locke, formerly Hill) 128, 131
Bullingham, John, Bishop of Gloucester and Bristol 134
Bullingham, Nicholas, Bishop of Lincoln, Worcester 131, 134
Bury, Elizabeth 183, 184, 185, 186, 187, 215
Bushe, Edith 127
Bushe, Paul, Bishop of Bristol 127

Caius, John 29
Calvin, John 124
Camberwell 132
Cambridge Group for the Study of Population and Social Structure 36, 57–9
capitalism 11, 93, 110; Capitalistic Industry 94
Capito, Wolfgang 121
Cary, Mary 215, 217, 219, 220, 226, 227
cathedral close 135, 136
Cavendish, Margaret: see Newcastle, Duchess of
Caversham, birth intervals 32, 33, 34

Cecil, William, Lord Burghley 135, 153
celibacy, clerical 118, 122
Cellier, Elizabeth 219
Centlivre, Susannah 217
Chaderton, Katharine 136
change, economic, and women in Oxford 98–100, 109–10; in York 110
Chanel, Elinor 214
charivari 80
Charles I 223
Charles II 223, 225
Chaytor, Miranda 9
Chesham, wet-nursing 29, 30, 31, 33, 35
Chidley, Katherine 213–14, 218, 221, 224
childbirth 164, 196–7, 227
children: in Stuart women's diaries 195, 196–8; of clergy 123, 126, 133–4, 135; of bishops 120, 121, 136, 137, 138; of recusant parents 153; remarriage of their widowed mothers 66–8, 73; see also maternity
church fathers 80
Civil War(s) 26, 41, 75, 99, 130, 141, 172, 200, 211, 212–14, 222, 223, 231
Clare, E. 113
Clark, Alice 6, 8–12, 14, 15, 93–4
Clark, Peter 125
classical languages 124, 170, 215, 227, 229
Clement, Margaret 168
clerical marriage 118–23; hostility to 126; under Henry VIII 122–3; legalized under Edward VI 123, 126; legislation repealed under Mary 126; position under Elizabeth 133
Clifford, Lady Anne 24, 193, 198, 200, 201
Clifford, Margaret 24
Clitherow, Margaret 156, 158, 163, 165

cloth-making 77–8
Cockburn, Catherine 220
coitus interruptus 22
Coldwell, John, Bishop of Salisbury 134
colostrum 27
Commissions, Ecclesiastical 150, 151, 153
common law 103, 133
Commons, House of 123, 151, 154, 155; see petitions to Parliament
compounding 156
concubinage, concubines 120, 125
Congreve, William 54
Connebere, John and Elizabeth 39–41
Constable, Lady 154
Constantine, George 130
consumer society 14, 99
continental reformers: related to early bishops' wives 121–2, 124; return to Continent 126–7
contraception 23–5
contracts 103
convents 166–9
Conway, Anne 211
cooking, 4–5, 13
Cooper, Amy 139–40
Cooper, Thomas, Bishop of Lincoln, Winchester 137–8, 140
Copland, Robert 81, 82
copyhold 74
Cotton, Priscilla 224
Council of the North 110
Counter-Reformation 149, 166, 168, 173
Coverdale, Miles, Bishop of Exeter, and Elizabeth his wife 124, 127
Cowper, Dame Sarah 188, 193, 200–1
Cox, Jane (née Awder, formerly Turner) 131, 138
Cox, Richard, Bishop of Ely 131, 135, 138
Cranbrook 29, 130

Cranmer, Edmund 122
Cranmer, Margaret 122, 129, 131–2; see also Osiander, Whitchurch, Scott
Cranmer, Margaret, the younger: see Norton
Cranmer, Thomas, Archbishop of Canterbury 122–3, 124, 126, 128, 131, 133
Cranmer, Thomas, the younger 132
Cressy, David 216
Crockford, Frances 38
Cromwell, Elizabeth 220
Cromwell, Oliver 225
Crowley, Robert 123
The Crown, Oxford 97–8, 106, 108
Culpepper, Thomas 125
Cunningham, William 6
Curteys, Richard, Bishop of Chichester 134
Custance, Christian 54

Davenant family 97–8, 100
Davenant, Jane: see Hallom
Davenant, John 97–8, 100
Davenant, William, the poet 97
Davis, Lady Eleanor 225–6
Day, Elizabeth (née Barlow) 136
de Carvajal, Luisa 175
Delaval, Lady Elizabeth 181, 189, 191, 192
depravity of women 119–20, 123
de Tserclas, Anne: see Hooper
Dickens, A. G. 126
dilapidations 136, 147 (n. 104)
dispensations 122
division of labour between sexes 94–8, 120
divorce 127, 135
Docwra, Anne 217
domestic industry 6–7, 11, 30, 94
domestic routine 189–90
domestic skills 9, 12–13
double standards 138, 230
Douglas, Eleanor 213, 220, 223
dower 123, 126, 134, 154, 156

Downham, William, Bishop of Chester 134
Dowriche, Anne 219
Dryden, John 216–17
Dulley, Frank 35

education 10, 13, 169–70, 215–16, 228–9
Edward VI 123–4, 126
Elizabeth I 129, 131, 133, 134, 135, 136, 137, 218
Elstob, Elizabeth 220
Elstree 30
employment 77–9, 95–6, 102–14, 227
enclosure of women's communities 168, 171, 173
'English Ladies': see Institute of the Blessed Virgin Mary
equality of women 10–11, 112, 119–20, 128, 129, 173, 229–30; see also feminist writings, priesthood of all believers
Erasmus, Desiderius 119
Evans, Arise 214
executorship of wills: see remarriage: factors affecting
exertion, physical 25–6
Exeter 102, 107, 124
exile, Marian 127–30, 131, 132, 140

factories, women in 6–7
Fall, the 94–5, 165, 228
family: and state 154–5, 160; effect of industrial revolution on 9–10, 11; recusant families 150, 153; see also intermarriage, nepotism
Family Industry 94
family reconstitution 23, 33, 36, 129, 140, 141
family size 22, 38, 42
Farr, William 61
Fawcon, Mawde: see Bentham
Featley, John 186
feme coverte 103
feme sole 102, 110

feminist writings 228–31
Ferrar, Robert, Bishop of St David's 128; his wife 125, 128
fertility 16, 22–5, 36–9, 44; age-specific 36–9, 42; naturally controlled 23, 43
Fiennes, Celia 181, 201
Finch, Anne 214, 220, 226–7, 229
fines 152
Fletcher, Richard, Bishop of Worcester, of London, and his second wife 135, 136
foetal loss 39
Forster, Mary 228
Foxe, John 124, 175
Frankfurt Fair 131
freemen: no women freemen in Oxford 108, 112, 113; women freemen in York 110; trading rights of freemen and their widows in Oxford 103; see also apprenticeships, guilds, widows
Freke, Elizabeth 192, 199
fugitives: see recusant women
Fusco, Horatio 81

Gardiner, Stephen, Bishop of Winchester 131
Garnet, Henry 158, 165
Geneva 130
gentlewomen: activities revealed in diaries 190; as diarists 184–5; in religious communities abroad 167; published writings 214, 219–20; recusant 154; remarriage 71; see also rich women
Gerard, John 172
Gibbons, Orlando 104
Gibbons, Mary and William 104
Gifford, Mary 163–4
Girton College 6
Godwin, Susan (née Wolton) 136
Godwin, Thomas, Bishop of Bath and Wells 134
Gotherson, Dorothea 225

government, effect of centralizing tendencies on women 14
Green, Alice Stopford (Mrs J. R. Green) 4
Green, Mary Anne Everitt 3–4
Greenhill, William 218
Grymeston, Elizabeth 222
guilds 14, 96, 103, 110–13
guardianship 73, 103
Guillemeau, J. 28

Hadleigh 123, 130
Hales, Sir James 128
Hales, Joyce 128
Halkett, Anne 221
Hallom, Jane (née Davenant) 98, 100, 106, 108
Hallom, Thomas 97, 100
Hammer, Carl 100
harbouring priests 156–60; see also recusant women
Harley, John, Bishop of Hereford, and his wife 128
Harrington, Mrs 113
Harrison, Matthew 101
Hatton, Sister 97–8
Haughty, Lady 55
Hawte, Sir William 125
Hayward, Amey 219
Heal, Felicity 134, 137
Hebrew 124, 215
Henry VIII 122–3, 136
Henry, Louis 36, 37
Henry, Sarah 191; see also Savage, Sarah
Hertfordshire 23, 30, 35, 78
Heyman, Maria: see Ponet, Hill
Heyman, Peter 125
Hicken, Mary 24
Hickman, Rose (née Locke) 128, 131
Hill, Georgiana 4–5
Hill, John, second husband to Maria Heyman 128
Hill, Richard, first husband to Elizabeth Bullingham 131

Hirons, Mary 113
Hit-Him-Home, Joane 230
Hobbes family 43
Hoby, Lady 186
Hohenheim, Ottilie von 121
Holbeache alias Randes, Joan (née Mannett) 125
Holden, Mary 227
Holgate, Barbara (née Wentworth) 126, 127
Holgate, Robert, Archbishop of York, 124, 126, 127
Hooker, John 124
Hooper, Anne (née de Tserclas) 124, 128, 129
Hooper, Daniel 128, 129
Hooper, John, Bishop of Gloucester and Worcester 124, 128
Hooper, Rachel 124, 129
horticulture 12, 13
household economy 8–9, 10, 11, 12; see also division of labour
household size 105
Hungerford, Lady 80
human milk 26–33
husbands responsible for recusant wives 150, 151, 153, 154, 155, 156, 160, 161; see also recusant women
Hutchinson, Lucy 182
Hutterite women 25
Hutton, Frances 134
Hutton, Matthew, Bishop of Durham, Archbishop of York 134

immigrants, urban 100
imprisonment of recusants 150, 151, 152, 153, 154, 155, 156; see also recusant women
industrial revolution 6, 7, 8–10, 94
infant mortality 27, 29, 30, 31, 33, 37, 41, 45, 46
infanticide 22, 29
innovations 13–14
Institute of the Blessed Virgin Mary 169–74, 180 (n. 103); houses and

schools 169, 172; international intake 171; opposition to 171–2; support for 170
Interregnum 213, 231
interrogations, replies to 150–1; see also recusant women
intestacy 134
Ireton, Bridget 220

James I 215
James II 219
James, Eleanor 213, 219, 223
Japanese women 25
Jeffreys, Joyce 14, 111, 181
Jegon, Dorothy (née Vaughan) 136
Jesuits 154, 162, 163–4; attitude towards Institute of the Blessed Virgin Mary 171, 172–4; harbouring 158–9
Jinner, Sarah 227, 228, 231
Joceline, Elizabeth 214, 222
jointure 152, 156
Johnson, Elizabeth 224
Jones, John 27
Jones, Sarah 226
Journal or Diary of a Thankful Christian, The 185
journeymen 105, 108

Karlstadt, Andreas 119
Kelfe, M. L. 113
Kelso, Ruth 81, 138
King, Gregory 100
Kingsmill family 130
Kinnaird, Joan 230
kinship networks 102, 106–8, 125
Knowles, Lillian 6–9, 11
Knox, John 131
Kuczynski, R. 24
Kung women 25

lactation 23–5; contraceptive effect of 23–5; intercourse during 22; see also prolactin, suckling stimulus
land tenure 71, 74

Lanyer, Aemilia 228
Laslett, Peter 105
Latimer, Hugh, Bishop of Worcester 123, 128, 138
Latin: see classical languages
law: factors discouraging remarriage of widows 75, 79–80; position of women in trade 102–3; position of recusant women 150–60; bishops' families 133–4; bishops' wives 123, 125, 126
Lawrance, Hannah 18 (n. 2)
Lawson, Dorothy 156, 163
laywomen 163–5; 169; in communities; 174–5
Lead, Jane 213
Leigh, Dorothy 212, 222
Levellers, the 213, 223
Levinz, William 101
Lewis, Jane 9
life expectation 63
life stages 191–9
life styles, varying 11, 12
Lincoln, Countess of 28, 224
Line, Anne 158, 159
literacy 183, 184, 216
Locke, Anne (née Vaughan) 131
Locke, Elizabeth: see Bullingham
Locke, Jane (née Wilkinson) 131
Locke, John, philosopher 220
Locke, Rose: see Hickman
Locke, Sir William 131
Lollardy 119, 125
London 30, 103, 131; environs of 29, 30
London School of Economics 6, 8
Long Wittenham 74
longevity 44, 61–5, 88 (n. 17)
Lords, House of 123, 255
loyalty: see remarriage
Luther, Katharine (née von Bora) 121, 124
Luther, Martin 119–20, 121, 124, 129

Macaulay, Catherine 18 (n. 1)

Maccabeus, John 124
MacCaffrey, Wallace 102
Major, Elizabeth 217, 226
Makin, Bathsua 220, 229
male and female realms 199–200; see also spheres, separate
malt-making 78
Mantel, Walter 125; his widow 128
mantua-making 111, 113
Mapledurham 33–4
marriage: age of 38–9, 42; purpose of 165; diarists on 191–200; of urban immigrants 100–1; women risk marriage by writing 225–6; women writers' views of 228; see also clerical marriage, remarriage
marriage settlements 134
martyrs: Catholic 157–60; Protestant 123, 128
Mary I, position of bishops' wives under 126–9
Mary, Queen of Scots 2–3
mass 150–1, 157, 163–4, 170, 175
Massinger, Philip 54
maternal mortality 43–4
maternity 26, 198, 221–2, 226, 229; see also children
Mathew, Frances (née Barlow, formerly Parker) 134, 139
Mathew, Maria (née White, formerly Bridgman) 104, 107, 109
Mathew, Toby, Bishop of Durham, Archbishop of York 134, 136
matriarchal households of recusant women 161, 162
matrilineal family trees 100–1
Mauriceau, François 27
menarche 25, 39
Mercers' Company 110–13
middle-class women 4, 7, 9, 33, 94, 183, 190
Middleton, Marmaduke, Bishop of St David's 134
midwives, midwifery 10, 219, 220, 227

milk, human: see human milk
milliners 111–13
Minehead: economy of 35–6; marital fertility and birth intervals 36–43; parish registers 36–7, 41
modesty 217
Moffat, Thomas 29
Montague, Mary Wortley 215
Mordaunt, Elizabeth 187, 192, 196
More, Dame Gertrude 168
More, Sir Thomas 120
Morrell, Anne 106, 107, 108, 112; see also Turton, Anne
Morrell, William 106, 108
motherhood: see maternity
Munda, Constantia 229

Napier, Richard 79
nepotism 121–2
Newcastle, Duchess of 182, 195, 215, 218, 226, 228
Newcastle, Duke of 55, 147 (n. 96), 215, 218
Newcome, Henry 24–5
Newdigate, Anne 28
Newstead, Christopher 81
nobility, bishops marrying into 122, 125, 136
Nonconformists 58, 67, 76, 81
Norton, Margaret (née Cranmer) 132
Norton, Thomas 132
nuns 166–8, 174; ex-nuns 121; Notre Dame sisters, Ursulines, Visitation nuns 172
nurse children 30–2, 35; mortality amongst 29, 31; successfully reared 32
nutrition: and fertility 25; and repeated pregnancies 44

occupations: effect on lifestyle 12; effect on remarriage 66–7, 69–72; of Oxford widows in trade 106–7; of wet-nurses' husbands 30, 31
Olave, Mary 113
Oldsworth, Edward 129

oligarchies, urban 102
Osiander, Andreas 122, 129
outlawry 152
ovulation, and breastfeeding 23, 24
Overton, Margaret (née Barlow) 136
Owen, Jane 220, 226, 231
Oxford: councillors 100, 102; economy 99, 102, 109–10; freedom of, entry into 100, 108, 112, 113; mortality 109; records 94; see also change, economic
Oxfordshire 23, 36

Page, William 81
Paine, Thomas 111
Palliser, David 110
Parker, Frances: see Matthew
Parker, M. 113
Parker, Margaret 121, 135, 139
Parker, Matthew, Archbishop of Canterbury 121, 123, 133, 134, 135
Parkhurst, John, Bishop of Norwich, and his wife 127
Parliament, members of 221, 223–4; see also Commons, House of; Lords, House of; petitions to Parliament
Parr, Susanna 215, 219, 225
Partridge, Dorothy 220
patriarchy 102, 106
Patrick, Simon 189
Peck, Catherine 76
peine forte et dure 158
Pembroke, Countess of 199
Pepys, Elizabeth 184
Pepys, Samuel 183, 184
Percy, Lady Mary 168
Perry, Ruth 230
petitions to Parliament 109, 213, 223–4, 225, 228
Petty, William 24
Philips, Katherine 231
Pilkington, Alice (née Kingsmill) 130, 139
Pilkington, James, Bishop of Durham 130

Pinchbeck, Ivy 6, 15
Plus, Lady 54
Poll Tax, 1667 105–6
Ponet, John, Bishop of Rochester, Winchester 125–6, 127; his first wife 125
Ponet, Maria (née Heyman, later Hill), second wife of John Ponet 125, 126, 127–8
Poole, Elizabeth 217, 223, 226
Poor Clares 171
poor law, Elizabethan 13
poor relief: see Abingdon
poor widows 59, 68, 75, 78, 79, 82
poor women 25, 27, 38, 45
Pope, Mary 217, 221, 223, 226, 227
Popham, Chief Justice 153
Pophley, Isabel 76
population change 23, 46, 49
Poulett, Katherine 45
Poullain, Valérand 124, 129
Power, Eileen 8
precedence 134
pregnancy 22–53, 195–6
princesses: see royalty
priesthood of all believers 120, 129, 140, 141
priests 154, 165, 167, 173, 174; see also harbouring priests, recusant women
Privy Council 151, 153, 154
professions: women excluded from 10; effect of exclusion 215–16
prolactin 23–4, 25–6
property and remarriage 74–5; see also copyhold, dower, feme coverte, feme sole, jointure, outlawry
prophetic writings 213, 222–5
Proudie, Mrs 138
providences, particular 164, 186–7
Puritans: and bishops 137; on remarriage 80, 81

Quakers 8, 9, 175, 213, 217, 218, 221, 222, 224, 225
queens: see royalty

Radcliffe, Katherine 154
Ralegh, Sir Walter 73
rationality, stress on 164, 175
Reading 30
ready-made clothes 111
recusant women 128; at home 162–6; in the English Catholic community 160–6; in religious communities 166–74; martyred: see Clitherow, Line and Ward, Margaret; fugitive: see Attwood, Brudiman, Hancorne, Jefferies, Phillips, Strange 152; harbourers: see Sheldon, Tully, Williams, 157; Vavasour 158; imprisoned: see Searle 153; Babthorpe, Constable, Metham, Ingleby, Radcliffe 154; see also Clitherow, Lawson, Line, Wiseman; in Protestant custody 154; see also Throckmorton; interrogated (1576)–Bowman, Brierley, Geldart, Strychett 150–1; husband held responsible for wife's behaviour–Dinley, Goldsmith, Hall, Kinchingham 151; works of mercy by Arundel, Gifford, Skinner 164, Sister Dorothea 165; see also enclosure, 'English Ladies', Institute of the Blessed Virgin Mary, nuns, refusal to plead, and Ward, Mary
Redford, Elizabeth 225
'redundant woman', the problem of 96
refusal to plead 158; see also Clitherow, Margaret; Wiseman, Jane
remarriage 54–83; of bishops 135–6, 147 (n. 100); change in rate of 65, 74, 86, 89 (n. 29); factors affecting: attractions of independence 76, 77, 81, 82, of legal independence 55, 75, 77; children 69, 73; economic penalties 74; executorship of wife 66, 68–9; husbands' attitudes 72; husbands' occupations 67–8; husband's wealth 66, 68, 69; land

tenure 71, 74; legal disabilities of married women 75, 77; length of preceding marriage 62–5; love of first husband 76, 79, 83; loyalty to deceased husband 73, 76, 77, 79; mutual comfort 81; provision of poor relief 79; public disapproval 79–80; religious teaching 80
reproductive patterns 23
repudiation of wives 123, 127
rich widows 59, 66, 68, 71, 75, 76–8
rich women 22, 26, 27, 28, 38, 43, 45, 115; see also gentlewomen, rich widows, wet-nurses
Richardson, Elizabeth 220, 222
Ridley, Nicholas, Bishop of London 128
Rogers, Daniel 80
Rogers, Richard 186
Roget, Mme 113
role models, Biblical 24, 28, 223
Roll, Margaret 220
royalty 2–4
Russell, Lord John 3

sacerdotalism 140–1
St Albans 32
Saint-Omer 169, 170
Sandys, Cicely (née Wilford) 130, 140, 141
Sandys, Edwin, Bishop of Worcester, London, Archbishop of York 130, 133, 140–1
Sandys family 139–41
Sandys, George 126, 140
Sarah 28
Savage, Sarah 181, 184, 185, 190, 192, 193, 195, 197; see also Henry, Sarah
Scandinavia 72
Schofield, Roger 56, 60
Schurman, Anne Maria 229, 231
Scory, Elizabeth 125, 139
Scory, John, Bishop of Chichester, Hereford 127

Scott, Bartholomew 132–3
Scott, Margaret: see Cranmer
Scottesford, Dorothy 72
Selden, John 136
Seth Ward's College of Matrons 72
settlements, marriage 134
Seven Sorowes that Women have when theyr Husbandes be Deade, The 81
sexual promiscuity 77
sexuality, female writers on 230
Shakespeare, William 97
Sharpe, Jane 227
Shaw, Mrs Bernard 8
Shaw, Hester 225
Shaxton, Nicholas, Bishop of Salisbury 123, 130
Short, R. V. 23, 25
silence, a virtue 216
silhouettists 113
Simonds, Rose, the case of 133
single women 7, 9, 55, 102–3, 108, 110, 111–14, 150, 166, 169, 191, 193, 226
Slatter, Anthony 108
Slatter, Jane and Phillis 108, 110
Slatter, Thomas 106
Smith, Lucy Toulmin 4
social criticism 222–4
social work: see works of mercy
Somerset 35, 43–6; see Minehead
Sons of the Clergy 72
South Sea Bubble 109–10
Sowernam, Esther 229
Spain 151, 153, 154
Speght, Rachel 219, 221, 229–30
spheres, separate 229
spiritual diaries 185–90
Spufford, Margaret 216
State Paper Office 3
staymaking 111
Steyning, Alice 44
Steyning family 43
stillbirths 36
Stirling, Earl of 185

Stone, Lawrence 79, 99, 109
Strickland, Agnes and Elizabeth 2–3
Stuckley, Lewis 215
suckling stimulus 24
suffrage, women's 93
superstition 126, 164, 192
Sutcliffe, Alice 218
Swetnam, Joseph 229

Tailors' Company, Oxford 108, 110–12; Guild 111
Tattlewell, Mary 230
Thirsk, Joan 33
Thirty-Nine Articles 133
Thomas, Keith 221
Thornborough, John, Bishop of Limerick 135
Thornton, Alice 187, 188, 198, 199
Throckmorton, Margaret 154
Tipper, Elizabeth 217
tombs of bishops 140–1
Topcliffe, Richard 153
trades unions 113
Trapnel, Anna 213, 216, 223
Trent, Council of 119
Trevelyan family 43; see also wet-nurses
Trye, Mary 227, 231
Turner, G. Lyon 76
Turner, Jane, author 221
Turner Jane: see Cox
Turner, Peter 131
Turner, William 131
Turton, Anne 106, 107–8; see also Morrell, Anne
Turton family 107–8
Twysden, Lady Isabella 197, 200
Tyler, P. 126
Tyndale, William 120

universities 5–6, 99–100, 109, 215
Ursulines, the 172

Vaughan, Jane 159
Vaux, Anne 156, 158

Venn, Anne 221
Verney, Mary 26, 28, 32
vindications, personal 225
Virgin Mary, The 27, 28
virginity 166, 191
visions 195, 213, 227
Vitelleschi, Mutius, Rector General 172
Vives, Juan 80

wages 113
Walker, Elizabeth 183, 184, 189, 190, 192, 197, 198
Warcup, Agnes 128, 141
Warcup, Anne 128, 141
Warcup, Cuthbert 128
Ward, Sir Adolphus 4
Ward, Margaret 159
Ward, Mary 169, 170–3
Warner, Alice 128
Warren, Elizabeth 216, 218, 219, 226
Warwick, Countess of 187, 190, 194, 195, 196–7, 199; see also Boyle, Mary
weaning 27
Wellesbourne, Agatha: see Barlow, Agatha
Wentworth, Anne 226
Westfaling, Ann (née Barlow) 136
Westfaling, Herbert, Bishop of Hereford 134, 136
wet-nurses 22, 24, 26–33, 43, 44–6; a domestic industry 30; and their employers: Elizabeth Gilbert and the Trevelyans 44–5; Joan Jenkins and the Andrews 32; Mary Ogden and the Knollys family 32; Elizabeth Vicary and the Trevelyans 45; attitude of church to use of 27; geographic concentration of 30
Whitchurch, Edward 132
Whitchurch, Margaret: see Cranmer, Margaret
White, Dorothy 224
White, Sir Thomas 107

Whitelocke, Bulstrode 80
Whitelocke family 33
Whittington, Richard, mayor of London 102
Whittington, Richard, mayor of Oxford 101–2
Whitrowe, Joan 225, 226
whores 120, 232
widows: ages of 63; bishops' 134, 136–7, 'cohort widows', defined 58, passim; diarists on 191, 198–200; older 65, 80; 'probate widows' defined 59, passim; recusants 150, 174–5; tracing, problems of 58, 59, 60, 86–7; untraced 59–60, 84–5, 86–7; widows continuing husbands' occupations 105; younger 62, 63, 80; see also bishops' widows; freemen's widows; poor widows; remarriage; rich widows; lower clergy; mortality
Wight, Sara 223
Wilford (or Wilsford), Cicely: see Sandys, Cicely
Wilkinson, Jane 128, 129, 131, 141; for her daughter see Locke, Jane
William of Orange 200
Willoughby family 45
wills: of bishops 134; of bishops' wives 139, 147 (n. 113); of husbands in Abingdon 72–4; see also executorship

Wiseman, Jane 158
Wishfort, Widow 54
Withers, George 218
Wolf, Magdalen 72
Wolfe, Reyner 131, 132
Wolley, Hannah 227, 229
Woodforde, Mary 198
workhouses 13
working-class women 4, 7, 183; see also poor women, poor widows
works of mercy 164, 168; see also recusant women
Wright, Mrs 113
Wrigley, E. A. 36, 56, 60
Wyatt, Sir Thomas 125, 127
Wycherley, William 54
Wyclif, John 119
Wykeham, Anthonina (née Barlow) 136, 139
Wykeham, William, Bishop of Lincoln, Winchester 134, 136

York 110, 150, 152, 222
Younge, Jane (née Kynaston) 130, 139, 147 (n. 104)
Younge, Thomas, 130, 136, 147 (n. 104)

Zell, Katharine (née Schütze) and Matthew 121